D0022510

Russia and the GCC

Russia and the GCC

The Case of Tatarstan's Paradiplomacy

Diana Galeeva

I.B. TAURIS

LONDON · NEW YORK · OXFORD · NEW DELHI · SYDNEY

I.B. TAURIS
Bloomsbury Publishing Plc
50 Bedford Square, London, WC1B 3DP, UK
1385 Broadway, New York, NY 10018, USA
29 Earlsfort Terrace, Dublin 2, Ireland

BLOOMSBURY, I.B. TAURIS and the I.B. Tauris logo are trademarks of
Bloomsbury Publishing Plc

First published in Great Britain, 2023

Copyright © Diana Galeeva, 2023

Diana Galeeva has asserted her right under the Copyright, Designs and
Patents Act, 1988, to be identified as Author of this work.

For legal purposes the Acknowledgements on p. ix constitute an extension of this
copyright page.

Series design by Adriana Brioso
Cover image: Sheikh Hamdan bin Mohammed Al Maktoum and Rustam Minnikhanov, at
the 10th International Economic Summit, Kazan, Russia, 2018. (© Yegor Aleyev/ITAR-TASS
News Agency/Alamy Live News)

All rights reserved. No part of this publication may be reproduced or transmitted
in any form or by any means, electronic or mechanical, including photocopying,
recording or any information storage or retrieval system, without prior permission
in writing from the publishers.

Bloomsbury Publishing Plc does not have any control over, or responsibility for, any
third-party websites referred to or in this book. All internet addresses given in this
book were correct at the time of going to press. The author and publisher regret any
inconvenience caused if addresses have changed or sites have ceased to exist,
but can accept no responsibility for any such changes.

A catalogue record for this book is available from the British Library.

A catalog record for this book is available from the Library of Congress.

ISBN: HB: 978-0-7556-4615-9
ePDF: 978-0-7556-4616-6
eBook: 978-0-7556-4617-3

Typeset by Deanta Global Publishing Services, Chennai, India

To find out more about our authors and books visit www.bloomsbury.com and
sign up for our newsletters.

To my mother – Galeeva Venera Nurullovna

Contents

Tables

Acknowledgements

I would like to sincerely thank all the people who believed in this project, and acknowledge their efforts and generous support during its development over different periods of time. My greatest thank you's go to Sophie Rudland, Senior Editor, Middle East Studies and Islamic Studies at I.B.Tauris /Bloomsbury, and Yasmin Garcha, assistant editor, as well as all the editorial team of I.B.Tauris/ Bloomsbury for their interest in publishing this book. My deepest gratitude is due to Dr Khaled al-Dhaheri, the chancellor of Mohammad bin Zayed University for Humanities, for kindly offering support for the translation and publication of this manuscript in Arabic.

I was fortunate enough to conduct this research during my Academic Visitorship at St Antony's College, Oxford University (since 2019), assistant professorship at Mohammad bin Zayed University for Humanities (since 2021) and scholar-in-residence status at the Oxford Centre for Islamic Studies (2020–1). I cannot thank each of these precious institutions enough for the support I have received from them so that I could complete this research.

My deepest thanks go to St Antony's College Middle East Centre, where I began to work on this direction of research. Among my many fine colleagues, I wish to single out Professor Eugene Rogan, my mentor, whose knowledge, support and belief in this project has been so crucial for its completion. Also, Dr Michael Willis, who mentored me when Professor Eugene Rogan was on research leave (2021–2), was fundamental in my progress.

I am profoundly indebted to the Mohammad bin Zayed University for Humanities, which I joined in 2021, for their generous support of this project. Dr Khaled al-Dhaheri was particularly supportive and interested in the idea of a project dedicated to studying the development of Islam in Russia, and the role of the Islamic factor in developing relations between Russia and the Middle East/ Gulf Cooperation Council (GCC) states. Colleagues at the university, especially Dr Karima al-Mazroui, Dr Samira al-Nuaimi and Dr Saif al-Shaali, have always been very supportive of my research. In addition, I would like to sincerely thank my colleagues at al-Mesbar Studies and Research Centre for their support over the years.

I have many thanks to give to my colleagues at the Oxford Centre for Islamic Studies, where I was a scholar-in-residence (2020–1). Dr Farhan Nizami, Dr Moin Nizami and Dr Talal al-Azem provided kind backing for my academic initiatives. In particular, I thank them for their support during the international online conference, 'Russia and the Muslim World: Through the Lens of Shared Islamic Identities' that I convened (18–19 March 2021). Their support was crucial for attracting academics and experts on this subject, and findings from the event have enriched this book considerably.

My deepest thanks go to all my interviewees (political elites and academics from Russia and the GCC) who kindly agreed to provide their insightful and valuable perspectives on the study's topics and shared their treasured time – (in alphabetical order) Mr Ainur Akkulov, HE Shaykh Abdulrahman bin Mohammad bin Rashid al-Khalifa, Mr Marat Gatin, Mr Ruslan Karamyshev, Professor Rafael' Khakimov, Ms Taliya Minullina, Mr Ruslan Mirsaiapov, Dr Farit Mukhametshin, Mr Il'kham Nurullin, Mr Gadzhiamin Ramaldanov, HE Mufti Kamil' Samigullin and Mr Aydar Shagimardanov. Also, I extend my sincere gratitude to Nail' Galiaviev, for his incredible help and support over the project, especially in introducing me to representatives of *umma* in Russia, whose efforts in contributing to relations between Tatarstan and the GCC states are enormous. I would also like to thank Dr Michael Rose, Mr Zinatullin Ranel and the anonymous reviewers for their valuable suggestions, which have been crucial for delivering the final product.

Finally, I would like to thank my mother Galeeva Venera Nurullovna for her endless love, support and encouragement throughout my life. Many thanks for giving me strength to chase my dreams. I dedicate this book to her, as the sing of my love, respect and deepest gratitude.

Note on transliteration

The *International Journal of Middle Eastern Studies'* guidance on transliteration was referred to for this book for Arabic and Turkish words. For example, all technical terms from languages in non-Latin alphabets have been italicized and fully transliterated with diacritical marks. Words found in Merriam-Webster's have been spelled as they appear there and not treated as technical terms. Following the guide, for such terms diacritics have not been applied, nor have they been italicized – for example, mufti, jihad, shaykh. The *International Journal of Middle Eastern Studies'* Word List has been applied for exceptions that preserve 'ayn and hamza, for example, Qur'an, shari'a, Ka'ba. Given the closeness of pronunciation between Turkish and Tatar languages, the guide for Turkish spelling has been applied. For example, the word 'ulama' (Arabic) has been rendered as ulema (Turkish), as the IJMS's Word List offers this for both languages – Arabic and Turkish. The transliteration style of *Slavic and East European Review* for languages written in Cyrillic, including Russian, Tatar, Bashkir words has been applied. Finally, given the complexity of use within different languages, for transliteration of personal names, and places, 'accepted English spellings' have been used, where these have been widely written on websites, in publications or on social media.

Tatarstan and the Gulf states

A recurrent puzzle

This chapter demonstrates the recurrent puzzle of the links between Tatarstan and the Gulf states by offering a short historical background. A key feature is their shared Islamic identities, which provide the rationale for the case studies in this text, and help bring to the fore the overlooked role of Tatars in Moscow–Arabian relations over the past 100 years. This background is followed by an outline of the argument of the book and its situation as regards International Relations (IR) theory. A brief examination of the constructivist position in IR is given, leading to the theoretical framework developed through the course of this book. Finally, the original empirical work emerging from the case studies is contextualized, and the potential impact of the developed framework is discussed.

1.1 Introduction to a recurrent puzzle

The increased political leverage of relations between Russia and the Gulf Cooperation Council (GCC) member states has become gradually more visible, particularly over the past five years, such as the historic first visit of King Salman of Saudi Arabia to Moscow in November 2017.[1] In return, President Putin visited Saudi Arabia[2] and the United Arab Emirates in 2019.[3] In existing academic work, the signs of closer cooperation between Moscow and the GCC states are mainly viewed in terms of economic factors. The Gulf states are important foreign investments and a market for Russian weapons, as well as potential partners in the oil and gas sectors. There is also considerable stress in existing scholarship on Russia's increasing role in the Middle East, driven by the region's diversification of relations with external powers.[4] Yet the role of specific Russian regions, especially those that share Islamic identities with the GCC, has commonly been overlooked. Their role, especially the modern Tatarstan Republic and the historical role of the Tatars, should be acknowledged to better understand the deepening close relations between Moscow and the Gulf states. This reveals not only the complexity of Russia's internal politics and structures but also how these can be productively employed to overcome potential barriers to external relations.

For example, Karim Khakimov,[5] of Tatar origin and the first consul general, granted 'Abd al-'Aziz al-Sa'ud formal recognition as the king of the Hijaz and the Sultan of Nejd in February 1926. Thereby, the Union of Soviet Socialist Republics (USSR) became the first state to establish full diplomatic relations with the Kingdom of Hijaz and Nejd.[6] Over ninety years later, another politician of Tatar origin, Rustam Minnikhanov, the current head of the modern Republic of Tatarstan, was chosen to carry the invitation of the Russian president Vladimir Putin to King Salman of Saudi Arabia, during a business trip to Saudi Arabia in 2017.[7] The unprecedented visit of a king of Saudi Arabia followed in November 2017. Perhaps this moment cannot be compared with the seismic events of 1926, but the visit certainly indicated a new wave of cooperation between the two countries, and a change in world politics. There are certainly parallels with the unique privileges that have been granted to the Russian Muslim Republic of Tatarstan by the federal government and the acceptability of collaboration shown by Saudi Arabia, which is (or contains) 'the (nominal) spiritual homeland' of Russian Muslims, as Stephen Page put it in 1971.[8] Against this background, this book examines a recurrent puzzle concerning direct links between Tatarstan and the GCC states, strung over almost 100 years. The research asks first, to what extent shared Islamic identities can be said to have influenced their bilateral relations, and second, how Moscow's relations with both Tatarstan and the Gulf Cooperation Council (GCC) states have affected the latter's bilateral relations.

These two questions directly link with the history of Tatarstan, which has been part of the Russian state since 1552, and the development of Islam, which was accepted by Volga Bulgars (modern Kazan Tatars) in 922.[9] The development of the Arabian states, from where Islam originates, also forms part of the story. For a brief but illustrative explanation of this vast historical background, this book acknowledges the findings of Ravil Bukharaev's book on Islam in Russia, *The Four Seasons*,[10] where he proposed a chronology of 922 to 1800. This consideration does not prioritize Ravil Bukharaev's findings over other important scholarship on Russian Islam, but it puts forward an aptly poetic version of Tatar history, and periodization of Russian Islam; it is an evocative framework rather than a precise definition. As poet, playwright and novelist, Ravil Bukharaev brilliantly captures the periodization of Russian Islam for any reader (irrespective of prior knowledge) by dividing it into spring, summer, autumn and winter, to show how Islam, vis-à-vis Orthodox Christianity, and in the Russian heartland, shaped its own highly sophisticated and extremely resilient civilization. I have developed Bukharaev's interpretations further, and included the development of Islam after 1800, the period where he ended his analysis. The chief point of interest here is that for the period under discussion – 1917–90, under Soviet rule – I describe a *cold winter of Islam*, whereas since the 1990s the situation has thawed somewhat, and can be seen as another *spring* period. Acknowledging that Ravil Bukharaev was not a historian, my interpretations also rely on many other scholars' work; one might see that he provided the vision, where scholarship has tested and developed these impressions. Importantly, his chronology has also been particularly useful to explain links with Arabian states, and the role of shared Islamic identities in this.

According to Ravil Bukharaev, the first period between 922 and 1229 is characterized as the *spring* of Islam, from the time it arrived on the banks of the Volga River until the onslaught of the hordes of Genghis Khan.[11] Arguably, the start of the first period might be placed even earlier, following Galina Yemelianova of SOAS, who brilliantly analyses the acceptance of Islam by proto-Tatars (Volga Bulgars), and theorizes the role of grassroots Islamization of the Volga Bulgars from Central Asia.[12] She suggests that when, in the seventh century AD, Islam was a new and influential religion in Arabia, the proto-Russians – who populated the riverbanks of the Dnieper, Pripyat, Bug and Volkhov rivers of present-day western Russia and Ukraine – were pagan. Relying on historical and archaeological sources, Yemelianova argues that the primary social and political organization of proto-Russians was influenced by the Khazars and the Biars (Volga Bulgars). In the mid-seventh century AD, the Khazars broke away from the Turkic Khaganate (552–745) and established their own state in the steppes between the rivers Volga and Don, and the Azov Sea. Itil', the capital of the state in the Lower Volga, by the mid-eighth century had turned into a powerful armed empire that covered much of Eurasia and even challenged the Arab Caliphate (along with the Byzantine Empire) for regional supremacy. At that time, Khazar rulers were largely pagan, and they allowed Manichaeism, Zoroastrianism, Nestorianism and Islam within their lands. Islam arrived in the Khazar Khaganate during the Arab–Khazar war of 708–37. In 737 the Arab General Mervan forced the Khagan and his subjects to adopt the new religion following his successful armed invasion of Khazar territory. Muslim Bukhara merchants who traded in the lower reaches of the Volga also added to the proliferation of Islam among some peoples of the Khaganate.[13]

From the seventh century, the Khazars desired domination over the eastern Slavs. Even according to the Arab sources, some proto-Russian tribes, known as Kasogi, allied with the Khazars against the Arab advance into the Caucasus. After defeat by the Arabs in 737, the Khazar leaders forced some Kasogi to move to the North Caucasus to support the Khazar defence there. The decision of the Khazar Khagan to introduce Judaism as the official religion in 740 was connected to geopolitical reasons: it offered an ideological counterweight to the Islamic Arab Caliphate and Christian Byzantine Empire. Nonetheless, the armed guard of the Khagan was largely Muslim.[14] The defeats of the Arabs at Talas in 751 and Poitiers in 753 aided Khazar expansion to the west, and by the mid-eighth century the Khazars had formed their rule over the southern part of the North Caucasus. However, further expansion westwards was prevented by the Biarmia, named after its main ethnic group, the Biars (a Turkic nomadic people) who lived along the valley of the rivers Volga and Kama. Like the Khazars, the Biars were originally under the political control of the Turkic Khaganate. At the end of the seventh century, they broke away and founded their own state. Birmia was multi-ethnic and poly-confessional: it included Turkic peoples (the Biars, the Bulgars, the Suvars, the Essengels, the Bersuls, the Barandjers, the Burtas) and Finno-Ugric peoples (the Mordvins, the Maris, the Komis, the Udmurts). In the ninth century the south-western province of Biarmia, known as Volga Bulgaria, developed into a separate state, and from the twelfth century onwards Biarmia ceased to be referred to in the chronicles.[15]

Volga Bulgars (proto-Tatars) split from Biarmia and established a separate state – Volga Bulgaria in Lower and Middle Volga – which continued to be dependent on the Khazar Khaganate.[16] The Volga Bulgars were Turkic people ethnically and culturally close to the Khazars. Yemelianova[17] applies the theory of Russian Islamic academics Vladimir Gordlevskii and Egor Kovalevskii, who believed that Central Asian merchants played a crucial role in the grassroots Islamization of the Volga Bulgars. Central Asia introduced the Volga Bulgars to the Hanafi *madhhab* (juridical school) of Sunni Islam and the specific Central Asian Islamic rites long before Volga Bulgaria's official conversion to Islam in 922,[18] where Ravil Bukharaev begins the first phase of Islam in Tatarstan, as he explains as follows. The acceptance of Islam by the Volga Bulgars[19] occurred due to a delegation from Baghdad led by Ahmad Ibn Fadlan,[20] sent by the Abbasid Caliph Jaffar al-Muqtadir to the ruler of the Volga Bulgars.[21] Given that Ibn Fadlan represented the Abbasid dynasty, this is an early partial link to the modern Arabian states.[22] In the time of the Prophet Mohammad, the founder of Islam (570–632), Mesopotamia and Persia united to establish the Sassanid Empire, governed by Khosroes. After the death of the Prophet, and on the succession of the Caliph Abu Bark, his general Khalid bin al-Walid led an army against the Sassanids, whose southern defences united at an enormous ditch running from Hit, on the Euphrates, to Kazama on the northern shore of Kuwait Bay. 'The Battle of the Chains' took place in 636, near the capital of the western province, Ubulla, the site of which was near the modern town of Zubair, which is south of Basra.[23] Khalid bin al-Walid was victorious, and all of Mesopotamia fell under Muslim rule. From 750 until 1250, the Abbasid Caliphate controlled Mesopotamia and its surroundings. The spread of Islam in the Volga region was a natural consequence, not least because for Volga Tatars acceptance of Islam also served political purposes, as Bukharaev argues:

> [T]the official acceptance of Islam by the King [*sic*] [though more accurately called baltavar'] of the Volga Bolgars from the hands of the Caliph of the time was consummated as well as the formal establishment of diplomatic liaisons between Volga Bulgaria and the Caliphate.[24]

It is also known that Ahmad, son of the Volga Bulgarian ruler Almush, visited Baghdad on his pilgrimage to Mecca, during the time of Caliph al-Muqtadir.[25] Therefore, along with hajji Amir Ahmad, who gained the Bulgar throne, he knew much more about Islam than his father did, and more and more Volga Bulgars travelled to perform hajj and returned to their homeland with the knowledge of the outer world.[26] This exchange created a deepening shared Islamic identity with what has become modern Arabia.

The second period of Islam in Russia according to Bukharaev was from 1229 to 1400 – described as the *summer* of Islam, covering the history of the Golden Horde until its ultimate collapse and split into separate Muslim polities. This period again refers to the Abbasid Caliphate,[27] after which Muslim prosperity and culture were curtailed in the thirteenth century, following the Mongol invasion of Genghis Khan.[28] Paradoxically, in the same period, arguably, there is a link, as earlier, Volga Bulgaria (which existed between 700 and 1238) also fell under the armies of Batu Khan in the late 1230s, and itself became a part of the Golden Horde.[29] In the Tatar case, Islam expanded from the coast of the Black and Caspian Seas to the northern Urals and beyond this mountain range, into Western Siberia. However, the Abbasid Caliphate was destroyed, as was much of Central Asia and Iran. Only the Turkish Mamluks of Egypt were able to repel the Mongol hordes and in 1260 Ayan Jalut stopped the Mongol advance in their direction.[30] The possibility of direct links with Arabia also occurred through hajj performance; however, as Ildar Nurimanov states, the period of the pilgrimage movement of Muslims who lived in the territory of modern Russia from the ninth to the fifteenth centuries is little studied, since in this time period many different states and khanates existed; some disappeared, others migrated, yet others merged with other cultures, losing their religion and past.[31]

The period between the 1400s and 1583, the *autumn* of Islam, incorporates the history of the Kazan, Astrakhan, Kasimov, Crimea, Nogai and Siberian Khanates; and within the context of this book, especially important in this period was that Kazan fell in 1552 into the hands of the Russian polity ('the Muscovy').[32] This period is also characterized as Eurasia's Turko–Tatar polities, which became the roots for closer links between modern Turkey and Tatarstan, based on both Turkic and Muslim identity, though only the latter is shared with the Gulf states. From the 1450s Moscow's rulers closely followed the internal scuffling in Kazan. They succeeded in the establishment of a pro-Moscow faction in the Kazan court.[33] It opposed the pro-Nogay groups which supported the pro-Crimean and Central Asia factions, backed by Ottoman Turkey. For two decades Moscow was confined to a policy of indirect political pressure on Kazan. However, in 1487, Moscow's Kniaz Ivan III conducted a successful armed campaign against the Kazan Khanate and built a Russian protectorate over it (1487–1506).

Moscow's annexation of the Kazan Khanate spread havoc among other descendants of the Golden Horde.[34] The Crimean Khanate – since 1477 a protectorate of the Ottoman Empire – and its rulers, the Giray dynasty, were worried about the increasing enlargement of Moscow, but they hoped that Ottoman protection would save them from Kazan's fate. Relations between Moscow and Bakhchisaray, the capital of the Crimean Khanate, were complicated. In 1506, in the context of Moscow's protracted conflict with Lithuania and Smolensk, the Girays offered vital armed help to the Khazanians that allowed the latter to regain their independence from Moscow. This contributed to the Crimeans playing a special role in Kazan affairs while Russian involvement declined to the politics of intrigue at the Kazan court. In 1519, pro-Moscow protege Shah 'Ali from the Kasymov dynasty remained in power until 1521, when he was replaced by an anti-Moscow Khan backed by the Crimeans, Poles and Lithuanians.[35]

Moscow consolidated its power over Smolensk and Ryazan by the 1530s, and resumed its active policy regarding the Kazan Khanate. The Russian Tsar Ivan IV (the Terrible, 1533–84) placed the armed suppression of the Kazan Khanate at the top of the Russian political agenda. Failed attempts in 1545 and

1547 by the Russian army led to a change in tactics, in favour of a lengthy siege of Kazan. In August 1552, Ivan the Terrible declared war on Kazan, which ended in victories for Moscow. Their shared past, cultural and religious ties with other Gengisid khanates did not help Kazan to gain protection: Turkic Muslim rulers of the Kasimov Khanate actively supported the Russian offensive against the co-religious and co-ethnic Kazanians. Additionally, some Nogay *murzas* supported Ivan the Terrible, while the Khan of Astrakhan stayed neutral. Even the traditional ally of Kazan – Crimea – decided to support Moscow.[36]

After 1552, Russia became a multi-ethnic and poly-confessional state and the Russian leaders were faced with the difficult task of redefining its state and national policy. After the annexation of Kazan, Moscow's strategic aim was the armed and political subjugation of the khanates. As a result, for example in 1556, Astrakhan fell under Russian military assault without any serious resistance. Attempts to defeat the Crimean Khans developed, though they failed in 1559 due to Ottoman Turk support.[37] Crimean rulers resumed their raids on the Russian lands in 1571. At the same time, Moscow focused on the Siberian Khanate from the 1580s, and in 1598 the last bastions of the Siberian Khanate's resistance fell under pressure from Cossack and the Russian troops. Russian–Nogay relations had a special character. By the end of the sixteenth century, the Nogay Horde, which represented a tribal alliance consisting of different clans, each controlling its own territories between the Kama and the Volga and along the Jaiyk river, split from what is known as the 'Great Nogay Horde'.[38] Its elite maintained a pro-Moscow course. The so-called 'Lesser Nogay Horde' was situated in the Kuban region, and its leaders were allied with the Crimean Khans against Russia. 'Alyul Horde', the third Nogay establishment, united those Nogay who moved within Kazakh and Uzbek political and cultural influence. For almost two centuries, the Kasimov Khanate remained a source of persistent Genghisid and Islamic influence on the Russian state, and militarily they fought with Russians against the Genghisid Khanates of Astrakhan, Nogay and Siberia. As Galina Yemelianova concludes, overall, the Genghisid and Islamized Eastern influence remained a powerful factor in the Russian state and society until the westernizing reforms of Peter the Great in the early eighteenth century. However, with the trend of the official Byzantization of the Russian state, and the Orthodox Church increasingly subordinated to the authority of the Tsar, the period moved towards the *winter* of Islam.

The period between 1583 and the 1800s includes the *winter* of Islam (which I extend until the end of the Russian Empire). It includes the history of its survival until the decree of Empress Catherine the Great, returning to Muslims the right to openly profess their faith and the lightening of the ban on Muslim books – printed in Russia.[39] Briefly, with the coming to power of the Romanov dynasty, the attitude of Orthodox Russia towards Islam had been officially enshrined in the tsar's decree of 16 May 1681, in which intolerance towards Mohammedanism acquired the character of a state political setting. In the era of Peter I, the policy of persecution against Islam, which consisted in the forcible Christianization of the Turkic-speaking population, and the destruction of the Muslim clergy and mosques, led to Islam being practically excluded from the active social and cultural life of the peoples who once professed it. However, under Catherine II, whom the Tatars called *Ebi-Patsha* ('The Granny Queen'), things changed, after she visited Kazan in 1767. With this visit, she officially ended the practice of forceful baptism and allowed the building of mosques by the Tatars. In 1788 the first official Muslim organization of Russian Muslims – Orenburg Muslim Spiritual Assembly – was founded. This period is also characterized by the emergence in the 1880s of *jadidism* (a form of Islamic modernism); the Tatars were active in its development.[40]

In the literature on the meetings of the Catherine Commission for 1767–69, it can be seen that the Tatars, who were representatives of different estates, local communities and sub-ethnic groups, acted as a united front in defending their religious rights as Muslims. One of their requirements was free travel to Mecca and back with the issuance of passports.[41] Without this, Russian Muslims were deprived of the opportunity to perform one of the main rites of Islam – the pilgrimage, hajj.[42] Only on 23 March 1803 did Emperor Alexander I sign the decree allowing Bukharans who live in Russia to receive passports and perform the hajj to Mecca.[43] Since the 1870s, the problems of the hajj of Muslim citizens of Russia had begun to be actively discussed in the foreign ministries – the Ministry of Foreign Affairs, the Embassy of Constantinople and the Consulate in Jeddah, which opened in 1891. From the late eighteenth to the nineteenth century, Russian pilgrims enjoyed special privileges in the Holy Land, which was under the control of the Ottomans.[44] However, the Russian authorities gave them passports with extreme reluctance, because they believed that 'the Hajj brings Turkey enormous material benefits from donations . . . used for military needs', and also believed that 'during the hajj, various epidemic diseases appear and develop, mainly cholera and the plague'.[45] For example, due to a withdrawal of the issuance of pilgrim passports, only 450 Muslims, and only sixteen from Kazan, performed hajj in 1898.[46] Clearly, links through shared identities had the potential to exist, but were hindered by their incompatibility with national political interests.

As noted earlier, I have further developed Bukharaev's chronology, into the atheist Soviet Union and the development of Islam. The rationale for choosing this period is that it uncovers an important history of the usage of the Muslim factor, and the Tatars, for political purposes by the USSR, towards Arabian states. Moreover, this period parallels the transformation and establishment of the modern Gulf states. In 1932 the two kingdoms of the Hijaz and Nejd were united as the Kingdom of Saudi Arabia.[47] Being under the former British umbrella of armed and political suzerainty, the Gulf monarchies were keeping more independent of each other.[48] However, in the early 1960s political conditions changed in the Gulf: the accession of Kuwait to full independence in 1961 serving as a message that Britain would finally abandon its total authority in that area.[49] The British began to encourage the smaller sheikhdoms of the so-called Trucial States to think about larger cooperation between them. In the 1960s, the British revealed to the Gulf rulers their plan to totally withdraw from the Gulf. In 1971 the Dubai Agreement was signed, under which Qatar, Bahrain and seven Trucial Sheikhdoms of Abu Dhabi, Sharjah, Dubai, Ajman, Fujairah, Ras al-Khaimah and Umm al-Quwain would join together in some kind of a federation or union. The next year, when Britain announced its withdrawal from its colonies and bases to the east of Suez, containing the Arabian Gulf, the nine sheikhs and amirs signed the agreement to form the United Arab Emirates (UAE).[50] However, only three years after the UAE came into being, Bahrain[51] and Qatar[52] decided to live as independent countries. Nonetheless, in the 1970s, all countries – with the former British-protected countries fully independent and with Oman having ended its era of isolation with the succession of power of Sultan Qaboos – were interested in cooperation and the establishment of unity.[53] The Gulf Cooperation Council (GCC) was founded in 1981 by Saudi Arabia, Bahrain, Kuwait, Qatar, Oman and the United Arab Emirates.[54]

Although the Tatars and Arabian states share Muslim identities, there are differences, with Tatars being Hanafis (the most flexible *madhhab*), while their counterparts are of the much stricter *madhahib* (Hanbali and Maliki) and, in the case of Oman, of the most inflexible, Ibadi school. Such differences were challenges, particularly after the collapse of the USSR, the period which I call the *spring* of Islam in Tatarstan; however, relations based on this Muslim factor flowered especially after the 2000s, and pragmatism has often overcome tensions between *madhahib*, as will be discussed throughout this book. The next section will situate this historical context within International Relations (IR) theory, while introducing further driving arguments behind this study.

1.2 The argument and its relation to IR theory

Among the key schools of thought in International Relations (IR) theory, we may count realist/neorealism/neoclassical realism, liberalism/neoliberalism and constructivism. Broadly, although there are disagreements about the keystones of realism, neorealism and neoclassical realism, realists of these three kinds are generally united in centralizing national power in their efforts to understand political power.[55] The liberal position is that violent conflict can be avoided, and that global prosperity can be increased, earning the description *utopian* or *idealist*. The liberal view holds that political and economic issues are more important in governing state behaviour than considerations of power.[56] By contrast, constructivists argue that global political relations between countries are socially constructed.[57] State relationships are thus based on three categories: norms (beliefs about what is successful and what is right in worldwide politics); strategic cultures ('sets of beliefs about the fundamental character of international politics and about the best ways of coping with it, especially as regards the utility of force and the prospects for cooperation')[58]; and identities.[59]

Constructivism is particularly relevant to describing Tatarstan–Gulf relations. Given the research question of the extent to which shared Islamic identities have influenced Tatarstan–Gulf relations, existing theoretical and empirical constructivist scholarship which focuses on identity and further cooperation between states can be helpful for understanding these relations. Alexander Wendt,[60] one of the key developers of the school, explains that 'social structure can matter in various ways: by constituting identities and interests, by helping actors find common solutions to problems, by defining expectations for behaviours, by constituting threats, and so on'. In other words, this might suggest that the Islamic factor boosts relations between Tatarstan and the GCC states, especially if there are other shared interests as well.

However, the second question addressed here, of how Moscow's relations with both (Tatarstan and the Gulf states) have affected the latter's bilateral relations, suggests some limitations within existing constructivist literature. Identity is largely considered by dividing between the state's conceptions of Self and Other. For example, Iver Neumann[61] in his book *Uses of the Other* traces the historical evolution of Christian European narratives, portraying the Turk as the Other. In *Orientalism*, Edward Said[62] focuses on relationships of power, of dominance, of varying degrees of complex hegemony between Occident and Orient, mainly considering European or Western relationships with the Orient. In other words, the existing literature considers relations between federal governments; none of it considers whether (and under which conditions) shared identities can be a boost to relations between independent states and the minorities of another state. This particular gap is where this manuscript aims to contribute, with a theory-development effort, examining Muslim GCC states and the Russian Muslim Republic of Tatarstan. The main argument of this book is that shared identities boost cooperation between 'Self(s)' and minority 'Self' of another state: (1) if 'Self(s)' and the 'Other' have interests in common, and the 'Other' is willing to integrate its minorities into this process; (2) if 'Self(s)' and minority 'Self' have shared interests.

1.3 Contributions to the argument and its relationship with existing explanations

This is the first book to examine Tatarstan–Gulf states relations during both Soviet and Russian eras, illustrating Moscow's relations with both players. The book also covers other Russian Muslim republics (Chechnya, Dagestan, Ingushetia, Bashkortostan) and their relations with the Gulf states. In doing so the volume fills a gap concerning other Russian Muslim republics' relations with the GCC states via shared Islamic identities; while acknowledging their importance, the volume helps current discussions to move beyond solely economic or geopolitical considerations, structuring a novel and increasingly important understanding of the role of minority cultures in underpinning international relations.

The research adopts an interpretivist epistemological position, with constructionist ontology. I combined a multi-country deviant case study with a grounded theory methodology to build on theory-development through an inductive process. During my Academic Visitorship at St. Antony's College, Oxford University (since 2019), Assistant Professorship at Mohamad Bin Zayed University for Humanities (since 2021) and Scholar-in-Residence status at the Oxford Centre for Islamic Studies (2020–1), a chain of evidence has been collected through primary and secondary sources in six languages (in Tatar, Russian, Bashkir, Turkish, Arabic and English) at the Bodleian Library, the Middle East Centre Library, St Antony's College Library (Oxford University), and the Library of Oxford Centre for Islamic Studies and the British Library. Additionally, online access to the National Library of the Republic of Tatarstan was especially useful, as it offers comprehensive sources in Tatar, Russian and Turkish, dedicated to the celebration of 100 years of the TASSR,[63] along with a range of collections, such as 'Tatarika',[64] which includes documents on culture, history, literature, art of the Tatar people and Tatarstan from the late nineteenth century to the present. Other vital resources have been the collection of Ivan Sakharov, which includes literature on the history of geography and theology, books on pedagogy of the writings of philosophy to the natural sciences – including on the Arabic language. I have relied on the online materials of the publishing house 'Medina',[65] established by the Spiritual Directorate of Muslims of Nizhny Novgorod, which specializes in the publication of literature on modern Islamic theology, mainly within the framework of the Hanafi school, as well as research in the history of Tatars and Muslims in Russia; these were beneficial for collecting sources on the history of hajj in the Soviet and modern Russian times (and earlier), the importance of the Mecca Congress 1926, the history of the development of Islam in Tatarstan and the contributions of Tatars to Muslim thought.

Archive analyses were conducted in the Middle East Archive (Oxford University), British Library, and with online documents on Soviet policies in the Middle East (in Russian). Archive documents of the Middle East Archive (Oxford University) and British Library allowed me to learn about British relations with the Gulf states in the context of this book, primarily with a focus on their view of Russia's policies. For example, the Monroe Elisabeth (1905–86) collection[66] includes translations of documents from Tsarist archives on the break-up of the Ottoman Empire, 1914–15; a note on the Arab Bureau, 1916–19, and Nasser's propaganda in the Persian Gulf, 1955–57. The Dickson, Lt.- Colonel Harold Richard Patrick (1881–1959)[67] collection contains administrative reports of the Kuwait Political Agency, 1918; 1921–32; Bahrain, 1920 – Ibn Saud; diaries of the mission in Bahrain, 1919–22; Saudi Arabia and UK: treaties and conventions; papers, slides and films relating to Rodney Giesler's[68] life and work for the Kuwait Oil Company Ltd Film Unit, and his later travels in the Middle East consisting of an extract from an oral history transcript 'Memories of Kuwait 1958–[19]61'; papers linked to Sir Richard Beaumont's[69] service in the Foreign Office, in particular his service as Consul in Jerusalem in 1948 and his role in the Burami Oasis dispute with Saudi Arabia in January–October 1960. In the British Library, File 3666/1925 'Arabia: Printed Correspondence 1924–1928' (27 December 1924–8, October 1929)[70] and File 61/11 II (D 42) 'Relations between Nejd and Hijaz'[71] were studied. Analyses of Soviet archive documents about the Middle East were based on Vitaly Naumkin's edited collection, which includes many diplomatic documents that shed light on significant aspects of the USSR's Middle East policy and reveal the most dramatic pages in the history of the Middle East conflict (Arab–Israel).[72] Moreover, documents of the foreign policies of the USSR are available at the historical documental department of the Russian Foreign Affairs Ministry, and these were also important for studying primary sources of Soviet policies towards the Middle East in 1943.[73]

During my fieldwork in Russian Muslim republics I have conducted semi-structured interviews with high-ranking political elites and political stakeholders, religious authorities, heads of religions organizations and academics. The areas covered include Tatarstan (February, December 2020; August, December 2021); Bashkortostan (February 2020); Dagestan (February 2020) and Moscow (February 2020). The views of the high-ranking Gulf political elites were obtained via email in Arabic. For example, the interview with Shaykh Abdulrahman bin Mohammad bin Rashid al-Khalifa, chairman of the Supreme Islamic Affairs Council of Bahrain, was conducted in January 2022. Given his important governmental position, this interview was crucial to establishing Bahrain's official view on Russia. Moreover, given his leadership of the Supreme Islamic Affairs Council of Bahrain and membership of the Group of the Strategic Vision 'Russia-Islamic world', his perspective was especially important for understanding the role of this group (from Bahrain's point of view), and the evaluation of the Islamic factor in building bilateral relations with Russia, along with the strategic objectives behind Bahrain–Tatarstan relations.

In Tatarstan, in order to demonstrate the shift of policies under the first president, Mintimer Shaimiev, and the current head, Rustam Minnikhanov, and their transformations with respect to the Gulf states, interviews with elites of both eras of leadership were conducted. For example, Dr Rafael' Khakimov can be identified among the political elites under Mintimer Shaimiev, as his chief advisor. He was also the director of the Institute of History at the Academy of Sciences of the Republic of Tatarstan. Ms Taliya Minullina is part of the political and economic elite under Rustam Minnikhanov. Before leading the Tatarstan Investment Development Agency (TIDA), she worked at the Ministry of Economy of Tatarstan Republic (specialist in Investment Department, leading adviser, leading consultant, Head of Department) (2007–10), and Office of the President of Republic of Tatarstan (head of division, head of department of civil service) (2010–14). TIDA further supported my research by also providing statistical data, and further evaluating and clarifying Tatarstan's paradiplomatic efforts towards the GCC states, which was very helpful for learning about current relations.

Interviews with officials who are directly responsible for building relations between Tatarstan/Russia and the GCC states were also conducted. Given Tatarstan's importance to the Group of the Strategic Vision 'Russia-Islamic world', as the head of the Republic Rustam Minnikhanov is the chair, in

Moscow I interviewed Dr Farit Mukhametshin, deputy chairman of the group, ambassador extraordinary and plenipotentiary, and deputy chairman of the Federation Council Committee on Foreign Affairs. This helped in understanding the importance of this group, as one of the mechanisms through which Tatarstan could carry out its paradiplomatic efforts, especially towards the Gulf. Also, policies under both Tatarstan's leaderships towards the Middle East were illuminated by talking to Mr Marat Gatin, who has extensive knowledge and experience in the development of Tatarstan's relations eastwards. Educated at al-Azhar University, he worked as the chief adviser of the sector of the countries of Asia and Africa of the Department of Foreign Relations of the President of the Republic of Tatarstan (2006–9), followed by an appointment as the head of the Sector for Asian and African Countries of the Department of Foreign Relations of the President of the Republic of Tatarstan (2009–10), and the Head of the Office of the President of the Republic of Tatarstan for Interaction with Religious Associations (2010–12). He continues to build further relations with the Muslim world, as the head of the Representative office of Rossotrudnichestvo in Egypt.

While the aforementioned interviews were crucial for learning about Tatarstan's paradiplomacy towards the GCC states, within the context of its position within the federal system and acknowledging its direct relations with Moscow, the second important question of this research on the role of shared Muslim identities could be studied thanks to crucial figures sharing their views on building religious policies with the Muslim world. Interviews with Kamil' Hazrat Samigullin, the Grand Mufti of Tatarstan, in February 2020 and December 2021, were fundamental concerning religious policies towards the Gulf states and more broadly the Muslim world. As Tatarstan's central figure for Islam, he is responsible for building such religious collaborations between Tatarstan and the Muslim world, and since 2013 has acted as the chairman of the Spiritual Board of Muslims of the Republic of Tatarstan.

The interview with Mr Aydar Shagimardanov, the president of the Association of Russian Muslim Entrepreneurs, was important for learning about the work of the Association (which also contributes to the mechanisms of Tatarstan's paradiplomacy), how business links are developed with the GCC states and a practical view on developments of Islamic banking and finance in Tatarstan, and more broadly in the Russian Federation. The interview with Mr Il'kham Nurullin, the former representative of the Ministry of Agriculture and Food of the Republic of Tatarstan, covered the potential prospects and challenges of Tatarstan–Gulf relations in this field. Meetings and conversations with representatives of Tatarstan's Chamber of Commerce and Industry, the Centralized Religious

Organization Spiritual Administration of Muslims of the Republic of Tatarstan Committee for 'Halal Standard' and the Bolgar Islamic Academy helped bring to the fore the wide-ranging engagements between Tatarstan and the Gulf states (and beyond that, the Muslim world).

Finally, prior to conducting the research, I have held internships at the President of Tatarstan's Office for the Department of Integration with Religious Associations, in 2012, and with the Cabinet of Ministers of the Republic of Tatarstan in 2011. These internships allowed me to better understand the mechanisms of Tatarstan's cooperation with foreign actors, including its paradiplomacy, which relies on effective interdepartmental cooperation and understanding the activities of other mechanisms central for cooperation with the Gulf states, including Islamic organizations, NGOs (such as the Association of Russian Muslim Entrepreneurs located in Kazan), and Islamic educational institutions. This personal experience was the primary inspiration for choosing to study Tatarstan's relations with the GCC states. In other words, the central focus of the book on Tatarstan's relations with the GCC states does not suggest any superiority or greater importance of Tatars and the Tatarstan Republic in such relations in comparison to relations of other Russian Republics with Muslim populations with the Gulf states; rather it is driven by my access to and awareness of a specific context. My practical experience and observations over a long period have particularly turned on how Tatarstan's dynamics have been shifting towards the Gulf states, especially since the 2010s.

As will be demonstrated over and over in the manuscript, especially the historical relations of Tatars and their links with the Arabian states, the dynamics with other Russian Muslim republics can be very close, especially Bashkortostan. The empirical research here significantly flourished due to the possibility of conducting an interview in Ufa with Mr Ruslan Mirsaiapov, who was the head of the Bashkiria State Committee for Foreign Economic Relations (2017–20), and who by then had just received a new appointment as the Trade representative of the Russian Federation in Azerbaijan. Mr Mirsaiapov is among the leading figures who conduct economic activities between Bashkortostan and the Gulf states, so his insights were particularly helpful. In addition, the interview with Mr Ainur Akkulov, vice-president of the Union 'Chamber of Commerce and Industry of the Republic of Bashkortostan' also added details to trade and economic links between the GCC and Bashkortostan. Finally, the interview with Mr Ruslan Karamyshev, the leading adviser to the Council for State Confessional Relations under the Head of the Republic of Bashkortostan, was helpful for learning about key objectives and directions of Bashkortostan in collaboration with the Gulf states. My fieldwork in Tatarstan and Bashkortostan culminated in studying their paradiplomatic efforts towards the Gulf states, after which a further visit to a Russian Muslim community was made possible, the North Caucasus.[74]

In Dagestan, the interview with Mr Gadzhiamin Ramaldanov, who was the deputy minister of Economics and Territorial Development of the Republic of Dagestan (2019–21), and is currently deputy head of Administration of Derbent city, exhaustively explained Dagestan's ongoing paradiplomatic efforts towards the Gulf states, mostly economic deals, and further elaborated on the mechanisms of such collaborations. He was particularly informative on how the Dagestan government builds such efforts. On Chechnya's efforts to build close links with the Gulf states, in-depth discussions occurred with representatives of the Chechen Republic on the subject. I also met with high-ranking Chechen representatives at the Fifth Forum for Promoting Peace in Muslim Societies in 2018 (Abu Dhabi, UAE), which allowed me to observe how Chechnya's paradiplomacy towards the Gulf states works in practice. All of this data collection has been crucial for achieving the goals of this book and offering an empirical contribution to the subject.

Overall, this book provides a new angle on relations between Russia and the Middle East/GCC states by bringing its minorities (and shared Islamic identities) into the discussion. Perhaps the closest existing scholarship to that of this book is in Russian and Bashkir, which acknowledges the importance of Muslim diplomats, especially Karim Khakimov's efforts, and religious authorities in attempts to develop relations between the Kingdom of Hijaz and Nejd (from 1932, Saudi Arabia) and the USSR. This includes works written by Professor Vitaly Naumkin, *Failed Partnership: Soviet Diplomacy in Saudi Arabia Between the World Wars*,[75] Oleg Ozerov's book, *Karim Khakimov: Chronicle of his Life*,[76] and L. Gadilov and F. Gumerov's *Karim Khakimov*.[77] By contrast, this book covers a crucial century of development (1920–2020) for both the Gulf states (Saudi Arabia, the United Arab Emirates, Bahrain, Qatar, Oman, Kuwait) and Tatarstan, during which the TASSR (modern Tatarstan) emerged as part of the Soviet Union. There is considerable overlap between this book and the themes of recent scholarships on the Russia–GCC states' relations, especially in comparison to the comprehensive volume *Russia's Relations with the GCC and Iran*, edited by Doha-based Russian scholar Nikolay Kozhanov, which offers the perspectives of Western and non-Western scholars on the subject. The book offers a great deal of historical context, details modern Russia's growing role in the Middle East, explains the rationale behind choices of regional alignment by

Moscow, the main aims, objectives and drivers in the region and, based on these assumptions, details Russia's foreign policy in the Gulf region. Nonetheless, the book lacks an account of Russia's Muslim minorities and their relations with the Gulf states, in comparison to this volume in particular, and is not able to cover the crucial role of Tatars in the Kremlin's policy-making.

Having said that, this book acknowledges the important contributions of the aforementioned authors, which provide significant insight into and support for the arguments presented here. Many other authors are also contributing to this growing field; the endnote that follows provides further details for extended reading, reflecting the current author's engagement with their important work. The nuances of this book are entwined with the specific identity of the author, beyond even this research basis. She is part of a Muslim minority within the Russian Federation – a Tatar – who has been brought up to be proud of her Tatar identity, but also strongly appreciating the benefits of the cultural richness of the multinational Russian state. One advantage is having the opportunity from childhood of speaking two languages – Slavic Russian and Turkic Tatar – while observing the tolerant relations and appreciation of both Muslim and Christian religions and cultures. Her professional life has also provided a range of perspectives feeding into this research, including experience of Tatarstan's paradiplomacy while an intern in the President of Tatarstan's Office for the Department of Integration with Religious Associations (in 2012), immersion in Gulf studies at university and stepping outside both these settings through living and working in the UK over seven years. This positionality permits interpretations and contributions that offer a new angle on Moscow–Gulf relations. This is done by looking at Tatar contributions to Kremlin–GCC relations over 100 years of history, along with a studied appreciation of other Russian Muslim-populated regions and their roles in a variety of developments.

Through this partly historical perspective, this book contributes to the literature on Russia and Middle East studies, including both Soviet and modern Russia.[78] The existing literature pays significantly less attention to the GCC–USSR/Russia relations, prioritizing USSR/Russia relations with Egypt, Syria, Yemen, Turkey, Afghanistan, Israel/Palestine and Iran. Examination of archive documents and available primary sources contributes substantially to existing literature on relations in the twentieth century, while interviews with political elites and stakeholders and analyses of primary sources have also been fundamental to elaborating on Russia–Gulf relations. Consequently, the book contributes to the study of GCC–Russia relations, which is a subject of increasing research interest but has yet to receive an extended targeted study.[79] Though a few academic works emphasize the importance of the Chechen government's efforts to build close relations with the GCC states,[80] studies on Tatarstan and other Russian regions, including Dagestan and Bashkortostan, and the GCC, are incomplete. Alongside its extended analysis of Tatar factors, an additional chapter provides an overview of other Russian Muslim republics (Chechnya, Ingushetia, Dagestan, Bashkortostan) and their relations with the Gulf states. In doing so the volume fills a gap concerning other Russian Muslim republics' relations with the GCC states via their shared Islamic identities.

Valuable scholarship of Islam in Russia[81] gives a good historical overview of the emergence of Islam in Russia and its Muslim republics, particularly modern Tatarstan. However, such scholarship tends to have a very limited focus on Islam as a contributing factor for developing relations between Tatarstan and GCC states/the Muslim world. Existing literature on the subject considers Soviet/Russia's usage of the so-called 'Islamic weapon' (often excluding detailed discussions on the TASSR/ Tatarstan and Gulf relations using Muslim identities).[82] Neither does other existing scholarship on Tatarstan look in detail at Tatarstan's paradiplomacy efforts towards the GCC states. Perhaps the closest contribution on the topic is Gulnaz Sharafutdinova's academic paper.[83] Others are mainly focused on the history of the Tatars and their relations with Russians,[84] the contributions of Tatar intellectuals to modern Islamic thought[85] and the identity of the Volga Tatars.[86] Existing literature also considers their national resistance,[87] research on radicalization[88] and other problems, such as the declining level of Tatar speakers.[89]

The book also offers a different perspective on the scholarship on Tatarstan and, consequently, Russian minorities studies. It adds an important dimension to the literature on minorities studies.[90] Meanwhile, the book also develops IR constructivists' scholarship[91] on the role of identities in developing relations between independent states and minorities of another state. Therefore, it helps the current discussions to move beyond solely economic or geopolitical considerations, structuring a novel and increasingly important understanding of the role of minority cultures in underpinning international relations.

Finally, the process of this book has been interrupted by geopolitical turbulence – the Ukraine crisis. The final chapter assesses the potential impact of the conflict, discussing the future of Gulf–Moscow–Kazan relations. In doing so, the manuscript also contributes to emerging academic literature on the impact of the Ukrainian moment on Russia–Gulf relations, and the potential impacts on Kazan–Gulf relations. On a broader scale, the manuscript offers a contribution on the Ukraine crisis by discussing the crucial regional players' positions on the conflict, closely linked to the energy-rich emirates and their role in the energy crisis. This includes analysis of possible external power shifts, and demonstrations of the multipolarity of the Middle East. Within these geopolitical complexities, the monograph follows its aim to consider the role of shared Islamic identities in future possible scenarios between Moscow and the GCC states, and the role of the Tatars in this process, thereby acknowledging the deeper currents of geopolitics than are necessarily visible to analyses which remain only at the level of the nation state.

1.4 The structure of the book

Chapter 1 demonstrates the recurrent puzzle of links between Tatarstan and the Gulf states by offering a short historical background, and pointing out their shared Islamic identities to explain the rationale behind the case studies and the overlooked role of Tatars in Moscow – Gulf relations over the past 100 years. This is followed by introducing the argument of the book and its relation to International Relations (IR) theory, by a brief examination of the constructivist position in IR, and the theoretical framework developed through this book. The chapter further stresses the contributions of the presented argument and its relationship with existing explanations. By stressing on empirical research, it presents the originality of the monograph.

Chapters 2 and 3 discuss any existing partnership between the TASSR and the Gulf states between 1917 and 1990, and the reasons for their shape and type. Chapter 2 particularly argues that during the Soviet time, direct engagements were very limited due to existing legislation. The USSR government did not grant TASSR the opportunity to conduct paradiplomacy, and this curtailed any direct links with the Arabian states. This, even though the Tatars were actively engaged, given their Muslim identities, in different Soviet mechanisms to build closer relations with the Kingdom of Hijaz and Nejd, notably in the 1920s and 1930s. Among two mechanisms that did facilitate some links were the appointment of a Tatar-origin diplomat(s) and the role of religious organizations. These efforts did not, however, contribute to TASSR and Arabian states having direct collaborations.

Chapter 3 brings Moscow to the discussion and argues that failed direct collaborations between the TASSR and the Gulf states are a prime cause in Moscow's relations with both. Potential challenges from the Tatars, such as the possibility of duality of power and the threat of pan-Turkism, led gradually to the erosion of the TASSR's status within the Soviet system. Arguably, similar concerns stopped the central government from permitting paradiplomatic efforts by the TASSR. Concerning shared Islamic identities, these also came under question during the Soviet period, as by the end of Soviet rule, Islam had retained only a ritual form, meaning that even limited collaborations through the religious field were limited. Also, relations between the USSR and Arabian states failed, mainly due to great power competitions, where the Gulf states had traditionally supported the Western bloc. This reason can be another explanation for the failure to build partnerships between TASSR and Arabian states between 1917 and 1990. In other words, based on the analyses provided in Chapters 2 and 3, the TASSR and the GCC states' relations were severely limited due to (1) the failed cooperation between 'Self(s)' and the 'Other', and (2) the damaged nature of their shared identities of 'Self(s)' and minority 'Self'.

Chapter 4 moves to the 1990s and the collapse of the USSR. The TASSR became the Republic of Tatarstan of the Russian Federation. The chapter demonstrates the emergence of relations between modern Tatarstan and the GCC states. At the political level, there were relatively few signs of cooperation in the 1990s, and most relations were built based on the religious factor. However, the situation changed after 2000. Since then, Tatarstan's paradiplomacy with the GCC states, relying on shared Islamic identities, has been mainly grounded in developing economic cooperation, including through Islamic finance and banking.

Chapter 5 brings Moscow into the discussion again and explains why active engagements between Tatarstan and the GCC states occurred, especially after 2000. The chapter examines Kazan–Moscow relations since the 1990s and illustrates the gradual erosion of the 'special status' of Tatarstan over time. However, it argues that, with growing federal centralized authority under Putin's leadership, Tatarstan has been productively integrated (along with other Muslim-populated regions) into federal policies to build closer relations with the Muslim world. Arguably, the federal centre has granted Tatarstan a 'special role' of bridging these relations between Russia and the GCC. Tatarstan–GCC economic collaborations reflect the Republic's status within the Russian Federation, along with the necessity to diversify the sources of its income. At the same time, economics have been crucial for the federal centre as well, as Russia has remained under sanctions, among other reasons. Improvements in relations between Tatarstan and GCC states are linked to growing geopolitical interests between Russia and the Gulf states, along with economic collaborations in energy, trade turnover and sale of weapons. Chapters 4 and 5 show that shared identities boost cooperation between 'Self(s)' and the minority 'Self' of another state, (1) if 'Self(s)' and the 'Other' have interests in common, and the 'Other' is willing to integrate its minorities into this process; and (2) if 'Self(s)' and minority 'Self' have shared interests.

Chapter 6 examines other Russian Muslim republics, such as Chechnya, Ingushetia, Dagestan and Bashkortostan, and their relations with the Gulf states. Due to similar factors to those presented earlier, direct relations barely occurred with the Arabian states until recently. For this reason, the chapter will briefly discuss the Soviet period, but mostly focus on modern Russia. The Bashkir Autonomous Soviet Socialist Republic's relations with the Gulf states are very similar to the TASSR developments. Relations have been actively developed since the 2000s, especially cooperation in economic fields (mechanical engineering, food supplies, construction and production of building materials). Further relations between Bashkortostan and the Gulf states rely on cooperation in religious and educational fields.

The chapter also explores the North Caucasus, another of Russia's key Muslim-populated areas, and the relations of republics such as Chechnya, Ingushetia and Dagestan with the GCC states. During Soviet rule, Chechnya, with Ingushetia, formed the Checheno–Ingush Autonomous Soviet Socialist Republic, and direct collaboration with the Gulf states had not occurred. After the collapse of the USSR, the GCC states supported the Chechen course during its wars against the Russian state. Over the next fifteen years, Ramzan Kadyrov, the head of Chechnya became known as a key supporter of Putin's policies. Chechnya uses its paradiplomacy, religious cooperation, including hosting different religious forums and conferences, to boost its close relations with the GCC states. Ingushetia also keeps links with the Gulf states, mainly relying on their shared Islamic identities. The Dagestan Autonomous Soviet Socialist Republic has had limited cooperation with the Gulf states. After the collapse of the USSR, Dagestan began developing economic operations with the GCC states, along with religious links. Cooperation mainly relies on the Dagestan diasporas in the Gulf states (another aspect of shared Islamic identity), serving as a unique mechanism for cooperation. The chapter concludes that these examples also illustrate how shared identities boost cooperation between 'Self(s)' and minority 'Self' of another state. In the Bashkortostan, Chechnya, Ingushetia and Dagestan cases, cooperation with the GCC states occurred mainly in the 2000s, when Russia had begun to integrate its minorities into its policies.

Chapter 7 has been produced during the finalization of the manuscript, and offers some possible scenarios resulting from the Ukraine conflict, specifically its impact on further relations between Moscow–Kazan–GCC states. Following the main argument of the book, the chapter draws on the GCC states' responses over the conflict, and consequently discusses its effects on current common interests between 'Self(s)' and the 'Other': to what extent such geopolitical turbulences might shape 'Self(s)' and 'minority Self' shared interests and what the visible prospects and obstacles are. The chapter also discusses the potential future of Kazan–Moscow relations, and argues that the federal centre will remain interested in further integrating its minorities – including the Tatars– into its policies, to boost relations with the GCC states. This may have legislative as well as practical or diplomatic implications.

Specifically, the chapter argues that, given the neutral responses of Bahrain and Oman to the conflict, it keeps the door open for further collaborations between Moscow and Manama/Muscat, including collaborations with Kazan based on shared Islamic identities. Relations between 'Self' and 'minority Self', such as between Kuwait and Tatarstan, might be limited, given Kuwait's stance on the crisis. Nonetheless, given the already limited interactions, it will not damage the situation much in bilateral relations. Qatar's position and interest in supporting the Ukraine, mainly driven by its own national interests, such as the possibility to emerge as the alternative to Russia as gas supplier to Europe, along with strengthening its relations with Washington, might decrease the level of common interests between 'Other' and 'Self', which might also affect relations between 'Self' and 'minority Self' – in other words, relations between Doha and Kazan might decline, too. Alternatively, the balancing act shown by both Saudi Arabia and the United Arab Emirates might suggest further common interests with Moscow, in other words, between 'Self(s)' and the 'Other'. In some regard, these cases have also been crucial to support the argument of the book. Both states, having shared identities with the Tatars, have the most developed, in other words, the strongest, relations between 'Self(s)' and 'minority Self', and have also chosen to maintain relations with Russia. These positions are linked with national interests, such as responses to energy crises, from which energy-rich states have been winning in the short run, and also reflect relations with the great powers – especially the current low point in relations with Washington under the Biden administration. As the book demonstrates, Saudi Arabia and the United Arab Emirates' relations have been significantly developed with Tatarstan, and shared Islamic identities have contributed to the balancing acts of the Saudis and Emiratis. With this in mind, it seems the Kremlin will continue acknowledging this existing powerful force of shared identities between the Tatars (and other Muslim minorities) and the Gulf states, and so this book concludes on the largely positive expectation that despite many obstacles, relations between 'Self(s)' and 'minority Self' will continue to develop in the future.

TASSR and the Gulf states

Limited partnership

Chapters 2 and 3 discuss the partnerships that existed between the TASSR and the Gulf states between 1917 and 1990, and the factors influencing their type and scope. Chapter 2 particularly argues that there was little or no direct engagement during the Soviet era, due to the governing legislation. The USSR government did not grant TASSR the opportunity to conduct paradiplomatic efforts, curtailing links with the Arabian states. This was despite the fact that, particularly in the 1920s and 1930s, the Tatars were actively engaged, given their Muslim identities, in different Soviet mechanisms to build closer relations with the Kingdom of Hijaz and Nejd.[1] Among these mechanisms were the appointment of Tatar-Muslim-origin diplomat(s) and the role of religious organizations. These efforts did not translate into direct collaborations with Arabian states.

To demonstrate this, first, the chapter discusses the so-called Soviet 'Penetration into Mecca'; in this policy, the Muslim factor was crucial from the outset. In particular, the policy engaged a Muslim Tatar, Karim Khakimov, who was officially appointed on 14 April 1924 as diplomatic agent and consul general of the USSR in the Kingdom of Hijaz. The former red commander is illustrative of the range of applied strategies based on Muslim identities, including hajj, and small hajj – *umrah* – diplomacy and distributions of gifts, which were instrumental for building close relations between the USSR and the Kingdom. Further, the chapter illustrates another mechanism of Soviet usage of the Islamic factor for collaborations, involving Tatars, but not allowing direct cooperation between the TASSR and Hijaz /Saudi Arabia: a religious organization, namely the Central Spiritual Board of Muslims Internal to Russia and Siberia.

2.1 The Soviet 'penetration into Mecca'

The so-called 'Islamic strategy' [or more stridently 'the Islamic weapon']² became crucial for the Bolshevik government in both internal and foreign policies. Internally, considering the Russian Empire had a considerable Muslim population, the Bolsheviks began active steps to attract the Muslim population. Following the bourgeois-democratic revolution of February 1917, the majority of the Tatar leadership maintained allegiance to constitutional democracy and supported the creation of the national-cultural autonomy of the Turko-Tatars of Inner Russia and Siberia within Russia.³ In addition to the liberal majority, there was a nationalist minority which pressed for full political independence and the establishment of a Tatar state. After the Bolshevik revolution, Tatar nationalists tried to revive Tatar statehood by acknowledging an Islamo–Turkic state of Idel-Ural.

Ayaz Iskhaki was one of the leading figures of the Tatar political and cultural renaissance, and he was also among the first Muslim 'radicals' to make the curious political evolution from Revolutionary Socialism to nationalism and Islam. He played a major role at the First All-Russian Congress held in Moscow in May 1917, and was elected chairman of the Central Executive Committee of the National Council (*Milli Shura*) established in Moscow (See Chapter 3). In his famous Idel-Ural essay he notes:⁴

> The purpose of this essay is to give a brief historical and political [account of] the descendants of the first group, i.e. about the Turks who occupy the territory between the Idel River (Volga) and Turkestan, starting from the Sura River to the Caspian Sea, which includes, according to the old (pre-revolutionary) administrative division, part of the Nizhny Novgorod province, the entire Kazan and Samara provinces, part of the Simbirsk and Saratov provinces, all Astrakhan, Orenburg and Ufa provinces and, finally, a part of Perm and Vyatka. History tells us that this land has belonged to the Turkic peoples since ancient times.

In other words, according to this view, the Middle Volga region remained mainly Islamic and non-Russian, and whenever there was a major revolt against Russian colonial rule, the Tatars were likely to be joined by the Chuvash, Bashkir, Cheremish (Mari), Mordova and other nations.

Following his contribution, Idel-Ural was expected to include the entire Kazan and Ufa guberniyas (governorates) and separate districts of Orenburg, Perm, Simbirsk, Samara and Vyatka guberniyas, which were mainly populated by the Turko-Tatars. Additionally, the Chuvash and Cheremish people were expected to enter the state.⁵ The project of the 'Volga-Ural State' was the first application of the idea of establishing Soviet Socialist Republics (States) in Russia.[6] The Idel-Ural State, or Idel-Ural Republic, was thus a short-lived Tatar republic, though defeated by the Red Army located in Kazan, on 28 March 1918, that claimed to unite Tatars, Bashkirs, Volga Germans and the Chuvash during the turmoil of the Russian Civil War. In May 1920 the Bolsheviks forced the Volga Tatars into a new administrative unit, the Tatar Autonomous Soviet Socialist Republic,[7] the borders of which included the modern-day Tatarstan territories, resulting in a territorial delimitation that left many Tatars living outside their ethnic republic.[8]

The path of the formation of the TASSR, including the role of the Muslim factor in its establishment, will be further explained in Chapter 3; however, within the context of this chapter, it should be mentioned that the TASSR did not have rights for the implementation of direct foreign policies; consequently, direct formal links between TASSR and Arabian states did not occur. This is expressed in the All-Russian Central Executive Committee Decree dated 27 May 1920 about the Autonomous Tatar Socialist Soviet Republic. In the note to Part II of paragraph 3 it is stated that 'Foreign affairs and foreign trade remain entirely under the jurisdiction of the Central bodies of the RSFSR'.[9] Khodorovsky comments on this as follows:

> This means that they [TASSR] are part of the all-Russian (federal) Soviet Republic, and not at all independent in all their affairs. The Tatar republic does not have its own People's Commissariat for Foreign Affairs. It cannot conduct any of its own independent foreign policy, cannot enter into treaties and, in general, in relations with other states. On behalf of all of Soviet Russia (and therefore on behalf of the autonomous republics of Bashkir, Tatar, Turkestan, Kirgiz and etc.) that are part of this Russia, international relations are conducted by the Council of People's Commissars of the Russian Republic and the People's Commissariat for Foreign Affairs of this republic.[10]

He continues to note that this is functionally necessary, rather than merely a restriction:

> such an order is quite understandable, and any other order would only lead to serious [*sic*] misunderstandings and complications. It is impossible to create a situation in which separate parts of Soviet Russia would conduct their own independent foreign policy, conclude independent treaties with other states, reconcile and fight with whom and when they pleased, etc.[11]

In other words, the Soviet government had no facility for TASSR to establish paradiplomatic efforts, but instead – especially in the period between

1920 and 1930 – involved Tatars in its foreign-policy objectives at the federal level (including towards the Arabian states).

In its emerging foreign policies, the Bolshevik government also made the southern, 'Muslim' direction one of its main priorities, which at first was very strongly influenced by ideological attitudes. In the early years of the existence of Soviet Russia, having undergone the Intervention and the Civil War, its activities in the foreign East, not counting work with communist organizations, did not go beyond the framework of agitation appeals and sporadic contacts, primarily with leaders of national liberation movements. Before the Revolution of October 1917, Vladimir Lenin, the founder of the Bolsheviks, wrote that the duty of socialists was to support the struggle of oppressed peoples for their complete national emancipation 'in whatever form, right down to an uprising or war'.[12] The key policy for achieving this was an 'alliance' between the 'victorious proletariat' of the USSR (the Bolsheviks), and the 'opposed peoples of the East' in their opposition to 'imperialism' (the West).[13] The appeal addressed 'To All the Working Muslims of Russia and the East' of 20 December 1917 stated that the Arabs and all Muslims had the right to be the masters of their country and to decide their own destiny as they wished.[14] Though the Middle East was still under the control of the Western powers of Great Britain and France, the new Soviet leadership started to show an interest in the region.[15] The Soviets started to establish normal, even friendly, relations with 'Muslim' states: they developed relations with Turkey, where Mustafa Kemal led the Turkish people's struggle for the establishment of a republic; in 1921 the Soviet–Iran treaty was signed, which has been seen by Soviet scholars as an 'example of equal relations'.[16] Further, when Britain launched a third war against Afghanistan in 1919, Soviet Russia had been the first to recognize the sovereignty of Afghanistan in March 1919.[17]

However, the priority was not only cast by ideology – the spread of communism and anti-colonial ideas. With the strengthening of the Soviet statehood and its increasing role, trade and economic interests began to accumulate.[18] The People's Commissariat for Foreign Affairs of the Russian SFSR was tasked with establishing contacts with the Arab world, whose population, after Turkey's defeat in the First World War, experienced a rise in national feelings. At the same time, special attention was paid by the government of the Russian Soviet Federative Socialist Republic (RSFSR) (since 1922, the Soviet Union) to those countries that were dependent on the colonial powers, including the Hijaz. Vitaly Naumkin[19] of the Russian Academy of Sciences lists the reasons for Moscow establishing relations with an Arabian state: establishing relations with states south of the borders of the USSR into the Arab world; attracting the population of Muslim states to their side; finding a market for Russian goods in the Middle East; and opposing the activities of Great Britain.[20]

To achieve this, the Politburo of the Central Committee of the RCP (b) quickly decided in principle to restore official relations with Hijaz. During the conference, back in December 1922, the Russian delegation in Lausanne had entered into a contract with the Hijaz delegation.[21] On the instructions of Sheriff Hussein, his representative Naji al-Asyl, who had several meetings with the Russian delegate, the plenipotentiary of the RSFSR in Italy Vatslav Vorovsky, and with the first people's commissar for Foreign Affairs, Georgy Chicherin himself, raised the issue of establishing diplomatic relations between the two countries.[22]

Significantly, the so-called 'Penetration into Mecca', which was of great importance for the USSR, as described by Georgy Chicherin, was boosted by using the Muslim factor, specifically a Muslim Tatar, the former red commander Karim Khakimov, who was officially appointed on 14 April 1924 as diplomatic agent and consul general of the USSR in the Kingdom of Hijaz. Vitaly Naumkin quotes Chicherin's note to Stalin on 18 December 1923[23] where he expressed a wish for the consul to also be a doctor, which 'would make it possible for the King to explain to the British his presence through the need for passports and sanitary supervision of pilgrims from the USSR'. The second wish, concerning the ethno-confessional affiliation of the candidate, touches on the strategic appointment of a Muslim. Chicherin aimed to reach the very heart of the Muslim world:

> The establishment of Mecca is undoubtedly of the most serious important focus. If Comrade Ibragimov[24] had found us an appropriate Muslim plenipotentiary who would be called a consul, but in fact a plenipotentiary, this would greatly increase our influence not solely in Arabia.

The doctor was not found, but a Muslim diplomat, in this case a Tatar, was appointed to the post.

The ethno-confessional affiliation of candidates for the posts of diplomatic representatives abroad was often, but not always, taken into account when making appointments.[25] The Russian government had established a consulate in 1891 to respond to the growing number of hajjis and their needs, and the first Russian consul in Jeddah was the aforementioned Muslim Bashkir Shagimardan Ibragimov.[26] However, Ibragimov died less than a year after the appointment in 1892, and after him, no Muslim was posted to Jeddah until the withdrawal of the consulate due to the World War in 1914. As a result, as Ildar Nurimanov states:

> an inevitable blow to the Hajj was struck [*sic*] during World War I, when the Russian and Ottoman Empires found themselves on opposite sides of the front.

Even the censored Muslim press spoke of the deep feelings of believers because of the impossibility of performing the Hajj.[27]

Also, Norihiro Naganawa argues that 'the rivalry with Britain in Arabia made Russian diplomats aware of the necessity of Muslim personnel at the Jeddah consulate.'[28] One example was the suggestion of the Russian consul in Jeddah, M. Nikolsky, to appoint a Muslim as secretary of the consulate, learning from the British experience.[29] The great power competition between the USSR and Britain/US will be discussed in relation to the limited relations between the USSR and Arabian states, in Chapter 3.

Moreover, a Tatar Soviet diplomat Iusuf Tuimetov (1893–1938) was the first secretary general of Jeddah, who also served as secretary of the Soviet Embassy in Yemen. He was arrested in 8 December 1937, and shot in 1938; however, in 1965 he was rehabilitated as a victim of the political terror in the USSR.[30] Nonetheless, the contribution of another Tatar – Karim Khakimov, who is especially known for applying strategies that relied on the shared Muslim factor with Arabia in his diplomatic activities – will be discussed specifically in the next section. The author likewise appreciates the necessity to consider other ethnic Tatars' roles in decision-making and their contributions to building relations between the Soviets and the Arabian states. For example, it is known that there were Tatars in the Jeddah–Medina area – only around ten families of ethnic Bashkir and Tatar origins – at that time, based on the document sent by Khakimov to the economic-legal department of the People's Commissariat for Foreign Affairs of the Russian SFSR (NKID); such seemingly small details can make it difficult to draw a historically precise account of the Tatar community, when seeking to apply the Muslim factor to relations with the Kingdom of Hijaz and Nejd (since 1932 known as Saudi Arabia).[31] However, it is possible to establish a coherent analysis of Karim Khakimov's diplomatic activities and applied strategies based on shared Muslim identities using the existing records, as further details that follow will demonstrate.

2.2 Tatar Khakimov as a mechanism of the Soviet 'penetration into Mecca'

2.2.1 Communist with a Muslim background

Karim Khakimov, known 'Red Pasha', or 'Tatar Lawrence of Arabia' or 'the Arabian vizier of the Kremlin',[32] was born on 28 November 1892[33] in the village of Dyusyan (now Dyusyanovo) in the Il'-Kul'minskaia volost' of the Beleevskii district of the Ufa province of Russia (today the Republic of Bashkortostan),[34] but he was of Tatar origin.[35] He came, as Vitaly Naumkin states, from either a family of land-poor peasants, as he himself reported in a questionnaire, or a far-from-poor family that owned ten tithes of land (as reported in the 'revision tales') (registers of birth), which he apparently concealed. The version that he was from a wealthy family was supported by Russian scientist Ruslan Khayretdinov,[36] but Oleg Ozerov states that this version is based on much later information, when Khakimov was no longer in the village.[37] Ozerov, rather, describes his family as 'middle peasant' like many that lived in Dyusyanovo.[38] His analysis is also similar to that of Gadilov and Gumerov, who argue that the large family had only 3.5 tithes of land, a cow and a horse.[39] Such family background details appear important, as this is directly linked with his non-systematic education[40] and his path to becoming a proletarian. However, it should be noted that the foundation of his education was in the Islamic environment, which became crucial for establishing relations with Muslim, especially Arabian, states during his career path as a diplomat.

Given his family background, he did not have much choice initially, as the only available school was a *mekteb*, which he attended from 1903 to 1905. There he learned Islamic prayers, knowledge of which became important for him when he was in his high post in Jeddah.[41] In the autumn of 1906, Karim Khakimov began to study at the 'Sadik' madrasa of the Khazret in Kargalinskaia Sloboda, a suburb of Orenburg.[42] He was respected among *shakirds* and mullas, due to his determination and performance, though he did not like the cramming system on which all the studies in the madrasa were built. In their book on Khakimov, Gadilov and Gumerov share an anecdote which foreshadows his emergence as *Revolutionary – Diplomat* (the title of the book): 'He began to get and secretly read Russian books. One of the *shakirds*, having learned about this, reported him. The reading aroused the anger of the mulla.'[43]

This illustration of preferring an internationalist rather than nationalist path, despite a strong Muslim background, is similarly seen in his other life experiences. Karim lived in constant financial need, which eventually meant he had to stop his studies at the madrasa.[44] He left, with his friend Gaziz Galimov, to go to Orenburg, where Galimov remembered it was extremely difficult to get money for food. In the end, having worked at first as a janitor in a butcher's shop, Karim managed to work for a blind man who lived at a madrasa. He was an expert on the Qur'an and Muslim prayers. Knowing the Holy Book by heart, he received alms for his labours and shared bread with Karim for his companionship.[45] Gaziz was satisfied with everything and got a job as a janitor in the tavern of the Tatar owner. Karim was looking for work with Russians, believing that having learned the Russian language, he would have access to much more knowledge. Oleg Ozerov[46] comments: 'For the first time, the breadth of his soul and the complete absence of xenophobia and nationalism emerged. He was ready to learn from any people who could give him new knowledge.'[47] However, his early attempts were unsuccessful. The Russian merchant he approached refused the young man a job, believing that he did not understand Russian well. In the summer of 1907, Karim was forced to get a job with a Tatar bey (in Tatar a title of address, corresponding to 'Mr') at the Chelkar station, but then, seeing no future prospects, he joined the Tashkent railway as a worker. Even while working there, he did not waste any time and studied Russian with the help of a clerk. Habib Khasanov remembers that when he met Khakimov a few years later, in 1915, he told Khakimov that he did not know Russian; Khakimov immediately promised to study with him. 'Without Russian language it is impossible,' he said, 'we live in the same family with a great people, we live and work together. And we have to fight together. Without the Russians, it will be difficult for us, brother.' To begin with, he gave him a book – *Self-study Guide to the Russian Language* and explained in detail how to use it.[48]

His path as a proletarian begun with working at Dzhela and Kumpula railway stations in 1907.[49] After spending the summer of 1908 in a Kyrgyz village, where he taught the children of wealthy nomads for money, in the late autumn of 1908 he returned to Orenburg, and again entered the madrasa, trying to find the truth and meaning of life in the Qur'anic texts.[50] He spent the winter of 1909 in the village of Nikol'skoe, in Orenburg province, where he taught the Qur'an.[51] He returned again to the madrasa, this time having saved up money in order to obtain the best education possible. His options were limited to 'Khusainiia' in Orenburg and the prestigious six-year-old 'Galia' in Ufa. These had been opened in the wake of the new national policy of the Tsarist autocracy, which after the 1905 Revolution presented the opportunity to create national schools. The main content of the educational process in them was inspired by ideas of a prominent Islamic enlightener, the founder of *jadidism* and pan-Turkism in Russia, Ismail-bey Gaspinsky.[52] He studied at 'Galia' madrasa but, having quarrelled with local *shakirds*, he was forced to quit his studies in 1911 and left for Tashkent.[53] Then he worked as a miner in the Tajik city of Konibodom, which gave him the opportunity to present himself as a proletarian in the future, which in those days helped to make a career.[54] There he also received an initial knowledge of Marxism and became interested in revolutionary ideas.[55] However, in the spring of 1917, he took an external examination for a certificate of maturity at the second male gymnasium in Tomsk,[56] which offered him the opportunity to pass exams and prepare to enter higher education. Nonetheless, as his brother Khalik Khakimov states: 'October 1917. Karim Khakimov postponed his studies to devote himself to the revolution.'[57] Tomsk in this case was crucial, as for the first time, Khakimov got the opportunity to get to know the revolutionary movement better. In his autobiography he wrote:

> The path in my youth and later developed in such a way that if I did not get into the small working centres of Russia, without receiving the necessary political education, I was deprived of the opportunity to conduct more rational political work. The opportunity arose only since 1915, upon arrival to Tomsk, where, colliding with student committees, I also met with the social democrats.[58]

In October 1917, the Socialist Revolution triumphed in Petrograd. The interim government was overthrown. All power passed into the hands of the military revolutionary committee. However, the Soviet regime did not immediately prevail everywhere. On the outskirts of Russia, it was established after a struggle; so it was in the territory of the Orenburg province, while Khakimov worked at the Ak-Bulak Tashkent train station.[59] At the end of November 1917 in Orenburg, in the Caravan-Sarai, the organizations of the Tatar bourgeoisie *Milli Shura* (National Council) and Muslim officers' *Herbi Shura* (Military Council) convened a meeting of Muslim soldiers. Civilians were also present. The initiative at the rally was seized by representatives of the Tatars, Bashkir bourgeoisie and Muslim officers. In their speeches, they

> urged Muslims not to recognise Soviet power and slandered the Bolsheviks, claiming that they were destroying national culture and religion. Most of the soldiers and workers present did not agree with this fiction, but none of them dared to line up.[60]

At that moment, Khakimov rose to the podium, and said that the Bolsheviks opposed the continuation of the imperialist war, national oppression, that they stood for the transfer of land to the peasants and working Cossacks, for the nationalization of factories. The speaker ended his speech with a call to recognize Soviet power and establish it in the Orenburg province.[61] Garif Alparov, who met and knew Khakimov in 1917 in Orenburg, concludes:

> The soldiers listened to him attentively, and then they heard exclamations of approval. However, the organisers of the rally [who were opposed to Bolsheviks] and their henchmen did not like Khakimov's speech. They made a noise, trying to drown out the speaker. Not having achieved the desired result, under the whistle and roar of the soldiers masses, they were forced to leave the hall.[62]

This was the first public speech by Khakimov, and it was successful. In April 1918 Khakimov officially joined the ranks of the Bolshevik Party.[63] In March 1919, Gabdulla Davletshin met Khakimov in Kazan. He was then one of the organizers of the First Volga region (*Privolzhskaia Tatbrigada*). Davletshin remembered well his heartfelt words: 'I, he [Khakimov] said, joined the Bolshevik Party and from that moment completely devoted myself to the Party, because the Party business is my own business, and I have no higher goal than serving the Party.'[64] After working in Orenburg as People's Commissar for Education, in April 1920 he was appointed as assistant to the head of the Political Directorate of the Turkestan front.[65] In December 1920, Khakimov was appointed the plenipotentiary representative of the RSFSR in the Bukhara People's Republic.[66] On 15 September 1921, by decision of the Politburo, Khakimov was appointed to diplomatic work: as the consul general in Mushhad (Persia), and in May 1923 Khakimov was appointed consul general of the USSR in Rasht (Persia);[67] on 24 April 1924, a decree of the Consul of People's Commissars of the USSR was signed appointing Karim Khakimov as consul general in the Kingdom of Hijaz.

This appointment eventually proved hugely significant and provides an opportunity to elaborate further on the lack of direct links between TASSR and Hijaz – in other words, within the context of this manuscript, developing the concept of relations between 'Self(s)' and minority 'Self' who shared Muslim identities. Kosach,[68] having analysed many documents of that time, describes the future diplomat as a person brought up in a Bolshevik international environment, where 'the leading role was played by Russian workers', alien to the concepts of the *Jadids* with their adherence to the national idea, which they tried to combine with Bolshevism, and often its left-wing radical sense. This view was mostly supported, for example, by V. Kuibyshhev, who wrote about Khakimov: 'Comrade Khakimov I know since 19-20 [*sic*] in Turkestan. He is of the Muslim workers, he was the most communist and alien to the nationalist hopes. . . . He is a proletarian by birth.'[69] That is why Khakimov came into conflict with the *Jadid* leadership of the All-Russian Central Bureau of Muslim Organizations of the RCP (b) and the Commissariat for Muslim Affairs of Internal Russia. Khayretdinov has also stressed that working in Orenburg as People's Commissar for Education, he took the position of an ardent communist internationalist. In this city, Karim Khakimov drew a clear line between his views and the positions of the leaders of the national movement, emphasizing his affiliation with the Bolshevik Party; he had a negative attitude towards the national movement in Bashkortostan.[70] Khakimov rejected their concept of Tatar–Bashkir autonomy within the framework of Russian statehood, and even denied them the right to classify themselves as Bolsheviks. Karim was also opposed to the concept of Tatar autonomy, just as he was earlier against the Tatar–Bashkir equivalent (though he changed his position later).[71] The role of the Tatar and Muslim identity in building its republic during the Soviet times will be further explained in Chapter 3, to further explain why TASSR as the republic was not given the necessary rights for its paradiplomatic efforts towards the Gulf states. However, within the context of this chapter, the impact of a Tatar diplomat in office who nonetheless had strong loyalty to the Bolsheviks, over nationalist concerns, can be seen in the evolving status of the republic, and the resulting limitations on its (para)diplomatic capacities.

2.2.2 Khakimov's applied strategies of Muslim identities towards the Kingdom

On 14 April 1924, Khakimov was officially appointed 'diplomatic agent and consul general of the USSR' in the Kingdom of Hijaz. His Muslim identity gave him a straightforward advantage, as Khayretdinov clarifies: 'In comparison to the consuls [*sic*] of other European countries, the Soviet diplomat had an undoubted advantage – he was a Muslim, so he was given the opportunity to visit the capital Hijaz'.[72] This advantage was used for policy-making decisions. Despite his being a communist, Muslim identities were central to Khakimov's strategies towards the Kingdom. In general, hajj diplomacy, including small hajj – *umrah* – and another Muslim manner of distributing gifts, were clearly very important for building closer relations with the Kingdom's elite.

An example of the first is when a direct introduction to Ibn Saud occurred through the hajj discussion. Interestingly, British colonial intelligence officer and adviser to Ibn Saud in 1930, Harry St John Philby, had good relations with Khakimov, and he convinced Ibn Saud to accept Khakimov as a person who wanted to help defend the right to pilgrimage of Muslims from the USSR (15,000 people). The problem at that time was that the British did not let them through the straits, fearing the strengthening of the Russian presence and the penetration of the 'communist infection'. At a personal meeting, Khakimov asked Ibn Saud to help organize the hajj. However, as Ozerov clarifies, 'perhaps it was about some other political issues, which received different interpretations from us [USSR] and from the British'.[73] Nonetheless, as noted earlier, the work of the consulate in Jeddah, which operated from 1891 in the Russian hajjis and the Russian Empire in the Red Sea until the First World War, began again only in 1924, when the Soviet government restored diplomatic relations with the Hijaz. Consequently, there is no need to talk about hajj during this period.[74] Nonetheless, this diplomacy was a useful tool for meeting with Ibn Saud.

Another example of the Muslim factor is the performance by Khakimov of *umrah* (small hajj) in Mecca, in the midst of a confrontation between King Hussein of Hijaz and Amir of Riyad, Ibn Saud.[75] This strategic move in many respects changed the alignment of forces in the Middle East by giving Soviets a 'cover' for contacts with the new king. On 7 April Karim wrote a letter to Ibn Saud informing him about his trip by car[76] and asking him to 'give an order to your respective authorities to facilitate our trip to Mecca'.[77] Khakimov behaved honestly and with dignity, having simultaneously informed Sharif Hussein about the 'pilgrimage' and the intentions of himself and two colleagues.[78] The latter did not object, realizing that he was already cornered, and even asked that in the conversations of Ibn Saud, the consul should help to facilitate the conclusion of peace, that is to carry out a mediating mission.[79] As a result of an exchange of letters with Ibn Saud, an agreement was reached on the trip on 10 April 1925.[80] During this trip, Khakimov had two lengthy conversations with Ibn Saud and several conversations with his Meccan governor (most likely Faisal) who contributed to the formation of a more objective and capacious understanding of the Saudi line in Arabian affairs on the Soviet side.[81] Russian ambassador Ozerov argues that, in fact, with this trip, Karim Khakimov brilliantly and masterfully fulfilled the task of Moscow, and laid the foundations for the establishment of official relations between the USSR and the Saudi monarchy.[82] The British version of events was recorded in a report for the period 20 March–9 April 1925, as stated by Sd. R. W. Bullard, H. B. M. Agent and Consul:

> Mr Khakimoff [*sic*], the Soviet Agent in Jedda, is paying a visit to Mecca, nominally in the private capacity of a Moslem desirous of performing the minor pilgrimage. As he scoffs openly at the Moslem religion one may suppose that his visit is not prompted by piety alone. He is taking with him a young Persian, the son of a merchant, who is at present in charge of Persian interests. This boy is completely in Mr. Khakimoff's pocket, and repeats all the Bolshevik cant about Persia having been saved by the noble Soviet Government from the imperialistic claws of Great Britain.[83]

Discussing the meeting between Ibn Saud and Khakimov, he concludes:

> There is good reason to believe that Mr Khakimoff publicly engaged in violent propaganda against the 'imperialistic' powers, especially His Majesty's Government.[84]

This might suggest that Khakimov's *umrah* diplomacy promoted Soviet interests with the Kingdom.

Further, Norihiro Naganawa explains that hajjis' lodges (*takiya* (Arabic)) or (*tekke* (Turkish)) developed a new political significance during Khakimov's tenure in Jeddah.[85] This means that Khakimov tried to restore the rights of the Soviet republics from which their founders had originally hailed.[86] In August 1925 Khakimov suggested to Chicherin to obtain details from Tatar, Azerbaijani and Crimean Republics on awqaf (an Islamic endowment of property to be held in trust and used for charitable or religious purposes) in the Hijaz. The Tatar Section of the OGPU (United State Political Directorate) confirmed five *tekkes* belonging to Kazan Tatars in Mecca.[87] Despite such initiatives, which had the potential to create some direct links between TASSR and the Kingdom, in other words, between 'Self(s)' and minority 'Self', this did not happen to any significant degree. In 1927, the Soviet Consulate in Jeddah decided that the awqaf that had been created by Russian Muslims should remain, to enact their initial purposes based on Islamic legal tradition (shari'a); additionally, a special philanthropic association should be established to control these awqaf, with financial support from the USSR republics concerned.[88]

In December 1925, Jeddah fell, and Ibn Saud was proclaimed king of the Hijaz and the sultan of Nejd and the annexed territories (until that time, starting in 1920, he was only the sultan of Nejd).[89] The position of Khakimov and the staff of the Soviet mission, accredited by the enemy of Ibn Saud, was rather difficult: the Hashemite government fell, and the new one had not yet established diplomatic relations with Soviet Russia.[90] Under these conditions, Khakimov believed that the only correct way forward was the urgent establishment of direct contact, and then diplomatic relations with Ibn Saud. There was permission for this: the Soviet government decided to recognize the new state.[91]

Khakimov immediately took up this important mission on behalf of his government. On 16 February 1926, he himself got behind the wheel of a passenger car, and without taking any of the employees with him, left Jeddah. Hostilities by this time had ceased, but individual skirmishes still occurred. It was not safe to drive. As the recent front line was crossed, Khakimov sighed with relief.[92] The meeting with the king took place in a tent, in the camp of his troops, about whom many tales were told at that time, for their fanaticism and severity. Ibn Saud, the king of the new state, warmly received the Soviet representative, treated him to camel milk, which his bodyguards served in large clay cups. During the conversation, Khakimov informed Ibn Saud about the decision of the Soviet government to recognize the new Arabian state and Ibn Saud personally as its head, and to establish diplomatic relations with the Kingdom.[93] From the conversation Khakimov understood[94] that Ibn Saud attached great importance to the recognition of the Kingdom of Hijaz and Nejd by Soviet Russia: the new state needed international support. Alexander Stupak, honoured worker of Culture of the RSFSR, states: 'In the memory of the workers of the Soviet mission, this meeting between Khakimov and Ibn Saud in a tent has been preserved under the name of the "meeting in the desert".'[95] Thus, the Soviet Union became the first foreign state to recognize the Kingdom. Ten weeks after Ibn Saud ascended the throne, apart from the USSR and Great Britain, he was also recognized by France and the Netherlands, but not yet by any of the Muslim states.[96] The speed with which Moscow made the decision allowed Karim Khakimov to become a doyen of the diplomatic corps in Jeddah.[97]

The diplomatic mail was slow in those years. Only at the beginning of April did the People's Commissar of Foreign Affairs react to the exchange of notes between Khakimov and the king.[98] On 2 April, a letter was sent to Ibn Saud, in which the People's Commissar confirmed that the Soviet government 'was pleased with the exchange of notes'. It noted: 'My Government will be very happy if Your Majesty will accept modest gifts that would be a reminder of the establishment of diplomatic relations between the two countries', and expressed the 'hope that the work of the USSR representative in the state of Ibn Saud will be facilitated'.[99]

Both sides expressed a desire to strengthen cooperation. In his letter, King Ibn Saud highly appreciated the activities of Khakimov: 'I received through the representative Mr Karim Khakimov your friendly letter containing noble feelings . . . I can praise it and honour his tact and ability to conduct business, which contributed to the strengthening of friendly relations between both sides.'[100] On 4 April 1926, after establishing direct relations with King Ibn Saud, Khakimov wrote to deputy people's commissar for Foreign Affairs of the USSR, Lev Karakhan:

Recognition of the Soviet rule for Ibn Saud played a significant role as I was told in the circles of the King, prompting England and other powers to recognise Ibn Saud. The recognition of England, which was rather hasty, can be considered as forced. However, our recognition, which turned out to be the first, also had the significance that it very clearly underlined our friendly policy towards Ibn Saud and the fact that he can find moral support from us in his steps towards the emancipation of his country.[101]

Indeed, relations with Ibn Saud developed to be very close with Khakimov, which assisted several political goals. Alexander Stupak, honoured worker of the Culture of the RSFSR, whom Khakimov invited to go to work at the Diplomatic Agency and Consulate General of the USSR in Jeddah in 1927, recalls that Ibn Saud always received Khakimov with 'pleasure and warmth'. The conversations were held in a 'friendly atmosphere, and the questions raised in them often received the permission desired by the Soviet side'.[102]

Along with development of the hajj mission and *umrah*, facility with another Muslim identity characteristic also seems to have carried political importance – distribution of gifts. According to Soviet intelligence, obtained from the circles of foreign diplomats, Khakimov gained many friends among the Hijaz nobility and ordinary people, 'the result of the distribution of many gifts', which the Soviet representative did not skimp on.[103]

Applied strategies based on Muslim identities used by Karim Khakimov assisted in establishing good informal relations with the Arabian ruler, and his family, upon which rested his impact in building relations between the Soviets and the Kingdom. Khakimov's wife Khadicha Khakimova remembered in 1957:

> In 1932, the King's son, Amir Faisal came to Moscow. . . . When Prince Faisal exited the carriage, seeing an old acquaintance of Khakimov, he was so delighted that, approaching him, he opened his arms and kissed him. Seeing such a meeting with a Bolshevik, the Polish officials were so dumbfounded that everyone stretched out and stood at attention in front of the Prince and Khakimov. They never understood the reason for such respect for the 'Bolshevik diplomat'.[104]

Bennigsen, Henze, Tanham and Wimbush also argue that until the Second World War, which was a turning point for Soviet policies, Stalin's policy towards the Muslim world abroad demonstrates

> strong evidence of his belief either that the possibilities of revolution there were limited if not non-existent or that the Soviet Union was in no position to exploit whatever opportunities might exist to stimulate a wider revolutionary conflict among Muslims, or both.

Stressing the exceptional character of Khakimov's role, the authors continue:

> It is significant that with only one exception – that of Kerim Khakimov [*sic*], a Tatar, who was the first Soviet Consul-General in Jeddah and representative at the court of the Imam Yahya in Yemen (1928) – Stalin avoided using Soviet Muslim diplomats abroad in visible positions and no Muslim 'clerics' from the official Soviet Islamic establishment served as diplomatic instruments.[105]

This statement requires some qualification, as Muslim Kazakh Nazir Tyuryakulov was appointed and assigned to the Hijaz on 15 December 1927, when at the beginning of 1929, Khakimov was appointed the plenipotentiary representative of the USSR in Yemen. In 1935 Khakimov was again appointed as plenipotentiary representative in the Kingdom, but now to the Kingdom of Saudi Arabia, the official title of which emerged in 1932 following the unification of the Kingdom of Hijaz and Nejd. Further historical factors should also be taken into account. Khakimov was a victim (along with Tyuryakulov) of Stalin's political terror, and in the modern discourses there are ongoing evaluations of the impact of this on Saudi–Soviet relations:

> The fate of such a respected man in the East has gone unnoticed for the history of relations between the two countries.... News of his [Khakimov's] demise had the effect of detonating a bomb on the monarch [Ibn Saud], and he decided to freeze relations with the Soviet Union. This situation was to last for 60 years.[106]

As this section attempts to demonstrate, shared Muslim identities assisted in the building of relations between two countries, and a Tatar, Karim Khakimov, skilfully used it in diplomatic efforts towards the Kingdom's leadership (although this occurred at the Soviet level, rather than on behalf of the TASSR).

2.3 Religious organizations as a mechanism of the Soviet 'penetration into Mecca'

Along with a Tatar diplomat, another mechanism of involvement with Tatar origins (again at the Soviet level rather than the autonomous republic level (TASSR)) can be identified in terms of religious organization. This refers particularly to the Central Muslim Spiritual Board of Inner Russia and Siberia (TsDum),[107] by then the main religious organization in the Volga–Ural region (and historically in Russia) and traditionally of importance to the Tatars, although located in Ufa rather than in Kazan. This mechanism can be identified as Soviet 'religious diplomacy', a term coined by Fred Halliday.[108]

Illustrative of this case is the World Muslim Congress, which took place in Mecca in June–July 1926. Inviting sixty-eight delegates from fifteen states and regions, Ibn Saud positioned himself as the new protector of the hajj, instead of the defeated Sheriff of Mecca, Hussein.[109] In contrast to the plans of the pro-British caliphates, Ibn Saud in 1925, even before his occupation of Medina, intended to hold a Congress under his auspices in Mecca, though the situation did not allow him to implement this plan until later.[110] He returned to this idea again in 1926. In fact, he almost achieved recognition for himself from the Islamic world as the custodian of Islamic shrines, although there were still many supporters for transferring them to the control of the International Islamic Committee.[111] For example, documents between Nejd and Hijaz (from 7 November 1924 to July 1925), by then 'confidential',[112] from the president of the Syrian Union, Subhi Barakat, to His Majesty 'Abd al-'Aziz bin al-Sa'ud, king of Nejd state:

> We and the Syrians are prepared to come to complete terms with Your Majesty in respect of the administration and [...] regulations for the Holy places conformable to the wishes of the Islamic world in order that the Hajj pilgrim routes should be safe and open for Moslems in general. We have received information about Your Majesty's demand for the despatch [*sic*] of representatives for this purpose to Mecca and we have done the necessary so that this glorious object should be achieved. But in view of the international aspect which is peculiar of the Hajj organization we deem it necessary to refer the question to the Governments under mandate.

So, Ibn Saud developed a completely different agenda for the Congress, which was in line with his purely statist interests.[113] However, there was also the project of the Cairo Congress held under British rule.[114] In a telegram from secretary of state, London to Viceroy (F. & P. Dept.) dated 24 (recd. 25) October 1924, it is suggested:

> In the opinion of the President of Supreme Religious Council in Egypt difficulties in Hijaz might be solved by placing Holy Places and the surrounding Territory under a Governor subordinate to a Council representative of Moslem countries. He has sounded British Representative confidentially as to the likely view such a proposal would meet with in India. It is proposed to inform British Representative that His Majesty's Government consider that it is undesirable that they should act as intermediaries in this matter between Moslem Leaders in various countries and would prefer not to depart from complete neutrality.[115]

Naturally, Moscow's sympathies were on the side of the Meccan, being directly opposed to the Cairo Congress. Asma-hanum Sharaf, daughter of the Mufti of the Central Muslim Spiritual Board of Inner Russia and Siberia (TsDum), Mufti Rizaitdin (Riza) Fakhretdinov (Fakhretdin),[116] wrote in her memoirs:

> In Spring of 1926, my father received an invitation from Arabia to the First World Congress of Muslims, which was to be held in the summer of the same year in Mecca. It was necessary to decide: to go or not? When they gathered

about this, my father [Mufti Rizaitdin Fakhretdinov] said: 'First of all, in order to resolve this issue, it is necessary to turn to the government. As it decides for its political reasons, so it will be'.[117]

Two letters were sent to Kalinin and Chicherin, and there were no objections. As Vitaly Naumkin explains, Chicherin understood that for this it was still necessary to solve several problems, in which the participation of the Soviet Muslim clergy in the Meccan All-Muslim Congress could be of great help: 'the use of our Islam by sending a delegation to Hijas'.[118] By sending the delegation, the Soviets, in other words, pursued two main goals: (1) opposing the British plans for the appointment of a candidate for the Caliph to England at the All-Muslim Congress; (2) ensuring the participation of Russian Muslims in those international Muslim bodies that may be created to control the 'Holy places'.[119]

To achieve these set goals, the People's Commissar came up with an interesting scheme with two delegations: official and unofficial[120]:

> Several influential people in the Muslim world will join the official delegation of our Muslims to the Congress in Mecca to serve the issues of the protection of 'Holy Places' and pilgrimage. These people will not have formal mandates, i.e. they will be just pilgrims. Due to the personal weight of the members of the delegation, it will be able to have a serious impact on the formation of mood among the pilgrims, without being bound at the same time by the official quality, as will be the case with the first delegation.

The 'unofficial' delegation, aiming to

> oppose the British plans in the Caliphate issue, is secret and does not act as a delegation as a whole, but individually. All significance depends on the personal influence of its members in the Muslim world. . . . The members of this 'delegation' are mere pilgrims and nothing more.[121]

The main, 'open' official delegation of Soviet Muslims formed to participate in the Meccan Congress, headed by the head of the Central Muslim Spiritual Board of Inner Russia and Siberia (TsDum) Mufti Rizaitdin Fakhretdinov, included the following representatives: Kashaf Tarjemani (Kashafutdin Tarjemanov) (Ufa),[122] Gabderrahman Homer (Astrakhan), Tagir Ilyas (Kazan), Moslakhetlin Khalil (Crimea), Mahdi bin Maksud (Siberia), Abdel-Wahid al-Kari (Turkestan), most of whom were of Tatar origins. Indeed, the 'unofficial' delegation was especially well designed to be deniable, and their names remain unknown. Nonetheless, it is highly probable that they included ethnic Muslim Tatars.

What we know for sure is that Tatars, as members of the Central Muslim Spiritual Board of Inner Russia and Siberia (TsDum) were very supportive of Soviet policies at that stage, closely connected to how they were indispensable as a mechanism used by the Soviets too. This is reflected in the translation of an interview with the secretary of the delegation of Soviet Muslims, Tagir Ilyas from Kazan, given by him upon the arrival of the delegation of Russian Muslims in Constantinople and published together with other materials on the Congress in Mecca in the Turkish newspaper 'Cumhuriyet' on 28 August 1926.[123]

> Of course, in the era of Tsarism, Russian Muslims could not take part in such a Congress. . . . But at present, the entire Muslim world sees how much Russian Muslims have gained thanks to the laws of the Soviet regime on freedom of belief and religious teachings.

Unlike the Cairo one, the Meccan Congress, as can be judged from the list of participants, was very representative.[124] The fact that Mufti Rizaitdin Fakhretdinov was elected one of the two co-chairmen of the Congress could not but cause satisfaction in Moscow. In an interview, Mufti Fakhretdinov described the events in Arabia as follows: 'After a stubborn and victorious struggle against the British protege Hussein and his sons 'Ali, the Wahhabite leader Ibn Saud united a significant part of the Arab lands and created an independent Arab state.' The sympathies of the Soviet delegation, acting in accordance with the instructions received from the authorities, were clearly on the side of the Saudis.[125] The final example of this, is coverage of the Journal *Ogonek* dated 1926, which reported on the trip of a delegation of Soviet Muslims to Mecca. In it, under the heading 'To Mecca', there is a photograph of them, and the caption reads:

> Delegation of the Muslims of the Soviet Union that left for the All-Muslim Congress in June in Mecca. At the same time, another All-Muslim Congress opens in Cairo, staged by the British who want to turn it into an executor of their imperialist goals. The Congress in Mecca will declare the protest of Soviet Muslims against the Congress in Cairo.[126]

Alongside strong support by TsDUM for Soviet policies, the Congress also facilitated personal meetings of the Soviet delegation with Ibn Saud (which clearly also contributed to Kremlin–Hijaz rapprochement). For example, based on the travel notes of Abdrakhman Umerov,[127] who was also part of the delegation, and written in old Tatar language, in his memories of the Soviet delegation's participation at the Congress from the first days until returning home, he stated that the Soviet delegation met with Ibn Saud:

On 14 June, we were picked up by Ibn Saud's personal car. Arriving, we had a conversation [with him] for an hour. Ibn Saud turned out to be a very open, cheerful person, he constantly spoke, we listened. Our conversations centred around the topic of weakening Muslims and opposing countries, which, in fact, are enemies of Islam. [It was also said that] the strengthening of Islam and the development of Muslims are in a dire condition.[128]

Later, hajj was also performed by the Soviet delegation.[129] The Soviet delegation met Ibn Saud for a second time on 11 July. Umerov stated:[130]

The audience with the ruler took one hour. He expressed his deepest gratitude to us for participation in the Congress and added that he was very pleased with [the work of the Congress]. After that, having said goodbye and relying on Allah, we returned home [. . .]. On 12 July, just before our departure, representatives of Ibn Saud came to us and presented each of us with valuable gifts from the King: a warm Arabian dress for men, a vessel with Zamzam water [pilgrims performing hajj and *umrah* drink this water], a diarrheal in a jug and cups.[131]

The People's Commissar was right in its calculations that the situation contributed to the rapprochement of the Soviet Union with Ibn Saud, who then needed support from Moscow.[132] In that time the Bolsheviks shared the language of anti-imperialism with the Soviet Islam leaders, while the Central Muslim Spiritual Board of Inner Russia and Siberia (TsDum) referred to Ibn Saud as 'uniting Arabs and liberating tyrannized Muslims from imperialists'.[133]

Interestingly, despite their differences in *madhahib*, it did not serve as a challenge for building these relations, but, rather, pragmatism prevailed. For example, Hafiz Wahba, who was the first adviser to Ibn Saud, and between 1924 and 1926 a governor of Mecca, presented the position of the Kingdom to the Congress, and addressed the delegates after Ibn Saud's brief greeting, saying:

Muslims were destroyed by their division into numerous *madhahib*. Let's think together about how we can unite, how to cooperate with each other in order to extract from this a common cause and benefit from preventing enmity and misunderstanding between representatives of *madhahib*.[134]

Despite this success, the position of TsDUM began a slight decline. In 1927, pilgrims entered Mecca through the Odessa port.[135] In another source it is stated that only a Tatar, Musa Bigiev,[136] performed the hajj that year.[137] The hajj continued until the complete closure of the southern borders of the USSR at the very beginning of the 1930s, and the number of pilgrims dropped sharply.[138] In the 1940s, to boost the patriotism of all peoples of the USSR in response to the

Nazi German invasion, the Stalin government relaxed its anti-Islamic stance.[139] In 1944 Stalin authorized the establishment of the Spiritual Directorate (Muftiate) of Muslims in the North Caucasus (in Buynaksk, Dagestan), and the Spiritual Directorate of Muslims of the Transcaucasia (based in Baku, Azerbaijan), along with the Muftiate of Central Asia and Kazakhstan (in Tashkent). In 1948, the USSR acknowledged the principal role of the Tashkent Muftiate in the Soviet *umma*.[140] In other words, the TsDUM lost its central functions, and Tashkent replaced Ufa. Consequently, in 1948, at the Congress of Muslim clergy, the TsDUM was transformed into the Spiritual Administration of Muslims of European Russia and Siberia (DUMES).[141]

Even this Islamic factor used 'offensively' (1973–80) by the Soviets[142] under Brezhnev's leadership, and following these policies, meant particular emphasis on relations with Saudi Arabia, Morocco, Jordan, Tunisia, the Gulf states [*sic*] and North Yemen.[143] The role of the Tatars in this policy was limited. The role of Central Asian Muslims was more prominent, and Tatars were distinctly missing from leading roles in such policies by the Soviets. This role was taken up by the Mufti of Tashkent – Ziaudddin Babakhanov.[144] For example, in 1974, along with other delegates he led a hajj to Mecca and also visited Saudi Arabia, where the Soviet delegation was received by King Faisal, by the rector of the University and by the chairman of the Muslim World league. The delegation also travelled to Abu Dhabi and met with Shaykh Zayed al-Nahyan.[145]

Moreover, another mechanism was the convening of international conferences by the Mufti of Tashkent. For example, to celebrate the tenth anniversary of the establishment of the journal *Muslims of the Soviet East*,[146] the international conference was held in Tashkent on 3 July 1979. This conference was chaired by the Mufti and was attended by high-ranking delegates from the Middle East, including representatives from the Arabian states, such as Kuwait.[147]

Further, Galia Golan,[148] explaining the appointments during the Andropov and Gorbachev periods, also demonstrates the limited usage of this Islamic factor, along with the emphasis laid on the limited number of Muslims in powerful positions, and their limited autonomy (including Tatars):

> Aside from the use of Muslims as ambassadors to some Muslim countries, those involved in foreign-policy decisions regarding these countries were not Muslims nor in any way linked culturally to the Muslim countries. As pointed out by Halliday, even the few Soviet Muslims who reached significant positions in Soviet foreign-policy matters, notably Geider Aliev who was named to the Politburo under Andropov and removed under Gorbachev, did not deal with this part of the world in particular. [. . .] Those who were sent and employed as

representatives of Soviet Islam were, like all other religious officials in the Soviet Union, state functionaries. They were clearly subordinate and limited by strict restrictions on their behaviour and pronouncements. While they may or may not have been respected in their own communities, it is most unlikely that they had any influence beyond these communities.

In almost the last decade of the existence of the USSR, the Soviet invasion of Afghanistan in December 1979 contributed to a substantial setback in the usage (or viability) of the Muslim factor in general.[149] For example, again with an absence of Tatars in important roles, at the Tashkent Conference in September 1980, of 500 people invited from Muslim countries, only 76 attended. As a protest against the Soviet invasion, Saudi Arabia, Bahrain, Oman, Qatar, and (as Bennigsen, Henze, Tanham and Wimbush call them) 'the Gulf states' did not attend the conference.[150]

After this fiasco, the Soviets did make changes to how they attempted to make use of the Islamic factor, such as making alterations to the upper level of the Islamic hierarchy, appointing a new Tatar Mufti in Ufa, Talgat Tadzhuddin, who replaced Abdul Bari Isaev as Mufti in July 1980. However, this had little impact on the possibilities of TASSR–Gulf relations. Situating the centre of the Spiritual Administration of Muslims of European Russia and Siberia (DUMES) in Ufa rather than in Kazan also somewhat inhibited links between TASSR and Arabian states. As will be discussed in Chapter 5, after the collapse of the USSR, the first Tatarstan president Mintimer Shaimiev's government vision was to integrate ideas of moderate Tatar nationalism into its politics and national ideology, while simultaneously distancing itself from 'radical' nationalists. As part of this strategy, the official separation between religion and the state, as stipulated in the Constitution in 1992, has been accompanied by a policy of allowing an indirect role to be played by Islam within Tatarstan politics. Consequently, the Tatarstan authorities favoured the secession in 1992 of the Tatarstan Muslim clerics from the Federal Islamic centre in Ufa and the formation of a separate Muslim Spiritual Board of the Republic of Tatarstan, (DUMRT), based in Kazan. The latter has been perceived as an indispensable attribute of Tatarstan's sovereignty, and since then has played an effective role in further building Tatarstan–Gulf relations, as will be demonstrated later.

2.4 Conclusion

This chapter has illustrated the limited direct links between TASSR and Arabian states between 1917 and 1990. Nonetheless, this period is important for consideration as it assists the development of the wider argument of the manuscript, particularly in regard to shared identities between minorities of a state and independent states – 'Self(s)' and minority 'Self' – which have the capacity to become or facilitate collaborations if both federal governments consider the importance and viability of the factor. As shown, the Soviets were not interested in offering TASSR the opportunity to conduct paradiplomatic efforts. Despite the importance of Tatars within Soviet mechanisms towards the Kingdom of Hijaz and Nejd, especially during the 1920s to the 1930s, they were not beneficial for TASSR–Gulf relations. Karim Khakimov's efforts for building closer links with Ibn Saud were vital, along with shared Muslim identities, to successfully conducting hajj, *umrah* diplomacies and distributions of gifts, contributing to Soviet strategies towards the Kingdom. However, his efforts did not contribute to direct links between TASSR and the Kingdom. At the same time, an Islamic organization with significant contributions by Tatars – TsDUM – was crucial, as illustrated, but the centre of it remained in Ufa, and it gradually lost its leading place to Tashkent; this again contributed in only very limited ways to direct collaborations between TASSR and the Gulf states. All of these can be explained by the internal dynamics between Kazan and Moscow, along with the Soviet's limited relations with the Gulf states between 1917 and 1990 in general, which the next chapter will address.

TASSR and the Gulf states

The Moscow factor

Chapter 2 demonstrated the general failure to establish direct collaborations between the TASSR and the Gulf states, in other words between 'Self(s)' and minority 'Self' through shared Muslim identities. This can be traced to the dominating Moscow factor in relations with both. The potential challenges raised by the Tatars within the USSR (as perceived by the Kremlin), such as demands for duality of power and the threat of pan-Turkism, led gradually to the erosion of the TASSR's status within the Soviet system. Arguably, similar concerns worked against the acceptability of paradiplomatic efforts by the TASSR, which explains the very limited relations with Arabian states (compounded by the surrounding legislative framework). Concerning shared Islamic identities, these were generally suppressed during the Soviet period, as by the end of Soviet rule, Islam was reduced to a purely ritual form, meaning that even limited collaborations through the religious field were blocked. Also, relations between the USSR and Arabian states failed, mainly due to great power competitions, where Gulf states have traditionally supported the Western bloc. This can be another explanation for failed partnerships between TASSR and Arabian states. To show this, first, this chapter will focus on Moscow–Kazan relations; and second, on Moscow's relations with the Arabian states.

3.1 Moscow and Kazan: The impact on TASSR–Gulf relations

3.1.1 The path towards the formation of TASSR: Nationalism, Islam and the threat of power duality for RSFSR

The prerequisites for TASSR can be traced to the political and social activities of Russia's Islamic community, which gained momentum mainly during the first

Russian Revolution of 1905–7. Following the February Revolution of 1917 in the Russian Empire, socio-political changes took place,[1] including through several Muslim congresses in Kazan in 1917.[2] The First All-Russian Muslim Congress in May 1917 was funded and largely controlled by the Tatars.[3] The Tatars dominated key boards of the Moscow Congress, as Aydar Khabutdinov explains:[4]

> The prevalence of the Tatars, similar to the situation at the All-Russian Muslim Congresses of 1905-1906 and 1914, was met with resistance on the part of most representatives of ethnic groups, each of whom wanted the interests of his community to prevail over the general interests of Russia's Muslims.

However, the Congress of 1917 was a double blow to Turkic unity. The conservatives and part of the socialists proclaimed territorial autonomy and created the purely declarative All-Russian *Milli Shura* (National Council). Most of the Tatars believed that it would be impossible to reunite territories split among various governorates and populated with Russians.[5]

The Second All-Russian Muslim Congress in Kazan was held in July 1917, where the cultural and national autonomous government formed the dominant Tatar national movement.[6] National liberal and moderate socialist leaders had nearly full control over the *Waqitli Milli Idara* (Provisional National Government) and focused their attention on administration rather than political activities.[7] Two more Muslim forums took place in Kazan at the same time: the Islamic Clergy Congress (17–21 July 1917, about 250 delegates), and the Muslim Soldiers' Congress (17–26 July 1917, about 200 delegates).[8] The summer of 1917 was a time when the 'all-Muslim' movement split into regional and ethnic factions, political forces became more disparate and many forms of 'egotism' came to the fore, especially those based on class, ethnicity and group.[9] Under these circumstances the 'traditional' leaders of the Tatar national movement had to review their future and the part they were to play. The Kazan congresses, which for concrete reasons became more of a 'Tatar' Congress than an 'all-Muslim' one, determined the future of the Tatar national movement.

National-cultural autonomy was declared under the title 'The Muslim Turko-Tatars in Inner Russia and Siberia' at the joint meeting of Muslim congresses on 22 July 1917.[10] The three prospective ministers of self-government established at the Second All-Russian Muslim Congresses in Kazan in July 1917 by the *Waqitli Milli Idara* (the Provisional National Government) represented the three most powerful professional corporations in the Tatar world. The *Milli Idara* was composed of three *nazarate* (ministries): *Magarif* (education), *Malia* (finance) and *Dinia* (religion). Kazan, Ufa and Orenburg-Troitsk were among the three centres, with a representative in each *nazarate*.[11] 29 November 1917 was the day when the National Assembly adopted the historic resolution to recognize the necessity of establishing the territorial autonomy of the Turko-Tatars of Inner Russia and Siberia as the 'Idel-Ural State'.[12] The republic was short-lived, and some accommodation of the Tatars had to be arranged. This impelled the Soviet authorities to set up a Tatar Autonomous Socialist Republic, with Mirsaid Sultan-Galiev as its leader.[13]

Here it might be useful to refer again to Karim Khakimov, and elaborate further claim to his importance, despite the limited contribution he made ultimately to links between autonomous republics and the Gulf states (see Chapter 2). In contrast to Karim Khakimov, Mirsaid Sultan-Galiev, a son of a Tatar school teacher, led a widely spread movement of Muslim *Jadids* (modernists) who supported the Soviets in conquering Bukhara. His modernism was anti-clerical and anti-feudal, and sought to reform Islam. This instigated hostility among many Muslims, but he was influential among a group of intellectuals.[14] He joined the Bolshevik Party in November 1917 with a number of his followers. Initially, due to his authority among the Muslims of Russia, none had contributed more to the consolidation of the Bolshevik regime than Sultan-Galiev.[15] However, the differences between Khakimov and Sultan-Galiev expressed during the Second Congress of the Organizations of the Peoples of the East demonstrate why Khakimov's Muslim factor worked successfully in Soviet diplomacy, while the TASSR possibly lost any opportunity to develop links with Arabian states. The key point for Khakimov was the accusation that the Central Bureau of Muslim Organizations was founded on 'the basis of bourgeois nationalism' and not proletarian internationalism.[16] Most importantly, Khakimov spoke out against the double subordination of party organizations, for them to be part of the general party structures, and for the elimination of any parallelism and isolation.[17] However, Sultan-Galiev constantly brought to the fore the question of the right of nations to self-determination. Ozerov comments:

> It is meaningless to object to it – this is Lenin's key idea, the main nerve and thesis of the Soviet government and its national policy, and on this basis it mobilises the national outskirts of the country to support socialist transformations.[18]

In Sultan-Galiev's stubbornness on the Tatar–Bashkir issue, Stalin apparently saw a challenge to the formation of a unified state and ultimately, together with Lenin, 'nullified' both the 'Little Bashkiria' project and the Tatar–Bashkir Republic, replacing them with their creation in 1920 of two separate centre-dependent autonomous formations,[19] which opened the way to the consolidation of power in the RSFSR and then the formation of the USSR, which under Stalin followed a more nationalist and parochial view of 'Mother-Russia'.[20,21] Bennigsen, Henze, Tanham and Wimbush[22] explain:

> the Russian Communist Party had become a home for a number of influential Muslim radical [*sic*] nationalists, who viewed co-operation with the Bolsheviks was the best way to achieve independence or autonomy from Russia in the post-revolutionary political order. These Muslim national communists played an important role in ensuring the final Bolshevik victory; in exchange for their support, Lenin wisely agreed – at least for the short term – to treat them as partners. It was a marriage of convenience, and it was to be short-lived.

Moreover, as Jennifer-Anne Davidson[23] argues, during the Russian Revolution period of 1917, Tatar nationalism was one of the most substantial nationalist movements to arise among Muslims of the Russian Empire and later, the early USSR government pursued a particularly anti-Tatar policy, 'as a result of the threat to Soviet control over the middle Volga'. In other words, ethnic and nationalist movements were considered threats to the stability of centres of power and to attempts by the RSFSR to consolidate federal power. Naturally, this directly impacted on any paradiplomatic efforts by the TASSR towards the Arabian states, despite their strong shared Muslim identities.

3.1.2 TASSR and the Gulf states: The impact of pan-Turkism

Another reason for limited collaborations between the TASSR and the Gulf states can be linked to the Tatars identifying more closely with Turks rather than Arabs, the roots of which were discussed in the account of the so-called *autumn of the Islam* period, with its focus on Eurasia's Turco–Tatar polities; see Chapter 1. Moreover, the same factor also appears to have contributed to the decline of the TASSR's status within the USSR, being perceived as a potential challenger especially during Stalin's leadership. Another concern for Moscow has been the support of some intellectuals of an idea of pan-Turkism, beginning in 1914, which meant the supranational unity of Turkic-speaking peoples (including the Turks of Turkey but also the linked ethnic groups in the Tatar areas of the Volga–Ural region, Turkic populations in Siberia, Persian and Soviet Azerbaijan, in Crimea and in Central Asia among Turkoman, Uzbek, Kazakh and Kirgiz groups).[24] These ideas were also popular among the Turkic intellectuals of Russia. For example, a Bashkir, Zeki Velidi Togan, saw it as a search for unity among Turkic, Mongol and Finno-Ugrian groups.[25] These ideas were also popular among Tatars. For example, Fatykh Karimi believed that Volga–Ural should be a centre of the Turkic world and suggested calling Volga Tatars 'Northern Turks'.[26] Another Tatar, Iusuf Akchura, who was one of the organizers and leaders of the aforementioned party 'Ittifak al-Muslimin', presented the central role of Russian Turks on pan-Turkism.[27] In his famous work *Üç Tarzı Siyaset*,[28] he encouraged Turks to leave the multi-ethnic Ottoman Empire and turn to Turkish nationalism and pan-Turkism. He was also a member of the Kazan Committee of the Party of Constitutional Democrats. In 1906 he took part in the work of the Second Congress of this party, and was elected to its Central Committee.

However, this became a concern for the Bolsheviks, and Stalin had already attacked pan-Islamism in his famous speech in 1913 on the national question. Ivo J. Lederer states that 'in the early 1920s pan-Turkism was attacked as a perversion of bourgeois nationalism and the movement was emasculated'.[29] The repressive mechanisms of the country reached their peak in 1937–8, with the persecution of regimental leaders of Muslims and groups in non-Muslim regions. Among them are two cases born in the bowels of the Main Directorate of State Security of the NKVD of the USSR and its republics and regional institutions: 'The Chain of Qur'an' (1940) and 'Case of TsDum' (1936–8).[30] Both cases directly explain the consideration of Tatars as potential challengers, and the decline of importance of the Tatar Muslim intelligentsia and clergy in the USSR. In other words, most Muslim clergy and intellectuals (including diplomats), who were instrumental in conducting the policies based on Muslim identities illustrated in Chapter 2, faced Stalin's repressions[31] – mainly due to accusations of supporting pan-Turkism.

'The Chain of Qur'an' and its repressions against the Muslim elites in the USSR[32] was a fabricated 'conspiracy of the leaders of the TsDUM, in which hundreds of mullas were accused of involvement in different regions of the USSR, including the Volga-Ural region and the Republic of Central Asia'.[33]

As Guseva details, supposedly[34]

[t]he intelligence agencies of two foreign powers [Japan and Turkey – Yu.G.] created in the USSR an espionage and sabotage counterrevolutionary organisation among Muslims, headed by the TsDUM (Rizaitdin Fakhretdinov, Kashaf Tarjemani[35]). In July [1936 – Yu.G.] the Counterrevolutionary Center was liquidated in Moscow and its branches were liquidated on the territory of the USSR.

One piece of evidence referred to the 'World Congress of Muslims' meaning the Meccan Congress of 1926, held in agreement with the Soviet authorities (see

Chapter 2), and beneficial for the Soviets for reaching their political objectives towards Arabia. The case stated that on the instructions of the TsDUM and personally Kashaf Tarjemani, Rizaitdin Fakhretdinov, Magdiy Magjulov, 'the asset of the Pan-Islamist organisation was obliged to conduct spy-intelligence work', in order to report to the TsDUM on the attitude of the population to the measures of the Soviet government.[36]

More specific repressions against the religious authorities of the TASSR occurred in the 'Idel-Ural organization case' (1938), which was developed alongside the 'TsDUM case'. The religious-national elite of Moscow, the Volga–Idel region and Central Asia were accused of planning to establish a nationalist pan-Turkic state.[37] Of note is that in 1938, the NKVD of the Tatar Autonomous Soviet Socialist Republic, as one of the main directions of its work, singled out the elimination of the 'widely spread anti-Soviet espionage-sabotage-insurgent organisation . . . led by agents of the Japanese and German intelligence services, with a Pan-Islamists line going to the TsDUM'.[38]

The efforts against the Tatar Muslim authority can be represented by the case of Kashaf Tarjemani. The view of the 'Pan-Islamist', generally 'anti-Soviet', nature of Kashaf Tarjemani and the structure of the TsDUM itself was laid down by the employees of the court intelligence service in the 1920s. In the 'eastern developments' memorandum dated 28 December 1922, the Tatar political department of the State Political Directorate (GPU), called 'Kazan mulla' Tarjemanov a 'Pan-Islamist'.[39] From February 1923, undercover surveillance was carried out on him.[40] Moreover, in the report of the Tatar Joint State Political Directorate (OGPU) from August 1923, it was written that a member of the Central Dispatch Office – Kashaf Tarjemanov – who was in Moscow on behalf of the Congress of the clergy (the All-Russian Congress of the Central Administrative Department, held in Ufa, 10–25 April 1923) was trying to petition for the 'teaching of religion' at mosques.

The work being done in Tataria was frequently linked with what was happening in the 'eastern republics – in Turkestan, Bashkiria, Siberia'.[41] All this assisted the later task of expanding the spread of the 'Pan-Islamist' threat, and the activity of the Ufa Muftiate in developing and preserving its socio-religious positions in the 1920s became a suitable pretext for organizing repressions throughout the Union.[42] It was not a coincidence, then, that the role of the Tatars dramatically declined, as mentioned in Chapter 2. Indeed, among those several influential Tatar figures who were instrumental in early relationship-building with Arab states, most were killed in the later period of repression, which naturally contributed to the possibilities of Tatar–Gulf relations fizzling out.

During the Second World War, this phenomenon of pan-Turkism recurred as an anti-Soviet arrangement, again supported by Turkey and Germany.[43] In an attempt to win over Turkey, Germany tried to attract the Turks by a distinct motivation: support for pan-Turkism.[44] By then, with the advance of the German armies into the Turkish-speaking and Muslim areas of the Soviet Union, such as the North Caucasus and Crimea, an opportunity occurred to revive the pan-Turkian idea. George Lenczowski states: 'Long chafing under Russian rule, the Crimean Tatars and the Kalmyk, Karachai-Balkar and Chechen-Ingush peoples of the Caucasus greeted the invading Germans as liberators, while certain groups and individuals among them offered the Nazi Reich their collaboration.'[45] As a result, in 1944, Chechens, Ingushs, Kalmyks, Karachais, Balkars, Crimean Tatars and others[46] were accused of large-scale collaboration with the Nazis, and deported to Central Asia. Kazan Tatars were affected to a lesser extent, as they showed strong loyalty to the Soviet regime during the Second World War. Nonetheless, policies of Russification, such as stressing the pivotal role of the Russians in the Soviet states continued under Stalin during 1940–55,[47] and the damage done by the aforementioned cases could not make the Tatars an ethnicity to lead Muslim Russia, as stated in Chapter 2. In the Kremlin's eyes, Tatars and TASSR had a closeness to pan-Turkist ideas, and connections with outside Muslim states were perceived as a threat (including with Arab states). This, despite the much stronger historical links between Tatars and Turks, sharing much culture, language and form of religion. Suspicion extended to other Muslim states largely because of Soviet 'atheist' policies against Islam. By the end of the Soviet period, Islam in TASSR had been reduced to a purely ritual form, as subsequent sections will elaborate.

3.1.3 TASSR–GCC states: Impact of Soviet policies towards Islam

The previous point also directly links with the development of Islam in TASSR under 'atheist' Soviet rule, and Soviet policies against Muslim Tatars. The Bolsheviks, against a background of more powerful institutional atheism in the Russian Empire, reserved the Spiritual Board as a means of controlling Soviet Muslims by moulding an Islam that was 'fundamentally loyal to the Soviet state and generally pliant'.[48] With the establishment of the Tatar ASSR (and other ethnic homelands), the state offered a secular education for all of Russia's Muslims and presumed jurisdiction over most other social functions previously coordinated by the Muftiate.[49] In the late 1920s, as the state began persecuting clergy and destroying mosques, the Spiritual Board was allowed to perform only narrowly identified religious rituals.[50] Beginning in 1923, Stalin began a strong anti-nationalist offensive against the Muslim nationalist communists, which led by the late 1930s to their virtual extinction.[51] Stalin liquidated nearly all the nationalist Muslim intellectuals, and most of the pre-revolutionary Muslim intelligentsia, including Kazan Tatars. Benningsen and Broxup explain:

> In 1928 Stalin augmented the systematic elimination of the Muslim intellectual elite with a frontal assault on the USSR's Islamic infrastructure. Mosques were closed and destroyed by the thousands, clerics were arrested and liquidated as 'saboteurs' and, after 1935, as spies. By 1941, of the 25,000–30,000 mosques open in 1920, only about 1000 remained: all of the 14,500 Islamic religious schools were forcibly shut down [sic], and fewer than 2000 of the approximately 47,000 clerics survived.[52]

Moreover, the press also followed this tendency. For example, in their analysis of 'Krasnaia Tatariia' ('Red Tataria'), Mukhamadeeva and Faizullin[53] cite an article on the holiday of Eid al-Adha that parades the worthlessness and falsity of the Muslim pilgrimage to Mecca. The readers had 'explained' to them that this 'fairy tale', with the sacrifice of an animal instead of a man, was taken entirely from the Bible. In general, according to the author of the article, hajj is a major source of income for the ruling circles of the Hijaz and Hijaz-Nejd Kingdom in general, whose population is not engaged in productive labour at all and subsists only on income from the hajj. Foreign exchange earnings from the hajj in 1929 amounted to 4.5 to 5 million pounds. Citing this 'incriminating' information, the author concludes that the hajj is 'a shameful page in the history of mankind'.[54] It may be no coincidence that relations between the minority 'Self' and 'Self(s)' – TASSR and Saudi Arabia – did not develop, not only despite, but also because of their shared Islamic identities, which risked attracting the ire of central Soviet policies.

By the middle of 1941, due to mass atheistic propaganda, repressions against clergy and believers and three all-union anti-religious campaigns, the religious associations of the TASSR were on the verge of complete destruction.[55] The position of the believers and the clergy changed significantly with the beginning of the Great Patriotic War.[56,57] The appeal of the Central Muslim Spiritual Board stated: 'The Central Muslim Spiritual Board of the USSR urges all true believers to rise in defence of their native land, to pray in mosques for the victory of the Red Army, and to bless their sons, fighting for a just cause.'[58] The rigid control established by Stalin over all subjects, including their spiritual life, was impossible in the conditions of the war.[59] Instead, non-atheist beliefs became an important mobilizing tool. Ruslan Ibragimov explains: 'In periods of social cataclysms, the stabilizing and integrating functions of religion become manifest and are in particular demand'. In September 1942, Stalin held a meeting with the heads of the Russian Orthodox Church, which led to the discussion of a new stage in relations between the state and the confessions. This also resulted in permission being granted to a group of seventeen believers to perform hajj.[60]

Between May 1945 and December 1947, there were registrations of sixteen Muslim religious associations in the TASSR.[61] That period also saw a peak of religious activities among the population. For example, in 1945, celebration of the Kurban Bayram [Eid al-Adha] was held in the republic on an uncommonly solemn and grand scale. According to a report by the Representative for Religious Affairs within the TASSR, approximately 24,000–25,000 people took part in the Namaz festivity in Kazan on 15 November (held in 6 places, despite only one Marjani Mosque and Muslim community being registered by the authorities).[62] In 1948, for the first time in twenty-two years, the Majlis of the Central Muslim Spiritual Board (renamed the 'Muslim Spiritual Board of European Russia and Siberia' at the Congress) was called, which in itself was an exceptional event in the history of relations between the state and religious confessions. Despite this, the decisions made at the Congress only confirmed the limited rights which the clergy and believers had possessed between the 1920s and 1940s. The Soviet short-term policies of permissiveness regarding religion ended in the post-war period. From 1958, a massive new attack on religion began.[63] The religious life was presented as the inevitable process of 'degeneration' and 'decline'.[64]

The common Islamic practice of 'taqiyya' that allowed Muslims to hide their true belief for the sake of confession became especially significant during the years of the Soviet power. The rules of Islamic rites played a key role, because in contrast to the Orthodox rites, it was possible to perform them in the houses and flats of Muslims and thus to stay out of sight of the controlling authorities. The state policy began to use less severe methods against religion after Nikita Khrushchev's removal from power.[65] The practice that had been in use since the early 1960s when some mosques of the USSR were chosen to illustrate the authorities' loyal attitude towards Islam became common in the 1970s. The Marjani Mosque in Kazan was among them. When delegations from Islamic countries visited TASSR, its members always visited the mosque, met the imam and then wrote in the guest book that 'the Soviet government does not interfere with the activity of religious organisations'. However, as Ruslan Ibragimov[66] states, 'some facts unpleasant for the authorities were so obvious that they were impossible to hide'. He gives an example of the visit of a Muslim delegation from Turkey to Kazan in 1979, when its members expressed their surprise that there were sixteen mosques in Tashkent and only one in Kazan.[67] By the *perestroika* era, only eighteen mosques were officially operating (only one was open in all of Kazan), and only about thirty registered Muslim clergy were active in the Tatar ASSR.[68] This is why I called this period a 'cold' winter of Islam in Chapter 1; within our context, Islamic identities were extremely damaged, diminishing the possibilities of contact between TASSR and Gulf states, in other words, between the minority 'Self' and 'Self(s)'.

3.2 Moscow and Gulf states: The impact on TASSR–Gulf relations

3.2.1 USSR–Arabian states' limited partnership

Moscow's limited relations with Arabian states remains a major explanation for why TASSR – as part of the USSR – could not build relations with states independently, as the following sections will demonstrate. The Soviet–Gulf relations can be divided into three categories: relations between Saudi Arabia and USSR; Kuwait and USSR; and other small monarchies (Bahrain, Qatar, UAE, Oman) and USSR. In other words, in the context of the argument, there were only limited common interests between 'Self(s)' and the 'Other'.

3.2.1.1 *Saudi Arabia–USSR*

Despite the USSR being the first country to establish full diplomatic relations with the Kingdom of Hijaz and Nejd in 1926, this did not lead to long-term partnerships between them. These diplomatic relations lasted until 1938.[69] Khakimov's execution, as noted earlier, was both a cause and illustration of this chilling effect. Another factor was the great ongoing power competition, which will be discussed in more detail later. Yodfat explains that trade relations between the USSR and Saudi Arabia were recognized as a danger by Western powers, who applied pressure to put an end to Soviet interference.[70] At the same time, Mark Katz[71] explains that the Soviets viewed that 'Abd al'-Aziz cooperated with London, rather taking active measures to challenge the British place in Arabia'. Hitler's Germany grew stronger, and as Katz explains:[72]

> Whether it was to improve relations with London or for some other reasons, in 1938 the Soviets withdrew their diplomatic mission from Saudi Arabia as well as from Yemen, Turkey, Afghanistan and Persia. This was a move that the Soviets

must deeply regret, for unlike Yemen, which agreed to resume diplomatic relations with Moscow in 1955, the Saudis did not do so.

Admittedly, there were some positive moves between the Saudis and Soviets in the 1950s. However, Yodfat states that while the Soviets were 'under the illusion that they would be able to renew their ties with Saudi Arabia', Saudis used this occasion 'to bring pressure to bear on Britain and the USA rather than to turn towards the Soviets'.[73] The Soviets were gladdened by King Saud's refusal of US armed aid in February 1954, and his refusal to join the Western-funded security pact that was to become the Central Treaty Organization (CENTO) in 1955.[74] The USSR was also hopeful of renewing friendship with the Saudis, as King Saud appeared keen to follow Nasser's lead by signing a security pact with Egypt and Syria in October 1955, and permitting Egyptian armed advisers into Saudi Arabia. With the support of the Soviets, Egypt, Yemen and Saudi Arabia also worked to weaken the British position in Aden.[75] Nasser and King Saud did not stay on friendly terms for long, and in August 1956 the King expelled all Egyptian armed advisers. They began to exchange hostile polemics in October 1956. The Soviets tried to avoid a deterioration of relations with both states, but the Saudis turned closer to the United States. In 1957 the Saudis renewed the US lease on Dhahran air base.[76] With King Faisal's leadership beginning in 1958, there were some positive moves and expectations on the part of the Soviets. In 1961 they were delighted when the Saudis declared that the lease on Dhahran air base would not be prolonged in 1962, when it was expected to expire. The two governments seemed to restore relations in September 1962. However, the North Yemeni revolution on 26 September 1962, instead, fostered extremely cold relations.[77]

The Soviet position changed again after the June 1967 Six-Day War, when the Saudis undertook to offer financial aid to Egypt and other Arab countries. By then, the Soviets had tried to re-establish diplomatic relations, but without positive results.[78] During the October 1973 war, the Soviet approaches towards Saudi Arabia again became friendly while King Faisal supported the use of the Arab 'oil weapon' against any state friendly to Israel, particularly the United States.[79] Despite speculations of possible resumption of bilateral relations, King Faisal, seeing that the Soviets were connected to Israel and that both opposed the Arabs,[80] continued his hostility towards the USSR until his death in March 1975.

Under the new leadership of King Khalid, the Soviets and Saudis released some more friendly statements, as when Crown Prince Fahd said that Riyadh wanted good relations with both the East and the West and that Saudi Arabia might 'settle' its relations with the USSR.[81] However, relations were developed 'without embassies' following the Saudis' wish.[82] At the end of December 1979, relations became much more hostile again with the USSR's invasion of Afghanistan; Riyadh became one of the key organizers of the Islamic summit conference that met in January 1980 to denounce this action.[83] Moscow strongly objected to Saudi funding of Pakistan and the Afghanistan rebels.[84]

3.2.1.2 Kuwait–USSR

With regard to smaller monarchies, the USSR established relations mainly with Kuwait.[85] The administrative report of the Kuwait Political Agency for the year 1932[86] noted two attempts again made by the representatives of the Soviet Company known as the 'Sharq' of Mohammarrah to persuade the ruler to allow Russian ships to call at Kuwait. However, 'The Ruler after consultation with the Political Agent rejected these advances out of hand',[87] which illustrates strong British influence, the key reason why relations with the Gulf states had a limited nature, as will be discussed in detail later. Nonetheless, it should be noted that Kuwait – USSR relations were the most developed in comparison to others, and the dynamics of Soviet–Iraq relations were directly affected by the Soviet–Kuwait relations. Soviet diplomats provided UN support to Iraq during the Kuwait crisis in 1961, when Iraq made claims to Kuwait as part of its territory.[88] Nonetheless, in March 1963 the Soviets concluded an agreement to establish diplomatic ties with Kuwait, while the Ba'thist regime in Iraq was persecuting communists, ignoring Soviet protests.[89] Melkumyan, Kosach and Nosenko[90] argue that the establishment of diplomatic relations between Kuwait and the USSR in 1963 after the change of regime in Iraq was due to Kuwaiti diplomacy.

By the early 1970s, Soviet–Kuwait relations had become outwardly friendly, but the signing of the Soviet–Iraq treaty of friendship and cooperation in April 1972 resulted in fears for Kuwait, along with Saudi Arabia and Iran.[91] This also brought the country closer to the United States, but due to inter-Arab and internal considerations, Kuwait supplemented this transformation with verbal attacks on the United States and a refusal to join Western-initiated defence treaties.[92] Kuwait was determined to have closer relations with the Soviets so that Moscow would not support Baghdad in any future Iraq–Kuwait crisis.[93] Kuwait sought to achieve this by buying arms from the Soviets, and in January 1974 a Kuwaiti military delegation visited Moscow for the first time.[94] The Soviets refused to sell arms to Kuwait, concerned that this might affect their relations with Iraq.[95] Kuwait persisted and another delegation visited Moscow in the autumn of 1975. However, shortly after the United States denied Kuwait's arms request, the Soviets relented and sent a military delegation to Kuwait with arms offers in March 1976.

In the 1980s, relations between the two countries expanded. The Iran–Iraq War, which began in September 1980, became a factor that stimulated the development of relations between the USSR and Kuwait, as both countries sought to end it as soon as possible, because it led to a drop in oil prices and, as a result, economic difficulties in both countries where oil was the main source of government revenue.[96]

In 1980 the Soviets sold Kuwait $200 million worth of arms, but Kuwait refused to permit a Soviet military mission. Kuwait diversified its arms purchases by arrangements with Britain, France and the United States, and engaged Western military instructions. In 1984, the United States, which limited the supply of modern types of weapons to the Arab countries – enemies of Israel, whose security they guaranteed – refused to supply Kuwait with a batch of modern missiles. Then Kuwait turned to the Soviet Union, which in these conditions willingly agreed to sign a new military agreement and expanded the supply of Soviet weapons, serviced by Soviet specialists.[97] In January 1985 some Kuwaiti military personnel were finally sent to the USSR for training.[98] Another aspect of Kuwait–Soviet relations was trade, which had grown from 700,000 rubles in 1960 to 36.6 million rubles in 1978, but fell to only 6.1 million rubles in 1982.[99] A Soviet–Kuwait cultural and scientific collaboration agreement was signed in March 1967, and several two-year exchange programme accords have been agreed to since then.[100] However, these collaborations were limited.

In 1987, Kuwait fell victim to the 'tanker war' unleashed by the belligerents of Iraq and Iran with the aim of internationalizing their conflict. The Kuwaiti government asked the world's leading powers to protect its tanker fleet.[101] The USSR was quick to accept Kuwait's invitation to reflag the emirate's tankers, and as a result, obtain 'legitimate' entry to Gulf waters.[102] Moscow used its links with both sides in the Iran–Iraq War to show to other Gulf states the advantages of diplomatic relationships with the Soviets, and the 'relevance' of such ties to the maintenance of regional diplomacy. As Chubin surmises, 'This had been a basic component of Kuwaiti diplomacy since 1961 that ties to the Soviet Union afforded a form of protection.'[103] He also adds that the value of building diplomatic links with the USSR gained greater credence among other Gulf states, as the USSR showed a 'conservative' approach to the Gulf War, 'eschewing blatant opportunism for the promotion of stability and an end to the conflict'.[104]

The Iraq crisis of 1990–1 became a turning point in relations between the USSR and the Gulf states. The Soviet Union, as a permanent member of the UN Security Council, played an important role in the adoption of resolutions demanding that Iraq immediately withdraw its troops from Kuwait and recognize its independence and sovereignty. The principled position of the USSR was appreciated not only by Kuwait but also by its partners in the GCC. Saudi Arabia restored diplomatic contacts in that period and facilitated the establishment of relations with another member of the GCC – Bahrain.[105]

3.2.1.3 The United Arab Emirates (UAE), Bahrain, Qatar, Oman–USSR

In comparison to other states in the Arabian Peninsula, the Soviets paid less attention to building relations with the UAE, Bahrain, Qatar and Oman.[106] The USSR delegation arrived in Abu Dhabi[107] on 29 January 1972 and on 14 February the sides declared that they had agreed to exchange diplomatic representatives at embassy level.[108] However, the pressure from Oman, Iran, Saudi Arabia, Qatar and other Arab states on the UAE prevented the establishing of diplomatic ties.[109] The USSR looked to have accepted this setback and continued to release positive commentaries about the UAE. They changed their view on the Saudi–UAE border dispute and began supporting the UAE instead.[110] Contacts between the USSR and the UAE have grown since the 1980s.

When Bahrain formally declared independence on 16 August 1971, it immediately concluded a defence agreement with Britain. The Soviets were critical of this move but could not afford to recognize Bahrain.[111] In general, the Soviet position towards the country grew increasingly positive and friendly, even though the PDRY and PFLOAG (which the communist Bahrain National Liberation Front [BNLF] had joined) declared Bahrain's independence 'false'. The Soviets repeatedly asked to establish an embassy in Bahrain, but Manama 'shelved' the request due to pressure from 'some neighbours'.[112] In February 1980 the communist BNLF marked its twenty-fifth anniversary, sending a representative to Moscow to express support for the Soviets and their policies.[113] Moscow also welcomed unity between the BNLF and another Marxist group – the Popular Front of Bahrain, in March 1981.[114] Only in 1990 were diplomatic ties formally established between Bahrain and the USSR.

Qatar declared its independence in September 1971.[115] Leonid Brezhnev, chairman of the Presidium of the Supreme Soviet, the head of the Soviet Union, sent a telegram to the Amir recognizing the new state. He did not mention establishing diplomatic relations.[116] Qatar did not have any diplomatic relations with the USSR and Doha's regime was viewed as 'feudal' and 'archaic' by the Soviets. The USSR criticized Qatar for its close ties with the West and for being a part of the Arab Military Industrial Organization, though complimenting it for opposing America's Middle East policy.[117] In September 1980, on the occasion of Qatar's independence date, Brezhnev greeted the Amir, delivering good wishes to him and 'the friendly Qatari people'. The Amir thanked Brezhnev and wished 'further progress to the Soviet people'.[118] Following Saudi Arabia, Qatar refused for many years to build diplomatic relations with the USSR. Only in 1988 were relations built, and in 1989 the USSR finally opened its embassy in Doha, and Qatar its embassy in Moscow.

The Sultanate of Muscat and Oman (the name was changed to Oman in August 1970) had no relations with the Soviets until 1985. In 1987 embassies were opened in Moscow and Muscat. The slow establishing of diplomatic relations can be explained by Oman being viewed as nominally independent but actually serving British interest, and, in later stages, American interests.[119] Among the complicated issues between the two countries were the problem of the Arab communist parties; divisions in the Arab world; and the fluidity of Middle East politics.[120] Oman and the USSR also took different stances on regional events. Oman condemned the Soviet invasion of Afghanistan and was critical of the Soviet–Cuban role in Ethiopia and Angola.[121] Moscow criticized Muscat for its ties with the United States and Britain, and Oman's efforts to link the GCC states with the West.[122]

As these summaries suggest, limits to collaborations can primarily be linked to the great power competitions, and the Gulf states' frequent support of the Western bloc rather than the USSR. Using Soviet terminology, the GCC states belonged to 'pro-Western conservative countries'.[123] As Khaled al-Tamimi,[124] an officer of the Ministry of Foreign Affairs of the Kingdom of Bahrain, put it, rather than acting as mere strategic footholds in the Middle East for Great Britain and the United States, in fact, from the moment of gaining independence, the Arabian monarchies increased their intensity of contacts along the line of the cross-Atlantic partnership, by default reducing their value to other centres of power.[125] In economic theory, this situation is described in terms of the difficulties of a new player entering an already divided market.[126] Almaqbali[127] states:

> The aggravation of international relations in the region was also the result of the competition between the Great Powers, and their respective political ambition. In the light of 'West-East' political-military confrontation, the Soviet Union took immediate interest in the latest regional developments.

The next section will discuss in detail the impact of the great power competition and illustrate that the absence of TASSR–Gulf relations can specifically be explained through this chief reason.

3.2.2 TASSR–Gulf States: The impact of great power competition

Before the Revolution of October 1917,[128] Lenin wrote that the duty of socialists was to support the struggle of oppressed peoples for their complete national emancipation 'in whatever form, right down to an uprising or war'.[129] The key policy for achieving this was an 'alliance' between the 'victorious proletariat' of the USSR (the Bolsheviks) and the 'opposed peoples of the East' in their opposition to 'imperialism' (the West).[130] This was the foundation of Soviet policies in the Middle East – to counter Western policies in the region. Though the Middle East was still under the control of the Western powers, Great Britain and France, the new Soviet leadership started to show an interest in the region in the period between the two world wars.[131] The Soviets started to establish normal, even friendly, relations with Turkey,[132] Iran,[133] and Afghanistan.[134] This was primarily because their governments had also declared a struggle for independence against the Western powers. Diplomatic relations were established in 1924 between the USSR and the Hijaz, while the Soviets also recognized Yemen's independence in 1926, which by that time was in a confrontation with Italy and Britain.[135] In 1940, in negotiations with Nazi Germany, the Soviets announced territorial aspirations 'south of the national territory of the Soviet Union in the direction of the Indian Ocean'.[136] However, Nazi Germany's aggression against the Soviets meant that the Middle East policy of the time was largely determined by the logics of war and survival. On 25 August 1941, the USSR occupied Iran, whose leaders were pro-Nazi.[137] In 1943, diplomatic relations were established between the USSR and Egypt.[138]

The end of the Second World War changed the global balance of power. Notably, in the Middle East, France and Britain, the historical enemies, were not welcomed as friends among Arabs. Such anti-Western sentiments among Arab states were linked to populist political movements (whose leadership later came to power in many Arab states), and their national attempts to strengthen sovereignty and independence from the West.[139] Given the Soviets' 'anti-imperialist' policies in the region, the image of the USSR became increasingly positive. The Soviets supported demands for the withdrawal of British troops from Egypt and for granting independence to Syria and Lebanon, and later to Libya.[140] Talal Nizameddin[141] divides Soviet policies towards the Middle East between the periods 1945 and 1985. These phases correspond to three dominant leaders between the years 1945 and 1986: Stalin, Khrushchev and Brezhnev.[142] In the first phase – between 1945 and 1955 – Europe and the United States were the overwhelming preoccupation of Moscow – and the second stage (1955–67), when the USSR's interests in the Middle East gained their peak in term of priority and success. Similarly, Robert O. Freedman[143] believes that both superpowers – the United States and the USSR – and the leaders of the Middle East states, were all locked into the two-camp approach established by President Harry S. Truman and John Foster Dulles on the one hand and Joseph Stalin and Viacheslav Molotov on the other. Khrushchev continued to believe in this rivalry between communism and capitalism; however, his policies relied on the prevailing realities at the time, which linked the need to divert the Cold War from direct hostility to the Third World.[144]

Finally, returning to Nizameddin's division of Soviet policies towards the Middle East between 1967 and 1985, the more calculated approach occurred by balancing between aggressive pursuit of low-risk opportunities and cautious manoeuvring in high-risk or complicated situations.[145] Specifically, George W. Breslauer,[146] analysing Soviet policy in the Middle East during the years between 1967 and 1972, rejects the common views of the literature that the USSR did not want another Middle East war to break out during these years.[147] Rather, he suggests that Soviet behaviour from 1967 to 1972 specified 'intense Soviet interest in a political settlement that would remove the escalatory potential from the conflict – but not at any price; and neither the United States nor Israel was willing to pay the Soviet price'.[148]

Carol Saivetz,[149] with regard to the Middle East, argues that since 1985, the USSR's stance in the region had been relatively weak. Specifically, Nizameddin[150] analyses Gorbachev's New Thinking policies and implications towards the Middle East, and concludes that the Gulf War was an illustrative lesson for Moscow that the idealism of New Thinking would be unproductive if it did not take into account national interests and national security. New Thinking also transformed the viewpoint from Moscow about the inevitability of a bipolar world, and a new concept was established which stimulated the cooperation and coordination of key regions; therefore Europe, the Far East and the Middle East started to have increasing importance of their own.[151] As Rahr states: 'Soviet diplomacy must no longer view world politics exclusively through the prism of US-Soviet relations.'[152]

These great power competitions can be illustrated in specific cases. As Hurewitz[153] argues, the United States and the USSR, in the late 1960s, moved into a collision course at the heart of which was the Middle East. These two superpowers were supporting rival sides in regional disputes.[154,155] During the 1950s and the 1960s, the most tense period of the Cold War, the United States and the USSR treated the Middle East as a battleground for their competition, following a 'zero-sum game' with direct loss for one side or another the assumption of their strategies.[156] Moscow believed that Americans were using the area to weaken the USSR; in return the United States suspected the USSR of attempts to enlarge their influence southwards towards the Gulf, and beyond, into Africa. In the Arab–Israeli conflicts of 1967 and 1973, the two superpowers were on opposite sides. Hurewitz[157] believes that in the Arab–Israel zone, the USSR was pursuing a diplomacy of polarization, aiming to increase its own influence and decrease American influence in the Arab world. The USSR declared itself the protector and patron of the Arab cause in the dispute with Israel and presented the United States as the protector and patron of Israel. After the Arab defeat in June 1967, the USSR began to offer military support, while the United States supported Israel militarily.[158] Documents of the Middle Eastern conflict between 1957 and 1967, from the Foreign Policy Archive of the Russian Federation, have also confirmed this view that the Soviets openly stated their military support for the Arab allies in 'defending the region from imperialists and their allies, particularly Israel'.[159] According to some observers, the Six-Day War of June 1967 mostly accomplished the aim of displacing the United States from its positions of influence in the Arab countries.[160]

The dynamics of the Arab–Israel conflict contributed to making the USSR and Egypt key partners, especially between 1956 and 1974.[161] The crucial elements for bilateral relations were arms supplies (along with economic aid)[162] and countering Western policies in the region.[163] This is shown by the 1 January 1957 telegram of the USSR ambassador to Egypt, Kiselev, to the Russian Foreign Office.[164] It stated: 'Nasser has agreed to meet with me on the evening of 31 December. He wants to thank the Soviet government . . . [and] for agreeing to continue weapons supplies.' This arms supply occurred at the request of the Egyptians, and Moscow confirmed the continuation of shipments of military equipment to Egypt under previous agreements. The Western states' activities also were mentioned, as Nasser thanked the USSR government for their congratulations on the withdrawal of Anglo–French troops from the territory of Egypt (as a result of the Suez crisis of 1956).

In the records of correspondence of the ambassador of the USSR in Egypt, Kiselev, with the Chief of the Office of the president of Egypt, Ali Sabri, on 8 January 1957, Kiselev states that Sabri invited him, on behalf of the president, to exchange views on Eisenhower's statement on the Middle East. He expressed his personal thoughts to Sabri, sharply criticizing Eisenhower's plan. He drew Sabri's attention to the consequences of an official statement addressed to this American plan by those Arab countries directly concerned: '[S]ince it was a matter of preserving independence and sovereignty, as well as peace and security in the Middle East, the Soviet Union would undoubtedly support these statements of the Arab countries with all its authority.'[165] The British report on Egyptian efforts to dominate the Arab world[166] explained:

> The USSR has found that Nasser's ambitious have made him a useful instrument for the establishment of their influence in the Middle East. . . . The climate of rabid anti-Western nationalism of which Nasser has become the main spokesman in the Middle East is an ideal breeding-ground for the National Fronts, incorporating Communist elements which will eventually control them, which the USSR hopes to see gaining power in the Arab countries. Khaled Bikdash, the Syrian Communist leader, speaking in Parliament on March 17th, spoke of the 'National Front and its leader, . . . Nasser' which would succeed in foiling American 'conspiracies and plans'.

Additionally, the USSR's military aid[167] went to Syria, another important ally between the 1950s and 1960s. The Syrian Baathist version of Arab nationalism and socialism allowed a number of links with USSR policy in the region, especially based on their anti-Western and anti-Israel position. Moreover, the coup of 23 February 1966 resulted in the victory of the left-wing Baathist faction under the leadership of Atasi, and strengthened bilateral relations.[168] Military aid from the USSR increased, along with the agreement of a joint project for building the Euphrates Dam and building a large hydroelectric power station.

Soviet–American competition in the Middle East went beyond Israel and the Arab East.[169] After the Second World War, the Soviets began to challenge US influence among the non-Arab Muslim states (Turkey, Iran, Afghanistan and Pakistan).[170] In this zone the competition between the great powers remained high due to the establishment of the American and British initiative, the Baghdad Pact in 1955, and its conversion four years later into the Central Treaty Organization (CENTO).[171] Turkey, Iran and Pakistan, as regional members of CENTO, concluded a bilateral alliance with the United States. The rivalry took a more benign form after 1962, due to Soviet efforts to lure its non-Arab Muslim neighbours into 'normalising' their relationship with the USSR and to end their alliances with the United States.[172]

Clearly, the dynamics in the Arabian region were similar, if opposite – as the Gulf states remained traditionally allied with the Western countries. The legal basis of Britain's informal empire in the Gulf had been established in the early twentieth century,[173] using (the British term) its 'Protected States'.[174] Initially, the centre of Britain's establishment in the Gulf relocated southwards.[175] Relations between the Arabian states and Britain can be explained by usefully adopting the correspondence of Harold Dickson, Lieutenant Colonel, Colonial Administrator:[176]

> Kuwait 'an independent Arab State, under British protection, but not British protectorate', . . . His Majesty's Government are pledged to protect against foreign aggression, and in time of need the actual implements of this responsibility would – if military assistance were required – most probably fall on the Indian government.

The headquarters of the Political Residency was originally located in Bushehr in southern Persia, and moved to Bahrain in 1946.[177] Although the Gulf remained but a side show in the global fighting that took place in the Second World War from 1939 to 1945, the theatre was significant for several reasons. It offered Great Britain and her allies a chief source of petroleum.[178] In 1909, the Anglo-Persian Oil Company, which later became the Anglo-Iranian Oil Company (AIOC) and then British Petroleum (BP) was established to exploit the oil deposits that were found in south-west Persia.[179] The association of the Gulf with the discovery of oil, just strengthened relations.[180] In 1932, oil was found in Bahrain, followed by Qatar in 1940.[181] In Abu Dhabi the exploration for oil began in 1948, the first sign of hydrocarbons was exposed in 1953–4, and export of oil began in 1963.[182] In other words, by seizing the region, Axis leaders expected to take energy supplies, and use the greater Gulf area as an embarkation point for a potential attack on the USSR's southern underbelly.[183] Nonetheless, there were reported cases of competition between British and American interests over oil. For example, the administration report of the Kuwait Political Agency for 1932 states:

> On the 14th April the Anglo-Persian Oil Company Ltd., suddenly and mysteriously abandoned these operations much to the disappointment of the [Kuwait] Ruler. It is presumed that this was as a result of American pressure in London. There followed what might be termed 'open Oil War' in London, between the American and British interests, the details of which need not concern the report. . . . His Majesty's Government had decided not to insist upon confining the concession to a 'purely British concern'.[184]

Also, during the Second World War the Gulf remained the principal lifeline for London and Washington's strategic initiative to offer financial aid to their beleaguered Russian ally.[185]

The two world wars had a long-term impact on Britain's informal empire.[186] It was believed that to boost its alliance with the United States, to build 'special relations',[187] the threat of the USSR remained the key to keep strategic relations with the Gulf states. From the US point of view, Britain's imperial influence provided a useful shield against Soviet growth.[188] Washington in the early 1940s still had little influence over affairs on the Arabian Peninsula.[189] However, within three years of Pearl Harbor, America had become the biggest benefactor of King Ibn Saud, beating Britain, and the United States would begin to rival Britain in its overall influence there.[190] At the same time, Chubin also clarifies that in the half century following the Second World War, the main determinant of USSR policy in the Gulf, similarly to everywhere in the region, was Moscow's rivalry with the United States.[191] As the Cold War emerged, American and British wartime dissimilarities in the Gulf lessened. London agreed to the superpower's increasing presence in two Persian Gulf states, Saudi Arabia and Iran.[192] During the 1940s and 1950s Americans offered both growing amounts of military and economic aid, and an increasing number of military advisers.[193] In the 1960s, the American view on the British leadership in the Gulf was clear: American interests were promoted by the UK's continuing to act as security guarantor for the region.[194]

The period from 1968 to 1971 witnessed a colossal change in the Gulf, not solely bringing to a close over a century of British supremacy in the region, but during this time a new political order in the Gulf also emerged.[195] In early 1968 the Labour government under Wilson declared their intention to withdraw from the Gulf.[196] The importance of keeping an alert eye on the USSR acted as another marker of US policy in the Gulf after Great Britain's declaration of withdrawal, and it manifested in a continuation of policies pursued since the Second World War, rather than a shift.[197] The impending power vacuum was a matter of concern for the United States, as it might encourage the communist world's 'meddling' in the Gulf[198] (e.g. the emergence of the communist People's Democratic Republic of Yemen).

The Washington authorities did not want to see a *Pax Sovietica* established in the vacuum that would follow the British departure; however, they possessed very few means to avoid it. At the same time, Britain's departure from the Gulf did not open direct routes for Soviet influence.[199] By the end of November 1971, the British Navy had pulled out completely from the Gulf. Ashore, the Staffordshire Regiment sallied its last postings in Bahrain and Sharjah. The RAF, too, flew off from those two sites, leaving behind only a small staging post on Masirah, a small island off the coast of Oman.[200] Jeffrey Macris concludes: 'For the first time in 150 years, by the end of 1971 the Gulf was without the presence or the protection of a major Western power.'[201] Nonetheless, the historical and strategic ties of the Gulf states remained with the Western bloc.[202] Therefore, despite existing shared Islamic identities (which realistically did not work effectively for political purposes during that period) – minority 'Self' and 'Self(s)' – TASSR and Gulf states remained in different camps, which is clearly one of the key reasons for their minimal relations between 1917 and 1990.

3.3 Conclusion

The chapter has demonstrated that TASSR–Gulf relations barely existed due to two principal reasons. First, there were limits to any paradiplomatic efforts available to the TASSR due to Soviet concerns over the Tatars' historical importance and their capacity to challenge centralized power, in particular through their role in the ideal of pan-Turkism. Tatars also had links to Turkic nations, including shared Muslim identities, which are much closer than those with Arab nations. Any potential collaborations based on Muslim identities with Arabian states were diminished by Soviet policies against Islam, and repressions against famous Tatar Muslim clergy, intellectuals and diplomats. In general, shared Islamic identities were badly damaged, diminishing the possibilities of relations between TASSR and the Gulf states on this basis. Despite the USSR being the first country to establish full diplomatic relations with the Kingdom of Hijaz and Nejd in 1926, this did not lead to longer-term partnerships between them. As a result, TASSR – as part of the USSR – could not build paradiplomatic relations either.

With regards to the smaller monarchies, the discussion has shown that Kuwait, which kept the closest relations with the USSR, was among the recipients of Soviet military aid, but this was not linked with the Islamic factor. The second major factor of this chapter comes into play here, namely the competition between the 'Great Powers'. The Arabian Gulf states generally supported the Western bloc in its competition with the Soviets.

This chapter concludes the first part of the book, which focuses on any existing relations between TASSR and Arabian states between 1917 and 1990, with the key themes as follows: TASSR and the GCC states' relations were severely limited due to (1) the failed cooperation between 'Self(s)' and the 'Other', and (2) the damaged nature of their shared identities of 'Self(s)'.

Tatarstan and the Gulf states

Emergence of relations

This chapter discusses the emergence of relations between modern Tatarstan and the GCC states – the minority 'Self' and 'Self(s)'. At the political level, there were relatively few signs of cooperation in the 1990s, and most relations were built based on religious factors. However, the situation changed after the early 2000s. Since that time, Tatarstan's paradiplomacy with the GCC states, relying on shared Islamic identities, has been geared mainly towards developing economic cooperation, including through Islamic finance and banking. In order to demonstrate this, first, this chapter will focus on analyses of the relatively few steps taken towards cooperation by Tatarstan and the Gulf states between the 1990s and 2000s. Second, it will examine Tatarstan–GCC relations since the 2000s by looking at key reasons for the growth of relations, explaining mechanisms for collaborations, followed by a case studies survey of each Gulf state's relations with Tatarstan. The chapter concludes by reviewing the existing challenges and limitations of such relations.

4.1 1990s–2000s: Relatively few steps

Since their declaration of sovereignty in August 1990, Tatarstan's leadership have been active in building trade and diplomatic relations within the Russian Federation, with other former Soviet republics, and in the 'far abroad'.[1] With Tatarstan as a case study, John W. Slocum applies the concept of 'paradiplomacy', which identifies attempts by non-central governments to establish equally constructive agreements with political entities beyond the borders of their sovereign state. Slocum has identified three types of paradiplomacy: trans-border regional paradiplomacy, trans-regional paradiplomacy and global paradiplomacy.[2] This research applies the concept of global paradiplomacy when considering Tatarstan's relations with other global players, including the Gulf states.

In the 1990s, Tatarstan developed paradiplomatic efforts, building relations with non-Muslim and Muslim states. For example, in 1995, Tatarstan concluded over 120 treaties and agreements with other subjects of the Russian Federation, Commonwealth of Independent States (CIS) countries and other governments. These included forty-six Russian regions, all of the CIS countries except for Azerbaijan, Armenia, the governments of Germany, France, the United States, Hungary, Lithuania, Greece, the Czech Republic and Bulgaria.[3] Among the Middle Eastern countries, however, collaboration was developed only with Turkey. Turkey and Tatarstan signed a cultural and economic collaboration agreement on 28 May 1995.[4] The agreement resulted in the opening of a mission in Ankara by the Tatars, while the Turks opened a consulate in Kazan.[5]

The reason for this broad spread of connections is that in the 1990s Tatarstan's international relations were built purely pragmatically, as explained during my interview with Rafael' Khakimov of the Institute of History of Sh. Marjani:[6] 'We have worked equally well with both Islamic and Christian countries.' He also states: 'Moreover, in the 90s, the question was about the economic survival of Tatarstan.' In 1997, Tatarstan's foreign trade turnover was $2.97 billion, with exports surpassing imports by a factor of 2.5.[7] The structure of Tatarstan's exports relied on the following sectors: aircraft, oil, chemicals, machine-building, automobiles and instruments.[8] At that time, Tatarstan's biggest trading partners were CIS states: Ukraine, Uzbekistan and Kazakhstan; other key trading partners were Germany, Poland, Lithuania and Finland.[9] Tatarstan attracted foreign investments in 1997, reaching $697.9 million (foreign direct investment amounted to only $17.1 million).[10] Most investments came from Germany, the United Kingdom and the United States. Cumulative foreign investment in Tatarstan as of 1 April 1998 was $1.164 million, of which foreign direct investment totalled $121.3 million.[11] Oil, aviation and automotive industries were at the centre of Tatarstan's foreign economic activities. Relations with Muslim or other countries were built not for political or ideological reasons but based on purely pragmatic interests. Khakimov shared during the interview:

> At first we just had to survive, and later, when the republic got on its feet, we had to sell our products. We were not expected anywhere with Tatarstan goods. The markets had to be conquered. Competition has always been and remains fierce. Arab countries were interested in our helicopters.

Nonetheless, Gulnaz Sharafutdinova in her research published in 2003 somewhat challenges this view, stressing the cultural, religious and political factors for building such relations:

> The prevailing Islamic direction in Tatarstan's diplomatic activities cannot be justified on pure economic grounds. Therefore, a case could be made for cultural, religious and political factors, as driving forces behind these contacts. Owing to cultural and religious links, Tatarstan gets distinct attention and recognition from these states, which consider Tatarstan's 'statehood' more seriously than the countries of the West.[12]

As examples of diplomatic efforts that Tatarstan made via the Islamic factor she notes relations with the GCC states – UAE (and others such as Turkey, Egypt, Jordan).

I argue that both views are partially correct. Economically, in the 1990s and the 2000s, relations were developed more closely with Christian rather than Muslim countries. At the same time, Sharafudinova's argument that Tatarstan's 'statehood' was considered more seriously by the East than the West is also problematic, since this status still comes with several limitations. For example, there have been emerging contacts between the Organisation of Islamic Cooperation (OIC) and Tatarstan even since 1992, but as Rafael' Khakimov explains, 'It was impossible to take a separate seat in the OIC because of the Charter of the organisation itself. We discussed this issue with Ekmeleddin bey [Secretary General of the Organisation of Islamic Cooperation (OIC), Professor Ekmeleddin Ihsanoglu], even before he became Secretary General. He has always been an ardent supporter of Tatarstan.' Ultimately, Tatarstan's status as part of the Russian Federation prevents it from full-fledged state relations. Indeed, it can be considered that the Russian federal government would discourage free rein in building such connections, since it has increasingly recognized the value of integrating Muslim minorities and their regions into broader federal policies for relations with OIC countries.

Meanwhile, Tatarstan developed interests in relations based on Islamic shared identities, which suggests a shift in priorities from the situation sketched earlier. For example, the government of the first Tatarstan president, Mintimer Shaimiev, had a vision to integrate the ideas of moderate Tatar nationalism into its politics and national ideology, while simultaneously distancing itself from 'radical' nationalists. As part of this strategy, the official separation between religion and the state, as stipulated in the Constitution in 1992, was accompanied by a policy of allowing an indirect role to be played by Islam within Tatarstan politics. Consequently, the Tatarstan authorities favoured the secession in 1992 of the Tatarstan Muslim clerics from the Federal Islamic centre in Ufa and the formation of a separate Muslim Spiritual Board of the Republic of Tatarstan (DUMRT), based in Kazan. The latter has been perceived as an indispensable attribute of Tatarstan's sovereignty. Tatarstan established direct links to Muslim clergy in the GCC states, and especially cooperation with Saudi Arabia, specifically for the performance of hajj and *umrah* by the Republic's clergy and inhabitants. Marat Gatin, the head of the Russian Centre for Science and Culture in Alexandria, Egypt,[13] confirmed during my interview that 'for the first years after the collapse of the USSR perhaps first links between Russian regions with Muslim population (such as Tatarstan, Bashkortostan, the North Caucasus) occurred through religious organisations and religious authorities; connections also occurred through educational exchanges – notably a lot of Tatars went to the Muslim countries, including the GCC states, to study'.

It is important to recognize that religious and cultural variations required negotiating, since ideological components prevailed in the GCC which are not inherent in the region.[14] Some GCC states have been seen as challengers to so-called 'Tatar traditionalism' and its role as the sole 'official' Islam in the region,[15] based on the Hanafi *madhhab* (school of Islam jurisprudence) and prescribed by the state-linked Muslim Spiritual Board of the Republic of Tatarstan, which is charged with observing all mosques in the region. There is growing evidence that religious fundamentalism, mainly attributed in Tatarstan and Russia to Wahhabism and Salafism, is regarded as having been brought in from abroad, including from some of the Gulf countries.[16] However, it should be mentioned that Islamic fundamentalism, or 'Wahhabism', as it is called by Russian authorities, has spread more quickly in the North Caucasus than in the Middle Volga region.[17] Galina Yemelianova[18] in 2000 pointed towards low levels of professionalism and the corruption of the Tatarstan Islamic elite, as well as limited financial and material support from the state, as factors that created strong doctrinal and financial dependence on foreign Islamic sources. Missionaries and representatives of various Islamic institutions from Saudi Arabia and Kuwait, and other Muslim states (Turkey, Iran, Jordan, Syria, Malaysia, Libya, Egypt) had foreign influence. She continues:

> These have taken charge of Islamic education in the new *medresses [sic]*, Islamic colleges and the Islamic University, supplying Islamic literature published in their countries. [. . .] Foreign Islamic funds, such as those emanating from the University of Imam Muhammad ben Saud [*sic*] in Saudi Arabia, the Organisation

of Islamic Conference (OIC), the World Islamic League and the fund of Ibrahim Hayri have provided scholarships for Tatar Muslims wishing to study in Islamic institutions abroad. As a result, future Tatar imams have been taught alien forms of Islam, which have nothing to do with the Tatar Islamic tradition, itself based on the tolerant Hanafi *madhab [sic]* (juridical school) of Sunni Islam.

Marat Gatin,[19] during my interview, explained the situation from his practical experience:

The region of the Arabian Peninsula, according to its *aqidah* [religious belief system or creed] is just not what our grandfathers used to say. The guys began to return; they are all sincere and good but had absorbed not quite what we had before. Against this background, hotbeds of conflict began to arise between *babai*[20] and the younger generation.

Allen Derrick goes even further and relies on a 2009 interview with Valiulla Yakupov,[21] who used the terms 'Wahhabism' and 'Salafism' interchangeably, and even blamed the Saudi Embassy in Moscow for 'drawing on its considerable resources to finance the spread of their Wahhabi ideology among the *umma* of Tatarstan'. Yakupov also judged 'Saudi Arabia and other Arab countries for their "foreign interference" in the lives of the republic's *umma*, employing methods such as sending young Tatar Muslims abroad to receive an Islamic education'.[22] The flavour of this contention is further conveyed by Derrick's interview: 'upon their return home, he [Yakupov] contended, these young men sow seeds of discord in mosques in villages and cities throughout the republic by "forcing a foreign religious ideology" on Tatars accustomed to their own Islamic traditions'.[23]

These views presented by an academic, practitioner and religious authority might suggest that even with existing collaborations in religious fields between the Gulf states and Tatarstan, the limits of such collaborations were revealed in the urgency for re-establishing its own theological school, and the traditional form of Islam in Tatarstan. As Marat Gatin[24] states:

Tatarstan began to think in the 2000s – in the first decade when the Russian Islamic University arose[25] – on the importance of having its own universities rather than only at the level of mosque madrasa, but Tatarstan also began seriously to think that they had to start restoring their religious education, their theological school.

A quotation from my interview with the chairman of the Spiritual Board of Muslims of the Republic of Tatarstan and the Grand Mufti of Tatarstan, Kamil'

Hazrat Samigullin,[26] can instructively reflect religious collaboration over the period:

> If you do not recall 1000 years of history in Islam, but take it from the 1990s, when practically everything had to be regained from scratch, people were hungry [for knowledge]. If an Arab arrived, it seemed that this was everything – the ultimate dream of one nation with the Prophet himself; he speaks Arabic and [Tatars] listen and believe every word from these people. Today, Tatarstan has home-grown scholars who have even studied abroad, but who live here and feel a responsibility to understand that they are local [. . .], they live in their own land [Russia] and they are responsible. [. . .] Politically – this is one thing, but in religious sense – we no longer need them [the Arabs]. This need was problematic.

Thus, the Grand Mufti underlines the importance of education of one's own scholars 'who will understand the circumstances in which we live, and will be responsible for what they say. I think that these will save us from many mistakes.'[27]

This might suggest that in the 1990s and the 2000s, Tatarstan and the GCC states' relations began to emerge, and were mainly based on cooperation with Saudi Arabia, specifically to perform hajj and *umrah*. Relations were complicated by the different ideological components in the Gulf and Tatarstan. In other words, even with existing shared Islamic identities, Tatarstan and the GCC states were not able to establish sufficient mutual interests for close collaborations in the 1990s and 2000s. However, this began to change after the 2000s, especially after 2008, as the next section demonstrates.

4.2 Modern relations (2000s–21)

4.2.1 Key reasons for growth of relations

Since the first decade of the 2000s, Tatarstan has been the 'avant-garde, if not the leader of this avant-garde', in building relations between Russia and the GCC states, according to Marat Gatin during my interview. This includes developing its paradiplomatic efforts towards the Gulf. The key was the establishment of the Group of the Strategic Vision 'Russia-Islamic World' in 2006. From its establishment, this group has been coordinated through the Republic of Tatarstan, and the key role is given to its leadership.[28] Initially, the Group was established under the leadership of well-known Arabist and former Russian prime minister (1998–9) Yevgeny Primakov and the first president of Tatarstan

Mintimer Shaimiev.[29] After their meeting in 2009, for almost six years the group was not active. However, with the re-establishment of its activity, the Tatarstan leadership's essential role in building ties with the Muslim world has again been illustrated.[30] In 2014, the current head, Rustam Minnikhanov, was appointed as the group's chairman.[31] Chief Executive of the Tatarstan Investment Development Agency, Taliya Minullina,[32] explained during my interview that this means that the head of Tatarstan is today responsible for the development of relations between the Russian regions and the OIC countries.[33] The group consists of public political organizations, former prime ministers, ministers of the OIC countries, as well as representatives of Russian Muslim regions, religious authorities, academics, Arabists and experts in Islam. In total, the group consists of thirty-three high-ranking statesmen and public figures from twenty-seven Muslim states, including Kuwait, Bahrain, the UAE, Oman, and three representatives from Saudi Arabia. The role of this group in linking the Kremlin and the GCC states is highly appreciated by the Gulf's high-ranking representatives, as stated during my interview with Shaykh Abdulrahman bin Mohammad bin Rashid al-Khalifa, chairman of the Supreme Islamic Affairs Council of Bahrain, who is also the foreign member of the group:[34]

> The Strategic Vision Group played a major role in developing relations between the Russian Federation and the Kingdom of Bahrain, as well as between Russia and other countries of the Arab and Islamic world, given that the group represents the decision personally expressed by Russian President Vladimir Putin about the necessity of linking the countries of the Arab and Islamic world with the community of Islam within the Russian Federation of more than 30 million local Muslims. They can play a pivotal role in the development of Russian-Islamic as well as Russian-Arab relations, given that the Russian Federation has become an observer member of the Organisation of the Islamic Conference. This was welcomed by the Supreme Council of Islamic Affairs in the Kingdom of Bahrain, because Russia's presence in this organisation will give its decisions a lot of strength and effectiveness, and will contribute to developing international relations among all members of the organisation.

The significance of this group as an effective mechanism for Russia and the GCC states might be indicated by the number and profile of meetings held, which have taken place in several Russian cities (Moscow, Kazan, Ufa, Grozny, Makhachkala), as well as in Saudi Arabia and Kuwait. It was planned to hold the sixth Annual Meeting of the Group of Strategic Vision in Saudi Arabia, in April 2020, at the invitation of the King Salman.[35] However due to Covid-19 this was delayed until 23–25 November 2021.[36] Outcomes of the meeting can be examined in depth to illustrate the role of the group for the federal government, and the Republic of Tatarstan.

The seventh meeting of the group was held in Jeddah under the slogan 'Dialogue and Cooperation Prospects'. Opening the plenary part of the meeting, Rustam Minnikhanov read out a greeting to the participants, which had been sent by President Putin.[37] In this speech, the Kremlin placed great importance on developing friendly relations with Islamic countries, either at the bilateral level or through dialogue with the OIC.[38] At the conclusion of his speech, he extended his thanks and appreciation to the custodian of the two Holy Mosques, King Salman, for his interest in organizing the meeting of the group,[39] all of which provides positive signs for bilateral relations between the Kremlin and Riyadh.

On the sidelines of the meeting, bilateral contacts between the head of Tatarstan and a number of representatives of the official and business circles of the Kingdom took place, which benefited both federal and republic interests. For example, the head of Tatarstan held meetings with the first deputy minister of Hajj and Umrah of the Kingdom, Abdel Fattah bin Suleiman al-Mashat; Governor of the Meccan Province Prince Khaled al-Faisal; secretary general of the GCC states Naef al-Hajraf and deputy secretary general of the World Islamic League, Abdelrahman al-Zeid. The special role played by Minnikhanov as the chairman of the group can be seen in his meeting with first deputy minister of Hajj and Umrah of the Kingdom, Abdel Fattah bin Suleiman al-Mashat, where Minnikhanov discussed the possibility of the participation of Russian pilgrims vaccinated against Covid-19 in hajj in 2022. The Grand Mufti of Tatarstan, Kamil' Hazrat, who also participated in the meeting, commented during my interview:[40]

> I think the main victory is that Rustam Nurgaliyevich [Minnikhanov] raised the issue of what we need for Sputnik V to be accepted by the Saudi side and within two weeks this issue was resolved. [. . .] This is the authority of the President of the country, and as Rustam Minnikhanov spoke on his behalf, since he leads the Group, . . . I believe this is completely to his credit.

As for the advantages for Tatarstan's paradiplomacy, Rustam Minnikhanov took part in a 'round table' with the participation of representatives of the business community of Tatarstan and Saudi Arabia in the Chamber of Commerce and Industry.[41] Moreover, the delegation from Tatarstan concluded their visit by performing *umrah*,[42] showing how their shared Muslim identities helped to further bilateral relations, as will be discussed later in the section on Tatarstan–Saudi Arabia relations.

As the example of the meeting arranged in Jeddah illustrates, these events are an opportunity to discuss the development of relations between Russia, its regions (specifically Tatarstan) and Islamic countries, including the GCC states. Trade and economic, scientific and technical, cultural, educational, tourist and other areas of relationships are implemented through this group.[43] The economic wing is carried out by the Investment Development Agency of the Republic of Tatarstan, which holds the international 'Russia-Islamic world' Kazan Summit[44], again offering more advantages for Tatarstan's paradiplomacy. This is the only business platform for economic interaction between Russian regions and the OIC countries. Table 1 shows that the number of participants, along with the number of country-participants, increases every year. Specifically, with regards to the Gulf states, in 2019, eighty representatives from almost all Gulf countries took part in the Kazan Summit: forty-one people from the UAE, twenty-nine from Saudi Arabia, eight from Bahrain, six from Oman and two from Kuwait. These included officials, including those holding high government posts, and companies.

The Kazan Summit pays special attention to the halal industry and the export of products, along with treaties and agreements signed on the fringes of the summit. For example, among key agreements signed at the Kazan Summit in 2019 were that Sberbank (state-owned Russian banking and financial services company) launched the Payzakat project. Sberbank together with the DUMRT launched a fundraising campaign for the 'Virtual Mosque' project to provide people with disabilities virtual helmets. Sberbank also presented 'Sadakomaty' terminals for collecting non-cash and cash donations of *sadaka*; Ak Bars Bank (one of the twenty largest Russian banks by assets; in 2014 it became the first bank in Russia to apply shari'a banking) launched a new mortgage product: housing finance through the sale of real estate in instalments, in accordance with shari'a norms. The DUMRT has entered into a cooperation agreement

Table 1 Kazan Summit: Participants' Statistics by Years and by Countries

Kazan Summit participants by year:

2009	2010	2011	2012	2013	2014	2015	2016	2017	2018	2019
250	400	772	1000	700	500	745	1556	2641	3000	3598

Kazan Summit participants from number of countries by year:

2009	2010	2011	2012	2013	2014	2015	2016	2017	2018	2019
18	24	27	30	40	25	46	51	53	53	72

Source: Investment Development Agency of the Republic of Tatarstan.

with the Management Company 'Ak Bars Capital'. This agreement expanded the choice of securities for Muslims in accordance with the norms of Islam on the exchange market. As a result of the Summit, specialists from the Russian Islamic Institute who submitted their development to the Council of Ulema of the Muslim Spiritual Board of the Republic of Tatarstan (DUMRT) are engaged in the creation of a methodology for halal investment in securities. Consequently, key agreements signed in 2019 that were finalized at the Summit concerned developing Islamic finance and banking, and also the active role of the Muslim Spiritual Board of the Republic of Tatarstan (DUMRT). In this can be seen the second reason for the development of relations between the minority 'Self' and 'Self(s)' – Tatarstan and the GCC states after the 2000s – economic opportunity, merged with existing shared Islamic identities. In this regard, Marat Gatin's[45] comments appear particularly valuable:

> As I have already said, if before the mid-2000s, a great emphasis on regional interaction was of a religious nature, then in the last 10-15 years it has begun to move into the economic plane. Here, if we take Rustam Minnikhanov [head of Republic of Tatarstan], he promotes the importance of drawing on the experience of the Muslim countries of the Arab world in introducing Islamic banking tools into our daily life. Islamic banking is part of what he calls the 'halal lifestyle' (in the Arab countries it is called a little differently – it is called 'Islamic lifestyle'). It is very comprehensive, but with an emphasis on the economy; this includes developments of sectors, such as tourism, Islamic banking, and the production of relevant pharmaceuticals.

Internally, the meaning of 'halal lifestyle' is explained by the Grand Mufti of Tatarstan, Kamil' Hazrat, as follows:[46]

> Rustam Nurgaliyevich [Minnikhanov] showed us the direction of movement [towards 'halal lifestyle']. In the last year, for example, together with the Association of Russian Muslim Entrepreneurs, we began to implement their project by opening prayer rooms in 7 shopping centres in Kazan.

Some outcomes of the 'halal lifestyle' policy for external relations can be seen in the foreign trade turnover of Tatarstan and the GCC states between 2011 and 2019) (Table 2), which proves Gatin's point. Economic relations occurred mainly between Saudi Arabia and the UAE, because of existing shared interests in developing Islamic economy and banking. These will be illustrated in terms of Tatarstan's paradiplomacy towards the Gulf states in the next section, but first, a short section will show the mechanisms by which Tatarstan builds such relations.

Table 2 Foreign Trade Turnover of Tatarstan and the GCC States (2011–19)

Thousand, $	2011	2012	2013	2014	2015	2016	2017	2018	2019	Total in the country, thousand $
Bahrain	34.6	0.0	134.4	224.3	48.5	0.0	0.0	13.7	83.8	539.3
Qatar	736.7	1 652.9	916.1	1 951.3	711.8	6 238.1	5 176.3	3 898.5	7 547.1	28,828.8
Kuwait	1 467.8	1 520.7	634.1	0.0	808.9	91.5	532.6	164.5	786.7	6,006.8
UAE	11 903.6	5 798.4	7 090.7	14 110.0	20 194.6	25 986.2	21 409.7	34 103.2	20 151.6	160,748.0
Oman	269.5	0.0	283.4	375.7	51.4	1 604.1	56.9	119.7	138.0	2,898.7
Saudi Arabia	8 955.7	27 289.7	4 118.2	4 725.2	10 931.7	11 155.1	42 844.8	18 651.8	49 409.3	178,081.5
Total for the year, thousand $	23 367.9	36 261.7	13 176.9	21 386.5	32 746.9	45 075.0	70 020.3	56 951.4	78 116.5	377,103.1
Total trade turnover, bn $	22.9	23.1	25.8	21.1	12.7	11.9	16.9	16.9	15.7	167.1
% of total turnover	0.1%	0.2%	0.1%	0.1%	0.3%	0.4%	0.4%	0.3%	0.5%	average 0.3

Source: Tatarstan Investment Development Agency.

4.2.2 Tatarstan's paradiplomacy towards the GCC states (2000s–21): Mechanisms of integration

Neither the subjects of the Russian Federation nor its regions can be independent subjects of economic and political activity within the overriding legislative framework. As such, in 1996 the president endowed the Ministry of Foreign Affairs with coordinating functions in matters of foreign relations of the regions, and since 2004 the regions have been obliged to obtain the consent of the Ministry to conclude international economic agreements. In general, the paradiplomatic efforts of Tatarstan are conducted through effective interdepartmental cooperation and, given that they are mainly economic in focus, economic development institutions remain central.

The chief executive of Tatarstan Investment Development Agency Taliya Minullina views this as a coordinated policy in the Republic of Tatarstan between the Department for Foreign Affairs of the head of the Republic of Tatarstan, and the Ministry of Industry and Trade, which is responsible for foreign economic activity in general, and the Investment Development Agency, which is engaged in attracting investments. Moreover, the State Committee on Tourism, which promotes the region's brand and directs its activities to attracting tourists to the republic, the Chamber of Commerce and Industry, the Ministry of Foreign Affairs of the Russian Federation and the customs and migration services are involved. Additionally, Tatarstan's largest enterprises today also have production facilities abroad in some countries, and also conduct active operations. Other mechanisms are important for developing such relations: Islamic organizations, such as the previously mentioned Muslim Spiritual Board of the Republic of Tatarstan (DUMRT); NGOs, such as the Association of Muslim Entrepreneurs of Russia; and educational institutions such as the Bulgarian Islamic Academy and the Russian Islamic Institute. Consequently, relevant ministries, such as the Ministry of Culture of the Republic of Tatarstan and Ministry of Education and Science of the Republic of Tatarstan are also due for consideration.

4.2.3 Tatarstan and Saudi Arabia (2000s–21)

Representatives of Saudi Arabia visited Tatarstan for the first time in 2011 during the leadership of Rustam Minnikhanov.[47] The delegation was headed by the Saudi Chairman of the Chamber of Commerce and Industry.[48] Rustam Minnikhanov drew the guests' attention to the fact that Tatarstan could become a good platform for Saudi Arabian enterprises to enter the Russian market. At the same time, the main directions of cooperation were outlined.[49] In 2013, a delegation from Tatarstan paid a return visit to Saudi Arabia. Rustam Minnikhanov spoke at the opening of the international economic forum in Jeddah, and met with representatives of the OIC and heads of large enterprises in the country. A similar programme made up the visit of 2014 – among other things, representatives of Tatarstan participated in a reception hosted by the king of Saudi Arabia.[50]

Perhaps the most significant visit of the Tatarstan head to Saudi Arabia was in 2017.[51] This was because it was associated with federal-level advantages, as Minnikhanov carried the invitation of the Russian President Vladimir Putin to King Salman of Saudi Arabia, and the unprecedented visit of a king of Saudi Arabia to Moscow followed in November 2017. Marat Gatin, who accompanied Rustam Minnikhanov, comments on the existing friendly relations between both leaders, and illustrates how shared Islamic identities play a positive role in building relations for further collaborations:[52]

> They [King Salman and Rustam Minnikhanov] also met in 2014 [above-mentioned visit], when Minnikhanov went on hajj. [This meeting in 2014 was during the reception] on behalf of the former King [King Abdullah bin 'Abd al-'Aziz al-Sa'ud] (it was a reception in honor of the distinguished guests invited to the hajj), and Rustam Minnikhanov was the [former] King's guest [. . .] in 2014. There their first acquaintance happened. They were just sitting there together, communicating with each other, so in February 2017, a meeting had already taken place when he [King Salman] became King of Saudi Arabia.

During that visit, Minnikhanov conducted wide diplomatic and business programmes: meetings with the leadership of the Kingdom: ministers of industry and commerce, the president of the Islamic Development Bank, representatives of big companies and heads of global organizations of the Islamic world. The visit was concluded with a prominent business forum, 'Tatarstan–Saudi Arabia'.[53] The head of Tatarstan also received 'a ticket to the highest Islamic political circles'[54] by being allowed inside the Ka'ba, the holiest place of Islam, during *umrah*. Again, analyses of Marat Gatin's recall of this visit illustrate how effectively shared identities can serve for developing mutual economic interests:

> We are grateful to the Saudi side as we were well received at the highest level in all respects. And in terms of content, very meaningful meetings were held here. From the point of view of the protocol, they accompanied us at the highest level and from the point of view of the religious component – at the request of Minnikhanov, our delegation was allowed into the interior of the Ka'ba.

It seems quite important to also point to the delegation of the Republic of Tatarstan in the Kingdom of Saudi Arabia, which illustrates how Tatarstan's paradiplomacy operates based on collaborations of different mechanisms (see 4.2.2). It included deputy prime minister of the Republic of Tatarstan; minister of Agriculture and Food of the Republic of Tatarstan, Marat Akhmetov; assistants to the head of Tatarstan, Radik Gimatdinov and Kamil' Iskhakov, head of Tatarstan Investment Development Agency Taliya Minullina; trade and economic representative of the Republic of Tatarstan in Dubai, Timur Khairutdinov; deputy minister of Industry and Trade of the Republic of Tatarstan, Denis Valeev; head of the Muslim Spiritual Directorate of the Republic of Tatarstan, Mufti Kamil' Hazrat Samigullin; chairman of the Board of the Chamber of Commerce and Industry, Shamil' Ageev; general director of PJSC Tatneft, Nail' Maganov; chairman of the Board of Directors of PJSC Taif; first deputy general director of PPJSC Taif, Rustem Sulteev; chairman of the Management Board of PJSC 'Ak Bars' Bank, Zufar Garaev; deputy general of PJSC 'Kamaz', Sergei Afanas'ev; and deputy general director for Commerce of 'Kazanorgsintez', Timur Sulteev. This is one of the most illustrative examples of how Tatarstan paradiplomacy operates (not solely towards the Gulf states, but also generally); as noted earlier, its success depends on effective interdepartmental cooperation, which adds to achieving both political and economic objectives.

All these ongoing engagements resulted in foreign trade turnover between Tatarstan and Saudi Arabia between 2011 and 2019 being among the highest (see Table 2). Direct foreign investment from the Gulf countries in Tatarstan was $68 million by 2019. Investments from Saudi Arabia in Russia amounted to $185 million and in Tatarstan, to $3 million. All investments from Saudi Arabia in Tatarstan were from a shareholder of the Tatarstan International Investment Company of Islamic Development Bank. Tatarstan and Saudi Arabia work on Islamic banking and Islamic finance.[55] This work is particularly closely associated with the Islamic Development Bank, as stated by Taliya Minullina during her interview. She further explains that the Tatarstan–Saudi relationship is built on Islamic economy and banking development, which can be regarded as contributing to closer cooperation between minority 'Self' and 'Self(s)':

> We work with those institutions that in Saudi Arabia set the standards for organising accounting and auditing in Islamic institutions. We have a consultant in Saudi Arabia, specifically on Islamic banking, they help us. We have the Russian Islamic University in Kazan, we have a local bank, Ak Bars Bank, which recently launched a mortgage product in accordance with shari'a law [See 4.2.1.]. That is, we make Islamic contracts in accordance with these international standards and in order to be consulted, we work a lot with Saudi Arabia in this area.

She concludes that the importance of Saudi Arabia for Tatarstan is that it is the chair of the Organisation of Islamic Cooperation.[56] At the same time, suggestions of initiatives between Tatarstan and Saudi Arabia towards Islamic banking and finance (among other sectors such as energy,[57] agriculture,[58] and manufacturing[59]) are constantly discussed, and remain fields for further collaboration.

While hajj and *umrah* remain the key for developing relations with the Kingdom, additionally the introduction of 'de-Wahhabisation' reforms in the Kingdom also might boost these collaborations, including in the economic field, based on broader shared Islamic identities. This policy has been followed under the current ruler, King Salman since his ascension to the throne in 2015, and his son – Saudi Arabia's Crown Prince Mohammad bin Salman, who has emerged as the dominant political actor in the country.[60] He has presented himself as a reformer, pushing Saudi Arabia forward in a variety of fields, including reforms in religion concerning fundamental changes to the existing historical political-religious pact between Wahhabi ulema and the al-Sa'ud family.[61] Mohammad bin Salman vowed to return Saudi Arabia to 'moderate Islam', stating that Riyadh's turn towards radicalization occurred as the outcome of the Iranian revolution. This was followed by the United States' ambition to have regional partners such as Saudi Arabia applying religion as a tool to counter the Soviet Union in Afghanistan and the Middle East during the Cold War.[62] Also, there have been a variety of significant transformations within Saudi Arabia in the past several years, which can be seen as examples of such 'de-Wahhabisation', including efforts to distance official Saudi Arabian history from Wahhabism; limiting the religious police's powers; and allowing women to drive, live alone and travel without a male guardian.[63] Such transformations seem to play a very positive role in building relations between the minority 'Self' and 'Self', in our case study, Russian Tatarstan and the Kingdom of Saudi Arabia.

Among such positive signs is the fact that during the visit of King Salman to Moscow in 2017, he met with leaders of the Muslim clergy of the Russian Federation. The meeting was also attended by the head of the Muslim Spiritual Directorate of the Republic of Tatarstan, Mufti Kamil' Hazrat Samigullin.[64] Kamil' Hazrat commented on this meeting:

> He [King Salman] used an interesting phrase about today being a new milestone in the history of relations [between Russia and Saudi Arabia], therefore, you and we should use this. It should be emphasised that Saudi Arabia is turning its face to the whole world, and we feel that there is an absolutely new policy, including in the sphere of religion. The King has repeatedly stressed that they are against

takfirism [accusing other Muslims of being apostates], against radicalism, or any manifestation of intolerance.

Within the context of positive signs for connections between the minority 'Self' and 'Self', we can have some expectations from his concluding words: 'This, as we now see, is also happening in practice, which makes us very happy.'[65]

Further, during the interview in December 2021, in response to how relations have been developing after this historical visit of King Salman to Moscow, and how it will affect further development of relations between Saudi Arabia and Tatarstan, Kamil' Hazrat suggested:[66]

> There are changes in the sense that the non-madhhab lobby has weakened. If earlier Saudi Arabia was perceived as the centre of Wahhabism of the whole world, today it is certainly not completely, and this tension has been lifted. That is already pleasing. [. . .] We are glad that there is some of kind dialogue; we will wait for what will happen next.

This might suggest that Saudi Arabia will remain the key partner for Tatarstan in the future, despite, and perhaps also due to, its responses over the Ukraine conflict, as discussed in Chapter 7, along with another crucial partner – the UAE.

4.2.4 Tatarstan–UAE

The UAE is another GCC state with which Tatarstan has a history of close links, initially, learning from the UAE's experience, and later emerging as an equally important partner in different fields of collaboration. For example, in 2000 the first president of Tatarstan, Mintimer Shaimiev, visited the UAE, aiming to benefit from the experience of the UAE in economic and urban development, and economic openness to the countries of the world.[67] The president expressed his admiration for the great economic and cultural achievements, thanks to the leadership of Shaykh Zayed al-Nahyan. Relations were further developed, especially under the current head, Minnikhanov.

Currently, the only trade and economic representative of the Republic of Tatarstan among the GCC states is located in the UAE – in Dubai. The office was opened in 2013, and as Marat Gatin speculates and shares his personal view during the interview, it was opened there due to its convenient logistics and concentration of representatives of large companies.[68] Taliya Minullina commented on bilateral economic relations during the interview in 2020, stating that 'If we consider the Emirates, our trade with them is certainly growing'.[69]

Investments from the UAE in Russia amount to $764 million; and in Tatarstan to $65.1 million.

Tatarstan finds the UAE among its key partners for building Islamic banking. Marat Gatin recalls: 'When I was still working in the Department of the Office of the President of Tatarstan Republic, we actively interacted with the UAE – with the Dubai Islamic Economy Development Centre, which was a subordinated institution of the Ministry of Economy of the Emirates.'[70] For example, the Dubai Islamic Economy Development Centre signed a memorandum of understanding (MoU) with the Tatarstan Investment Development Agency at the Kazan Summit, 2018.[71] Through this signed agreement, the Dubai Islamic Economy Development Centre hosted a number of workshops in cooperation with the Group of the Strategic Vision 'Russia-Islamic World'[72] to share knowledge linked to Islamic banking and finance, identify leading developments and trends in the Islamic economy sector and transfer the experience of Dubai and the UAE in the progress of an integrated Islamic economic strategy.[73] This is an ongoing development in bilateral relations. Among recent events, during the meeting between the UAE minister of Economy, Abdulla bin Touq al-Marri, and head of Tatarstan Minnikhanov on 22 February 2021, cooperation on key areas, including the Islamic economy, halal industry, tourism, artificial intelligence and technology, was discussed.[74] The UAE delegation participated in the Kazan Summit in 2021 and the UAE and Tatarstan agreed on a partnership to benefit from the halal industry.[75] Such examples suggest that future collaborations in developing the 'halal lifestyle' are likely (despite emerging obstacles as outcomes of the Ukraine conflict, as discussed in Chapter 7).

Tatarstan is also among the frequent participants at mega-events organized by the UAE, which assist in implementing in practice these various areas for collaboration: it has organized its own expositions at the Annual Investment Meeting since 2011, through the company 'KAMAZ' (who manufacture heavy-duty trucks and have a regional representation office in the UAE), and the Zelenodol'sk shipyard has several times participated at the International Defence Exhibition (IDEX).[76] Traditionally, the head of Tatarstan acts as one of the invited speakers in such events. For example, in 2019, Rustam Minnikhanov was a speaker at the Second World Summit of Tolerance in Dubai.[77]

Moreover, Rustam Minnikhanov took part in the expert discussion 'Application of artificial intelligence technologies in solving global problems' on 1 October 2021, which showcased Dubai Expo 2020 as a platform for sharing the latest innovative developments. Russia's eye-catching matryoshka doll pavilion, located in the Expo's Mobility District, had Tatarstan as its first exhibition topic.[78] Minnikhanov visited the Seventh Annual Investment Meeting (AIM) in 2017, where he met with the minister of Economy of the UAE, Sultan bin Saeed al-Mansoori. Importantly, Rustam Minnikhanov's relations with the Emirati leadership are also 'very warm' – with both the president of the UAE, Mohammad bin Zayed al-Nahyan, and the prime minister, Mohammad bin Rashid al-Maktoum. It is no coincidence that Minnikhanov often visits the UAE, including following informal invitations. For example, in November 2018 both Minnikhanov and Kadyrov attended the Formula One Abu Dhabi Grand Prix, where Mohammad bin Salman of Saudi Arabia was also present.[79]

What may this mean for real projects between UAE and Tatarstan? In 2019, $2.7 million of investments from the UAE in Tatarstan included those made by TGT PRIME LLC (a former Tatarstan company that moved its head office to Dubai) and from a Turkish holding company HAYAT KIMYA LLC, which invested 10.5 million rubles.[80] Investments from the UAE come from the division of international holdings that has opened a business in Tatarstan. In 2017, 0.8 per cent of total investments in Tatarstan came from the UAE; in 2018, 8.4 per cent; and in 2019, 0.8 per cent.

The impact of Moscow–Abu Dhabi relations will be discussed in Chapter 5, but it is foreshadowed here: when the spike in 2018 occurred, the UAE and Russia signed a Declaration of Strategic Partnership to cooperate in various sectors, such as politics, security, economy and culture. Putin commented on this: 'The UAE has been a close partner for us in the Middle East for years, and today we will sign a Declaration of Strategic Partnership as a further step in strengthening our relations.'[81] This might illustrate both the impact of close links between Moscow and Abu Dhabi for Tatarstan–UAE relations, and the ongoing contribution of Tatarstan, primarily based on their Islamic identities, to developing collaborations in Islamic finance and economy (to implement the concept of 'halal lifestyle') for Moscow–Abu Dhabi partnerships (see Chapter 5). In other words, the Emirati (similar to the Saudi case) is illustrative of how shared identities can boost cooperation between 'Self' and the minority 'Self' of another state: (1) if 'Self' and the 'Other' have interests in common, and the 'Other' is willing to integrate its minorities into this process; (2) if 'Self' and minority 'Self' have shared interests.

4.2.5 Tatarstan–Qatar, Bahrain, Kuwait, Oman

Rustam Minnikhanov visited Qatar on an official visit and met with Shaykh Tamim al-Thani on 8 December 2015. Discussions included the development of trade, economic and investment cooperation. Both leaders also keep up 'good'[82] relations. Table 2 shows that Tatarstan–Qatar foreign trade turnover between 2011–19 was third in comparison to other Gulf states – \$28.9 thousand. There were discussions, especially on economic projects. In 2018 during St. Petersburg's International Economic Forum, the Tatarstan head also met Hassan al-Tawadi, Qatar FIFA World 2022 Secretary, and Tatarstan agreed to cooperation on the Qatar World Cup,[83] including further possibilities of contribution to the World Cup 2022, and cooperation in the oil and IT fields, along with enhancing trade and economic collaboration.[84] Interestingly, on whether the Gulf crisis in 2017 negatively affected dealings between the two sides (Qatar vs the Quartet, consisting of Saudi Arabia, the UAE, Bahrain and Egypt), Taliya Minullina explains that Tatarstan does not have projects with consortia consisting of several states. The Republic tries to build relations individually, which helps to avoid such conflicts.

Nonetheless, further discussed projects and future collaborations between Tatarstan and Qatar remain under question, considering all the obstacles raised by the Ukraine conflict, and Doha's pro-Ukraine stance. This will be discussed in Chapter 7, which explains that Qatar's position is linked with its national interests, especially as the alternative state-supplier of gas to Europe and efforts to boost relations with Washington; in the shadow of the build-up to the crisis, Qatar has been designated as a major non-NATO ally of the United States by the Biden administration. In other words, prior to the Ukraine conflict, relations between 'Self' and minority 'Self – Qatar and Tatarstan – had been developed based on their shared interests, and integration by Moscow into its policies to boost relations with Qatar, driven by common interests between 'Self' and 'Other' (Doha and Moscow), as will be discussed specifically in relation to the Ukraine conflict. There are several different scenarios for future relations between Qatar and Russia, and as a result, questions remain about the future of relations between 'Self' and minority 'Self'.

Minnikhanov has also developed 'very good' relations with the King of Bahrain, Hamad ibn Isa al-Khalifa.[85]Bahraini delegations with high-ranking representatives have actively participated in the Kremlin's mechanisms where Tatarstan plays key roles, for example, at meetings of the Group of the Strategic Vision 'Russia-Islamic world',[86] or delegations from Bahrain's economic and business institutions at the Kazan Summit.[87] Relations primarily rely on economic collaborations, as Marat Gatin recalls: during his work at the head's office, they built up close contacts with colleagues from Bahrain to develop Islamic banking and finance. Similarly, Shaykh Abdulrahman bin Mohammad bin Rashid al-Khalifa, chairman of the Supreme Islamic Affairs Council of Bahrain, said during his interview in January 2022:[88]

> The main interests of the two sides lie in the presence of many economic and commercial possibilities in the Kingdom of Bahrain and the Republic of Tatarstan, which need development, due to the presence of many factors and common denominators that can lead to the supply and linking of the business community between the two countries, especially in light of the holding of successive sessions of the Kazan Economic Conference [Kazan Summit], which contributed to the presentation of economic and commercial possibilities and opportunities available for cooperation, which are currently being studied by the concerned authorities in the two countries.

Among the central interests of the Bahraini delegation that participated at the Twelfth Kazan Economic Summit from 28 to 30 July 2021 – headed by the chairman of the Board of Directors of the Small and Medium Enterprises Association in Bahrain, Dr Abdul-Hassan al-Diri – were halal food, education, information technology, health, tourism and agriculture. Another potential field for cooperation has been the energy sector. For example, the meeting between Rustam Minnikhanov and the chief executive of the Bahrain Economic Development Board (EDB) (since September 2019 – chief executive Officer of Mumtalakat), Khalid al-Rumeikhi, took place on 9 April 2018. Bahrain expressed interest in the possibility of cooperation and exchange of technologies in the field of heavy oil production and its further processing. However, based on customs statistics for 2018 and 2019, there is no evidence that the export of equipment from Tatarstan to Bahrain has materialized.[89] Earlier, the Russian Direct Investment Fund (RDIF) had signed a memorandum of understanding with Bahrain's sovereign wealth fund, Mumtalakat, in 2014.[90] By 2018, Mumtalakat had invested more than $235 million in RDIF.[91] Tatarstan–Bahrain foreign trade turnover remains the smallest in comparison to all the GCC states – $539.3 thousand (Table 2). Nonetheless, two memoranda of understanding have been signed, aiming to consolidate Bahrain's role as a marketing arm for Russian products for the countries of the GCC and North Africa,[92] which may support further potential collaborations, including developing 'halal lifestyle', Islamic banking and finance, the halal food sector, tourism and pharmaceuticals. The neutrality of Bahrain during the Ukraine crisis helps to keep doors open for collaborations between Kazan and Manama (see Chapter 7).

Kuwait–Tatarstan foreign trade was $6.0006,8 thousand, while Oman–Tatarstan trade was $2.898,7 thousand between 2011 and 2019 (Table 2). The head of Tatarstan Minnikhanov by then was prime minister and met with his

Kuwaiti counterpart. Among the key issues for discussion were investments, including towards sport and football.[93] Oman (along with Bahrain) was interested in importing halal products from Tatarstan in 2017.[94] Taliya Minullina explained during her interview some facets of the limited interactions with Omani and Kuwaiti investors. She believes that 'they did not find here the partners with whom they wanted to work'. She continues:

> When we had the last Kazan Summit [2019], for example, delegations from the UAE of more than 40 people took part in it, and about 30 people from Saudi Arabia. Only 6 people came from Oman, and only 2 people came from Kuwait. That is, you see that their activity itself is not as high as we would like. But we are still working with Oman and Kuwait [and Qatar].

These examples clearly demonstrate where there are mutual interests along with shared Islamic identities, such as the development of Islamic banking and finance; relations have been built closely between Tatarstan and Saudi Arabia and the UAE. However, there have been challenges which have prevented flourishing relations between the minority 'Self' and 'Self(s)', despite common interests. The next section will identify some of the key obstacles, based on fieldwork in these areas; further limitations have also arisen as the outcomes of the Ukraine conflict, the implications of which will be discussed in Chapter 7.

4.2.6 Challenges and limitations

Even with increasing collaborations based on the shared Islamic factor, and with the growth of the so-called 'halal lifestyle' economy, relations have had their limitations and challenges (even prior to the Ukraine moment). Among the key factors is the fact that Tatarstan's authority is limited, and directly linked to rights granted by the Russian Federation. In other words, rather than diplomacy, it is able to conduct only paradiplomacy, due to its political status (see Chapter 5). For example, despite the fact that Tatarstan has one of the most active relations with Saudi Arabia, the opening of the Consulate General of Saudi Arabia had not progressed beyond a discussion for over nine years. However, on 18 February 2020, the Russian prime minister Mikhail Mishustin signed a decree to confirm the opening of the Consulate General of Saudi Arabia in Kazan. In accordance with the order, the consulate circle will include Bashkortostan, Dagestan, Ingushetia, Kabardino-Balkaria, Mari El, Mordovia, North Ossetia, Tatarstan, Udmurtia, Chechnya, Chuvashia, as well as Perm' Krai, Kirovskaya, Nizhegorodskaya, Orenburgskaya and Penza districts, Saratov and Ulyanovsk regions.[95] Nonetheless, as of the time of writing in 2022, the consulate has not opened. Kamil' Hazrat, during my interview in December 2021, noted:

> They have been talking about this for a long time, so I cannot comment. Probably this decision reflects both countries: Tatarstan is not a separate country, so things will be decided in Moscow, and by colleagues of Saudi Arabia.[96]

This is one of the key reasons why relations with the GCC states have been based mainly on economic cooperation, with the attendant limitations and challenges. Despite a number of discussions with Russian regions, including the above-mentioned discussions between Tatarstan and the GCC states, the Gulf states have paused investments in Russia and its regions directly, acting only through the Russian Direct Investment Fund, the country's sovereign wealth fund, with reserved capital of $10 billion under management.[97] Taliya Minullina,[98] the chief executive of the Tatarstan Investment Development Agency, explains this as due to the lack of existing global experience in investment projects in the Russian Federation (and the lack of successful previous projects to reassure investors), as well as the high expectation of state guarantees – 100 per cent return on investments – that most of the Gulf States have when investing through the RDIF. In response to my enquiry to TIDA about what can be done to reverse this trend and make the GCC states invest directly into the regions, they stated that 'this trend cannot change as long as there are sanctions against Russia[99] or until the world order in the global economy, where the United States is the main economy of the world, changes'. (This view might be relevant to the existing 'great power' competitions – see Chapter 5). Another point mentioned is that Arab countries are investing on the basis of 'you to me, me to you'.

Tatarstan's initiatives to leverage shared Islamic identities for economic prosperity have resulted in the development of Islamic banking and Islamic finance, but again with limitations. There remain continuing complications with this development, too, since Russian legislation does not yet accommodate all its aspects, such as legislative, regulatory, organizational and tax barriers.[100] For example, as briefly pointed out earlier, an agreement was signed for the establishment of the Tatarstan International Investment Company, and the first meeting of the founders of Tatarstan International Investment Company took place in Bahrain in 2009.[101] It was assumed that it would help strengthen cooperation between the republic and the Islamic Development Bank, as well as promote various investment projects.[102] One of the first projects of the Tatarstan International Investment Company was to create a centre for the production of halal products for the whole of Russia in Kazan. The second project is a development company, and the third is one of the largest business centres in the region.

However, after ten years, the only investment currently operating is the Eurasian Leasing Company. The Tatarstan International Investment Company is the initiator and one of the shareholders of Eurasian Leasing Company. Eurasian Leasing Company is active and offers *Ijara* [an Islamic finance technique used to finance the acquisition of assets on terms compliant with shari'a] Islamic leasing. One of the initiators of the republic's cooperation with Islamic financial institutions, president of the Islamic Business and Finance Development Fund, and president of the Association of Regional Investment Agencies Linar Yakupov, commenting about further limitations of activities of Tatarstan International Investment Company, touched on the barriers hindering the development of financial and business projects based on the principles of Islam. For example, Linar Yakupov draws attention to the following point: though the Western banking system entered the new Russia very aggressively and was heavily financed by the largest banks in the West, in the case of Islamic banking everything turned out to be completely different. He continues:

> Such an aggressive movement does not correspond to the position of the Islamic Development Bank. The Islamic Development Bank is not trying to impose anything on anyone, and if the country has an interest in working in this direction, then the bank is ready to provide some technical support in developing the necessary legislative framework. If there is no such desire, then everything is limited only by what can be done within the framework of existing legislation. Unfortunately, all our Islamic finance initiatives have serious limitations. Nobody was able to overcome the issue of double taxation.[103]

Indeed, the limitations of existing Russian legislation remain a serious challenge for developing Islamic banking and economy, and further collaborations with the Gulf states. However, Aydar Shagimardanov,[104] the President of the Association of Muslim Entrepreneurs of Russia also stressed another factor in his interview: the inner legal consciousness of a Muslim businessman:

> Yes, we do not have such an understanding of Islamic banking in our legislation, and the Islamic bank in the full format in which it operates in Islamic countries [. . .]. However, we have some so to speak, 'sprouts' of Islamic finance that have been opening for a long time in Kazan. This is the financial house Amal,[105] a member of our Association.[106] We are friends with them, we have been cooperating for many years, many members of our Association just use the services of the Amal financial house. [. . .] But the legal consciousness of

a Muslim is not yet so developed that they can completely abandon non-halal banks. And when a businessman with such an unstable sense of justice comes to Sberbank, where they can get a loan at 11%, and in the Amal financial house there is no loan, but property or equipment that interests you is bought, an extra charge is made on it and sold and given to you in instalments. That is, roughly speaking, it turns out to be 15% [. . .]. It depends very much on the inner world, the inner level of development of the Muslim himself. [Individuals struggle to] choose between 'more expensive' and *haram* [forbidden].

This may be linked with the history of development of Islam in Russia and demonstrates some limitations to building closer relations with the GCC states. Again, though to a lesser extent than in the 1990s, differences exist within the shared Islamic identities of the GCC and Tatarstan. As noted earlier (see Section 4.2), ideological components continue to divide approaches to Islam in different regions, though there are moves towards less restricted collaborations. This is linked with the emergence of a rather clearer pragmatic approach in relations between the GCC states and Tatarstan, accommodating differences in their ideological/religious and political stances. In response to the question of how Tatarstan's and the Gulf states' religious leaderships negotiate their *madhhab* differences, Kamil' Hazrat shared during his interview:[107]

As for the various *madhahib*, this cannot be overlooked. Since we are Hanafis, we have our own Council of Ulema in Tatarstan. It consists of all competent scholars and all shari'a issues are solved there. But in any question there are two aspects. For example, Turkish Muslims seem to be Hanafis, but our attitude to the Syrian issue will be completely different because we have our own television, we have our own propaganda, we have our own books. These all affect us. Therefore, the political aspect will always be different and this is normal. Given this, we cannot just turn to a foreign specialist and ask them to solve an issue; everything is solved internally and there are no problems.

Clearly, there are some limitations of Muslim identities as a connecting factor, not reducible to one simple aspect, applying also to links between Tatars and Arabs of the Gulf states. However, they are undoubtedly powerful initiators and facilitators for other fields. As Chapter 5 will explain further, both Tatarstan and the Gulf states are following pragmatism in their political relations, despite ideological differences. This is also influenced by relations between Moscow–Kazan and Moscow–Gulf states.

Finally, during my fieldwork in Tatarstan, Il'kham Nurullin,[108] the former representative of the Ministry of Agriculture and Food of the Republic of Tatarstan also shared during an interview that the absence of institutions (there is only a Trade-Economic Representation of the Republic of Tatarstan in Dubai (UAE)) limits GCC–Tatarstan collaborations. It is hoped that the Saudi consulate in the Republic of Tatarstan will increase opportunities. However, growing interactions with other Gulf states – Qatar, Bahrain, Kuwait and Oman – might be required to build similar institutions, along with more visits of governmental and business delegations, although this has again been complicated by the current challenges added by the Ukraine conflict (see Chapter 7). For example, it might occur also through NGOs, such as the Association of Muslim Entrepreneurs of Russia. The latter's head, Aydar Shagimardanov,[109] explained during his interview that 'our relations [are] built through religion'. Therefore, despite all the listed limitations and challenges, shared identities between Tatarstan and the GCC continue to play a vital role in collaborations, including in economic contexts.

4.3 Conclusion

The chapter has illustrated the modern relations between Tatarstan and the GCC states. Specifically, it has discussed how the limited collaborations so far between Tatarstan and the Gulf states are due to limited identification of mutual interests, even given their shared Islamic identities. At the same time, relations have grown since the 2000s, notably through developing a 'halal lifestyle' based on Islamic economy and banking. The growing interactions in this field explain the increasing collaborations with Saudi Arabia and the UAE, in particular. At the same time, since the 2000s, Tatarstan has been in the 'avant-garde' of relations between Russia and OIC states/Gulf states, even if not the leading region. The Kremlin has become ever more interested in utilizing Tatarstan and other Muslim-populated regions as part of its central foreign policy. These can be illustrated by considering the dynamics between Tatarstan–Moscow–GCC, which will be discussed in the next chapter.

Tatarstan and the Gulf states

The Moscow factor

The chapter brings Moscow into the discussion again to explain why active engagements between Tatarstan and the GCC states occurred, especially after the 2000s. In other words, as noted in Chapter 4, common interests have emerged based on the shared Muslim identities between the minority 'Self' and 'Self(s)'. The chapter examines Kazan–Moscow relations since the 1990s, and illustrates the gradual erosion of the 'special status' of Tatarstan over time. However, it argues that alongside growing federal central authority under Putin's leadership, Tatarstan was integrated (with other Muslim-populated regions) into federal policies, used to build closer relations with the Muslim world. Naturally, this includes the GCC states, given their importance as the 'spiritual homeland'[1] of Russian Muslims, and the location of the holy cities of Mecca and Medina in Saudi Arabia. Arguably, Tatarstan's 'special role' has been repurposed rather than eroded, to become a bridge with these increasingly important partners. In other words, the 'Other' has been actively integrating its minority, which positively boosts relations between 'Self(s)' and the minority 'Self'.

Tatarstan–GCC economic collaborations and mutual interests also somewhat reflect the republic's status within the Russian Federation, along with the necessity of diversifying the sources of its income. Economic priorities have similarly been crucial for the federal centre as Russia has remained under sanctions since 2014, among other reasons. Simultaneously, improvements in Tatarstan–GCC relations are linked to growing geopolitical interests between Russia and the Gulf states, along with economic collaborations in energy, trade turnover and sale of weapons. In other words, relations between 'Self(s)' and minority 'Self' have also been boosted due to established common interests between 'Self' and 'Other'. To demonstrate this, the chapter will examine Kazan–Moscow relations and their implications for Tatarstan–Gulf relations; thereafter, it will look at Moscow–GCC relations, which impact relations between Tatarstan and the GCC states.

5.1 Kazan and Moscow: Implications
for Tatarstan–Gulf relations

Increasing relations between Tatarstan and the GCC states, discussed in Chapter 4, are directly linked to Moscow–Kazan relations, which themselves took a different shape between the 1990s and the 2000s and between the 2000s and the present. The Gorbachev leadership is known for its reconfiguration of centre-periphery relationships in the former Soviet Union. By the late 1980s, restricted democratization and the failure of effective control over the economy caused the leaders of the union's republics to start issuing declarations of sovereignty, which normally included claims to republic-level legislation over all union laws.[2] The so-called 'parade of sovereignties' reached its peak in July 1990, when the supreme Soviet of the Russian Republic (under the governance of Boris Yeltsin) released its own statement of sovereignty.[3] In his power struggle with Gorbachev, Yeltsin's policy was to support regions and republics within Russia.[4] Accordingly, in August 1990, when Yeltsin visited Kazan, he made the famous declaration that Russia's autonomous republics should 'take all the sovereignty they can swallow'.[5] Consequently, the Supreme Soviet of the Tatar ASSR delivered a 'Declaration of State Sovereignty' on 30 August 1990, in the process unilaterally declaring the formation of the Tatar Soviet Socialist Republic.[6] Similarly, nearly all the ASSRs within Russia also made their own sovereignty declarations, joining Tatarstan in granting themselves a status equivalent to that of the union republics.[7] However, only Chechnya's declaration received international recognition.

On 31 March 1992, the Russian Federation signed three documents collectively referred to as the Federation Treaty, which established the key principles of Russian Federalism. Among the 'subjects (*sub'ekty*) of the Russian Federation' (as the regions, republics and other subunits of Russia were hereafter designated), only Tatarstan and Chechnya refused to sign the Federation Treaty.[8] Tatarstan, instead, held a referendum in late March,[9] with the question put to the electorate: 'Do you consider that the Republic of Tatarstan is a sovereign state, a subject of international law, entitled to develop relations with the Russian Federation and other states on the basis of treaties between equal partners?' With a voter turnover of 82 per cent, 61.4 per cent voted in favour.[10] Negotiations between Kazan and Moscow maintained a pragmatic attitude[11] and relations between Moscow and Kazan emerged as 'asymmetrical',[12] known as the 'Tatarstan model'.[13]

In December 1991 they signed economic agreements (*soglashenie*) designed to anticipate clarification of the elementary parameters of their mutual economic relationships. An 'Agreement on Economic Cooperation' was signed on 6 December 1991, and this document recognized Tatarstan's right to implement its own independent foreign trade, and consequent agreements covered issues such as customs duties and the right of Tatarstan to exploit the Russian oil distribution system.[14] In November 1992, the Supreme Soviet of Tatarstan accepted a constitution which included the language of the March referendum. The Tatarstan Constitution's Article 6 contains the key sentence: 'The Republic of Tatarstan is a sovereign state and a subject of international law, that is associated with the Russian Federation on the basis of a treaty on the mutual delegation of powers and jurisdictions.'[15]

In February 1994, Moscow and Kazan finally signed a bilateral treaty 'On the Dimension of Jurisdictional Authority and the Mutual Delegation of Powers between the State Bodies of the Russian Federation and the State Bodies of Tatarstan'.[16] Tatarstan was characterized as 'a state united with the Russian Federation' (preamble), which characterization neither directly recognizes Tatarstan's sovereignty nor accords with the Constitution of Tatarstan's assertion that the republic's relation with Russia is not one of union, but one of association.[17] However, the treaty granted Tatarstan broad rights to implement its own foreign policy and foreign trade, though it did not clearly recognize Tatarstan's status as a sovereign state (Art. II, sec. 11).[18] From the Russian point of view, Tatarstan gave up its sovereignty when it signed this treaty; however, the Tatarstan leadership's perspective was that the treaty was an agreement between two sovereign states.[19] As Sergey Sergeev concludes, 'The compromise was based on the de facto separation of spheres of influence: Tatarstan would be part of the Russian Federation but under special circumstances.'[20] The bilateral treaty between Tatarstan and Russia has been followed by a number of similar bilateral power-sharing agreements between Russia and a number of other republics (regions) of the Russian Federation; forty such treaties had been signed as of late 1997.

Since taking over power, Putin has sought to refocus power towards the federal centre, rather than at regional levels and their elites.[21] He has portrayed himself as 'President of all Russians', while his policies over 2000–2008 can be characterized as 'growing centralisation and a changing regional policy'.[22] Ortung believes:[23]

> Over the course of his first term (2000-4), Putin transformed center-regional relations and restricted the regions' political power. The changes [. . .] greatly strengthened the central executive's oversight and control of the regional administrations and limited the governors' capacity to make policy without the Kremlin's consent.

With regard to Tatarstan, however, the situation still remained stable to some extent for its relations with the federal centre. Graney believes that Shaimiev supported Putin during the Beslan crisis and in the process secured Putin's support for re-nomination as president of Tatarstan on 11 March 2005.[24] Putin participated in the 1,000th anniversary of Kazan celebrations in late August 2005, and this has been seen as an indicator of a less hard-line and more conciliatory approach to certain regions, provided they made concessions to Moscow.[25] For the Republic, it resulted in the February 1994 bilateral power-sharing treaty between Russia and Tatarstan being renewed on 29 October 2005, and according to Graney, after September 2004, Tatarstan

> pursued the same strategy that had brought them such success in the past – keeping the sovereignty project as robust as possible while accommodating it to new political and economic realities in Russia.[26]

However, in 2017, it became clear that the Kremlin would no longer prolong the treaty on mutual delimitation of jurisdictional subjects and delegation of authority between the state bodies of the Russian Federation and the state bodies of the Republic of Tatarstan; as Sergey Sergeev puts it: 'The 2007 treaty that the ruling elite hoped would be extended (at least in large measure) was to a great extent a symbolic document that underlined Tatarstan's special status among other constituent entities of the Federation.'[27] But Petr Kozlov of the BBC quotes the Kremlin: 'The contract ends and that's it. It retains the post of President in the Republic until the next elections [of the leadership of the republic in 2020]'[28] – although, Minnikhanov was re-elected as the president of Tatarstan in 2020 (nonetheless, following up orders and decree of the President of the Russian Federation Vladimir Putin, from 12 July 2022 the position of Rustam Minnikhanov in official documents has altered and referred to as the 'head of the Republic of Tatarstan'). These events are illustrative of a wider erosion of the 'special status' of Tatarstan in the federal system. In the summer and fall of 2017, a 'language crisis' occurred, when President Putin stated that no one should be forced to study non-native languages. As the result of this, most secondary schools teach the Tatar language only for two hours a week, and only with the written consent of parents.[29] Further, as Sergey Sergeev notes,[30] post-Crimea, revenue from the regions, especially donor regions, started to be seen as a source for 'replenishing' the federal budget. Part of the income revenue tax has increased in favour of the centre. (Until 2017, income tax revenue was separated between the regional and federal centre at a ratio of 18 to 2 per cent, but this transformed to a ratio of 17 to 3 per cent in 2017.)[31] This meant that Tatarstan perhaps lost around 3.5 billion rubles,[32] which promoted Minnikhanov's speech at the meeting of the State Council bemoaning 'the center's politics of dekulakization',[33] giving an analogy to Soviet campaigns of political repression, including arrests, deportations or executions of millions of kulaks (prosperous peasants) and their families in the 1929–32 period of the first five-year plan.

Paradoxically, despite this apparent erosion of the 'special status' of Tatarstan, these factors have contributed to the further development of relations between Tatarstan and the GCC states, especially since the 2000s. First, this is linked with economic objectives: given Russian legislation, Tatarstan is able to conduct economic activities (see Chapter 4) with foreign players; second, both Russia and Tatarstan aspire to develop their economic potential. Tatarstan is known as 'a small oil and economic model of the big Russian economy'[34] – this is despite having made serious attempts to diversify its economy, which broadly match the diversification efforts of Russia's economy, too. As part of the diversification of the economy, technoparks have been established, such as the IT-park, ZAO Innovative-production technopark 'Idea', industrial site KIP 'Master' and Technopolis 'Himgrad'. Additionally, the special economic zone of industrial production 'Alabuga' was created in 2005.

This was particularly necessary after 2015, as Tatarstan has had to find new revenues for its economic stability. Along with the traditional investments from the West, among the Middle Eastern partners, Turkey has historically been among the biggest investors in the Tatarstan economy. Both the Kazan Tatars and Turkish people are predominantly Muslim, Turkic nations with historical entanglement, as well as ethno-cultural and *madhahib* similarities; the reasons for this, relying on historical roots, have been discussed in Chapters 1 and 3. For example, Turkish companies became vital residents of the Special Economic Zone 'Alabuga'. Some examples: in 2010 Kastamonu Integrated Wood Industry LLC, with initial plans for 19.73 billion rubles of investment (by 2019, in fact – 21.2 billion rubles); Trakya Glass Rus JSC building a modern plant for the production of sheet glass, mirrors and coated glass in Russia, with planned investments of 6.78 billion rubles (in fact, by 2019 –7.2 billion rubles); in 2011, LLC 'Hayat Kimya' with a project for the production of sanitary paper (toilet paper, napkins, paper towels), with investment planned for 9.5 billion rubles (in fact, by 2019 – 11.1 billion rubles); and JSC 'Automotive Glass Alliance Rus', a project focused on the production of automotive glass, investing 1.83 billion rubles (by 2019 – 4 billion rubles).[35] Thanks to the trust established between Tatarstan and Turkey, which relies mainly on this common history and culture, over many years Turkey has remained the first among foreign investors in Tatarstan – for example, in 2021 with investments of $2.5 billion.[36]

However, when a Turkish Air Force F-16 fighter jet shot down a Russian Sukhoi Su-24M attack aircraft near the Syria–Turkey border in 2015, such cooperation was threatened. It was very illustrative that the response from the Russian government, but especially the Tatarstan government, was swift and encouraging. Within that month the Tatarstan head had sought to ease tensions and stress the value of collaboration, saying: 'These issues are resolved at the political level between our countries. As for investors, here we work within the framework of the law, we have no discrepancies. Here I find full support from the leadership of our state.'[37] He sought to ensure maximum comfort at that time for Turkish businesses in the territory of Tatarstan. However, at the same, this incident also showed the limitations of Tatarstan–Turkish relations, as they directly depend on complex wider Russia–Turkish relations. As mentioned in the interview by Kamil' Hazrat, quoted in Chapter 4, the Tatarstan leadership appreciate that there are different political stances over Syria, keeping pragmatic relations with partners. At the same time, arguably, this incident was one of the key reasons for developing further relations with wealthy GCC states, especially after 2015. From my personal observations in the Republic of Tatarstan, it was very notable how the Tatarstan leadership swiftly began working on the diversification of its relations with other Middle Eastern partners, especially with the Gulf states.

Second, increasing Tatarstan–Gulf relations are linked through the consideration of the Islamic factor by the federal centre, and trying to use such shared Islamic identities as a soft power tool for building relations with the Gulf states. Tatarstan was granted a special role in these policies towards the Muslim world – and eventually the GCC states. Arguably, Russian federal officials' consideration of Islam has moved through a number of stages, from viewing it as a threat or a challenge to state security, towards a pragmatic tool or as a religious soft power. Under Gorbachev's (communist) government, Islam was regarded as a custodian of moral values and an ally of the country, but with the rise of nationalism in the 1990s, and the collapse of the USSR, Islam became a political and social tool, as much among Muslims as among Islam's opponents[38]. After the fall of the Iron Curtain, new ideas, including radical ones, spread among Russian Muslims, making them aware of their religious identity and part in the worldwide Muslim *umma*.[39] Consequently, Putin's rise to power in the early 2000s was characterized by the threat of religious extremism from the North Caucasus.[40] These groups used connections with the GCC states to implement jihad in Russia (see Chapter 6). Relations with the GCC states were unsurprisingly tense, and as Fredholm observes, for example, the Chechen war involved several diplomatic crises between Qatar and Russia, because Gulf citizens were involved in fighting Russia, as well as the bomb attack that killed Yandarbiyev, the Chechen separatist living in Qatar.[41]

It would be too simple to regard this as a state-religion dichotomy, however, and gradually the Kremlin began to realize the potential advantages of Islam and its Muslim minorities, including ways in which they could be turned to *religious soft power*[42] in Russian foreign policy. Russia made its first move towards the Muslim world by obtaining the status of official observer at the Organisation of Islamic Cooperation (OIC) in 2005. In his speech at the opening of a two-day Malaysian summit of the OIC in 2003, in which he laid out the reasons for Russia's request for observer status, Vladimir Putin noted that no religion should be associated with terrorism, and stressed the importance of Muslim populations in all countries, including Russia. 'Russian Muslims are an inseparable, fully-fledged, and active part of the multi-ethnic and multidenominational nation of Russia.' He continued that 'Russia, as a unique Eurasian power, has always played a special role in building relations between East and West'.[43] Joining the OIC as an observer was possible mainly due to the support of Saudi Arabia. As Kreutz[44] explains:

> The best and probably the only way to achieve that [Russia's observer status at the OIC] was through a reconciliation with Riyadh, which held special prestige and influence among the Islamic nations due to its wealth and unique position as the guardian of the holiest Muslim sites.

The rapprochement between Russia and Saudi Arabia occurred principally due to the deteriorating relations between the United States and Saudi Arabia after 9/11 (resulting, among other things, in the Saudi leadership becoming increasingly interested in buying Russian weapons),[45] energy cooperation development since the 2000s, with Russia becoming an observer at the Organisation of Petroleum Exporting Countries (OPEC) meetings, and Russia's agreement to decrease oil supplies to the market.[46] At the same time, Saudi Arabia acknowledged Moscow's dominance over Chechnya.[47]

A further important early initiative for the development of relationships between Russia and Muslim states occurred through inter-civilizational and inter-cultural cooperation. As noted earlier, in 2006 the Strategic Vision Group 'Russia-Islamic World' was founded, in which Tatarstan's leadership plays the key role. Furthermore, in 2007, Putin, in his famous speech at the Munich

Conference on Security Policy, stated that unipolarity is impossible in today's world and that such a model of international relations 'itself is flawed'.[48] As part of Russia's corresponding multipolar strategy, Moscow began to establish closer cooperation with the Muslim world. One illustrative example is that the day after this Munich speech, Putin began a tour of the Middle East. For example, he visited Saudi Arabia, Qatar and Jordan between 11 and 13 February 2007,[49] thereby identifying alliances with the Gulf states as important to building a multipolarity and increasing their geopolitical role. Borrowing the words of Leonid Ivashov, Malashenko states that 'despite official statements professing love for Islam, the rapprochement with the Muslim world [was] a "tactical move".[50] All of these effected further development of policies of integrating Russia's Muslim population into federal foreign policies, a form of soft power, aimed particularly towards the Gulf states. More particularly, despite the gradual erosion of Tatarstan's 'special status', it was offered the opportunity to be the key 'bridge' between Russia and OIC countries/ GCC states.

After returning to the presidential office in 2012, Putin strengthened this vision and began integrating Muslim populations further into federal policies, including giving a primary role to Tatarstan and its leadership. However, when the Arab Spring occurred in 2011, Russia had to respond to new challenges and threats coming from the region. Risks to the stability of the country emerged, linked to Islamic-extremist threats and religious radicalization in the post-Soviet space. The 2000s also saw a new phenomenon, the Islamization of migrants and Russian Muslims joining the Syrian opposition to fight against the al-Asad regime. Russia's relations with Islam and its own Muslim population included clear tools for international connections, but not in a monolithic sense; it is a complex issue that required 'smart power' leadership from which to control and benefit. Since 2013 Islam might best be described as a pragmatic tool wielded by the Russian government. Among the key turning points was the meeting of President Putin with the heads of the Muslim Spiritual Boards in October 2013, where Putin legitimated political Islam and recognized that political Islam is not necessarily negative.[51] Most importantly, in 2014, Putin entrusted the head of Tatarstan, Rustam Minnikhanov, with the chairmanship of the Strategic Vision Group 'Russia-Islamic World'.[52] Notably, the role of regions with a Muslim population, especially the Republic of Tatarstan, has started to be used much more visibly since then.[53] Minnikhanov's appointment is an indicator of the vital role of the Tatarstan Republic in such federal policies. This is not solely recognition of the important role of the Tatarstan leadership, whose paradiplomatic efforts towards the Muslim world, where the Gulf states play a vital role, have proved successful.

It is also an indication of the transformation of relations between Tatarstan and the federal government – 'special relations' have perhaps gradually ended, but a new chapter of relations has opened: a leading role in 'bridging' between Russia and the OIC states, which has also strengthened Tatarstan–GCC relations since the 2000s. The second factor of growing Tatarstan–Gulf relations is linked to the increasing partnership between Russia and the GCC states during the same period. Within the context of the book's argument, the 'Other' has begun to integrate its minority 'Self', which contributed to further rapprochement between 'Self(s)' and the minority 'Self'.

5.2 Moscow and the GCC states: Implications for Tatarstan–Gulf relations

5.2.1 Growing geopolitical interests

Geopolitically the new Russia had become 'much weaker than its predecessor [the USSR]'[54] in the 2000s; likewise, in the eyes of Russians and the rest of the world, Saudi Arabia stood far above its smaller neighbouring monarchies – certainly until the first decade of the 2000s. However, the political status of both Russia and all the GCC states has been transformed by the outcomes of the Arab uprisings. The so-called Arab Spring surely became a turning point of geopolitical importance for both the GCC states and Russia, which also resulted in collaborations between them. Transformation of the GCC states into regional powers, and Russia's emergence (or return) as a great power, at least based on its military capacities, impacted on Tatarstan–GCC relations, becoming another fundamental factor for further collaborations.

The GCC states have emerged as vital players in the region since the Arab Spring. Their importance in the region lies in their economic strength, still based largely on the hydrocarbon sector, despite diversification efforts;[55] and such economic power remains crucial for the region's rising political status, especially as an outcome of the Arab Spring.[56] The transformed geopolitical balance of power in the MENA region shifted US foreign policy towards Asia, and fears of the local effect of the Arab uprising in the GCC states spread this influence within the Middle East.[57] The power vacuum that emerged in the Middle East due to the decreasing roles of the traditional leaders – Iraq, Egypt and Syria – in turn created leadership opportunities for the GCC states. Saudi Arabia, the UAE and Qatar, in particular, have been dominant in the Middle

East since 2011. The changing political environment and the active position of the GCC states have led to debates among scholars to adequately define the terms 'weak' and 'strong' in the region.[58] The growing status of all GCC states, not solely Saudi Arabia, encouraged Russia to build closer relations with all Gulf actors (though these developments may change course in some cases following the Ukraine conflict).

Due to its active approach towards the region (starting with the intervention in the Syrian War), Russia's great power status has to some extent been reclaimed.[59] Although most scholarship considers this great power status to have been gained thanks to military power, Russia's diplomacy was also crucial. In comparison to the Soviet policies in the region, a pragmatic approach of balancing adversaries was also adopted.[60] Russia has balanced relations between Turkey and Israel, and supported al-Asad's regime in the Syrian War along with Iran and Iran-backed militias (Hizbullah), despite clashes and disagreement between all these players at the geopolitical level. (As noted earlier, these analyses precede the Ukraine crisis, which may result in significant shifts again. The first signs of these potential transformations in policy are discussed in Chapter 7.) Moreover, this policy of balancing adversaries is applied to either bilateral disputes, such as protecting relations with both Israel and Palestine, or individual relations within the state, as in the example of Libya. In Libya, Russia militarily supported General Khalifa Haftar, the head of the Libyan National Army (LNA).[61] At the same time, Moscow brokered the 2020 talks between the two factions in the civil war – the National Accord (GNA) of Fayez al-Sarraj and the LNA.[62] Malashenko[63] stated that throughout the residual 'great power' narratives, 'Russia's politics gravitates towards pragmatism; it gives due consideration to potential partners regardless of their ideology and rhetoric'; in 2021, in the MENA region at least, it could be said that Russia had arguably returned to 'great power' status,[64] largely through such policies.

Without balancing relations with the GCC states, Russia could not have achieved its growing influence, as the Gulf states have often been Russia's geopolitical opponents. Nonetheless, there is another important view to consider, which Li-Chen Sim formulates thus: 'Russia's economic and political behaviours in the Gulf are not part of a grand, pro-active geo-political or geo-economic strategy per se, but are merely opportunistic reactions.'[65] This has a grain of truth in it, but is incomplete. It is worth mentioning that Russia's balancing policies meant careful calibrations of all adversaries, and findings routes towards mutual benefit. An example of this is the 2013 'chemical deal' between the United States and Russia. Alexander Shumilin and Inna Shumilina[66] explain:

[it] saved Assad from the defeat that would have resulted from an American and French intervention in Syria as punishment for his use of WMD. . . . this deal turned the Gulf leadership toward Moscow, [. . .], the Arab Gulf elites stopped concealing their disappointment with the US approach to Syria and started looking to Russia as a perhaps undesirable, but *de facto* only (by force of events) partner to deal with.

The GCC states, realizing the importance of Russia, despite disagreements, began to find common agendas. Cengiz concludes that this pragmatism played a major role in Saudi–Russian approaches in the Syrian War, and also towards each other.[67] Despite both states following a different route, they also found common ground on certain issues (e.g. the territorial integrity of Syria, and a mutual concern in the fight against extremism).[68] Saudi Arabia and Russia joined together in their attempts to unite the fragmented Syrian opposition.[69] In 2018, the UAE re-established diplomatic relations with Syria and recognized Asad's legitimacy.[70] In 2019, rapprochement between Syria and Qatar began – similarly to the Saudi Arabian strategy in Syria, Qatar backed Islamists to overthrow Syrian president Bashar al-Asad. Flights had been suspended in 2011, but eight years later Qatar Airways was granted a license to fly over Syrian airspace.[71] At the end of 2021 Bahrain became the latest Gulf nation to appoint an ambassador to Syria after nearly a decade of severed ties.[72] Without such calibrated policies, Russia's 'return' to the Middle East would not have been feasible. In other words, it is not only Russia's hard power, allied with its Iranian partnership, that saved al-Asad and secured Russia's 'great power' status; balanced adversaries, including all the GCC states, were also crucial. Another example is Moscow's careful calibration of all sides in the Libyan civil war, noted earlier. There is a myth circulating of Haftar as a Libyan Bashar al-Asad, which emerged in 2016 after Haftar's two visits to Moscow: speculation emerged that Russia had agreed to supply Haftar with weapons in exchange for a naval base in Tobruk or Benghazi. Actually, Russia had allied with the UAE and France to support Haftar, and reach its objectives,[73] to further cement its position in the region.

What has Russia offered to successfully implement such a model with respect to the GCC states? Leonid Issaev and Nikolay Kozhnov[74] call Russia's balancing policies with the Gulf states 'a bargaining strategy'. They explain that by applying such an approach, Russia has used its indirect and direct presence in the major regional conflicts (in Libya, Syria and Yemen, the Israeli–Palestinian conflict and Iran's nuclear issue) attempting to highlight its significance to the Gulf states; at the same time, Russia has aimed to build stronger economic collaboration with the GCC states by attracting a larger number of investments from the GCC to Russia, and coordinating attempts with Saudi Arabia in the global oil market (see Section 5.2.2.). Arguably, this view can be further developed geopolitically.

Russia was also keeping a balance by *not* interfering, if the dynamics demanded. For example, in the Yemeni case, Leonid Issaev and Andrey Korotayev[75] conclude:

> Russia's involvements in the Yemeni crisis is constrained by Russia's economic weakness and the prioritisation of Russia-Gulf relations. Russian policy in the Arabian Peninsula is based primarily on the importance of maintaining relations with the Arabian monarchies, rather than Yemen. Given that Russia has no strategic interests in Yemen, it is trying to use its loyalty to the Arab Coalition's policy in Yemen for leverage during talks with Riyadh and Abu Dhabi on bilateral issues.

Non-interference and neutrality in the Gulf's internal issues can be seen in the case of the Gulf crisis of 2017–21. During the Gulf crisis, Russia 'pursued an even-handed approach' and offered to mediate between the states.[76] This helped to boost its relations with both sides: the Quartet states (Saudi Arabia, UAE, Bahrain and Egypt) and Qatar.[77] Less than five months after the crisis arose, the unprecedented historical visit of Saudi Arabian King Salman to Russia occurred.[78] Shaykh Tamim of Qatar visited Moscow in March,[79] followed in May 2018, by Shaykh Mohammad bin Zayed (MbZ) of Abu Dhabi – the current president of the UAE.[80] In return, the official visit of the Russian leader Vladimir Putin, the first since 2007, to Saudi Arabia and the UAE occurred in October 2019.[81] A working visit of Russia's deputy foreign minister Bogdanov to Doha further developed ongoing cooperation with Qatar.[82] Among the key disagreements between the sides were different attitudes towards the Muslim Brotherhood; while the Quartet considered it a threat to domestic stability, Qatar built long-term relations with Islamists for pragmatic reasons.[83] Despite the Muslim Brotherhood being a banned organization in Russia, Russia did not pressurize the issue, and remained neutral to the Quartet's demands during the Gulf crisis of 2017. Importantly, Russian regions with Muslim populations also continued this non-interference and balancing policy. As noted in Chapter 4, Tatarstan did not find any difficulties in dealing with both sides – Qatar and the Quartet. At the same time, as will be discussed in Chapter 6 – while Chechnya maintained close links with the Quartet, Ingushetia seemed closer to Qatar. This also allowed Russia, as a federation, to foster links with both sides.

Finally, in changing the Moscow–GCC geopolitical dynamics, the Washington factor remained important, too. This also affected Tatarstan–Gulf relations.

The transformation of the traditional close alignment between the GCC and Washington over the years was another factor promoting further Moscow–GCC collaborations, and consequently Tatarstan–GCC. Under the presidency of George W. Bush, the turning point in relations was clearly the 9/11 attack, with the United States labelling Saudi Arabia as 'the center of evil'.[84] For example, Saudi capital began to flow out of the United States, and the Saudi leadership showed interest in buying Russian weapons. Although another Gulf neighbour – Qatar – seized this opportunity to build special relations with Washington, it also began dialogue with Russia.

When the United States needed to vacate Saudi Arabia's Prince Sultan Air Base in 2001, it provided an opportunity for Qatar to host the United States Central Command (CENTCOM)'s new forward headquarters, becoming home for a range of Special Forces and a CIA outpost.[85] The Amir of Qatar, Shaykh Hamad, oversaw the process of increasing bilateral relations with the United States, and the high construction cost of the al-Udaid Air Base and its increased capability demonstrated the strategic significance of being under the US security umbrella.[86] At the time, however, despite, by then, complex relations between Qatar and Russia, Qatar was Putin's second stop on his Middle Eastern tour in 2007.[87] During his visit, energy agreements were signed between Qatar Petroleum and Lukoil for joint ventures in gas and oil exploration.[88] The idea of setting up a 'gas cartel',[89] or 'Gas OPEC',[90] was discussed. This was expected to include Russia, Iran, Qatar, Algeria and Libya, and to build a united Russian Muslim 'gas front'.[91] However, efforts only resulted in a meeting of the Gas Exporting Countries Forum in Doha in 2007, and no documents were signed. In 2010, there was a bilateral agreement on Qatari investments worth $500 million to investigate polymetallic deposits in Russia's Yamalo-Nenets and Sverdlovsk regions. The real estate fund was completed by the investment of $75 million by Qatar's Barwa Real Company and Gazprombank in January 2011.[92]

During the Obama administration, the United States supported the Arab Spring uprisings, and this was considered by some Gulf states as their 'having abandoned two long-time allies, Egypt's Mubarak and Tunisia's Ben Ali, in their time of need'.[93] Also, as noted, the 2013 'chemical deal' over Syria was another stimulus for building closer relations with Russia. In other words, Russia's position on Syria demonstrated by contrast to the United States the reliability of its long-term support in the region – the al-Asad family friendship dates back to the days of the Soviet Union.[94] Moreover, in 2015, the nuclear deal negotiation between the United States (and other members of the P5+1) and Iran, was viewed negatively by the majority of the GCC states.[95] However, arguably, it was the Gulf crisis of 2017–21 that brought the importance of diversifying external relations into view for GCC states. Despite President Trump openly tweeting and supporting the Quartet at the beginning of the crisis, and publicly issuing a 'call on Qatar to end this funding . . . and its extremist ideology',[96] the United States also maintained close relations with both parties, and in return received considerable investments. Saudi Arabia's sovereign wealth fund held about $10 billion in the United States, adding $2 billion through its investment at the start of 2020 alone. In 2019, Qatar agreed to buy 'tremendous amounts of military equipment'.[97] Even by building an anti-Iran 'axis' consisting of Israel and two GCC states (Saudi Arabia and the United Arab Emirates), through withdrawal from JCPOA as part of the 'maximum pressure' on Iran', the United States arguably lost its leverage as the sole great power in the region, opening opportunities for others (Russia and China) to cement their presence. As Martin Indyk argues, the Trump administration abandoned half a century of American policy in the Middle East, and concludes that his course in the region was a 'fiasco'.[98] Steven Cook also put forward this case in 2021, under the title: 'Trump's Middle East legacy is a failure.'[99] All these events pushed the GCC states towards Russia.

The current US leadership is also viewed as risking driving Russia–GCC relations closer. The vision of the Joe Biden Administration is based on a return to traditional US diplomacy and multilateralism, stressing that 'America's going to reassert its role in the world and be a coalition builder', though Biden was at pains to distance himself from something resembling a third term of the Obama administration.[100] Under Biden–Harris, the United States plans to return to its leadership role, rather than Trump's isolationist policy. For example, by proclaiming itself as a defender of human rights, the Biden administration seems to be making stronger efforts to end wars and conflicts (e.g. in Syria, Yemen and Libya). President Biden announced the end of support for 'offensive' operations by the Saudis in Yemen. The new US administration halted arms sales to Saudi Arabia and UAE, including the $35 billion deal to sell Abu Dhabi F-35 fighter jets.[101] President Biden talked with King Salman of Saudi Arabia about putting America's old historical ally 'on a new footing'.[102]

By contrast, Moscow's approach towards the GCC states does not involve putting pressure on their human rights record (though Western positions are also various, vacillating between turning a blind eye to human rights abuses in the name of maintaining trade and relations, and advocating more strongly for 'democratic values'; the latter approach can promote action through greater international scrutiny, but often at the cost of deteriorating relations). Moscow was alert to the possibilities of taking advantage of such situations. For example, when the Kingdom of Saudi Arabia and its leadership were under attack over the Khashoggi case, during the G20 summit Putin greeted MbS with the now-famous high-five.[103] Moreover, during the official visit of Russia's foreign minister Sergey Lavrov to the GCC states (Saudi Arabia, UAE and Qatar) in March 2021, Lavrov became the first 'extra-regional' high-ranking diplomat to meet with Mohammad bin Salman, the Saudi Crown Prince since Washington had released an intelligence report of the killing of Jamal Khashoggi.[104] Despite the so-called oil prices war of 2020, when the energy market was shocked by the substantial drop in oil prices caused by Saudi's response to Moscow's refusal to reduce oil production in March, working relations were reinstated in October 2020.[105] Relations between Russia and Saudi Arabia, especially between their respective leaderships, has never reached such working productivity as that which had developed since 2015 and boomed under King Salman's leadership. Professor Vitaly Naumkin, full member of the Russian Academy of Sciences, along with his academic accomplishments, is also known for his membership of a number of Russian governmental positions. He has suggested that 'MbS is a brave leader, a brave reformist'.[106] This seems in line with Russia's general position on the current leadership of Saudi Arabia: prioritizing the new leadership's reformist nature, rather than focusing on its human rights record. More recently, new complications for collaboration have, of course, emerged, as Saudi and the other Gulf states decide on their specific responses to Russia's actions in the Ukraine. Not incidentally, the deterioration of relations between Saudi Arabia and the new Biden administration contributed to Saudi Arabia's neutral stance over the Ukraine conflict, which will be discussed in Chapter 7.

However, even while relations have become 'colder' between the traditional allies of the United States and the GCC states, Russia's relations have not reached the same level of collaborations as the long-term multilayered and multifaceted GCC–US relations.[107] Moreover, even with the decline[108] or even the predicted end of the so-called Pax-America,[109] the United States remains the largest economy of the world. In the short term, no country can replace the United States in offering security to the GCC states, either.[110] Therefore, as Carla Norrlöf explains, '[m]ilitary, great power resurgence has narrowed the gap between the United States and those on the next level in the global distribution of power, China and Russia. But in terms of raw power projection, American undeniably remains in a league of its own.'[111] For the GCC states, the continuing importance of retaining productive relations with the United States is clear, despite some disagreements; consequently, they should be regarded as diversifying their relations with Russia, rather than exchanging the United

States for Russia. Consequently, all of this has remained an obstructing factor for further collaborations with the GCC states on geopolitical issues, and the Gulf's economic cooperation, including with Russia's regions, including Tatarstan. Nonetheless, the geopolitical importance of Moscow–GCC relations has made shared Islamic identities useful for the Kremlin, and they continue to integrate Russian regions with Muslim populations – such as Tatarstan – into their federal policies, as leverage to strengthen collaborations, particularly in economic fields, as demonstrated in the next section. This also explains why Tatarstan's mutual interests are also primarily built on economic factors, which also receives more attention in what follows.

5.2.2 Moscow and Gulf states' economic cooperation

After the collapse of the USSR, the importance of the GCC states for modern Russia as a source of foreign investments, as well as a market for Russian weapons, and as potential allies in oil and gas, was already recognized. As noted earlier, Moscow particularly prioritized relations with Saudi Arabia in that period. Saudi–Russian political and economic relations were enhanced, with increasing engagement in energy affairs. For example, during the visit of then Crown Prince Abdullah to Moscow in September 2003, the leadership of both states stressed their political closeness on the issues of Arab–Israel peace in the Middle East, the situation in Iraq and criticism of extremism.[112] A major five-year agreement in the oil and gas sectors was made, to 'coordinate and cooperate in oil policy' and preserve 'an acceptable basket price for each oil barrel', alongside a 'gas initiative' that proposed joint development of gas fields, use of gas for desalinating sea water, geological surveys, the building of gas pipelines and gas-powered power stations.[113] The Saudi approach towards Moscow was identified as cooperation in regulating energy prices and to foster combined policy cooperation through the international Energy Forum.

Despite the focus on Saudi Arabia, even then, the importance of the other smaller GCC members was also acknowledged, largely because of their financial resources, while the importance of the UAE was due to its geopolitical location and its rapid economic development.[114] Moreover, the state had the largest population of Russian expats among the GCC states, with more than 30,000 by the 2000s. In February 2007, Russian foreign minister Lavrov estimated that Russian trade with the UAE had reached $1 billion.[115] The UAE was the biggest purchaser of Russian weapons among the GCC between 1998 and 2005, worth $900 million. UAE–Russia cooperation also included defence and security engagements. Barabanov concludes that 'Russia has captured a well-defined place on the UAE arms market and earned a degree of trust on the part of the military elite of this country as a reliable supplier of arms'.[116]

Notably, Kuwait also concluded contracts for buying weapons more regularly than others.[117] The military–technical relationships between Russia and Kuwait can be seen in the contracts between 2001 and 2002, with Russian state-owned companies used for delivery of parts for the Smerch multiple-launch rocket system, and the BMP-2 and BMP-3 infantry fighting vehicles.[118] By comparison, Oman–Russian cooperation in the military–technical area remained limited; despite reports of certain maintenance 'contracts', no details have been provided. Beyond this spending, the establishment of the Russia–Bahrain Business Council occurred, and Kreutz has explained that the rapprochement is related to political purposes.[119] Bahrain was interested in building cooperation with Moscow in the 2000s due to the Iranian nuclear challenge. The newest all-wheel-drive Mustang trucks were delivered to Bahrain and Qatar: in 2004 Rosoboroneksport supplied Bahrain with 40 Tatarstan-made KAMAZ-4350 double axel trucks for $1.1 million, and 500 KAMAZ-6350, KAMAZ-6350 (6*6) and KAMAZ-6350 (8*8) trucks, for a total of $20.1 million.[120] However, at that stage, such economic collaborations were limited.

The situation began to change with the geopolitical proximity of Russia and the GCC, along with the common threat of the dramatic drop in the price of crude oil. Consequently, engagements with the Gulf states were crucial for Russia's economic diversification and enlargement due to Western sanctions over the annexation of Crimea. Finally, the impact of Covid-19 and the drop in oil prices due to the Russia–Saudi 'oil war' in 2020,[121] on one hand, damaged collaboration (between Russia and Saudi Arabia), but on the other demonstrated the importance of all GCC actors' collaborations as part of OPEC+ to stability of the energy market.[122] These relations have been essential for the integration of the Russian energy industry into the global market. Given all of this, it is no coincidence that the Russian Foreign Policy Concept[123] of 2016 defines the Middle East as a region whose instability has a direct impact on Russia, and, importantly, most of the specified economic objectives are related to collaborations with the GCC states. For example, expansion of Russian presence in the regional markets for arms, nuclear fuel, oil and gas, food and so on; attracting investments to Russia, including from the rich countries of the Gulf; and maintaining energy prices by coordinating actions with key suppliers of oil and gas in the Gulf countries. These objectives, including security objectives (the containment and weakening of Islamic extremism and radicalism) and political objectives (the creation of a system of long-term political alliances), have been directly linked with successful collaborations with the Gulf partners.

All these factors have assisted in increasing economic collaboration. Shaykh Abdulrahman bin Mohammad bin Rashid al-Khalifa, chairman of the Supreme Islamic Affairs Council of Bahrain, during my interview in 2022, described the growing bilateral relations between Bahrain and Russia as follows:[124]

> The real reason for the growing relations between Russia and Bahrain is the Kingdom's desire to develop economic cooperation in trade, energy and other sectors. This cooperation has no political reasons, as evidenced by the fact that Russian-Bahraini relations have been developing steadily since the beginning of 1991, when diplomatic relations began between the two countries – that is, before the Syrian war. And before any wars in the region, because the Russian Federation is a great power, and one of the fundamentals of foreign policy in the Kingdom of Bahrain and the directives of His Majesty King Hamad bin Isa al-Khalifa is to maintain and develop good relations with Moscow. Manama wants to expand its international relations with all the decision-making capitals of the world.

For example, total trade between Russia and the GCC states increased dramatically, mainly with Saudi Arabia and the UAE (which particularly benefit from the dynamics of trade turnover between Tatarstan and Saudi Arabia–UAE, as discussed in Chapter 4). For example, trade between Russia and Saudi Arabia in 2018 totalled $1,054,857,321, up by 15.26 per cent in comparison to 2017.[125] In 2019, it totalled $1,667,159,568, an increase of 58.05 per cent from 2018. Even in 2020, among Covid-19 impacts and the oil price war between Russia and Saudi Arabia, total trade was $1,677,427,155, up by 0.62 per cent from 2019. Similarly, total trade between Russia and the UAE increased significantly in 2018. It was $1,689,188,234, up by 8.65 per cent and totalled $1,835,220,289 in 2019, while after Putin's visit to the UAE in 2019, in 2020, it was up by 77.64 per cent, and totalled $3,260,065,710. Qatar–Russia turnover was also positive: in 2018 it totalled $78,791,038, up by 7.47 per cent in comparison to 2017; in 2019 it was $82,605,597, up by 4.84 per cent in comparison to 2018; and in 2019 it totalled $100,616,522, up by 21.80 per cent in comparison to 2019.[126]

The GCC's investments have become important for Russia's economy. For example, in 2013, the Qatar Investment Authority (QIA) purchased a $500 million stake in VTB bank, and QIA became a 25 per cent stakeholder in St. Petersburg's Pulkovo airport.[127] In 2016, the QIA became a shareholder in Rosneft as a result of the Russian state-controlled oil giant's privatization. By 2019, the

Russian Direct Investment Fund (RDIF) had already committed to a $10 billion investment partnership with the Saudi Public Investment Fund (PIF), with more than $2 billion already invested in projects, such as oil refining, petrochemical, gas chemical and oilfield services.[128] A tranche of multimillion-dollar deals has been signed on the back of the historical visit of King Salman to Russia, and deals worth $1.3 billion were signed during Putin's visit to the UAE in 2019, notably in the energy, health and technology fields.[129] However, it should also be noted that GCC investments in Russia are limited in comparison to the West: for example, Saudi investments in Russia amount to only $185 million, while Saudi Arabia's sovereign wealth fund now holds about $10 billion in the United States, adding $2 billion in the latest investment at the start of 2020, alone.[130] This is connected to the aforementioned great power competition, under which Russia has remained under sanctions since 2014, and the United States remains the largest economy of the world. As illustrated in Chapter 4, this is one of the reasons for limited, but increasingly important, investments from the Gulf to Tatarstan.

Notably, Russia's share of the Middle East defence market has doubled since 2016; Saudi Arabia, the UAE and Qatar were the top buyers in 2019. In the fall of 2017, following the visit of King Salman to Moscow, several documents were signed in the field of military–technical cooperation. In particular, there were negotiations on the memorandum on the purchase and localization of production of TOS-1A 'Solntsepek' heavy flamethrowing systems, 'Kornet-EM' anti-tank missile systems and AGS-30 grenade launchers. In 2019, it was reported that Russia had begun deliveries of heavy flamethrower systems to Saudi Arabia. In August 2019, at the MAKS air show, the head of the Federal Service for Military-Technical Cooperation (FSMTC) of Russia, Dmitry Shugaev, said that Russia was supplying weapons to Saudi Arabia. In February 2021, the head of the Ministry of Industry and Trade of the Russian Federation, Denis Manturov, announced that the contract between Russia and Saudi Arabia on a joint venture for the production of Kalashnikov assault rifles was undergoing interstate approval.[131] Moreover, in November 2019, Dmitry Shugaev said that the UAE had ordered Russian weapons worth $0.5 billion. Shugaev also noted one of the most successful examples of cooperation with the UAE, in the field of military–technical cooperation, joint development and production of the Pantsir-S short-range air defence systems.[132] With regards to Qatar, discussions over the possibility of purchasing Russia's anti-aircraft missile systems S-400 were in progress; the matter was delicate since all the Gulf states were still carefully balancing their relations with the United States, as noted earlier. However, there were many areas of military cooperation, in particular in the field of personnel training, and there were corresponding agreements in this area.[133] They have a knock-on effect for Tatarstan–GCC relations, as covered in Chapter 4, though activity remained vigorous; the Tatarstan government regularly attended specialized military exhibitions, such as UAE-based IDEX, and scope for expansion in the deals on KAMAZ trucks and so on have already been mentioned.

Energy collaborations to stabilize the energy market between the GCC and Russia have been crucial. The GCC states are effectively Russia's opponents in the energy market. However, since 2015 Moscow has decided to cooperate, aiming to integrate the Russian energy industry into the global market. In 2016, Russia collaborated with OPEC on an oil production cut for the first time since 2016.[134] In 2019, OPEC+ emerged, mainly as a result of agreements between Moscow and Riyadh with respect to crude output levels.[135] Both states cooperated in sharing the burden of production cuts, in an attempt to stabilize prices.[136] Moreover, in 2019, during Putin's visit to the UAE, the Abu Dhabi National Oil Company agreed to sell a stake in the Ghasha gas project to Lukoil, and also signed a strategic framework agreement with Gazprom Neft on upstream, downstream and technology cooperation.[137] The UAE and Russia also increased bilateral energy talks, with their cooperation on the OPEC+ crude production cut agreement.[138] In 2020, Gazprom Neft and Mubadala Petroleum signed a memorandum of cooperation to jointly develop new technologies focused on oil production, and digitalization of production processes.[139] The United Arab Emirates' Mubadala holding company made its single largest investment in Russia in December 2021, purchasing 1.9 per cent of Sibur, Russia's largest integrated petrochemical company.

Meanwhile, Russia and Qatar are the world's largest Liquified Natural Gas (LNG) exporters and major natural gas producers, and compete to offer gas to Europe; this situation has in some ways intensified since the Ukraine conflict. There have been several collaborative projects in the energy field, rather than direct competition, though it remains to be seen how this will play out in the longer term. Joint projects, such as Doha becoming the owner of 19.5 per cent of Rosneft PJSC, played their role. Also, in April 2020, Qatar and Russia, who were between them Europe's leading sources of LNG, adjusted their tactics for shipping the commodity to the region. Due to a slowdown in global economic activity triggered by Covid-19 and intensifying competitive pressure in Europe – not solely from other LNG producers but other pipelines too – Qatar and Russia increased their exports in March, targeting specific destinations for maximum strategic effect.[140] Russia and Qatar had, prior to the Ukraine crisis, agreed to coordinate their energy policy in 2019, as major natural gas producers.[141] Given all such active engagements in the energy market, and considering that Tatarstan is rich in natural resources, including oil–gas–chemical industries, as discussed in Chapter 4, Tatarstan has been a recipient of investments from the Gulf in the energy field. Discussions in the energy field have been in progress, and real deals are expected to materialize in the future, depending on how the global market adapts in the medium term. This means potential economic deals which benefit the Russian Federation, as Tatarstan is part of it, too.

5.3 Conclusion

This chapter has discussed the key reasons for active engagements between the Tatarstan region and the GCC states since the 2000s, within the larger framework of Russia's federal governance and policy. Dynamics between Moscow and Kazan illustrate a gradual decline in the 'special status' of Tatarstan, but this has balanced against the Republic's increasing utility for the geopolitical objectives of the Kremlin. The latter began integrating its Muslim minorities and offering Tatarstan a leading role in building relations with OIC countries. Given the geopolitical importance of the Gulf states for Moscow in this direction, Tatarstan–GCC relations also increased, especially in the first decade of the 2000s (with the establishment of the Strategic Group 'Russia-Islamic World'). For Moscow and the Gulf states, growing geopolitical roles have become especially important as outcomes of the Arab Spring in the region. Moscow returned to its 'great power' status in the region, at least militarily, while the GCC states' importance grew geopolitically, with their emergence as key players in regional dynamics. At the same time, interests in economic collaborations, especially in energy, sale of military equipment and investments, have been crucial for Moscow–GCC relations. Given these interests, Tatarstan has facilitated common interests and relationship-building, while also working on diversification of its own economy, especially towards Islamic finance and banking (see Chapter 4). This supports the overall argument of this book, that shared identities boost cooperation between a state's 'Self' and a minority 'Self' of another ('Other') state (1) if 'Self' and the 'Other' have interests in common, and the 'Other' is willing to integrate its minorities into this process; and (2) if 'Self' and minority 'Self' have shared interests.

Russian Muslim Republics

Paradiplomacies towards the GCC

This chapter focuses on the dynamics of other Russian Muslim republics and their paradiplomatic efforts towards the Gulf states. The key localities are the republics of Chechnya, Dagestan, Ingushetia and Bashkortostan, the rationale for whose case studies has already been mentioned during earlier chapters. More concretely, although there are more than twenty-five million Muslims in modern Russia, they are most prominently located in densely populated regions: Bashkortostan, Dagestan, Chechnya, Kabardino-Balkaria, North Ossetia-Alania, Ingushetia and Tatarstan. Their shared Islamic identities with the Gulf states may immediately suggest that shared identities can boost cooperation between 'Self(s)' and the minority 'Self' of another state (1) if 'Self(s)' and the 'Other' have interests in common, and the 'Other' is willing to integrate its minorities into this process; and (2) if 'Self(s)' and the minority 'Self' have shared interests.

For this study, regions with less prominent Muslim populations, such as in central Russia (Moscow, Saint Petersburg, Nizhny Novgorod and so on) were not chosen, since their distribution is comparatively less dense and, consequently, the effects of the identity less visible. Further, the republics of Kabardino-Balkaria, North Ossetia-Alania and Crimea were excluded from the analysis due to their extremely limited existing paradiplomatic efforts towards the Gulf states, as well as the disputed status of the republic of Crimea, which includes Crimean Tatars.[1] Paradiplomatic efforts of all case studies chosen were limited during the Soviet time, for reasons similar to those explored in the TASSR case, and links were largely limited to hajj performance. Consequently, this chapter will briefly describe the specific historical links of Chechnya, Dagestan, Ingushetia and Bashkortostan with the Arabian states, while the main analysis will be devoted to post-1990 events and policies.

6.1 Brief historical analyses

Another centre of modern Russia's Islam is the North Caucasus. Its history of Islam dates back to the seventh century, when Islam began to spread in southern Dagestan among the Lezgins. In 685–6 the Arabs took the town of Derbent, which as a result became the pivotal point of Islamization of the north-eastern Caucasus, known as Bab al-Jihad (the gateway of jihad).[2] Despite the fact that the Arab Caliphate could not obtain a long-term position in Dagestan, the spread of Islam continued. Interestingly, these links were regarded by the political elites and stakeholders in Dagestan as long-term historical links with the Arabian states, serving as a foundation for current relations between the minority 'Self(s)' (the North Caucasus) and 'Self(s)' (GCC states) based on shared Muslim identities. During interviews it was explained in terms of roots that go back to when the forty companions of the Prophet – who in the Caucasus are called Ashabs – arrived with their new faith almost 1,500 years ago. They were buried in what is now the sacred Muslim cemetery of Kirkhlyar. Kirkhlyar, one of the oldest Muslim shrines in the North Caucasus, is located within the Northern City Cemetery of Derbent.

From the tenth to the twelfth centuries, Islam began to spread among the Avars, the largest ethnic group in Dagestan.[3] By the end of the fifteenth century most Dagestanis accepted the Shafi *madhhab* of Sunni Islam. In the fifteenth to the sixteenth centuries, Islam in the Shafi *madhhab* spread among the indigenous population of Chechnya and Ingushetia, the Vaynakhs. Islam had spread into the western Caucasus from the Golden Horde in the thirteenth and fourteenth centuries following the acceptance of Islam by Khan Berke.[4] Additionally, in the sixteenth and seventeenth centuries it spread into Kabarda, and then further spread to Ossetia. In the mid-eighteenth century Islam spread to the Balkars, and by 1782 to Karachai. In contrast to Dagestan and Chechnya, the mountain peoples of the western Caucasus adopted the Hanafi *madhhab*.[5] The North Caucasus is home to various Sufi tariqas, including Qadiriyya, Naqshbandiyya and Shadhiliyya.[6]

As for the Soviet period, there were very limited direct relations between the republics and the Arabian states, for similar reasons as in the TASSR case, as discussed in Chapter 3. Galina Yemelianova[7] states that after the Russian Revolutions of 1917, the German, Turkish and White Russian armies occupied Dagestan. A group of rebellious Chechens and Dagestanis attempted to revive the Islamic State and proclaimed a theocratic North Caucasian Empire. It was defeated in 1921 by the Bolsheviks, and Dagestan became the Dagestan Soviet

Socialist Republic of the Russian Federation of the Soviet Union. Gameer explains the reason for the creation of two national Autonomous Soviet Socialist Republics (ASSRs) within the Russian Soviet Federal Socialist Republic – the Checheno–Ingush ASSR and the Dagestani ASSR – as the result of Soviet policies to destroy the hold of Islam and the Sufi brotherhoods over society, to suppress all vestiges of resistance and to break up the unity of the Muslim community.[8] As noted in Chapter 3, the Chechens and the Ingush were 'deported' to Central Asia in 1944 and 'rehabilitated' in 1956.[9] The 'deportation' enhanced the Chechen national consciousness and negative attitude to Russian/Soviet rule. Islam therefore became the antithesis of everything Marxist and Soviet.[10] The year 1944 also saw the deportation of Dagestan's Chechen–Akkins from the Aukhovskii (Novolakskii) district (*rayon*). In the 1950s, most of the Chechen–Akkins returned to Dagestan, but their lands were taken by their neighbours, particularly the Laks.[11] Both republics' politics had remained secular until the end of 1994. Only the outcomes of the first war in Chechnya (1994–6) changed the situation. The war enhanced the Islamic dimension of mainly (but not only) Chechen identity. More importantly, the war triggered the Islamization of politics in Chechnya and catapulted the 'Wahhabis' and their ideology to centre stage in both republics;[12] this also prompted stronger relations with the Gulf states.

It should also be noted, in comparison to TASSR's case, that Muslim identities in these regions are of a form that permits closer alignment with the culture of the Gulf states. For example, Chechnya and Dagestan remained the strongest 'Islamic' areas in the USSR, despite seventy years of Soviet anti-religious campaigns. Moshe Gammer explains the survival of Islam thus: first, because both regions received less attention from the USSR than the Central Asian republics. More importantly, the strong Sufi character of Islam in these two republics gave it deep and resilient roots. From the eleventh century to the 1920s, Dagestan was a leading centre of traditional Muslim scholarship, and resistance to Russian conquest and rule under Tsarists and Bolsheviks was conducted under the banner of Islam and the leadership of Sufi brotherhoods.[13]

The Bashkirs held their land under the Mongol Khanate of Kipchak from the thirteenth to the fifteenth centuries, until the territory was invaded by Russians in 1552.[14] In the eighteenth century there were different uprisings, such as the famous *Pugachev* rebellion of 1773 that was strongly supported by the Bashkirs, who were led by their own Salavat Yulai.[15] During the Soviet era, as noted earlier, despite pre-existing Idel-Ural, Bashkirs were organized into the Bashkir Autonomous Republics in 1919, under the leadership of Zeki Velidi Togan.

Since 1992, the republic has transformed into the Republic of Bashkortostan. As illustrated throughout this book, the history of Tatars and Bashkirs and their links with Arabian states are very similar, along with parallels in their relations with Moscow and the history of Islam in the Volga region. The 'Khakimov factor' has also been a trump for both regions for closer relation-building with the Gulf states, and this will be discussed in the next section.

6.2 Russian Muslim Republics' paradiplomacies towards the GCC: 1990–2021

6.2.1 Chechnya and the Gulf states

Putin's rise to power in the early 2000s was characterized by the threat of religious extremism from Chechen separatists.[16] Importantly, these groups used connections with the GCC states to implement jihad in Russia, such as the 1995 arrival of Jordanian-born Habib Abdul Rahman Khattab, who also holds Saudi nationality.[17] Khattab became the main commander of the foreign Islamic extremists in Chechnya, and was the channel for Gulf-based patrons funding the jihad in the Caucasus, such as the Qatar Charitable Society, accused of funding extremists in Dagestan in 1999.[18] In Russia, several organizations with a political and ideological bias, such as Jamiat Ihia al-Turath al-Islamiya ('Revival of Islamic Heritage Society'), the International Islamic Relief Organization, 'Qatar', al-Harameyn ('The Two Holy Places'), al-Hairiya ('Charity'), Benevolence International Foundation, and groups such as the Muslim Brotherhood, al-Qaeda and Hizb ut-Tahrir have been active as 'a response to conflicts that developed in its domestic public and political life and to a crisis in people's consciousness.'[19] Russia's response to this threat was strict counter-terrorist operations in the North Caucasian region, or the so-called Second Chechen War, between 1999 and 2009. Relations with the GCC states were unsurprisingly tense, and as Fredholm observes, the Chechen war involved several diplomatic crises between Qatar and Russia, because Gulf citizens were involved in fighting Russia, as well as the bomb attack that killed Yandarbiyev, the Chechen separatist living in Qatar.[20]

As noted in Chapter 5, to integrate its Muslim minorities into federal policies, the Kremlin made its first move towards the Muslim world by obtaining the status of official observer at the Organisation of Islamic Cooperation (OIC) in 2005; the organization's headquarters are located in Jeddah. At the time, Saudi

Arabia acknowledged Moscow's dominance over Chechnya.[21] In January 2004, the Chechen president, Akhmad Kadyrov, was received by the Saudi leadership as the legitimate representative of the Chechen people. After the assassination of Akhmad Kadyrov on 9 May 2004, his son Ramzan became president (later the head of the Chechen Republic), and continued the diplomatic exchanges. Several trips to Saudi Arabia were arranged, in March 2007 and August 2007, which included performing u*mrah* and the ritual of washing at the Ka'ba in Mecca with the Saudi King Abdullah; these helped to secure Saudi Arabia's support for Kadyrov's leadership of Chechnya.[22]

Over the years, Ramzan Kadyrov became known as a key supporter of Putin's policies, and in the Middle East as 'Russia's Top Diplomat'.[23] He was the only head of a Muslim region to accompany Putin during his official visit to Saudi Arabia and the UAE in 2019.[24] This visit in 2019 was fundamental, cementing Moscow's political and energy links across the Middle East.[25] Demonstrably, key milestones in boosting relations between Saudi Arabia and Russia – 'reach[ing] a new qualitative level', to quote the Russian foreign minister Sergey Lavrov[26] – have directly involved Russian Muslim republics and their leaderships.

Shared Muslim identities are the vital element on which Ramzan Kadyrov builds close relations with the Gulf states, and especially with their leadership. Kadyrov's relations with the GCC leaders became so close that he began calling them 'brothers'.[27] This can be seen in all visits to the Gulf and from Gulf representatives, such as when in November 2018 both Minnikhanov and Kadyrov attended the Formula One Abu Dhabi Grand Prix, where MbS was present.[28] Both leaders also usually attend the International Defence Exhibition and Conference (IDEX) in the UAE.[29] In November 2019, Bahrain's delegation, led by royal representatives, visited Grozny.[30] In return, Kadyrov visited Bahrain and met King Hamad Ibn Isa al-Khalifa. The head of Chechnya, together with the Crown Prince of the Kingdom, Salman bin Hamad al-Khalifa, took part in the opening of the International Defence Exhibition and Conference, in 2019 in Manama.

Kadyrov's importance for the federal government has mainly been built on his personal contacts with leaders and the authorities in the Muslim world, which relied initially on his father's network. Akhmad Kadyrov was a respected spiritual leader, who interrupted his studies at a Muslim University in Oman in 1991 to join the rebellion at home and rose to the key position of Mufti. From that position he proclaimed jihad against Russia in 1995, but after four years he switched over to the side of Putin, then prime minister, who launched a war in Chechnya in October 1999.[31] Ramzan Kadyrov was thereby able to lay the foundations of his family's recognition in the Muslim world, and he began to further build close personal links. The Chechen Republic's paradiplomacy efforts therefore rely heavily on the individual factor of its head as 'a charismatic regional autocrat', along with strong Muslim shared identities.[32] Marat Gatin explains: 'Kadyrov is more active in the religious field, I personally believe, he is more active than us [Tatarstan], as Minnikhanov personifies the Islamic *umma* of Russia in the person of various economic projects'.[33]

Specifically, taking advantage of personal links in the Muslim world, Chechnya organized a variety of religious forums and conferences, which have allowed it to bring important Islamic scholars to Russia. For example, in 2019, Moscow and Grozny hosted the International Conference on Principles of Mercy and Peace in Religious Values, co-organized by the Muslim World League, which was 'the first of its kind in the history of Russia under government patronage'.[34] Beyond their theological goals, given that in modern Russia there is no Islamic authority in legal or theological issues, such conferences also served political purposes. The conference was held during the Gulf crisis (between Qatar and the Quartet states – Saudi Arabia, the UAE, Bahrain and Egypt – between 2017 and 2021), and was particularly beneficial for the deepening of relations with and between the Quartet states, especially the UAE. The conference identified Salafism/Wahhabism as a dangerous and misguided sect, along with extremist groups including ISIS, Hizb ut-Tahrir and the Muslim Brotherhood. Moreover, alignment between Chechnya and the Quartet, especially the UAE, can additionally be explained by the previous relations with the spiritual leader of the Muslim Brotherhood, Shaykh Yusuf al-Qaradawi, who has been hosted by Qatar, and has close links with Qatar's leadership. Commenting on Russia's support of the al-Asad regime, al-Qaradawi said: 'Arabs and the Islamic world must declare a boycott of Russia. We must regard Russia as our enemy number one.' It was the head of the Chechen Republic, Ramzan Kadyrov, who was the first to condemn al-Qaradawi's anti-Russian speech, defining it as 'blasphemous' and directed against millions of Muslims in Russia.[35] Relations have since then deteriorated between al-Qaradawi and Kadyrov. Chechnya has frozen its relations with Doha, while boosting its relations with the Quartet leadership.

It should be noted that the Grozny conference diminished relations with another Quartet member, Saudi Arabia, because of Grozny's fatwa.[36] Nonetheless, the Chechen leaders again leveraged shared Islamic identities to overcome challenges in their relations. The Chechen leadership strongly supported 'moderate Islam' in the Islamic world – as led by the Quartet, including Saudi

Arabia[37] and the UAE.[38] In 2019, Kadyrov gave a speech supporting 'moderate Islam' under the patronage of King Salman (for an assessment of the Saudi efforts, see Chapter 4), stating:[39]

> terrorism does not have a religion [. . .] Saudi Arabia, led by King Salman
> . . . unites Muslims in the fight against extremism and terrorism, spreads true
> Islamic values. . . . Therefore, I urge Muslims to stand in solidarity with Saudi
> Arabia.

The most striking developments and investments emerged during the period of the Gulf crisis, which explains the great number of visits of Kadyrov to the UAE, and such close relations with its leadership, which have materialized as investments in Chechnya,[40] such as building the five-star hotel 'The Local', and the construction of the International University.[41] In 2017, the Shaykh Zayed Foundation was established to support entrepreneurship and innovation in Chechnya, with $50 million capital to support the Chechen economy.[42] The federal government decided to reduce subsidies to Chechnya from 2017,[43] as such close cooperation between the UAE and Chechnya was needed to advance the republic's economy. For the federal government it was a way to diversify the economic budget of Chechnya to other spenders. In 2019, Leonid Slutsky, chairman of the State Duma Committee on International Affairs minuted that Russia appreciated the UAE's support for the economic reconstruction of Chechnya.[44] The UAE's 'taking care' of Chechnya was also helpful for the federal government, when the UAE sent five medical aid planes to Chechnya carrying 31.3 metric tons of medical supplies and 20,000 testing kits, benefiting 31,300 medical professionals during the Covid-19 pandemic.[45]

Arguably, despite the key factor of building relations through shared Muslim identities, the importance of Chechnya also lies in its strong military forces, in its own 'hard power' resource. For example, despite an initial denial of the presence of Chechen fighters among the Russian troops, the Chechen leader has since confirmed that an armed police battalion constituted by ethnic Chechens was in Syria as part of the Russian military forces. In 2017, Maxim Suchkov also noted that Kadyrov's closest adviser, Adam Delimkhanov, and Mufti of Chechnya Salah Haji Mezhiev, travelled to Syria to meet with Maher al-Asad, brother of the Syrian president.[46] This resulted in the decision by the Regional Public Fund named after Akhmad Kadyrov, Ramzan Kadyrov's father, to fund the restoration of the UNESCO World Heritage-listed Umayyad Mosque in Aleppo, which had been destroyed by the Islamic State. There is no evidence of collaborations on this basis with the Gulf states, though they remain distinctly feasible, with the proviso that Chechen hard power is at the current moment primarily involved in the Ukraine conflict,[47] rather than in the Middle East.

6.2.2 Ingushetia and the Gulf states

While Chechnya developed closer relations with the Quartet leadership and supported its religious agenda, by contrast, Ingushetia concentrated on developing some links with Saudi Arabia, while simultaneously trying to build closer cooperation with Qatar. The former leader of Ingushetia, Yunus-bek Yevkurov, during his visit to Doha, visited Ali al-Qaradaghi, the secretary general of the International Union of Muslim Scholars[48] (headed by Shaykh Yusuf al-Qaradawi, a spiritual leader of the Muslim Brotherhood). Yevkurov's Instagram account reported: 'I expressed gratitude to the Shaykh for his efforts to consolidate Muslim society, for his contribution to strengthening stability in our region.' Within the context of the Gulf crisis between 2017 and 2021, one of the drivers of which were the conflicting views on the Muslim Brotherhood, this is a good example of the balancing act performed between both sides by Russia's Muslim regions. The balancing of opposing sides during the crisis was no coincidence, also reflecting the internal dynamics of the two Russian republics, and especially so in the period when the Gulf crisis occurred.

The drawing of administrative borders between Chechnya and Ingushetia caused protests that began in October 2018 and continued until March 2019, adding to the already complex relations between the republics. (The controversy led to the resignation of Ingushetia's leader two months later.)[49] This also demonstrates the advantages for the Kremlin of integrating its minorities into its policies of balancing adversaries: when Chechnya dealt with the Quartet, its counterpart, Ingushetia, engaged with the Quartet's rival, Qatar); and this again demonstrates how shared Muslim identities between Russian regions and the GCC states have been central in such policies. In other words, relations have been developed between 'Self(s)' and the minority 'Self(s)' as a result of common interests, alongside 'Other' and 'Self (s)' relations following the integration of minority 'Self(s)' into the former's policies.

Consequently, based on Russian press sources, 'Qatar acts as an economic investor in Ingushetia since 2014 – from the beginning of the economic crisis'[50]. Agreements between Ingushetia and Qatar were made to establish a group to develop investment projects in 2018,[51] across a wide range of sectors of the economy: from housing and communal services to the automotive industry, tourism and technology parks on the sites of former Soviet factories.[52] At the time of writing, there have been only very limited details released about these plans. Moreover, there is limited information about the Islamic complex earlier agreed on to be built by Qatar in Ingushetia.[53] This subject remains an ongoing discussion with the Gulf states, as earlier in 2009, Kuwait also planned to build an Islamic complex with a mosque, but progress on this deal remains difficult to assess.[54] According to reports in 2020, chairman of the World Council of Muslim Communities, Ali Rashid al-Nuaimi, declared the possibility of the UAE joining the construction of the first cathedral mosque in Magas.[55] This might suggest expectations of further development of links based on the Islamic factor with any Gulf state which assists in religious construction, with the Magas cathedral mosque a key focus. Construction was started in 2010 and the facility was planned to be opened in 2013, but activity was frozen due to lack of funds.[56] Given the 'special' relations between Chechnya and the UAE, it will be interesting to follow the resulting dynamics: whether the UAE decides to stay close to Chechnya or further develop its links with Russian Muslim republics. (As noted earlier, Tatarstan–UAE relations are also close.) Earlier, the UAE had provided humanitarian aid to Ingushetia during the first wave of the Covid-19 pandemic, similarly to other North Caucasus republics (Chechnya, Dagestan, North Ossetia, Kabardino-Balkaria and Karachay-Cherkessia).[57]Indeed, the future of these plans also depends on the impact of the Ukraine crisis; the main obstacles are clarified in Chapter 7.

Traditionally relations with Saudi Arabia have been associated mainly with hajj and the religious factor, with limited economic activities. For example, a similar group to the Qatari initiative is planned, which is expected to deal with techno-economic relations in agriculture between Ingushetia and Saudi Arabia; this was initially agreed in 2016.[58] The former head of Ingushetia was the only head of Russian subjects to be part of the Russian delegation to Saudi Arabia, which met with King Salman on 1–2 November. In his presentation, he mentioned a joint business in the field of honey supplies beginning to develop between Ingushetia and Saudi Arabia. Business representatives of both sides are working on the issue of supplying fruit to Saudi Arabia.[59] More concretely, it appears relations with the Kingdom remain active via hajj performance,[60] based on shared Islamic identities.

6.2.3 Dagestan and the Gulf states

After the collapse of the USSR, the markets of the United Arab Emirates (and other Gulf states) and Turkey were open. This occurred mainly due to the

Table 3 Information on Trade and Economic Cooperation between the Republic of Dagestan and Saudi Arabia

Turnover	thousand, $								
	2011	2012	2013	2014	2015	2016	2017	2018	2019
Export	45.2	0	0	72.79	0	13.42	0	0	24.58
Import	18.7	44.8	272.82	339.33	370.23	676.47	433.32	492.01	270.89
Total	63.9	44.8	272.82	412.12	370.23	689.89	433.32	492.01	295.47

Source: Ministry of Economy and Territorial Development of the Republic of Dagestan.

Table 4 Information on Trade and Economic Cooperation between the Republic of Dagestan and the UAE

Turnover	thousand, $								
	2011	2012	2013	2014	2015	2016	2017	2018	2019
Export	12.0	0	295.56	0	100.91	244.64	13.85	23.29	8.98
Import	7957.5	934.3	110.20	57.16	53.29	174.49	287.84	535.16	501.54
Total	7969.5	934.3	405.76	57.16	154.19	419.13	301.69	558.45	510.52

Source: Ministry of Economy and Territorial Development of the Republic of Dagestan.

Islamic component of the region, along with economic possibilities offered by the Middle Eastern states.[61] However, in recent years, trade with the Gulf states (see Tables 3 and 4) has remained low. Available statistics provided by the Ministry of Economy and Territorial Development of the Republic of Dagestan show trade and economic collaborations with Saudi Arabia and the UAE. These are small numbers, but within them, UAE remains the largest economic partner. Relations with the UAE occur mainly via businessmen,[62] while with Saudi Arabia via DUM Dagestan,[63] prioritizing shared identities with the region.[64] The Republic of Dagestan developed yet another mechanism for engagements with the Gulf states, relying on economic cooperation based on ratified agreements between the federal governments. Moreover, as Gadzhiamin Ramaldanov, the former deputy minister of Economy and Territorial Development of the Republic of Dagestan[65] explained, there is also an 'unofficial' mechanism, through Dagestan's diaspora businessmen, who have become crucial for attempts to build relations with the GCC monarchies. Among the directions explored is the halal economy.[66] This pathway is not taken solely with the Gulf states, as Dagestan also maintains relations with the Middle Eastern states via its diaspora in Turkey (Istanbul, Ankara, Konya), Jordan and Israel.[67]

Among the key reasons for limited collaborations that have been identified (concentrating on those that existed before the 2022 Ukraine conflict) are the geopolitical dynamics in the Gulf, which have worsened relations between Iran and the GCC states, alongside the Gulf crisis of 2017–21, when Saudi Arabia, the UAE, Bahrain and Egypt cut diplomatic and trade ties with Doha, and imposed sea, land and air blockades on Qatar.[68] These factors negatively affected logistics, especially for import, since the traditional route to the Gulf states was via Azerbaijan – Iran – and the Persian Gulf.

These subtleties are most important within the context of this book and the issue of the clarification of 'Self' and 'Other' identities. Middle Eastern sectarian differences have also reached the North Caucasus. While Chechnya keeps close links with the Gulf states, especially the UAE and Bahrain, their competitor, Iran, is increasing its influence in Dagestan. First, Iran is importing huge quantities of mutton, mostly from Dagestan. The import has become so big that it has led to prices on the local market rising by 80–100 per cent in 2018. Allegedly, Iran is re-exporting the mutton meat to the Gulf countries. The trade comes with cultural influence in tow, as there are reports of several hundred former Sunnis converting to Shi'ism in Dagestan. They moved to Shi'ism largely through the pan-Islamist political organization Hizb ut-Tahrir.[69]

This contested Islamic space helps to explain why Chechnya is closer to the Gulf states than Dagestan, and plays out variously at the local level, too. The spread of Shi'ism in the North Caucasus and among different regions is perceived very differently by different groups. One example is the screening of Majid Majidi's film 'Mohammad: Messenger of God' in Dagestan. Dagestanis in the Muftiate promoted it despite very strong criticism from the Sunni side, accusing the film of being based only on Shi'ite sources. There was an aggressive reaction to Majidi's film from the Chechen Muftiate. On 24 June 2017 an online appeal was circulated by the Mufti of the Chechen Republic, Salah Haji Mezhiev, regarding the ban on the distribution of Shi'ite books. He said: 'Under the guise of its culture, Iran is spreading Shi'ite religious literature, thereby disturbing the true path of Islam'. Books such as 'Collection of Fatwas' by Ayatollah Sayyid 'Ali Sistani, 'The Personality of the Prophet of Islam' by Hussein Sayyidi, 'The Personality of 'Ali Ibn Abi Talib' and many others confuse young people.' This fatwa was a direct reaction to the screening of a 'Shi'ite' film in the neighbouring region. But in terms of inter-Muftiate relations, the Chechen Mufti did not mention the Dagestani Muftiate and Majidi's film directly, blaming Shi'ite 'propaganda' via books, instead, drawing a connection to Iranian influence.[70] In other words, secretariat dynamics in the Gulf also affect relations between Chechnya/Dagestan and the Gulf states. The popularity of Shi'ism in Dagestan can explain the comparatively limited collaborations with the GCC.

6.2.4 Bashkortostan and the Gulf states

The development of the chief argument of this book has been the matter of shared identities, and more so when the federal government integrates its minorities into interactions with independent states. Ruslan Mirsaiapov,[71] who at the time when I met him for an interview was the chairman of the State Committee of Bashkiria for Foreign Economic Relations, and currently the trade representative of the Russian Federation in Azerbaijan, clarifies how ties arise at the regional level with the countries of the Islamic world:

> [In such maters] we are talking about the official-level prerogative of the Ministry of Foreign Affairs of the Russian Federation, while at the regional level, we are talking about the business level, about possible financial relationships. Basically, what interests the Russian regions is increasing exports to the countries [*sic*] of the Islamic world [. . .] I think it pleases both the leaderships of the individual regions of the Russian Federation and the Ministry of Foreign Affairs of the Russian Federation, in general.

Modern Russia, building on the successful elements of earlier Soviet policies, has begun integrating its Muslim population for policy purposes, thereby creating opportunities to establish direct links with the Gulf states. Specifically, Karim Khakimov's contribution to the warm relations between Saudi Arabia and the USSR, especially in the 1920s and the 1930s, are remembered and acknowledged in the modern Republic of Bashkortostan. The legacy of Karim Kharimov (also appealed to in Tatarstan) grants opportunities for the development of relations between Saudi Arabia and Bashkortostan, because the Soviet diplomat was born there. For example, Ruslan Mirsaiapov[72] stated that Bashkortostan received an invitation to present its potential at OIC headquarters, based in Jeddah, precisely because of this 'Khakimov' factor. Moreover, the 'Khakimov factor', whose policies towards Saudi Arabia made use of shared Muslim identities (see Chapter 2), was acknowledged during the plenary part of the fifth meeting of the 'Russia-Islamic World' Group, which took place in Ufa, in 2019.[73] A memorial plaque was dedicated to him in the building housing the 'Galiya' madrasa, where he studied from 1910 to 1911.[74] Ufa also hosts the annual scientific forum known as 'Khakimov's Readings'. Ainur Akkulov,[75] vice-president of the Union of the Chamber of Commerce and Industry of the Republic of Bashkortostan, suggests that 'when Saudis visited Ufa, where the group took a meeting in 2019, they said that came to see the homeland of the diplomat who brought the USSR and the Kingdom very close, and who was a close friend of Ibn Saud'.[76] Yury Barmin explains:

Soviet-Saudi relations turned sour after Khakimov was executed in Moscow, which happened two months before the discovery of the largest deposit of oil in the world in March 1938 in Saudi Arabia. Arguably, had the Soviets not killed their sole link to the Saudi King and by extension to his gigantic oil wealth, the Middle East might well look very different today.[77]

Interestingly, this view was reflected in Akkulov's argument in 2020 during his interview: 'Who knows how history would have been changed if he had not been killed. Maybe today we would have very close relations.'[78]

In modern times, since the 2010s, Saudi Arabia and Bashkortostan have demonstrated bilateral interests and serious intentions for economic cooperation: Bashkortostan held an exhibition at the economic forum in Jeddah in 2010, and agreements were reached for cooperation in key areas (mechanical engineering, food supplies, construction and production of building materials).[79] In 2011, a delegation of businessmen from Bashkortostan visited Saudi Arabia; this visit was in response to the arrival of a delegation from Saudi Arabia at the first International Forum on 'Big Chemistry'. Other agreements were reached for cooperation in investments and trade in 2016.[80] In 2017, the former head of Bashkortostan, Rustem Khamitov, had a meeting with King Salman, where the development of trade-economic, cultural and multiregional ties were discussed.[81] However, hajj pilgrimage for Muslims of the republic and cooperation in religious and educational fields remains central to relations between Bashkortostan and Saudi Arabia. On the other hand, after 100 years, the fact that the 'Khakimov factor' is still recognized and leant on does indicate the importance for both the Kremlin and Riyadh of maintaining his legacy, as part of maintaining warm relations. This also remains a 'trump' for maintaining relations between Bashkortostan and Saudi Arabia.

In general, both Akkulov[82] and Mirsaiapov[83] stressed a common interest in economic projects with all Gulf states, in tourism, oilfield services, oil production and oil refining, among other areas. For example, in November 2019 the company 'Packer' took part in the international exhibition of the oil and gas industry ADIPEC, which took place in Abu Dhabi (UAE).[84] The event presents the latest research and innovative solutions and services in all sectors of the industry, including the latest technologies for development in the oil and gas fields, processing, storage and transportation of products of the oil and gas and petrochemical industries. According to the official response to a request from the Ministry of Industry and Innovation Policy Regarding the Republic of Bashkortostan, 'participation in international exhibitions for "Packer" is an essential element of establishing a reliable and long-term partnership'.[85] Also, the 'Packer' delegation took part in the ninth meeting of the Intergovernmental Russian-Emirates Commission on Trade, Economic and Technical Cooperation within the framework of the exhibition.[86] The key topics of the meeting were cooperation in the fields of trade and investment, industry and digital technologies, energy, transport and agriculture. Business meetings were also held with representatives of companies from Kuwait, Oman and Saudi Arabia, at which options for further cooperation were discussed.[87] For example, in 2011, a delegation of Bashkortostan went on a three-day study visit to Kuwait. They visited the al-Wasatiyya International Centre. In 2018, at the Agricultural Agency of the state of Kuwait, the delegation of Bashkortostan gave a presentation on the economic and investment potential of the republic.[88] In 2019, an agreement on the supply of dry kumis to Kuwait was reached during the visit to Bashkiria of the chairman of the board of directors of the Kuwaiti company 'Almasa', Salem al-Bianoni.[89] Ruslan Mirsaiapov recalls this visit, stating that he headed the Bashkortostan delegation:

> We made a presentation and the businessmen in Kuwait liked very much how within a few hours, you can make a drink from powder, which for the Gulf countries is primarily interesting for its properties of preventing lung diseases. This is a serious scourge for the Arabian Peninsula countries, including Kuwait, and here we can be very attractive for the production and export of our products.

Also, Mirsaiapov stresses the development of halal tourism, which is very similar to Tatarstan's halal lifestyle, as well as developing an Islamic economy based on Islamic identities shared with the Gulf states:

> we invest in the republic in expanding production because the topic of halal tourism has a lot of potential. We actually have highly competitive proposals and the effect of special novelty can play a role.

Nonetheless, Table 5, showing Custom Statistics, demonstrates that as of 2019 exports remain limited despite such active engagements. These were largely restricted to the UAE and Oman, in industry and digital technologies, energy, light industry, transport and agriculture.

Moreover, according to the official response to an information request made to the Ministry of Industry and Innovation Policy Regarding the Republic of Bashkortostan with the GCC states, 'we would like to inform that there are no signed cooperation agreements with countries'.[90] Ruslan Mirsaiapov,[91] who when interviewed in 2020, was the chairman of the State Committee of Bashkiria for Foreign Economic Relations, and is currently the trade representative of the Russian Federation in Azerbaijan, shared his thoughts on the (then) challenges

Table 5 Exports: Bashkortostan–GCC States

No	Name of the partner country and product group	Export January–December, 2019
1	Nuclear reactors, boilers, equipment and mechanical devices; their parts	
	UAE	$518.9 thousand
	Oman	$8.5 thousand
2	legumes, dried, shelled, peeled or unpeeled, chopped or not chopped	
	UAE	$1041.5 thousand
3	Optical, photographic, cinematographic, measuring, control, precision, medical or surgical instruments and apparatus parts and accessories	
	UAE	$13.2 thousand
	Oman	$0.2 thousand
4	Other plates, sheets, films and strips or tapes, of plastics, non-porous and unreinforced, non-laminated, without a backing and not bonded in a similar way to other materials	
	UAE	$2.3 thousand
5	Electrical machinery and equipment, their parts; sound recording and reproducing equipment, equipment for recording and reproducing television images and sound, their parts and accessories	
	UAE	$4 thousand
6	Furniture; bedding, mattresses, mattress supports, cushions and similar stuffed furniture; lamps and lighting fittings	
	Oman	$1538.3 thousand
7	Means of land transport, other than railway or tram rolling stock, and their parts and accessories	
	Oman	$0.2 thousand
8	Trailers and semi-trailers; other non-self-propelled vehicles and their parts	
	Oman	$0.2 thousand

Total export

Counterpart country	Export December 2019	January–December 2019
UAE	$27.5 thousand	$703.7 thousand
Oman	$4 thousand	$1077.9 thousand

Source: Ministry of Industry and Innovation Policy Regarding the Republic of Bashkortostan.

of engagements with the GCC states. On the question of why comprehensive discussions with Saudi Arabia did not result in investment projects, he stressed the presence of 'very serious competition'. He clarified:

> Many countries around the world are fighting for interest, including the investment interest of Saudi Arabia. We understand them as a country that has a very serious financial cushion that plans to diversify its business at the country level, including looking for investment opportunities and external investment [reference to Saudi Vision 2030]. Here so far regions of Russia have not been able to compete with whole countries that are actively attempting to get Saudi investments.

Mirsaiapov believes that one solution can be a consolidated platform to present the regions of Russia, for example, to have a united stand for the regions of the Russian Federation, at such platforms as the Annual Investment Meeting in the UAE. He concludes: 'It seems to us that we need to unite at some stage, step over the regional framework and go out together.'

Despite efforts towards the further building of a 'halal lifestyle', especially in the export of halal products, Bashkortostan products are not certified for the Arabian states' measures. Ainur Akkulov,[92] vice-president of the Union of the Chamber of Commerce and Industry of the Republic of Bashkortostan stated in February 2020:

> For example, we have halal products, but the certification system in the Russian Federation does not suit the requirements of the Gulf states. We have just sent our specialists to meet those requirements and conditions so that our halal products can be sent to these countries. They are trained, in other words, in the Chamber of Commerce and Industry; we are creating a certification centre for halal products, and we will try to increase this turnover [based on halal production]. Today, in general, there are still such export options so that we can send costless products there.

This might illustrate the potential for building up the halal economy, but with limited existing mechanisms, which limits collaborations. Nonetheless, developments in this direction might suggest further relations based on shared Muslim identities. In comparison to the North Caucasus, this issue does not remain such a challenge, since in Dagestan, for example, there is already a 'halal landscape'.[93]

It should also be noted that among other challenges of relations with the Gulf states, shared Muslim identities can themselves require some finesse. Karamyshev Ruslan, the leading adviser to the Council for State Confessional Relations under the Head of the Republic of Bashkortostan, shares that they intend to 'tread carefully' and, rather, 'observe how agreements will be developed'. This can be seen in comments on the Saudi efforts to follow the path of 'moderate Islam' under the current leadership, as Karamyshev speculates:

> In the first place, they have not created anything conclusive yet. Even from their statements that we can see today, it is clear for us that there is more politics than religion. We can not yet talk about serious shifts in the plan of religion – practice, especially dogmatics. Therefore, it is premature to call it a new Islam or something. Second, we carefully call it de-Wahhabisation. Here, in addition, in the religious or confessional sphere, quick action is not just in our nature, due to our historical experience [he refers here to activities of the Central Spiritual Board of Muslims Internal to Russia and Siberia located in Ufa]; we know they can lead to a whole chain of irreversible actions or irreversible results. Therefore, any decisions, including on cooperation, are worked out not just for months, but years, and the position is agreed several times in advance.

These differences with the *madhahib* of the GCC states remain of concern for both sides (particularly in the Volga region) and must be negotiated in the journey towards further close relations.

As a final interesting observation, with similarities to Tatarstan's position on the Gulf crisis, Mirsaiapov[94] concludes that Bashkortostan has attempted to develop relations with all states equally. Here we could view how those geopolitical dynamics in the region might affect the North Caucasus and their relations with the Gulf states. Both Tatarstan and Bashkortostan have prioritized the development of economic relations based on Islamic identities with the Gulf states, rather than considering Muslim identities and their usage for political purposes – largely due to the restrictions under which they carry out their paradiplomacy.

6.3 Conclusion

To support the argument of this book – that shared identities boost cooperation between 'Self(s)' and minority 'Self(s)' of another state (1) if 'Self(s)' and the 'Other' have interests in common, and the 'Other' is willing to integrate its minorities into this process; and (2) if 'Self(s)' and minority 'Self(s)' have shared interests – this chapter has looked closely at relations between other Russian regions with a dense Muslim population and the Arabian states. Similarly to the Tatar case, it can be concluded that relations have generally boomed alongside the Kremlin's interest in further developing collaborations and integrating its minorities into its federal policies. Shared Islamic identities have been crucial for this. As we look into it in greater detail, it can be seen how each republic has followed its own mechanisms to increase its links with the Gulf states. For example, in the Chechen case, relations have been mainly based on the personal links of its head Ramzan Kadyrov, and his authority and friendship with the Gulf leaders, which were in turn initially based on connections with his father's network; Akhmad Kadyrov's status in regional politics is considerable. This is further boosted by Ramzan Kadyrov's strategic policy of building relations based on shared Islamic identities. As a result, Chechnya has chosen a policy of organizing Islamic conferences and religious forums, aiming to connect or bridge Russia with Muslim authorities and the Muslim world in general. Dagestan meanwhile relies on such Islamic identities, and conducts policies that draw on diaspora businessmen, with one of the outcomes being the emergence of an economic 'halal landscape'. This chapter has attempted to demonstrate that the internal dynamics between republics also play a role, such as the Ingushetia and Chechnya border dispute, in conjunction with the Gulf crisis. By comparison with the North Caucasus style, which largely remains on the individual level – friendships between leaders (Chechnya), individuals links with specific diaspora representatives of businessmen (Dagestan) and religious authorities (Ingushetia) – Bashkortostan's paradiplomacy is more like the Tatarstan case – relying mainly on interdepartmental collaborations to conduct these policies. Bashkortostan profits from the Khakimov factor, especially in its relations with Saudi Arabia, aiming to develop a marketable 'halal lifestyle' based on Muslim identities to develop its economy. Nonetheless, these relations remain somewhat limited in comparison to its neighbour.

Afterword

The impact of the Ukraine conflict on Gulf–Moscow–Kazan relations

In closing this book, it is worth noting a little of the context of its production. It was written prior to the Russia–Ukraine conflict,[1] which began on 24 February 2022. In this transformative period of international politics, the future dynamics of Tatarstan–GCC relations (along with other Muslim republics and the Gulf states) have become even more complex, despite shared Islamic identities. Nonetheless, the context of the Ukraine conflict further assists in developing the main propositions that the book aims to offer. In this chapter the future of Moscow–Gulf states relations and their potential paths will be considered, including the potential political, economic and geopolitical outcomes of the Ukraine conflict. This analysis then extends to the implications of such geopolitical realities on federal–regional relations within the Russian Federation – relations between Moscow and Kazan – and then a discussion of what the future may hold for Tatarstan–GCC relations.

7.1 The impact of the Ukraine conflict: Moscow and the GCC states

As of April 2022, there have already been some indicators of shifts in Russia's policies in the Middle East. As noted earlier, prior to the Russia–Ukraine conflict, Russia's foreign policies relied heavily on pursuing 'win-win' strategies to advance key Russian interests in the region. However, emerging patterns seem to suggest that Russia may be adopting more 'zero-sum' strategies, and bilateral relations with some Gulf members appear to be heading towards a fork in the road.[2]

While the Gulf states were not forthcoming about their views on the annexation of Crimea in 2014, they had generally expressed support for the UN General Assembly's resolution on the territorial integrity of Ukraine in 2014. This cautious attitude can plausibly be linked to the Middle East's regional changes and security architectures as a consequence of the Arab Spring.[3] At the time, the international community regarded the situation as a confrontation between Russia and the West, rather than a confrontation between Russia and Ukraine. Since then, due to the political complexities surrounding Russia's active stance in regional affairs (and particularly since its intervention in Syria in 2015), each of the GCC states has pursued a policy of neutrality towards Moscow's actions in Eastern Europe. Today, the GCC states' voices resonate more loudly. They have expressed different views on the conflict, demonstrating how divided the Gulf remains; while some have remained strictly neutral and others have attempted to hedge their bets between Russia and the West, others have come out in full force for one side or the other, in part due to their own historical experiences. Existing competition between the Gulf states themselves has led some to gamble by showing direct or indirect support to both sides of the conflict, perhaps envisioning fundamental changes in the security order in Europe, and the coming change to the balance of power globally, as a result of the conflict.

7.1.1 Bahrain and Oman responses: Strict neutrality

Bahrain has not expressed a clear position on the Russo–Ukrainian conflict. However, likely due to its close security partnership with the United States, it has tended views friendly towards Washington, and by extension, the United Nations. In 2014, Bahrain supported the UN General Assembly resolution defending the territorial integrity of Ukraine. During discussions between Ukrainian deputy foreign minister Emine Dzheppar and Bahraini deputy foreign minister Abdullah bin Ahmad al-Khalifa, the latter reaffirmed[4] 'Bahrain's support for Ukraine's territorial integrity and emphasized his country's principled position on preventing Bahraini companies from carrying out any activities in the temporarily occupied Crimea.' At the same time, as noted in earlier chapters, from interviews with Bahrain's political stakeholders it is clear that Manama wants to expand its international relations with all major powers, and concerns over the Russia–Ukraine dispute have not been considered an impediment to that relationship. The importance of diplomatic solutions to resolve the conflict in Ukraine – discussed between Bahrain's king, Hamad bin Isa al-Khalifa, and Russian president Vladimir Putin in March 2022 – only support this view.[5]

This also suggests that Bahrain will seek to maintain a neutral stance on the current crisis. Potentially, this offers a pathway towards relations with Kazan in the future based on shared Islamic identities, drawing on a common agenda for both Moscow and Manama; as mentioned earlier, both Kazan and Manama seem positive on potential engagements and collaborations.

Similarly, the Sultanate of Oman took a relatively neutral stance. Oman expressed concerns over the escalating military build-up on January 25.[6] During his official visit to Oman in May 2022, the Russian foreign minister, Sergey Lavrov, met with Omani Sultan Haitham bin Tariq. During the press conference, Lavrov said that Muscat and Moscow have 'identical positions on most international issues', praising Oman's 'objective and balanced' stance on the Ukraine conflict.[7] Oman's reluctance to back one side or the other in the conflict can be understood within the broader context of its political course, as Oman is known for its policies of neutrality.[8] At the same time, economic considerations will likely play a role in any further developments. Although Oman is a relatively minor energy exporter compared to its richer neighbours, its oil revenue has continued to rise throughout the crisis. This has had two independent impacts on the Omani economy, one negative and one positive. As the writer and economic analyst Khalfan al-Touqi explained to the Times of Oman: 'The rise will cause inflation in countries importing goods, and that includes the Sultanate of Oman, since they import a majority of [their] goods. The positive side is that the government will pay off debts, and the credit level of the Sultanate will rise.'[9] Given this balance it does not seem that Oman will shift from its current neutrality at present, which also politically offers an open door to maintain relations with Tatarstan. That said, the quite limited collaborations that already exist between Muscat and Kazan may mean that engagements will remain relatively low.

7.1.2 Kuwait's response: Echo of its own past

By contrast, Kuwait's position on the Russian actions has been very clear – perhaps unsurprising considering its own historical experience. On February 24, the day of the 'special military operation', the state of Kuwait underlined the importance of respecting the independence and sovereignty of Ukraine and categorically rejected the 'use, threat to use, or displaying of force' in conducting relations between countries.[10] Such a statement draws an implicit parallel between Ukraine's experience in February 2022 and Kuwait's in August 1990, when Iraqi dictator Saddam Hussein ordered his army to invade Kuwait.[11] At the same time, a different analogy between the past can be made: as noted earlier, one of the five permanent members of the UN Security Council, the Soviet Union played an important role in the adoption of resolutions demanding that Iraq immediately withdraw its troops from Kuwait and recognize its independence and sovereignty. At the time, not only Kuwait but all its GCC partners appreciated the principled position of the USSR. Saudi Arabia restored diplomatic contacts with Russia in that period and facilitated Moscow's establishment of relations with Bahrain. In general, while other Gulf states remained in the Western bloc during the Cold War, Kuwait, which concluded an agreement with the Soviets to establish diplomatic ties in March 1963, remained the most receptive of all the GCC states to Moscow's interests. It is still unclear whether their former friendly past or current realities will shift relations between Kuwait and Russia. Ultimately, given the somewhat limited collaborations between Kazan and Kuwait to date, the impact of the Ukraine war may also have quite limited effects in this regard.

7.1.3 Saudi Arabia, Qatar and the UAE: Relations at the fork in the road?

Three further actors – Saudi Arabia, the UAE and Qatar – have been in the spotlight even prior to the Ukraine conflict, and the conflict may presage potential transformation in relations towards Kazan. Most clearly, this links to relations between Russia and Qatar, which are at a significant fork in the road. By prioritizing its national interests and maintaining close relations with the Western bloc, Qatar has perhaps most explicitly demonstrated its position through condemnations of Russian actions and gestures of support for Ukraine. On the day of the 'special operation', Ukrainian president Zelensky wrote in Twitter:[12] 'I continue negotiations with the leaders [of Qatar] . . . [Ukraine has] received support from the Emir of Qatar.' The Doha Forum hosted by Qatar on 26–27 March included representatives from Ukraine and Western countries, but no high-ranking representatives from Russia.[13] Along with the Amir of Qatar, Shaykh Tamim, and president of the United Nations General Assembly, Abdulla Shahid, President Zelensky addressed the Forum. Emine Dzhaparova, Ukraine's first deputy minister of Foreign Affairs, participated in several panels. The panel 'Crisis in Ukraine: A Defining Moment for European Security' included Dzhaparova. The rest of the panel members – Pawel Jablonski, a Polish Undersecretary of State; Patrick Turner, NATO assistant secretary general for Defense Policy and Planning; and Karin von Hippel, director general of the UK-based think tank RUSI – represented various Western powers and organizations. Russian officials were not invited to participate. This rather obvious show of support for the Ukrainian cause at such a sensitive time may spell danger for the bilateral relationship between Doha and Moscow in the short- to medium-term, including damage to all initiatives with Tatarstan discussed earlier.

This potential scenario of downgraded relations between Doha and Moscow, within the context of this manuscript, reflects limitations to the common interests between 'Self' and the 'Other', which will also affect relations between 'Self' and the minority 'Self' of another state, meaning downgraded relations between Kazan and Doha, too. A rupture in Qatar–Russia relations is made more probable by the emergent economic competition between the two states. Indeed, Qatar has become one of Europe's best hopes of weaning itself off Russian natural gas. Germany, France, Belgium and Italy have all begun talks with Qatar to buy liquefied natural gas (LNG) on a long-term basis.[14] Germany has already agreed to a long-term energy partnership with Qatar, although the complexity of negotiating energy flows must be considered when judging the potential of such an arrangement.[15] In a recent interview, Dr Nikolay Kozhanov, a research associate professor at the Gulf Studies Center of Qatar University, explained:[16]

> In the short run, the GCC countries that can theoretically play an important role in the diversification of European supply sources are unlikely to be able to significantly increase the exports of their hydrocarbons to the EU. However, the trend of a growing Middle Eastern presence in the European oil and gas market has been set, and within the next five to seven years it might lead to a decrease in the Russian share of the regional market.

In this sense, while Doha has already demonstrated its readiness to come to the aid of Western countries over the last six months, physical limitations on the ability of Qatar to increase export volumes remain. These obstacles will continue to hamper Europe's efforts to rid itself of Russian gas. Other challenges, such as Moscow's demand that European states pay for Russian gas in rubles, place immense pressure on Western states.[17] How Europe will respond to these developments remains uncertain. It also remains to be seen how Western sanctions on Russian hydrocarbon exports will impact the international financial system. Russia has sought ways to circumvent the dollar-dominated financial system – including the possibility of using the Chinese renminbi to sell its gas and oil abroad.[18] Qatar, which seeks to expand its LNG export profile and maintain the current oil trading system, may view Russia's actions as inimical to its long-term interests.

The Ukrainian conflict is not merely an energy issue, however. Long-term security cooperation between Qatar and the United States has driven the emirate to align more closely with Washington in recent years. For the same reason, Doha has drifted away from Moscow. The current strength of the US–Qatar relationship is based on ties developed during the Shaykh Hamad era, as well as Qatar's overriding security concerns as a small state. The centrality of al-Udeid Air Base to US deployments in the region, Washington's recognition of Qatar as a 'Major Non-NATO Ally' and ongoing Qatari mediation efforts – such as liaising between the United States and the Taliban in Afghanistan – all exemplify the depth of US–Qatar ties and the symbiotic nature of the relationship.

The Ukraine crisis may force Qatar to align even closer to the United States, bandwagoning with its powerful partner. This behaviour would be highly unusual, given that Moscow is not a major threat to Doha's security and remains a relatively tangential actor within the Gulf region. Despite this, states within the international system have come to recognize Russia's potential for aggression and Moscow's willingness to use force to further its interests. Given such developments, relations between Moscow and Qatar could be downgraded in the short- to mid-term, moving Doha closer to the West. In turn, this might shift the strategic calculations of Qatar's neighbours. Although ties between Doha and several Gulf monarchies have been on the mend recently, many of Qatar's fellow GCC member states remain wary. Qatar's continued movement towards the United States opens the doors for Qatar's neighbours, such as Saudi Arabia and the United Arab Emirates, who have thus far demonstrated a marked neutrality in the Russia–Ukraine conflict, to develop relationships with other states on either side of the conflict.

For example, Saudi Arabia, the region's biggest player, has perhaps the most challenging balancing act to maintain between Russia and the West. Prince Turki al-Faisal, the former chief of the General Intelligence Directorate and former US, UK ambassador, commented in his interview for Arab News's Frankly Speaking programme on the Kingdom's stance on the conflict:[19]

> The Kingdom has publicly declared and voted in the UN General Assembly to condemn the aggression against Ukraine that was passed by the UN General Assembly. But also [. . .] the Kingdom offered to mediate between Russia and Ukraine as a mediator. It will have to maintain a link – if you like – and the ability to talk to both sides. So that is where the Kingdom is coming from and how it is dealing with the Ukraine issue. We've had good relations with both countries

over the years, and of course in general, as I mentioned, the Kingdom is against the aggression in Ukraine. But also, most recently, of course, the Kingdom has contributed to the fund that was established by the UN to provide support for the Ukrainian refugees in Europe. So that is where the Kingdom stands.

Riyadh's careful position can be explained by a variety of reasons – from prioritizing their national interests to their links with the external powers, especially Washington. With the Ukraine crisis, oil prices have dramatically increased over recent months. For example, on 12 December 2021, it was $65.57 per barrel, but reached a peak on 8 March 2022 of $123.70 per barrel. It decreased, then increased again, and by the end of April had reached $104.69 per barrel.[20] Nonetheless, it should be mentioned that the energy market was also reacting to other events, including the Hothi attack on Abu Dhabi on 17 January,[21] and Hothi attacks on an oil depot in Jeddah.[22] Returning to the context of the Ukraine crisis, citing the need to preserve the production agreement among OPEC and non-OPEC countries in the OPEC+ deal, Saudi Arabia refused President Biden's call to pump more oil as prices jumped past the $100 per barrel mark after the Russian 'operation' in Ukraine.[23] Bloomberg has even suggested that if the war creates any winners, one of them will be Saudi Arabia, which can benefit from a drop in competition to its reliable oil supply.[24] Nonetheless, as Dr John Sfakianakis, chief economist and head of research for the Gulf Research Centre in Riyadh, and associate fellow at Chatham House, explains, he sees both short- and medium-term impacts on Middle Eastern oil production:[25]

> One is the short-term impact, and other is the medium-term. The short-term, of course, is that the macroeconomic optics look very good for the Gulf countries: of course, because of the higher oil price, better revenues, surpluses, GDP, everything will look good this year as long as oil stays at these levels, if not rise a bit further. [. . .] Now, for the medium-term, views differ, if the Ukraine crisis continues, and this is a trigger for a global recession, of course, this is not the only trigger. This is not going to end up being so good for the Gulf oil-producing states because we will go into a demand-destruction environment. Oil prices will go down and the break-even for the entire Gulf, give or take a few dollars, is around $65 to $70 a barrel. So, if we go into a global economic recession, oil is not going to be at $70, of course – it will go below that.

Based on his analyses, in the short run we might expect continuation of the relatively neutral stance of the Kingdom, as currently the economic implications of the conflict serve their national interests.

At the same time, along with crucial energy markets, US policies under the Biden administration towards Riyadh and its leadership have influenced the Saudi balancing act.[26] As discussed in earlier chapters, this is linked with the Biden administration's stance on the Khashoggi case, and deteriorating personal relations with the Crown Prince Mohammad bin Salman, while Russia's pragmatic approach was supportive of the Saudi Crown Prince. In one interview with *The Atlantic* on 3 March 2022, a week after the beginning of the Ukraine conflict, the Saudi Crown Prince said that 'he does not care whether US President Joe Biden misunderstood things about him, saying Biden should be focusing on America's interests'.[27] Along with the Emirati leader Mohammad bin Zayed al-Nahyan, Saudi Crown Prince Mohammad bin Salman also reportedly declined US requests to speak to Mr Biden.[28] American voices reacted negatively to this, even suggesting that 'Biden should punish Saudi Arabia for backing Russia'.[29]

In response, again it might be useful to consider the Saudi voice, as presented by Prince Turki al-Faisal, who wrote a column that spread worldwide across social media, under the title 'America should laugh with the Kingdom, not scowl'. The piece gives his interpretations of differing American coverage of current events, and still offers some optimism in relations:[30]

> American politicians of all political persuasions shoot arrows at the Kingdom to criticise and demean, even to the extent of calling for a carrot and stick approach to dealing with Saudi Arabia. I tell them that we are not school children who accept such chastisement and reward. Our friendship with the US stems from our shared interest in finding peace in the Middle East, combating terrorism, and challenging Iran's aggression and its declared animosity to both of us. [. . .] We also share mutual benefits from the business exchanges and development projects in the Kingdom, ties that have grown over the years and will continue to grow in the years to come.

Despite such polarized positions, the view of Kristian Ulrichsen, a non-resident Senior Fellow at the Arab Centre, Washington DC, who eloquently puts forward his analyses on 'The GCC and the Russia–Ukraine Crisis', can be considered the most accurate future scenario for consideration:[31]

> It may be premature to speak of a post-American Gulf in the networks and structure of US force posture in the region (and it is a matter of some irony that the pivot to Asia that so raised Emirati and Saudi apprehensions of US disengagement referred to a pivot not from the Gulf but from Europe). Still, however, it could be the case that the Russian invasion of Ukraine has accelerated the process of geopolitical drift between American interests and those of its partners in the Gulf, or some of them.

Within the context of this book, it is clear that further relations between Riyadh and Washington are important to consider further, as these relations will in turn shape upcoming relations between Moscow and Riyadh. With existing mutual interests, and existing economic and investment interconnections between Riyadh and Washington, it is expected that relations will be normalized over time. Nonetheless, Riyadh might choose to further maintain neutral relations between the two poles of Moscow and Washington. What may this mean for Kazan and Riyadh relations, and Russian Muslims in general? Given the special status of the Kingdom as the guardian of Muslims worldwide, especially being the guardian of holy places for Muslims, such as Mecca and Medina, Riyadh will always be important to Russia's 20 to 25 million Muslims. In other words, in any scenarios of relations between Moscow and Riyadh, however affected by Washington, for the Kremlin and Riyadh this factor of Muslim identities will always have the potential to serve as common ground, and as a link for maintaining relations based on this factor. The question might emerge whether the role of Tatars will become similar to that between 1920 and the 1930s, when ethnic Tatars (diplomats and religious authorities) played a vital role in creating and boosting these relations. Alternatively, will relations between modern Tatarstan and Saudi Arabia continue to develop, given that Tatarstan's leadership play a crucial role in the Group of the Strategic Vision 'Russian-Muslim world'? This will be examined alongside the dynamics between Kazan and Moscow, after the examination of another important regional player and their stance on the Ukraine conflict – the United Arab Emirates.

The UAE appears to have calculated the potential advantages of actively balancing both sides. On February 23, Russian and Emirati foreign ministers Sergey Lavrov and Shaykh Abdullah bin Zayed discussed the two countries' friendly relations and strategic partnerships, stressing their 'keenness to enhance the prospects of UAE-Russian cooperation across various fields for the higher good of their peoples', in a joint statement.[32] Subsequently, on February 25, the day after the beginning of the Russian military operation, Shaykh Abdullah and US secretary of state Antony Blinken discussed the Russian attack over the telephone.[33] On February 26, the UAE abstained from the US-backed United Nations Security Council resolution opposing the Russian military operation against Ukraine,[34] calling for immediate de-escalation and cessation of hostilities.[35] There were only three abstainers in total – China, India and the UAE.

The position of the UAE towards the Ukrainian crisis is expressed precisely by the Dr Ebtesam al-Ketbi, who is the president and founder of the Emirates Policy Centre. Her explanations are especially important, as it is known that her powerful voice advocates for and expresses the UAE's position. In her paper 'Prospects of UAE-US relations in a New Strategic Environment'[36] she explains the UAE stance on the crisis as follows: while emphasizing the safeguarding of its national interests and pursuing an independent policy, the UAE reiterates its commitment to the OPEC+agreement with Russia and other countries. Also, the UAE has tried to avoid polarization among the great powers. The UAE has called for de-escalation of tension between Russia and Ukraine, supported diplomatic resolutions to the crisis and encouraged mediation to end the war. Finally, the UAE has continued its contacts with all parties to the crisis and provided humanitarian aid.[37]

Within the context of this book, the argument that Dr al-Ketbi makes about the Emirati efforts to avoid polarization among the great powers deserves particular attention. She explains that while the UAE abstained from the vote on the United Nations Security Council resolution, the UAE nonetheless joined the UN General Assembly in denouncing Russian interference in Ukraine. Interestingly, she also stresses that 'the UAE reaped the dividends of its balanced position when Moscow favored renewing the arms embargo on Yemen and designating Houthis as a "terrorist movement" in the UN Security Council'.[38] This balanced position regarding Moscow and the increasing geopolitical relationships between Moscow and Abu Dhabi was discussed in earlier chapters, noting the influence of the Washington factor in these moves. As this chapter offers potential scenarios and the impact of the Ukraine conflict on Abu Dhabi–Moscow–Kazan relations, it must also consider the Emirati perspective on UAE–US relations, as this factor has a direct effect on the former.

It should, indeed, be noted that UAE–US relations have been strong since the opening of the US Embassy in 1974, while the United States was among the first to recognize the UAE immediately after its inception in December 1971.[39] The strong relations can be illustrated in bilateral trade – $23 billion.[40] This dwarfs the equivalent trade between Abu Dhabi and Moscow, which was only $4 billion in 2021, notwithstanding the story of strengthening collaborations that this book has demonstrated.[41] The UAE has participated in the US-led military operations in Kuwait, Afghanistan, Serbia and Iraq, as well as the NATO US-led mission in Libya.[42] Nonetheless, as illustrated earlier, the UAE has attempted to maintain a balance between both powers. Abdulkhaleq Abdulla, an Emirati political science professor commented in the Financial Times:[43] 'We no longer need a green light from America or any other western capital to decide on our national interest.' He continued, 'We are not with or against – that is the position.

If America is upset, they will just have to level with that.' This provides a strong echo of the explanations given by Dr al-Ketbi.

Specifically, in the paper 'UAE-US Relations: What Went Wrong?' published by the Arab Gulf States Institute in Washington, Mohammad Baaroon, the director general of b'huth, explains how the relationship reached such a perceived crisis, which he explains as rooted in the United States' strategic shift, specifically the 'pivot East' foreign policy of the administration of former President Barack Obama. The finalization of the JCPOA in 2015 without consultation with the GCC countries was perceived by the Gulf states as an effort to reduce US security involvement in the Middle East. The great blow was the US position on the offensive of the Iranian-supported Houthi movement in Yemen.[44] Dr Ebtesam al-Ketbi argues that tensions between Abu Dhabi and Washington are the outcome of a long-running accumulation of factors, including the uncertainty regarding Washington's continued commitment to regional security, the US elections and overcoming Trump's legacy. On the final point she returns again to the great power factor, suggesting that a divergence of America and the Emirati implies closer interests and ties with China and Russia.

Among the potential scenarios for dealing with the current tension in UAE–US relations, Dr al-Ketbi considers the following: continuation of the status quo; enlarging and deepening of the strategic framework of relations and redefining relations; and signing a bilateral defence treaty, establishing a regional defence umbrella scenario. She concludes that 'the Ukrainian crisis presents an opportunity to redefine the UAE–US relations. It is a time to suggest new approaches to enhance, develop, and institutionalise the Emirati-American strategic partnership to contain tension; guarantee, and expand, mutual interests; develop the UAE's defence capabilities; and confront threats to safeguard its larger interests.'[45] It is unclear at this stage in which direction relations move, though clearly from the Emirati views expressed, the country is following its own national interests, and will develop relations with the external powers based on these. Finally, the author's trip to Abu Dhabi in March 2022 only strengthened the impression that the country will continue its balancing act. The country aims to welcome and be open to everyone – citizens' representatives of all parties involved in the conflict. It consequently seems likely that the UAE will continue to balance relations with all sides, including relations with Russia. This may also offer positive scenarios for relations with Tatarstan, and the continuation of ongoing projects with the republic, including whose which are based on shared Muslim identities.

Despite a generally positive prognosis, obstacles remain. Among them are the sanctions introduced by the West, especially in the economic and financial fields. For example, the EU has restricted access to US primary and secondary capital markets for certain Russian banks and companies, prohibited transactions with the Russian Central Bank of Belarus, introduced a SWIFT ban for certain Russian and Belarussian banks, prohibited the provision of euro-denomination banknotes to Russia and Belarus, blocked public financing or investment in Russia and halted investment in or contribution to projects co-financed by the Russian Direct Investment Fund.[46] The United States' sanctions include economic measures to ban new investment in Russia, severe sanctions on two Russian financial institutions (Alfa Bank and Sberbank) and sanctions on critical major state-owned enterprises. Meanwhile, the United States has committed to ending all imports of Russian coal and oil by the end of 2022.[47]

Although it has not applied similar sanctions against Russia, the Abu Dhabi Wealth Fund, Mubadala, has paused investments in Russia.[48] Moreover, the Qatar Investment Authority (QIA) has also reportedly decided to place a hold on Russian assets worth billions of dollars.[49] That said, Mubadala, which has at least $3 billion worth of exposure to Russia, is 'unlikely to unwind its partnership with the Kremlin-run Russian Direct Investment Fund, as the company does not want to hamper the relationship with Kremlin'.[50] This suggests that beyond the short term there are more positive prospects for relations with Tatarstan, which is a major beneficiary of these funds. Assuming the flow will continue, there is potential for more future collaborations between Tatarstan and UAE based on such investments. Similarly, it is also clear that the QIA, which has a roughly 19 per cent stake in Rosneft PJSC, considers the investment key to supporting Doha's relations with Moscow.[51] This also potentially offers the opportunity and expectation of investment from Qatar to Tatarstan, discussions over which had been in progress prior to the Ukraine crisis.

It can even be argued that Western sanctions may have a positive effect on the Gulf–Russia relations. Displaced by sanctions and unwelcomed in the West, Russian oligarchs are reportedly fleeing sanctions and, instead, hunting for houses in Dubai.[52] The UAE facilitates such a diaspora of wealth through a 'golden visa' programme, which provides long-term residency for foreigners if they invest at least 10 million dirhams ($2.7 million) in a local company or investment fund; this may naturally plant seeds for further investment collaborations between the UAE and Russia in the future.[53] It is unclear to what extent Tatars ethnic businessmen moves in circles likely to relocate to the emirate, but such a diaspora can emerge as another link for flourishing relations between Tatarstan and the UAE. Shared Muslim identities can only complement potential business projects, including further development of the so-called 'halal lifestyle', which was a priority for the Tatarstan leadership prior to the Ukraine moment. In the broader context, the movement of Russian citizens, potentially representatives of the Russian Muslim republics, from the West to the Gulf offers new opportunities. As mentioned earlier, there are already established examples of the important role of diaspora populations in building connections, even as far back as Dagestan's attempts to boost relations between the Gulf states and the Dagestan republic through appeal to an ancient lineage. It is consequently timely that Gulf representatives will attend the XIII International Economic Summit 'Russia-Islamic World: Kazan Summit 2022' (19–21 May), which is dedicated to the 1100th anniversary of the adoption of Islam by the Volga Bulgaria. The event and its themes are another positive indicator for future collaborations, despite all current obstacles, and will specifically rely on shared Islamic identities. In some respects, Islamic banking and Islamic economics might serve as an alternative to the Western sanctions, so that while boosting relations between 'Self' and the 'Other', there can be positives for the minority 'Self' and 'Self' relations, too.

7.2 Future relations between Moscow and Kazan

Even with potential positive expectations for the relations between Russia and the GCC states, especially with Saudi Arabia and the United Araba Emirates, states which already have good working collaborations with Tatarstan based on shared Muslim identities, it appears another vital question must be considered: Will the Kremlin continue to be interested in integrating Muslim communities into federal polices and bilateral relationships with the GCC states? This book was written during a discussion about the law and public power – specifically the project entitled 'On the general principles of the organisation of public power in the subjects of the Federation' by Andrey Klishas and Pavel Krasheninnikov.[54] The propositions of this important work had been discussed intently in Tatarstan, as the republic retained the only remaining 'President' status, and this was abolished on July 12, 2022. On November 9, the Duma adopted this initiative at the first reading, and on December 14, it successfully passed the second and third readings. Russian president Vladimir Putin signed it into law in December 2021. The federal government is expected to appoint heads of regions and even ministers. According to this law, heads of regions are banned from being called presidents.

The change went through despite opposition from Tatarstan, and such transformations also add to uncertainties around the current leading role of Tatarstan as the chairman of the Group of the Strategic Vision 'Russia-Muslim world'. This includes potential changes in the (formerly) President's status in terms of both internal and external relations. Will relations between the federal centre and the region become more asymmetrical? Will a more direct line of authority to the Kremlin mean the Tatarstan leader will be granted more responsibility for building closer relations with the Muslim world through the Group of the Strategic Vision 'Russia-Muslim world', or the opposite, reducing him to a mere figurehead? Ultimately, will the deliberate integration of Tatars into the process of building relations with the Muslim world, including the GCC states, continue as an important part of strategy, or will their role decline?

This final thought does not aim to reflect changes in the federal legislation, but, rather, to highlight the powerful force of the Russian Muslim regions, and their shared Islamic identities – which can be perceived as needing to be controlled by the central government, yet may also have deep positive potential. Paradiplomatic efforts – so often overlooked in current scholarship – help to build closer diplomatic and cultural ties along with economic links, which is particularly beneficial for Russia to further strengthen its presence in the Middle East. This becomes more apparent in comparison with other external powers, whose access to viable shared identities is more limited, such as the Western states or China (whose policies include oppression of its own Muslim Uygur population).[55] In some respects the European response to the Ukraine crisis has thrown this into sharp relief, because of the stark contrast in the response to the Ukrainians' suffering compared to similar conflict sites around the world, notably Syria and Yemen. In essence, Europe has identified Ukrainians as more 'like us' than Muslim populations in the Middle East. This is despite huge Muslim populations in France, Germany and the UK, who nonetheless appear not to have the deep roots of Muslim populations in Russian regions. This has a strong effect on the dynamics of 'Self' and 'Other', and reflects Russia's ability to mobilize a minority 'Self' in ways that the West cannot or chooses not to do. In France there has been a long debate about the place of Muslims, and the French government's efforts to reconcile secular arrangements with greater respect for religion,[56] along with controversies about the treatment of refugees from the Middle East and Afghanistan, for example. In British society the situation is less stark, at least legally, and the state sees clear advantages in having greater flexibility in institutional arrangements, particularly in building partnerships with Muslim elites and selecting its interlocutors from a variety of organizations.[57] However, the

Brexit vote, when different identities were among the main reasons for many to vote to exit the EU, showed a euro-centric bias, too. Despite some racism towards eastern Europeans (with Ukrainians lumped together with Poles, for example), the current Ukraine crisis has contributed to making them 'more European', and defenders of European democratic values. This form of cultural xenophobia cannot have gone unnoticed in Muslim circles, both within and outside the UK, and may have subtle but extensive effects on future relations with the Gulf.

By contrast, as this book has argued, Russia has currently put itself in a very strong position to further integrate its minorities, leaning on a long history and build stronger relations with the Gulf states, along with other Muslim countries. Moscow has in some ways come to terms with the 'mistakes' of repressing Muslim diplomats and Muslim authorities that led to frozen relations with the Arabian states, and since the 2000s these same Muslim actors have contributed to Russia's return to the Middle East. In other words, Russia can derive benefits from its multinationalism and multiethnicity, and giving more opportunities to Russian regions to conduct paradiplomatic efforts would not only be beneficial to those regions and the Gulf states but also be crucial to the success of Moscow's foreign policies, its political objectives and its economic future.

7.3 Conclusion

This chapter has offered a set of considered scenarios and outcomes of the Ukraine conflict, considering the responses of each of the GCC states, offering possible developments of relations with Moscow, and consequently Kazan. The Ukraine crisis illustrated several of the fundamental arguments of the book as a whole, bringing into view the role that can be played by shared identities and appeals to a commonly understood history. Shared identities boost cooperation between 'Self(s)' and minority 'Self(s)' of another state (1) if 'Self(s)' and the 'Other' have interests in common, and the 'Other' is willing to integrate its minorities into this process; and (2) if 'Self(s)' and minority 'Self(s)' have shared interests. The responses of the GCC states to the Ukraine crisis will shape interests in common between 'Self(s)' and the 'Other'. Given the balancing act of both Saudi Arabia and the UAE it is expected that relations will be further developed between these two states and Moscow, and Muslim identities, most powerfully through relations with Tatarstan, have an important role to play. Western sanctions have both created diplomatic and practical obstacles, and opened the door to an appeal to common culture as well as common interests. The question might remain how relations between the federal centre and the regional centre will be further shaped, and whether Moscow will still willingly integrate its (Tatar) minorities into federal policies. Clearly, the policy has immense potential. It is worth noting that the two Gulf states whose attempts to balance relations have been most visible and substantial are also those with the strongest existing relations with Tatarstan and other Russian Muslim regions. While their primary motivations are the protection of national interests, and direct relations with Washington, the often overlooked factor of a shared Muslim identity with Tatarstan/Russian Muslims doubtless contributes to the manner and substance of their largely neutral positioning.

On a concluding note, the author would like to stress that this manuscript has been produced in very challenging and transformative times, driven by great power competitions and the struggle for the future of the international system. At this stage, in the early days of May 2022, there are many remaining questions, and fewer clear answers: What is next? How will the world move on from here? What does the threat of nuclear weapons say about the fragility of the status quo? Given the fact that the war in Europe is an indirect confrontation between the great powers, it is worth reminding the reader that there is a tendency in the West to measure everything that is happening in the Russian Federation through the prism of this conflict. Partisan narratives seek to reduce the 'Other' to a simplistic villain, while distracting away from one's own involvement in competing national interests and contested histories. If nothing else, this book aims to provide a reminder that every country is a construct from many diverse aspects, pursuing goals both visible and elusive, and that forces of pragmatism, personal relationships and cultural history can play a defining part in questions of policy and diplomacy. Above all, there is a diversity of identities within any nation, which should not be overlooked by scholarship, or other interested parties. Particularly in the writing of this book, the author would like to express her greatest appreciation to all Tatar ethnic diplomats, religious scholars and politicians, those involved in business and political process and those who have been contributing greatly to establish close relations between Soviet/ modern Russia and the Gulf states. They provide an example to the international community of the important role of Muslim minorities in Russia, even if their actions can be hard to perceive without knowledge of the context. Similar situations exist in many other countries, and the model put forward in this book seeks to assist in bringing these factors to the fore. Finally, I have a personal hope that the book will prompt further interest in the culture and history of Russian Muslims, both as bridges in foreign policy during turbulent times and as unique and resourceful agents in their own right.

Notes

Chapter 1

1   Patrick Wintour, 'Saudi King's Visit to Russia Heralds Shift in Global Power Structures', *The Guardian*, 5 October 2017. Available at: https://www.theguardian .com/world/2017/oct/05/saudi-russia-visit-putin-oil-middle-east.

2   Al Jazeera, 'Putin Visits Saudi Arabia in Sign of Growing Ties', 14 October 2019. Available at: https://www.aljazeera.com/news/2019/10/14/putin-visits-saudi-arabia -in-sign-of-growing-ties.

3   Al Jazeera, 'Russia's Putin Signs Deals Worth $1.3.bn During UAE Visit', 15 October 2019. Available at: https://www.aljazeera.com/economy/2019/10/15/russias-putin -signs-deals-worth-1-3bn-during-uae-visit.

4   Section 1.3, Contributions to the argument and its relationship with existing explanations offers a broad literature review. As an example of this point, a recent volume on Russia–GCC–Iran relations, see Nikolay Kozhanov (ed.), *Russia's Relations with the GCC and Iran* (Singapore: Palgrave Macmillan, 2021).

5   Karim Khakimov was general consul of RSFSR/USSR in Mushhad and Rasht (Persia) during 1921–24, consul general, then plenipotentiary of the USSR in Jeddah, between 1924 and 1928, plenipotentiary representative in the Kingdom of Yemen during 1929–31 and the head of Soviet representation in Saudi Arabia between 1936 and 1937.

6   Vitaly Naumkin, *Failed Partnership: Soviet Diplomacy in Saudi Arabia Between the World Wars* [*Nesostoyavsheesya partnerstvo: Sovetskaya diplomatia v Saudovskoi Arabii mechdu mirovymi voynami*] (Moscow: Aspect Press, 2018).

7   Olga Kudrina, 'Rustam Minnikhanov Boosts Links with the Muslim World' ['Rustam Minnikhanov ukreplyaet svizi s Islamskim mirom'], *Kommersant*, 8 February 2017. Available at: https://www.kommersant.ru/doc/3213546

8   Stephen Page, *The USSR and Arabia: The Development of Soviet Policies and Attitudes Towards the Countries of the Arabian Peninsula, 1955–1970* (Michigan: University of Michigan, 1971).

9   See Z. Ishtvan, 'Volzhskie Bulgary I Islam' [Volga Bolgars and Islam], *Minbar Islamic Studies* 4, no. 2 (2011): 52–6. Available at: https://www.minbar.su/jour/ article/view/92

10   Ravil Bukharaev, *Islam in Russia: The Four Seasons* (Richmond: Curzon Press, 2000), x. As the author explains, his analyses mostly rely on studies of the Muslim

regions of Tatarstan, Bashkortostan, the federal districts of the lower Volga region, Ural and Siberia, as well as populations in Moscow, Saint Petersburg and all the major cities of Russia.

11 Bukharaev, *Islam in Russia: The Four Seasons*, x.

12 Galina Yemelianova, 'Islam in Russia: An Historical Perspective', in *Islam in Post-Soviet Russia: Public and Private Faces*, ed. Hilary Pilkington and Galina Yemelianova (London; New York: Routledge, 2003), 16–17.

13 A. A. Alov, N. G. Vladimirov, and F. G. Ovsienko, *Mirovie Religii* (Moscow: Nauka, 1998), 247.

14 P. Golden, *Khazar Studies: A Historical-Philological Inquiry into the Origins of the Khazars* (Bibliotheca Budapest: Orientalist Hungarica, 1980), 62–4.

15 V. V. Trepalov, 'Vostochnie elementy Rossisskoi gosudarstvennosti', *Rossia i Vostork, Porblemy Vzaimodeistviia* (1993): 42.

16 Yemelianova, 'Islam in Russia: An Historical Perspective', 18.

17 Ibid., 19.

18 V. A. Gordlevskii, *Pamiati Akademika Ol'denburga* (Moscow: Nauka, 1934), 164.

19 Today's Kazan (or Volga) Tatars are descendants of the Volga-Kama Bolgars, the Qypchaq Turks from Central Asia. See Gustav Burbiel, *The Tatars and the Tatar ASSR, Handbook of the Major Soviet Nationalities* (London: The Free Press, 1975), 392. For more on Kazan Tatars, see P. Znamenskoy, *Kazan Tatars [Kazanskie Tatary]* (Kazan: Publisher of Imperator's University, 1910), Available at: https://kitap.tatar.ru/ru/dl/nbrt_tatarica_Inv_373_63; Aristah Speranskyi, *Kazan Tatars [Kazanskie Tatary]* (Kazan: Central Publisher, 1914). Available at: https://kitap.tatar.ru/ru/dl/nbrt_tatarica_Inv_F_1633843. Also see differences with Crimean Tatars and their language, for example: A. Samoylovich, 'About the History of the Tatar Crimean Language', [K istorii Krysko-Tatarskogo literaturnogo yazyka], *Vestnok nauchnogo obshestva Tatarovedeniya*, vol. 7 (Kazan: Academy of the Centre of the People's Commissariat of Education of the TSSR, 1927), 27–33.

20 See in Russian and Tatar: V. Smolin, 'To the Opening of the List of Works of Ibn Fadlan' [*K otkrytiu spiska sochineniyya Ibn – Fadlana*], *Vestnik narodnogo obshestva Tatarovedeniya* 1–2, January–April (Kazan: Academy of the Centre of the People's Commissariat of Education of the TSSR, 1925), 10–15; Anvar Khhayri, *Writings of Ahmad Ibn Fadlan of His Travels to the Bolgar Government in 921–922 [Ahmed ibne Fadlannyn 921–922 ellarda Bolgar deuletene kulgende yazgan seyahetlere]* (Kazan: Suz, 2013).

21 Bukharaev, *Islam in Russia: The Four Seasons*, 19.

22 For example, Arabs originating from modern-day Saudi Arabia, the Hijaz in particular, founded the Rashidun (632–61), Ummayyad (661–750), Abbasid (750–1517) and Fatimid (909–1171) caliphates.

23 Rodney Glesler, *The Story of Kuwait* (n/a, 1959), 4.

24 Bukharaev, *Islam in Russia: The Four Seasons*, 49–50.

25 Ibid., 48.

26 Ibid., 94–5.

27 Glesler, *Story of Kuwait*.

28 Ibid., 4.

29 Ravil Bukharaev, *Tatarstan: A 'Can-Do' Culture – President Mintimer Shaimiev and the Power of Common Sense* (Kent: Global Oriental, 2007), 25.

30 Bukharaev, *Islam in Russia: The Four Seasons*, 121.

31 Ildar Nurimanov, 'Hajj of Russian Muslims: From Past to Present' ['*Hajj Musulman Rossii. Iz proshlogo k nastoyzshemu*'], *Medina al-Islam* 1, no. 25 (2007). Available at: http://www.idmedina.ru/books/history_culture/hadjj/1/nurimanov.htm

32 Bukharaev, *Islam in Russia: The Four Seasons*, x.

33 Galina Yemelianova, *Russia and Islam: A Historical Survey* (New York: Palgrave, 2002), 28.

34 Ibid., 29–30.

35 Ibid., 30.

36 Ibid.

37 Ibid., 32.

38 Ibid., 33.

39 Bukharaev, *Islam in Russia: The Four Seasons*, x.

40 This book will refer to *jadidism* throughout; for details, for further reading, see Edward J. Lazzerini, 'Ethnicity and the Uses of History: The Case of the Volga Tatars and *Jadidism*', *Central Asian Survey* 1 (1982): 61–9; M. Kemper and S. Shikhaliev, 'Qadidism and Jadidism in Twentieth-Century Daghestan', *Asiatische Studien* 69, no. 3 (2015): 593–624; Mustafa Tuna, '"Pillars of the Nation": The Making of a Russian Muslim Intelligentsia and the Origins of Jadidism', *Kritika: Explorations in Russian and Eurasian History* 18, no. 2 (Spring 2017): 257–81.

41 Ocherki, *Islam and Muslim Culture in the Middle Volga Region: Past and Present* [*Islam and Musulmanskaya kultura v Srednem Povolzhie: istoriya i sovremennnost*'] (Kazan: Master Lain, 2002): 96–101.

42 Nurimanov, 'Hajj of Russian Muslims'.

43 U. Arapov, *Islam in the Russian Empire (Legislative Acts, Descriptions, Statistics)* [*Islam v Rossiyskoy imperii (zakonodatelnye akty, opisaniya, statistika)*] (Moscow: Akademkniga, 2001).

44 Nurimanov, 'Hajj of Russian Muslims'.

45 Ibid.

46 Medina, 'The Hajj of Russian Muslims and the Sanitary Conditions of the Pilgrimage' [*O hajje russkih musulman i o sanitarnyh usloviyah palomnichestva*]. Available at: http://www.idmedina.ru/books/history_culture/hadjj/2/glava-5.htm? For example, see the hajj performed by Almushev Khamidulla (1855–1929), who was 'alim and educator, deep connoisseur of Islamic culture, imam-khatib of the 4th

4

rcathedral mosque (built in 1887) in Petryaks, Nizhny Novgorod in 1899–1901. On his way to Arabia, he described the lives and traditions of local residents, met with famous scientists of those years and wrote in the Old Tatar language. This narrative can be found in the book 'Hajj-Name', see Khamidulla Almushev, *Hajj-Name [Hadj – Name]*. Available at: http://www.idmedina.ru/books/history_culture/hadjj/1/almushev.htm.

47 On the historical development of the Kingdom of Saudi Arabia, for example, see Gary Troeller, *The Birth of Saudi Arabia: Britain and the Rise of the House of Sa'ud* (Letchworth: The Garden City Press Limited, 1976); Joseph Kostiner, *The Making of Saudi Arabia, 1916–1936: From Chieftaincy to Monarchical State* (Oxford; New York: Oxford University Press, 1993); David E. Long, *The Kingdom of Saudi Arabia* (Gainesville: University Press of Florida, 1997); Askar H. Al-Enazy, *The Creation of Saudi Arabia Ibn Saud and British Imperial Policy, 1914–1927* (London; New York: Routledge, 2010); J. E. Peterson, *Saudi Arabia under Ibn Saud: Economic and Financial Foundations of the State* (London; New York: I.B. Tauris, 2018).

48 J. Christie, 'History and Development of the Gulf Cooperation Council: A Brief Overview', in *The Gulf Cooperation Council: Moderation and Stability in an Interdependent World*, ed. J. A. Sandwick (Colorado: Westview Press, 1987), 14.

49 On the historical development of Kuwait, for example, see Jill Crystal, *Kuwait: The Transformation of an Oil State* (Boulder: Westview Press Inc, 1992); Isam Al-aher, *Kuwait – The Reality* (Pittsburgh: Dorrance Publishing Co, Inc, 1995).

50 On the historical development of the United Arab Emirates, for example, see Anthony Axon and Susan Hewitt (eds.), *United Arab Emirates, 1975/76–2018*, Vol. 2 (Leiden; Boston: BRILL, 2019); Muhammad Morsy Abdullah, *The United Arab Emirates: A Modern History* (London; New York: Croom Helm, 1978); Christopher M. Davidson, *Abu Dhabi: Oil and Beyond* (London; Oxford: Hurst & Co.; Oxford University Press, 2011); Kristian Coates Ulrichsen, *The United Arab Emirates: Power, Politics and Policy-Making* (Abingdon: Routledge, 2016).

51 On the historical development of Bahrain, for example, see Emile A. Nakhleh, *Bahrain* (Toronto; London: Lexington Books, 1938); Mahdi Abdala al-Tajir, *Bahrain, 1920–1945: Britain, the Shaikh and the Administration* (London; New York; Sydney: Croom Helm, 1987).

52 On the historical development of Qatar, for example, see Allen Fromherz, *Qatar: A Modern History* (London: I.B. Tauris, 2010); David Roberts, *Qatar: Securing the Global Ambitions of a City-State* (London: C. Hurst & Co, 2017); Mehran Kamrava, *Qatar: Small State, Big Politics* (New York: University Press, 2013); Diana Galeeva, *Qatar: The Practice of Rented Power* (Abingdon: Routledge, 2022).

53 On the historical development of Oman, for example, see Miriam Joyce, *The Sultanate of Oman: A Twentieth-Century History* (Westport: Praeger Publishers, 1995); Raghid El-Solh, *The Sultanate of Oman, 1939–1945* (Reading: Ithaca Press, 2000); Calvin H. Allen and W. Lynn Rigsbee II, *Oman under Qaboos: From Coup to*

Constitution, 1970–1996 (London; Portland: Frank Cass, 2000); Francis Owtram, *A Modern History of Oman: Formation of the State since 1920* (London; New York: I.B. Tauris, 2004); Jeremy Jones and Nicholas Ridout, *A History of Modern Oman* (Cambridge: Cambridge University Press, 2015).

54 On shared identities between the GCC states and development of relations between members, see Diana Galeeva, 'How National Identity Will Shape the Future of Liberalism: The Consequences of Brexit in the EU, and of the 2017 Crisis in the GCC', *Al Mesbar*, 5 February 2018. Available at: https://mesbar .org/national-identity-will-shape-future-liberalism-consequences-brexit-eu-2017 -crisis-gcc/

55 See Hans J. Morgenthau, *Politics Among Nations: The Struggle for Power and Peace*, 3rd edn. (Chicago: University of Chicago Press, 1954); Kenneth N. Waltz, *Theory of International Politics* (Reading: Addison-Wesley, 1979); Stephen Walt, *The Origins of Alliances* (Ithaca; London: Cornell University Press, 1987); Gideon Rose, 'Neoclassical Realism and Theories of Foreign Policy', *World Politics* 51 (October 1998): 144–72; John Mearsheimer, *The Tragedy of Great Power Politics* (New York: W. W. Norton & Company, 2001); Steven Lobell, Norrin Ripsman and Jeffrey Taliaferro, *Neoclassical Realism, the State, and Foreign Policy* (Cambridge: Cambridge University Press – M.U.A., 2009).

56 See Joseph S. Nye, *The Paradox of American Power: Why the World's Only Superpower Can't Go It Alone* (Oxford: Oxford University Press, 2003); Robert O. Keohane, *After Hegemony* (Princeton: Princeton University Press, 2005); G. John Ikenberry, *Liberal Leviathan: The Origins, Crisis, and Transformation of the American World Order* (Princeton: Princeton University Press, 2012).

57 Aaron L. Friedberg, 'The Future of US-China Relations: Is Conflict Inevitable?', *International Security* 30, no. 2 (2005): 34.

58 Ibid.

59 Alexander Wendt, 'Collective Identity Formation and the International State', *American Political Science Review* 88, no. 2 (1994): 384–96; Alexander Wendt, 'Constructing International Politics', *International Security* 20, no. 1 (1995): 71–81; Alexander Wendt, *Social Theory of International Politics* (Cambridge: Cambridge University Press, 1999).

60 Wendt, *Social Theory of International Politics*, 24.

61 Iver B. Neumann, *Uses of the Other: 'The East' in European Identity Formation* (Manchester: Manchester University Press, 1998).

62 Edward W. Said, *Orientalism* (New York: Pantheon Books, 1978).

63 See National Library of the Republic of Tatarstan, 'TASSR–100 Years'. Available at: https://kitaphane.tatarstan.ru/TASSR100.htm; Also see the website dedicated to 100-years since the establishment of the TASSR: http://100tatarstan.ru/.

64 See National Library of the Republic of Tatarstan, *Statistics of Collections [Collection Statistics]*. Available at: https://kitap.tatar.ru/ru/ssearch/ecollection/.

65 See Publishing House 'Medina'. Available at: https://www.idmedina.ru/about/concept/.

66 See Middle East Centre Archive, St Antony's College, 'Guide to Collections Regarding the Gulf', 1 February (2020): 3. Available at: https://www.sant.ox.ac.uk/sites/default/files/mec-archive-gulf-guide.pdf.

67 See ibid., 2.

68 See ibid.

69 See ibid., 1.

70 See File 3666/1925 'Arabia: Printed Correspondence, 1924–28', IOR/L/PS/10/1155: 27 December 1924–28 October 1929. Available at: https://searcharchives.bl.uk/primo_library/libweb/action/display.do?tabs=detailsTab&ct=display&doc=IAMS040-000546630&displayMode=full&vid=IAMS_VU2&_ga=2.110433856.413039908.1626276110-1358129400.1626276110.

71 See File 61/11 II (D 42) 'Relations between Nejd and Hijaz' IOR/R/15/1/565: 7 November 1924–10 July 1925. Available at: https://searcharchives.bl.uk/primo_library/libweb/action/display.do?tabs=detailsTab&ct=display&fn=search&doc=IAMS040-000228024&indx=2&recIds=IAMS040-000228024&recIdxs=1&elementId=1&renderMode=poppedOut&displayMode=full&frbrVersion=&dscnt=0&scp.scps=scope%3A%28BL%29&frbg=&tab=local&dstmp=1626276466337&srt=rank&mode=Basic&&dum=true&vl(freeText0)=Soviet%20Muslims%20%20and%20Arabia&vid=IAMS_VU2.

72 Vitaly Naumkin, ed., *Middle East: From Foreign Policy Archive Documents* [*Blizhnevostochniy conflict: Iz dokumentov arhiva vneshney politiki*] (Moscow: MFD, 2003). Available at: http://history-library.com/index.php?id1=3&category=voennaya-istoriya&author=naumkin-vv&book=2003&page=220.

73 Ministry of Foreign Affairs of the Russian Federation, *Documents of the USSR's Foreign Policy* [*Dokumenty vneshney politiki SSSR*], 2 January–31 August 1943. Available at: https://idd.mid.ru/dokumental-nye-publikacii/-/asset_publisher/5H3VC9AbCsvL/content/publikacii-podgotovlennye-istoriko-dokumental-nym-departamentom-v-2004-2015-gg-?inheritRedirect=false&redirect=https%3A%2F%2Fidd.mid.ru%3A443%2Fdokumental-nye-publikacii%3Fp_p_id%3D101_INSTANCE_5H3VC9AbCsvL%26p_p_lifecycle%3D0%26p_p_state%3Dnormal%26p_p_mode%3Dview%26p_p_col_id%3Dcolumn-2%26p_p_col_count%3D1.

74 Alexei V. Malashenko, 'Islam in Russia', *Social Research* 76, no. 1 (Spring 2009): 321–58.

75 Naumkin, *Failed Partnership*.

76 Oleg Ozerov, *Karim Khakimov: Chronicle of his Life* [*Karim Khakimov: letopis' zhini*] (LitRes: Samizdat, 2020).

77 L. Gadilov and F. Gumerov, *Karim Khakimov* [*Kerim Khakimov*] (Ufa: Bashknigoizdat, 1966).

78 For example, Mark Katz, *Russia and Arabia: Soviet Foreign Policy toward the Arabian Peninsula* (Baltimore: Johns Hopkins University Press, 1986); Page, *The USSR and Arabia*; Michael Confino and Shamir Shimon, *The USSR and the Middle East* (New York: J. Wiley, 1973); Galia Golan, *Soviet Policies in the Middle East: From World War Two to Gorbachev* (Cambridge: Cambridge University Press, 1990); Robert Freedman, 'Russia and Middle East under Yeltsin, Part II', *Milwaukee* 6 (1997); Evgeny Primakov, *Russia and the Arabs: Behind the Scenes in the Middle East from the Cold War to the Present* (New York: Basic Books, 2009); Alexei Vasiliev, *Russia's Middle East Policy: From Lenin to Putin* (Abingdon: Routledge, 2018).

79 For example, Mark Katz, 'Saudi-Russian Relations since the Abdullah-Putin Summit', *Middle East Policy* 16, no. 1 (2009): 113–20; Katerina Oskarsson and Steven Yetiv, 'Russia and the Persian Gulf: Trade, Energy, and Interdependence', *The Middle East Journal* 67, no. 3 (2013): 381–403; Charap Samuel, 'Is Russia an outside Power in the Gulf?', *Survival* 57, no. 1 (2015): 153–70; Alexander Shumilin and Inna Shumilina, 'Russia as a Gravity Pole of the GCC's New Foreign Policy Pragmatism', *The International Spectator* 52, no. 2 (2017): 115–29; E. Melkumyan, G. Kosach and T. Nosenko, 'Russia in the Foreign Policy Priorities of the Council of Cooperation of the Arabian Gulf States After Events of the Arab Spring', *Vestnik MGIMO-Universiteta* 4, no. 55 (2017): 139–53; 'Russia's Relations with Gulf States and Their Effect on Regional Balance in the Middle East', *RUDN Journal of Political Science* 20, no. 4 (2018): 536–47; Kozhanov, *Russia's Relations with the GCC and Iran*; Leonid Issaev and Nikolay Kozhanov, 'Diversifying Relationships: Russian Policy Toward GCC', *International Politics* 58, no. 6 (2021): 884–902.

80 Andrej Kreutz, *Russia in the Middle East: Friend or Foe?* (Praeger: Praeger Security International, 2007).

81 For example, Akiner Shirin, *Islamic Peoples of the Soviet Union* (London: Kegan Paul International, 1983); Rafiq Mukhametshin, *Islam in the Social and Political Life of Tatarstan: Ethnicity and Confessional Tradition in the Volga-Ural Region, [Islam v obshchestvenno-politicheskoy zhizni Tatarstana: Etnichnost' i konfessional'naya traditsiya v Volgo-Ural'skom regione]* (Moscow: Vostochnaya Literature, 1998); Michael Kemper, *Sufis und Gelehrte in Tatarien und Baschkirien, 1789–1889: Der Islamische Diskurs unter russischer Herrschaft* (Berlin: Klaus Swartz Verlag, 1998); Yemelianova, *Russia and Islam: A Historical Survey*; Galina Yemelianova and Hilary Pilkington, *Islam in Post-Soviet Russia: Public and Private Faces* (London; New York: Routledge Curzon, 2003); Hunter Shireen, Thomas Jeffrey and Alexander Melikishvili, *Islam in Russia: The Politics of Identity and Security* (New York; London: Armonk, 2004).

82 Marlene Laruelle, ed., 'Russia's Islamic Diplomacy', *CAP Paper* 220 (2019), 'Islam in Russia, Russia in the Islamic World' Initiative, *Central Asia Program, Institute for European, Russian, and Eurasian Studies of the George Washington University.*

Available at: https://centralasiaprogram.org/wp-content/uploads/2019/07/CAP
-paper-220-Russia-Islamic-Diplomacy.pdf; Alexander Bennigsen, Paul B. Henze,
George K. Tanham and S. Enders Wimbush, *Soviet Strategy and Islam* (London: The
Macmillan Press Ltd, 1989); Carol R. Saivetz, *The Soviet Union and the Gulf in the
1980s* (Boulder: San Francisco; London: Westview Press, 1989), 9–28.

83 Gulnaz Sharafutdinova, 'Paradiplomacy in the Russian Regions: Tatarstan's Search
for Statehood', *Europe-Asia Studies* 55, no. 4 (2003): 618–19.

84 For example, Mikhail Artamonov, *History of Khazars* [*Istoria Khazar*] (Leningrad:
Izd-vo Gos. Ermitazha, 1962); Alfred Khalikov, *Tatars and their Accessors* [*Tatarskii
narod I ego predki*] (Kazan: Tatarskoe knizhnoe izd-vo, 1989); Devin DeWeese,
*Islamization and Native Religion in the Golden Horde: Baba Tükles and Conversion
to Islam in Historical and Epic Tradition* (University Park: Pennsylvania State
University Press, 1994); Ravil Bukharaev, *The Model of Tatarstan under President
Mintimer Shaimiev* (New York: St. Martin's Press, 1999).

85 For example, Alfrid Bustanov, 'Shihabaddin Marjani and the Muslim Archive
in Russia', *Islamology* 9, no. 1–2 (2019): 138; D. Mardanova, 'Controversy as a
Mechanism for Search and Approval of Truth (The Case of Debate on 'Aqibah
between Shihabetdin Marjani and His Opponents in the Volga Region in the Last
Third of the 19ᵗʰ Century)', *RUDN Journal of Russian History* 17, no. 3 (2018): 513–37.

86 For example, Galina Yemelianova, 'The National Identity of the Volga Tatars at the
Turn of the 19ᵗʰ Century: Tatarism, Turkism and Islam', *Central Asian Survey* 16, no.
4 (1997): 543–72; Allen Frank, *Islamic Historiography and 'Bulgar' Identity Among
the Tatars and Bashkirs of Russia* (Leiden: Brill, 1998).

87 For example, Azade-Ayse Rorlich, *The Volga Tatars: A Profile in National Resilience*
(Stanford: Hoover Institution Press, 1986).

88 For example, Alfrid Bustanov, 'The Language of Moderate Salafism in Eastern
Tatarstan', *Islam and Christian Muslim Relations* 28, no. 2 (2017): 183–201.

89 Teresa Wigglesworth-Baker, 'Language Policy and Post-Soviet Identities in
Tatarstan', *New York, USA: Cambridge University Press, Nationalities Papers* 44, no. 1
(2016): 20–37.

90 For example, Egdunas Racius, *Islam in Post-communist Eastern Europe: Between
Churchification and Securitization* (Leiden; Boston: Brill, 2020).

91 For example, Wendt, *Social Theory of International Politics*; Said, *Orientalism*;
Neumann, *Uses of the Other: 'The East' in European Identity Formation*.

Chapter 2

1 The chapter focuses mainly on relations between the USSR and the Kingdom of
Hijaz and Nejd (Saudi Arabia since 1932), as Tatars were especially involved in the

Soviet mechanisms during the 1920s to the 1930s to build closer relations with the Kingdom. The limited focus on relations with other Arabian states in this chapter, but which is part of the broader focus in Chapter 3, is largely because the other smaller monarchies did not gain independence until after the British withdrawal in 1971.

2 Marlene Laruelle, ed., 'Russia's Islamic Diplomacy', *CAP Paper* no. 220 (2019), 'Islam in Russia, Russia in the Islamic World' Initiative, *Central Asia Program, Institute for European, Russian, and Eurasian Studies of the George Washington University*. Available at: https://centralasiaprogram.org/wp-content/uploads/2019 /07/CAP-paper-220-Russia-Islamic-Diplomacy.pdf; Alexander Bennigsen, Paul B. Henze, George K. Tanham and S. Enders Wimbush, *Soviet Strategy and Islam* (London: The Macmillan Press Ltd, 1989); Carol R. Saivetz, *The Soviet Union and the Gulf in the 1980s* (Boulder, San Francisco; London: Westview Press, 1989), 9–28.

3 Galina M. Yemelianova, 'Islam and Nation Building in Tatarstan and Dagestan of the Russian Federation', *Nationalities Papers* 27, no. 4 (December 1999), 607.

4 Gaiaz Iskhakyi, *Idel-Ural* (Kazan: Tatarskoe knizhnoe izd-vo, 1991), 10.

5 Dilyara Usmanova, 'The Kazan Muslim Congresses and the Proclamation of "Cultural National Autonomy"' in *The History of The Tatars Since Ancient Times Tatars: and Tatarstan in the 20ᵗʰ -Beginning of the 21ˢᵗ Centuries*, vol. 7 (Kazan: Academy of Sciences of the Republic of Tatarstan, Sh. Marjani Institute of History, 2017), 234.

6 Ibid., 247.

7 The Tatar National Library of the Republic of Tatarstan offers a comprehensive collection of books for the 100-year anniversary of TASSR, in Russian and Tatar languages, with a focus on General Information and State Structure; History; Economics; Science; Culture; Linguistics. See National Library of the Republic of Tatarstan, *Electronic Collections of Books for 100-Year Anniversary of TASSR*. Available at: https://kitaphane.tatarstan.ru/TASSR100/elibrary.htm

8 Yemelianova, 'Islam and Nation Building in Tatarstan and Dagestan of the Russian Federation', 607.

9 I. Khodorovsky, *What is the Tatar Soviet Republic?* [*Chto takoe Tatarskaya Sovetskaya Respublika?*] (Kazan: Gosudarstvennoe Izdatelstvo, 1920), 5. Available at: https://kitaphane.tatarstan.ru/file/kitaphane/File/1.%20Inv_18459_93.pdf; p. 5.

10 Ibid., 17–18.

11 Ibid.

12 Vladimir Lenin, *A Caricature of Marxism and Imperialist Economism: Collected Works* (Moscow: Progress Publishers, 1968): 34.

13 Alexey Vasiliev, *Russia's Middle East Policy: From Lenin to Putin* (Abingdon: Routledge, 2018): 14.

14 Documenty vneshnei politiki SSSR [*Documents of Foreign Policy of the USSR*],
    Vol. 1 (Moscow: Gospolitizdat, 1957), 34–5, cited in Vasiliev, *Russia's Middle East
    Policy*, 11.

15 Wilbur Green, *Soviet Strategy in the Middle East* (Carlisle Barracks: Army War
    College, 1973), 4.

16 Documenty vneshnei politiki SSSR [*Documents of Foreign Policy of the USSR*], vol.
    3 (Moscow: Gospolitizdat, 1959), 598–601, cited in Vasiliev, *Russia's Middle East
    Policy*, 18.

17 Vasiliev, *Russia's Middle East Policy*, 18–19.

18 See A. Rodriguez, *'Establishment of the Trade Relations between the Soviet Union
    and the States of the Arabian Peninsula', (1920–1930)* [*Y istokov vneshnetorgovyh
    svyzei SSSR so stranami Araviyskogo poluostrova' (1920–1930)*] (Vostk-Zapad:
    Kontakty i Protivorechiya).

19 Professor Vitaly Naumkin is full member of the Russian Academy of Sciences
    and academic director of the Institute of Oriental Studies, Russian Academy of
    Sciences. He is a member of the Science Council, Russian foreign ministry and the
    Russian Security Council; president of the Centre for Strategic and Political Studies
    (since 1991), and Goodwill ambassador for the Alliance of Civilisations by the UN
    secretary general (since 2007). He is the author of over 500 publications in Russian,
    English, French, Arabic and other languages, dealing with the history of Asia, the
    Arab world, Central Asia and the Caucasus.

20 Vitaly Naumkin, *Failed Partnership: Soviet Diplomacy Towards Saudi Arabia
    Between the World Wars* [*Nesostoyabsheesya Partnerstvo Sovetskaya Diplomatiya
    v Saudovskoi Aravii mechdu Mirovymi Voinami*] (Moscow: Aspect Press, 2018):
    72–3.

21 L. Z. Gadilov and F. H. Gumerov, 'Karim Khakimov' [in Bashkir: 'Karim
    Khakimov'] (1966): 105.

22 See O. B. Nikonov, 'The USSR's Role in Forming the State Sovereignty of the
    Kingdom of Saudi Arabia', [*Rol' SSSR v stanovlenii gosudarstvennogo suvereniteta
    korolevsta Sauvskaya Aravia*]; *Prepodavatel 21 vek* 94, no. 53 (2017): 302–16.

23 Chicherin – Stalinu [*Chicherin to Stalin*], 18 December 1923, Arhiv vnseshnei
    politiki Rossii [*Archive of Foreign Policy of Russia*], F. 0127, Op. 1, p. 1, d. 2., pp.
    6–7, cited in Naumkin, *Failed Partnership*, 81–2.

24 Oleg Ozerov clarifies that this refers to Shaimardan Nurimanovich
    Ibragimov, who in 1921 became chairman of the Plenipotentiary Commission
    of the Central Committee of the All-Union Communist Party of Bolsheviks,
    the All-Russian Central Executive Committee and the Council of People's
    Commissars of the RSFSR for Crimea, and then a member of the Collegium
    of the People's Commissar for Nationalities of the RSFSR. See Oleg Ozerov,
    Karim Khakimov: Chronicle of His Life [*Karim Khakimov: letopis' chizni*] (LitRes:
    Samizdat, 2020): 372.

25 Naumkin, *Failed Partnership*, 83.

26 Arkiv vnseshnei politiki Rossiskoi imperii [*Archive of Foreign Policy of Russian Empire*], f. 149 (Turetski stol) [*Turkish Table*], op. 502a, d. 425, II, 3–4, 9–10; f. 180 (Posol'stvo v Kostabtinople) [*Embassy in Constantinople*], op. 517/2, d.5322, 1. 97; E. A. Masanov, 'Sh. M. Ibragimov – Drug Ch.Ch. Valikhanova', *Vestnik Akademii nauk Kazakhskoi SSR* [*Kazakh SSR*] 9 (1964): 53–60.

27 Ildar Nurimanov, 'Hajj in Soviet Period' ['*Hadzh v Sovetskiy Period*'], *Hajj of Russian Muslims № 4, Annual Collection of Hajj Travel Notes* [*Jadzh rossiskih musulman №4 Ezhegodniy sbornik putevyh zametok o hadzhe*], 7 September 2012. Available at: http://www.idmedina.ru/books/history_culture/?4751

28 Norihiro Naganawa, 'The Red Sea Becoming Red? The Bolsheviks', *Commercial Enterprise in the Hijaz and Yemen* (1924–1938): 8.

29 Ibid.

30 Naumkin, *Failed Partnership*, 96; About the diplomatic activities of Tuimetov, Naumkin explains, see pp. 229–45. Also see Jusuf Galyatdinovich Tuimetov (1893). Available at: https://ru.openlist.wiki/Туйметов_Юсуф_Галяутдинович_(1893)

31 Naumkin, *Failed Partnership*, 113.

32 Group of the Strategic Vision, 'Russia-Islamic World', Karim Hakimov – "'Red Pasha" and the Arabian Vizier of the Kremlin', 25 May 2020. Available at: https://russia-islworld.ru/kultura//karim-hakimov-red-pasha-and-the-arabian-vizier-of-the-kremlin/.

33 Gadilov and Gumerov, 'Kerim Khakimov', 17.

34 Naumkin, *Failed Partnership*, 88–9.

35 The significance of Karim Khakimov's legacy for establishing the Soviet– Saudi relations is particularly remembered in both the modern Republic of Bashkortostan (where Khakimov grew up) and the Republic of Tatarstan – as is his ethno-confessional affiliation.

36 Ruslan Khayretdinov, 'Karim Khakimov – Revolutionary, Diplomat' [*Karim Hakimov – revlucioner, diplomat*], PhD Thesis, Bashkir State University, 2006. Available at: https://www.dissercat.com/content/karim-khakimov-revolyutsioner -diplomat/read.

37 Ozerov, *Karim Khakimov*, 27.

38 Ibid., 26.

39 Gadilov and Gumerov, 'Kerim Khakimov', 7.

40 Despite this, his willingness to study throughout his life resulted in his entering the Institute of Red Professors in 1932.

41 Ozerov, *Karim Khakimov*, 35.

42 Ibid., 40.

43 Gadilov and Gumerov, *Revolutionary Diplomat* [*Karim Hakimov – revlucioner, diplomat*] (1966), 14.

44 Ibid.

45 Ozerov, *Karim Khakimov*, 40.

46 Oleg Ozerov has amassed significant diplomatic experience since 1981, largely in the MENA region. Among the most relevant points, he was the former ambassador extraordinary and plenipotentiary of the Russian Federation to the Kingdom of Saudi Arabia and Permanent Representative of the Russian Federation to the Organization of Islamic Cooperation in Jeddah, Saudi Arabia, concurrently (2011–17).

47 Ozerov, *Karim Khakimov*, 42.

48 L. Z. Gadilov and G. G. Amiri, *Memories of Karim Khakimov*, [*Vospominaniya o Karime Khakimove*] (1982), 12.

49 Ozerov, *Karim Khakimov*, 42.

50 Ibid., 45.

51 Ibid.

52 Ibid., 46.

53 Naumkin, *Failed Partnership*, 89–99.

54 Ibid.

55 Ibid.

56 Gadilov and Gumerov, 'Kerim Khakimov', 20.

57 Gadilov and Amiri, *Memories of Karim Khakimov*, 36.

58 Gadilov and Gumerov, 'Kerim Khakimov', 20–1.

59 Ibid., 23.

60 Ibid., 24.

61 Ibid.

62 Gadilov and Amiri, *Memories of Karim Khakimov*, 9.

63 Gadilov and Gumerov, 'Kerim Khakimov', 27.

64 Gadilov and Amiri, *Memories of Karim Khakimov*, 18.

65 Arhiv vneshnei politiki Rossii [*Archive of Foreign Policy of Russia*], F. 110, Op. 2, D. 6, p. 233; cited in Khayretdinov, 'Karim Khakimov – Revolutionary, Diplomat', 19.

66 Arhiv vneshnei politiki Rossii [*Archive of Foreign Policy of Russia*], F.25859, Op. 1., D. 51, p. 66; cited in Khayretdinov, 'Karim Khakimov – Revolutionary, Diplomat', 19.

67 Arhiv vneshnei politiki Rossii [*Archive of Foreign Policy of Russia*], 'From the personal case of Karim Khakimov': 9, cited in Khayretdinov, 'Karim Khakimov – Revolutionary, Diplomat', 20.

68 G. Kosach, 'Karim Khakimov: Years of Life in Orenburg] (A Person and His Time)' [Karim Khakimov: Gody zhizni v Orenburge (chelovek I ego vremya), in V. Naumkin and I. Smilyanskaya, eds., *Unknown Pages of Russian Oriental Studies* [*Neizvestnye stranicy otechestvennogo vostokovedeniya*] 2 (2004): 125–48.

69 Gadilov and Amiri, *Memories of Karim Khakimov*, 3.

70 Khayretdinov, 'Karim Khakimov – Revolutionary, Diplomat', 18.

71 Naumkin, *Failed Partnership*, 90.
72 According to the protocol, diplomatic representatives of non-Muslims in Mecca were not allowed to present their credentials. The procedure for presenting them to the king took place in Jeddah.
See R. F. Khayretdinov, 'Unknown Heroes of the Past: Karim Khakimov' [*Neizvestniye geroi proshlogo. Karim Khakimov*], *Vestnik of Bashkir State University* 15, no. 4 (2010): 1.
73 Ozerov, *Karim Khakimov*, 761.
74 Nurimanov, 'Hajj in Soviet Period'.
75 On their rivalry, see Martin Strohmeier, 'The Exile of Husayn b. Ali, ex-Sharif of Mecca and ex-king of the Hijaz, in Cyprus (1925–1930)', *Middle Eastern Studies* 55, no. 5 (2019): 733–55; Alexey Vasiliev, *The History of Saudi Arabia (1745–1973)* [*Istoria Saudovskoy Aravii (1745–1973)*] (Nauka: Moscow, 1982); Madawi al-Rasheed, *A History of Saudi Arabia* (Cambridge: Cambridge University Press, 2012).
76 Note that this request was made in conditions when Jeddah was blocked by the forces of Abdullaziz, and Karim Khakimov took great risks for conducting his policies.
77 See Khayretdinov, 'Unknown Heroes of the Past: Karim Khakimov', 1344.
78 Ozerov, *Karim Khakimov*, 777.
79 Ibid., 777.
80 Ibid., 778.
81 Ibid.,781.
82 Ibid., 787.
83 MicROFILM, 'Relations Between Nejd and Hijaz from 7-11-24 to 7-25', R/15/1/565, 10R, NEG 9871, F. 61/11-II, D. 244: 7–8.
84 Ibid., 253: 5.
85 Naganawa, 'The Red Sea Becoming Red? The Bolsheviks', 12.
86 Ibid.
87 Arhiv vneshnei politiki Rossii [*Archive of Foreign Policy of Russia*], F.180, Op.517/2, D. 5322, II., 203–203ob.
88 Naganawa, 'The Red Sea Becoming Red? The Bolsheviks', 12.
89 Naumkin, *Failed Partnership*, 143.
90 Gadilov and Gumerov, 'Kerim Khakimov', 91.
91 Ibid.
92 Ibid.
93 Ibid., 92.
94 Ibid.
95 Gadilov and Amiri, *Memories of Karim Khakimov*, 31.
96 Naumkin, *Failed Partnership*, 143
97 Ibid.

98 Ibid., 144.

99 Ibid.

100 Gadilov and Gumerov, 'Kerim Khakimov', 93.

101 Arhiv vneshnei politiki SSSR [*Archive of Foreign Policy of the USSR*], X, Doc. 77, Moscow (1965): 134.
Cited in Gadilov and Gumerov, 'Kerim Khakimov', 93.

102 Gadilov and Amiri, *Memories of Karim Khakimov*, 25.

103 Naumkin, *Failed Partnership*, 195.

104 Gadilov and Amiri, *Memories of Karim Khakimov*, 38.

105 Benningsen, et al., *Soviet Strategy and Islam*, 23.

106 Republic of Bashkortostan, 'The Friend of the King, Soviet Diplomat' [*Drug korolya, Soviet Diplomat*], 30 October 2020. Available at: https://resbash.ru/articles/cotsium/2020-10-30/drug-korolya-sovetskiy-diplomat-758145. It might also be useful to mention that the above-mentioned visit of Prince Faisal was linked with the request of economic support from Moscow. However, the Soviets showed a refusal, and the entire oil concession, as oil was found in 1938 in Saudi Arabia, went to the United States, which until today occupies the place of the strategic partner for Saudi Arabia.

107 The origin of the organization can be traced back to 1788, when Catherine II signed a decree proclaiming the establishment of the Spiritual Mohammedan Assembly in Ufa. This was renamed the *Orenburgskoe magometnaskoe duhovnoe sobranie* (the Orenburg Mohammedan Spiritual Assembly, or OMDS). See Renat Bekkin, 'The Central Spiritual Administration of the Muslims of Russia (TSDUM) and Its Strategy of Subordinate Partnership in Dialogue with the Russian Orthodox Church', *Journal of Interdisciplinary Studies* 4, no. 2 (2017): 7–28.

108 Galia Golan, *Soviet Policies in the Middle East from World War II to Gorbachev* (Cambridge University Press: Cambridge, 1990): 198.

109 Martin Kramer, *Islam Assembled: The Advent of the Muslim Congresses* (New York, 1986).

110 Naumkin, *Failed Partnership*, 191.

111 G. Kosach, 'Saudi Arabia: Power and Religion' [Saudovskaya Aravia: Vlast' I Religiya], *Politichsekaya nauka* (2013): 102.

112 MicROFILM, 'Relations Between Nejd and Hijaz from 7-11-24 to 7-25', R/15/1/565, 10R, NEG 9871, F. 61/11-II, D. 1.

113 Naumkin, *Failed Partnership*, 191.

114 On the Cairo and Mecca Congresses, see also Kramer, *Islam Assembled*.

115 MicROFILM, 'Relations Between Nejd and Hijaz from 7-11-24 to 7-25', R/15/1/565, 10R, NEG 9871, F. 61/11-II, D. 28.

116 Rizaitdin Fakhretdinov is well known for the development of Tatar Jadidism; from 1921 he served as the de facto Mufti of the Russian Soviet Republic (RSFSR). See Michael Kemper, 'From 1917 to 1937: The Mufti, the Turkologist, and Stalin's

Terror', *Die Welt Des Islam* 57 (2017): 162–91. In Russian and Tatar there are
important contributions on Fakhretdinov's view on the model of state; his ideas
for the reformation of Russian Muslims; the major religions in the world; aspects
of religious and world outlooks in Tatar theological thought at the beginning of
the twentieth century; developments of ideas on the *kadimist* system of education;
activities to preserve the teaching of religious doctrine in Bolshevik Russia, among
others. See A. U. Khabutdinov, 'Rizeddin Fakhretdinov (1859–1936): About the
Model of State in Modern Time' [*Rizeddin Fakhretdinov (1859–1936) O Modeli
Gosudarstva Novogo Vremeby*], *Islam in Modern World*, 17, no. 3 (2021): 107–19;
Damir Mukhetdinov, 'Rizeddin Fakhretdinov: Ideas of Reforms in the Muslim
World of Russia [*Rizeddin Fakhretdinov: idei reform musulmanskogo mira Rossii*],
*Educational traditions of Islam in the Ural-Volga Region: First Fakhretdinov
Readings*, 15 April 2009. Available at: http://www.idmedina.ru/books/materials/
?1209; Aysilu Unusova, 'Riza Fakhretdinov's activities to preserve the teaching
of religious doctrine in Bolshevik Russia' [*Deyatelnost' Rizy Fakhretddinova po
sohraneniu prepodavaniya religioznogo verouchheniya v bolshevistskoy Rossii*],
*Educational Traditions of Islam in the Ural-Volga Region: First Fakhretdinov
Readings*, 15 April 2009. Available at: http://www.idmedina.ru/books/materials/
?1213; Salavat Khusainov, 'Riza Fakhretdinov about main world religions' [*Riza
Fakhretdinov on the Main Religions of the World*], *Educational Traditions of Islam
in the Ural-Volga Region: First Fakhretdinov Readings*, 15 April 2009. Available
at: http://www.idmedina.ru/books/materials/?1237; Dina Mukhametzynova,
'Kadimist Education System in the Writings of Rizeddin Fakhretdinov
[*Kadimistkaya systema obrazovaniya v trudah Rizeddina Fakhretdinova*],
*Educational traditions of Islam in the Ural-Volga Region: First Fakhretdinov
Readings*, 15 April 2009. Available at: http://www.idmedina.ru/books/materials/
?1241; Radik Mukhametshin, 'Riza Fakhretdinov and Some Aspects of Religious
and World Outlook in the Tatar Theological Thought of the Beginning of the XX
Century', [*Riza Fakhretdinov and nekotorye aspecyt religiozno-mirovozzrencheskih
iskaniy v Tatarskoi bogoslovskoy mysli nachala XX veka*], *Innovative Resources
of Muslim Education and Culture: Second Fakhretdinov Readings*, 31 May 2011.
Available at: http://www.idmedina.ru/books/materials/?2355.

117 Asma Sharaf, *Memories of My Father. Rizaitdin Fakhretdinov: Scientific-
Bibliographic Collection* [*Vsopominaniya ob otce. Rizeddin Fakhretdinov: nauchno-
bibliographicheskiy sbornik*] (Kazan, 1999).

118 Naumkin, *Failed Partnership*, 192.

119 Ibid., 192–3.

120 Ibid., 193.

121 Ibid., 194.

122 Kashaf Tarjemani played a key role as a murid and a close associate of Galimjan
Barudi (Mufti of Central Spiritual Administration in Ufa between 1917 and

1921). After Barudi, Rizaitdin Fakhretdinov became the Mufti, and Tarjemani became his deputy. In 1935, in connection with the mass closure of mosques and arrests, Tarjemani proposed closing the Central Spiritual Administration in Ufa. After the death of Fakhretdinov, he served as chairman of the Central Spiritual Administration in Ufa, but the authorities did not allow the holding of Mufti election. See Ramazanov Readings [Ramazanovskiy chteniya], 25 May 2020. Available at: http://www.idmedina.ru/ramazan/

123 Naumkin, *Failed Partnership*, 198–9.

124 On differences between the Mecca and Cairo Congresses, and views of the Soviet government on both, see I. Nurimanov, 'Meccan Congress and Hajj in 1926: Based on the Travel Notes of Abdrakhman Umerov' [*Mekkanskiy Kongress i hajj 1926 goda: Po motivam putevyh zapisok Abdrahmana Umerova*], *Islam in Modern World*, 17, no. 1 (2021): 148–9. Available at: http://www.idmedina.ru/pdf/web/viewer.html?file=/pdf/content/ism/ism-1-2021.pdf#139.

125 Naumkin, *Failed Partnership*, 199.

126 *Ogonek*, 23, no. 167 (1926): 13.

127 Abdurahman Umerov (1867–1933) is a well-known Russian theologian, educator, publisher, journalist and scientist, born in Astrakhan into a peasant family. He received his primary education in a village school. In 1881 he entered the madrasah of the most prominent theological scholarly educator Sh. Mardjani in Kazan. In 1892 he returned to Astrakhan, where he became the Imam of the Cathedral Green Mosque and created a mekteb 'Nizamiya'. In 1917, he was ousted by the imam-mukhatasib of the Astrakhan province and the chairman of the provisional Bureau of the Muslim clergy in Kazan. He headed *Milli Idare* in Kazan. In 1923 he was an elected member of TsDUM. See A. Umerov, 'Based on the Travel Notes of Abdrakhman Umerov' [*Po motivam putevyh zapisok Abdrahmana Umerova*], *Hajj of Russian Muslims*, no. 10 (2021): 8–67. Available at: http://www.idmedina.ru/pdf/web/viewer.html?file=/pdf/content/hajj/hajj-10-r.pdf#27.

128 Umerov, 'Based on the Travel Notes of Abdrakhman Umerov', 29.

129 Ibid., 30.

130 Ibid., 32.

131 The Memorial Museum of Riza Fakhretdinov was opened in the village of Kichuchatovo, Almetyevsky District (Tatarstan) in 25 May, 1995. The holdings of the Museum, as of 2015, are 2345 units of storage in the objects of the main holdings and 2061 units of storage in the scientific and auxiliary archive. The most valuable exhibits of the museum are the lifetime editions of the books of the scholar, and gifts presented by the King of Saudi Arabia to Fakhretdinov in 1926 as the vice-president of the world Congress of Muslims in Mecca – a tray and a jar of incense. See Fakhretdinov Rizeddin Fahretdinovich. Available at: https://kitap.tatar.ru/ru/site/42317029a/pages/Fahretdin/.

132 Naumkin, *Failed Partnership*, 192–3.

133 Ismail-zade, Hajj to Mecca [*Palomnichestvo v Mekku*], *New East* [*Novyi Vostok*], 8, no. 9 (1925): 230–43.

134 Umerov, 'Based on the Travel Notes of Abdrakhman Umerov', 30.

135 Nurimanov, 'Hajj in Soviet Period'.

136 Musa Bigi (Bigiev) was a liberal theologian, public figure and one of the leaders of the social movement. He played an important role in the formation and revival of Tatar spiritual culture. He studied at Apanaev madrasa in Kazan, which had not yet been reformed to the *Jadid* pattern, but was considered a good example of traditional Muslim religious education. Musa continued his religious education in Bukhara, then went to Istanbul, and studied at al-Azhar University in Cairo. He later studied for two years in Mecca and Medina, and in India. Returning to Cairo, he was engaged in scientific research and wrote the work of Tariq al-Qur'an wa-l-Masarif' (History of the Qur'an and its Lists'), which was published in 1904 in the Cairo magazine al-Manar, and a year later in Kazan a separate book was published. See Ramazanov Readings [*Ramazanovskiy Chteniya*], 25 May 2020. Available at: http://www.idmedina.ru/ramazan/. Also see in Russian and Tatar, Musa Bigiev's writings on performance of hajj in 1927, Aydar Khairutdinov, [*Unique Notes of Musa Bigiev's performance of hajj in 1927*'] [*Unikalniy zapisi Musy Bigieva o ego hadje 1927 goda*], *Hajj of Russian Muslims* [*Hajj Rosiyskyh Musulman*], no. 8 (2017): 7–14; Musa Bigiev, 'Hajj performance of Musa Bigiev' [*Musa Bigievnen 1927–nche elgy hachnamese*], *Hajj of Russian Muslims* [*Hajj Rosiyskyh Musulman*], no. 8 (2017): 15–53.

137 Nurimanov, 'Meccan Congress and Hajj in 1926', 150.

138 Nurimanov, 'Hajj in Soviet Period'.

139 Galina Yemelianova, 'Islam, Nationalism and State in the Muslim Caucasus', *Caucasus Survey*, 1, no. 2 (2014): 5.

140 Ibid., 14.

141 Gabdurrahman Rasuli, 'Trip to Hajj in 1945' [*Poezdka v hajj v 1945 godu*], *Hajj of Russian Muslims № 4, Annual Collection of Hajj Travel Notes* [*Jadzh rossiskih musulman №4 Ezhegodniy sbornik putevyh zametok o hadzhe*], 7 September 2012. Available at: http://www.idmedina.ru/books/history_culture/?4752.

142 Benningsen, et al., *Soviet Strategy and Islam*, 35.

143 Ibid., 38.

144 Ibid., 50–2.

145 Ibid., 44.

146 The journal was established in 1968 by the Muslim Religious Board for Central Asia and Kazakhstan. It was the only Islamic periodical carrying the official seal of approval of the Soviet government. The journal was published in Uzbek, along with Eastern languages, such as Arabic, Persian and Dari and Western languages, French and English. Available at: https://www.eastview.com/resources/journals/muslims-soviet-east/

147 J. G. Tewari, *Muslims under The Czars and the Soviet* (Lucknow, India: Academy of Islamic Research and Publications, 1984), 413.

148 Golan, *Soviet Policies in the Middle East from World War II to Gorbachev*, 199.

149 See Benningsen, et al., *Soviet Strategy and Islam*, 57–65.

150 Ibid., 59.

Chapter 3

1 Ramzi Valeev, 'Projects of National State-Building and the Establishment of the Tatar Autonomous Soviet Socialist Republic', in *The History of The Tatars Since Ancient Times: Tatars and Tatarstan in the 20th -Beginning of the 21st Centuries*, vol. 7 (Kazan: Academy of Sciences of the Republic of Tatarstan Sh. Marjani Institute of History, 2017), 242.

2 See, G. Kasymov, *Essays about Religious and Antireligious Movements Among Tatars Before and After Revolution* [*Ocherki po relizioznomu I antireligioznomu dvicheniy sredi Tatar do I posle revolucii*] (Kazan: Tatizdat, 1931).

3 Aydar Khabutdinov, 'All-Russian Muslim Congresses of 1917, the National Assembly and Their Importance: Declaration of National Autonomy in 1917–1918', in *The History of The Tatars Since Ancient Times*, 214.

4 Ibid.

5 Ibid.

6 Aydar Khabutdinov, 'Spiritual Boards During World Wars and Totalitarianism' *(1917-1950)* [*Spiritual Boards in the Years of World Wars and Totalitarianism (1917–1950)*]. Available at: http://www.idmedina.ru/books/history_culture/minaret/5/habutdin.htm?

7 Aydar Khabutdinov, 'Kazan from the February Revolution until the Creation of the Tatar Autonomous Republic (1920) [Kazan ot Fevralskoy Revolucii 1917 goda do sozdaniya Avtonomnoy Tatarskoy Respubliki v 1920 godu]', *Islam in the Modern World* 13, no. 3 (September 2017): 115–36. Also see Almaz Faizullin, 'Conditions and Activities of the Tatar-Muslims after the February Revolution in the Government of Kazan (February–October 1917) [Polozhenie I deyatelnost' Tatar-Musuulman posle Fevralskoy Revolucii v kazanskoy Gubernii (Fevral'–Octyabr' 1017 goda)]', *Islam in the Modern World* 15, no. 3 (2019): 138–49.

8 Dilyara Usmanova, 'The Kazan Muslim Congresses and the Proclamation of "Cultural National Autonomy"', in *The History of The Tatars Since Ancient Times*, 225.

9 Ibid., 226.

10 Aydar Khabutdinov, 'Organs of Tatar Autonomy in 1917–1919', in *The History of The Tatars Since Ancient Times*, 218.

11 Ibid.

12 Dilyara Usmanova, 'The National Assembly and National Autonomy Projects', in *The History of The Tatars Since Ancient Times*, 233.

13 J. G. Tewari, *Muslims under The Czars and the Soviet* (Lucknow, India: Academy of Islamic Research and Publications, 1984), 95.

14 More on Sultan-Galiev's political view, see Ilmira Islamgulova, 'Political View of Mirsaid Sultan-Galiev [Politichsekie vzlyady Mirsaida Sultan-Galieva]', PhD Thesis, Bashkir State University, 2005.

15 Tewari, *Muslims under The Czars and the Soviet*, 95.

16 Oleg Ozerov, *Karim Khakimov: Chronicle of his Life* [*Karim Khakimov: letopis' zhini*] (LitRes: Samizdat, 2020), 179.

17 Ibid., 180.

18 Ibid.

19 On the establishment and development of TASSR, see I. Klimov, *Establishment and Development of Tatar ASSR* [*Obrazovanie I razvitie tatarskoy ASSR*] (Kazan: Kazan University Press, 1960); Daishev, ed. *History of TASSR* [*Tatarstan ASSR tarihy*] (Kazan: Kazan University Press, 1960).

20 Ozerov, *Karim Khakimov*, 188–9.

21 Alexander Benningsen, Paul Henze, George Tanham and S. Enders Wimbush, *Soviet Strategy and Islam* (London: The Macmillan Press Ltd, 1989), 22.

22 Ibid., 19.

23 Jennifer-Anne Davidson, 'Power Dynamics in Russian-Tatarstani Relations: A Case Study', MA Thesis, University of Victoria, 2008, 12.

24 On pan-Turkism, see M. A. Czaplicka, *The Turks of Central Asia in History and at the Present Day* (Oxford: Barnes & Noble Books, 1918); Charles Warren Hostler, *Turkish and the Soviets: The Turks of the World and Their Political Objectives* (London: George Allen & Unwin, 1957); Serge A. Zenkovsky, *Pan-Turkism and Islam in Russia* (Cambridge, MA: Harvard University Press, 1960); and Firuz Kazemzadeh, *The Struggle for Transcaucasia, 1917–1921* (New York: Philosophical Library; Oxford: George Ronald, 1951).

25 Zeki Velidi Togan, 'Unification Cases of Turks ['Türkistanlıların Birleşme Davaları']', *Serdengeçti*, (1952): 15–16.

26 F. Karimi, *Compliments from Istanbul* [*Istambul maktuplary*] (Orenburg, 1913, B. 415).

27 Aydar Uzeev, 'Islamism, Turkism and Tatarism in Components of the Social-Political Establishment of Tatar at the Beginning of the XXth Century ['Islamism, Turkism and Tatarism kaka komponenty obshestvenno-politicheskogo coznaniya tatar nachala 20 veka]', *Islam in the Modern World* 14, no. 1 (March 2018): 175.

28 Usuf Akchura, *Three Policies* [*Üç Tarzı Siyaset*], ed. H. B. Parsoy (Routledge: Abington, 1995).

29 Ivo J. Lederer, 'The Soviet Union and the Middle East: The Post-World War II Era', in *Historical Introduction*, ed. Ivo J. Lederer and Wayne S. Vucinich (Stanford: Hoover Institution Press, Stanford University, 1974), 8.

30 Guseva, 'The Gloomy Echo of the "TsDUM Affair": "The Chain of the Qur'an" and the Repressions against the Muslims Elite in the USSR (1940)' ['*Mrachnoe echo "Dela TsDUM": :Cep' Korana" I Repressii protiv msuslmanskoy elity v SSSR (1940)'*], *Novyi Istoriceskij Vestnik* 52, no. 2 (2017): 85.

31 On repressions of Tatars, see Rafael Mustafin, *Tatars Who Were Repressed* [*Repressiyalengen Tatar ediplery*] (Kazan: Tatarstan Kitab Neshriyaty, 2009); Repressions of Muslims from Moscow, see D. Khayretdinov and B. Ahmadullin, 'Manifestations of the Repressive-Ideological Dictatorship of the Authorities on the Muslims of Moscow during the Years of Soviet Rule' [*Proyavleniya repressivno-ideologicheskogo diktata vlastei na musulman Moskvy v gody sovetskoy vlasti*]. Available at: http://www.idmedina.ru/books/materials/faizhanov/5/hist_haretdinov.htm?

32 Guseva, 'The Gloomy Echo of the "TsDUM Affair"', 89.

33 Ibid., 85–102.

34 Ibid., 90.

35 See Chapter 2 – notes 115 and 121.

36 Guseva, 'The Gloomy Echo of the "TsDUM Affair"', 89.

37 Ibid., 91.

38 Ibid.

39 Ibid.

40 Ibid.

41 Ibid., 96.

42 Ibid.

43 Lederer, 'The Soviet Union and the Middle East', 8.

44 George Lenczowski, *Soviet Advances in the Middle East* (Washington: American Enterprise Institute for Public Policy Research, 1972), 43–5.

45 Ibid., 43.

46 Lubomyr Hajda, 'Ethnic Politics and Ethnic Conflict in the USSR and the Post-Soviet States', *Race, Gender and Ethnicity* 19, no. 2 (1993): 220.

47 Andrey Schberbak, 'Nationalism in the USSR: A Historical and Comparative Perspective', *Nationalities Papers* 43, no. 6 (2015): 872–3.

48 Yaacov Ro'I, *The Limits to Power: Soviet Policy in the Middle East* (London: Croom Helm, 1979), 155.

49 Matthew Allen Derrick, 'Placing Faith in Tatarstan, Russia: Islam and the Negotiation of Homeland', PhD Thesis, University of Oregon, 2012, 116.

50 Ibid.

51 Bennigsen, et al., *Soviet Strategy and Islam*.

52 Cf. Alexander Benningsen and Marie Broxup, *The Islamic Threat to the Soviet State* (London: Croom Helm, 1983), 44–50.

53 L. A. Mukhamadeeva and A. R. Faizullin, 'The Anti-Religious Policy of the Tatarstan Government (1920s) ['Antireligioznaya politika v Tatarstane (1920s)]', *Minbar. Islamic Studies* 12, no. 2 (2019): 438–50.

54 Ibid.

55 Ruslan Ibragimov, 'Islam among the Tatars in the 1940–1980s', in *The History of the Tatars since Ancient Times*, vol. 7 (Kazan: Kazan University, 2017), 454.

56 Ibid.

57 On Government–Muslim relations in the USSR in 1944–1949, see Arzamaskin Uryi, 'Government-Muslim Relations of the USSR in 1944–1949' [Gosudarstvenno-Musulmanskie Otnosheniya v SSSR v 1944–1949 godu], *Islam in the Modern World* 13, no. 4 (December 2017): 25–35.

58 V. A.Kuroyedov, 'Religion and Law' [Religiya i zakon], Moscow: Znanie, 1970, 92–3.

59 Ibragimov, 'Islam among the Tatars in the 1940–1980s', 454.

60 Ibid.

61 National Archive of the Republic of Tatarstan, File R-873, List 1, Act 4, Sheet 33; cited in Ibragimov, *Islam among the Tatars in the 1940–1980s*, 455.

62 SA HPD TR, Fund 15, Inventory 5, File 1844b, Sheet 1]; cited in Ibragimov, *Islam among the Tatars in the 1940–1980s*, 455.

63 Ibragimov, *Islam among the Tatars in the 1940–1980s*, 458.

64 Ibid.

65 Ibid., 461.

66 Ibid.

67 National Archive of the Republic of Tatarstan, Fund R-873, List 1, Act 93, Sheet 58.

68 Usmanova et al., 'Islamic education in soviet and post-Soviet Tatarstan', in *Islamic education in Soviet Union and Its Successor States*, ed. By Michael Kemper, Raoul Motika and Stefan Reichmuth (London: Routledge, 2010), 46.

69 Mark Katz, *Russia and Arabia: Soviet Foreign Policy toward the Arabian Peninsula* (Baltimore: Johns Hopkins University Press, 1986), 131.

70 Aryeh Y. Yodfat, *The Soviet Union and the Arabian Peninsula: Soviet Policy Towards the Persian Gulf and Arabia*, 1.

71 Katz, *Russia and Arabia*, 132.

72 Ibid., 133.

73 Yodfat, *The Soviet Union and the Arabian Peninsula*, 2.

74 Katz, *Russia and Arabia*, 133.

75 Ibid., 134.

76 Ibid.

77 Ibid.

78 Yodfat, *The Soviet Union and the Arabian Peninsula*, 8.

79 Ibid.

80 Katz, *Russia and Arabia*, 136.

81 Ibid.

82 Ibid.

83 Ibid., 138.

84 Ibid.

85 Kuwait obtained independence in 1961.

86 H. R. P. Dickson Box 3, File 3, Administrative reports of the Kuwait Political Agency, 1928–32, DN3/3/135: VI.

87 Ibid.

88 E. C. Meljumyan, G. G. Kosach and T. B. Nosenko, 'Russia in the Foreign Policy Priorities of the Council of Cooperation of the Arabian Gulf States after the Events of the "Arab Spring"' [Roosiya vo vneshnepolitichsekih prioritetah Soveta Sotrudnichestva Arabskih Gosudarst zaliva posle sobytiy 'arabskoy vesny'], *Vestnik MGIMO-Universiteta* 4, no. 55 (2017): 141.

89 Yodfat, *The Soviet Union and the Arabian Peninsula*, 9.

90 E. C. Meljumyan, G. G. Kosach and T. B. Nosenko, 'Russia in the Foreign Policy Priorities of the Council of Cooperation of the Arabian Gulf States after the Events of the "Arab Spring"', 141.

91 Katz, *Russia and Arabia*, 163.

92 Yodfat, *The Soviet Union and the Arabian Peninsula*, 10.

93 Katz, *Russia and Arabia*, 163.

94 Ibid.

95 Bennigsen, et al., *Soviet Strategy and Islam*, 117.

96 E. C. Meljumyan, G. G. Kosach and T. B. Nosenko, 'Russia in the Foreign Policy Priorities of the Council of Cooperation of the Arabian Gulf States after the Events of the "Arab Spring"', 141.

97 Ibid., 141.

98 Bennigsen, et al., *Soviet Strategy and Islam*, 117.

99 Katz, *Russia and Arabia*, 165.

100 Ibid.

101 E. C. Meljumyan, G. G. Kosach and T. B. Nosenko, 'Russia in the Foreign Policy Priorities of the Council of Cooperation of the Arabian Gulf States after the Events of the "Arab Spring"', 142.

102 Shahram Chubin, 'Soviet-American Rivalry in the Middle East: The Political Dimension', in *The Soviet Union in the Middle East: Policies and Perspectives*, ed. Adeed Dawisha and Karen Dawisha (London: Royal Institute of International Affairs, 1982), 64.

103 Ibid.

104 Ibid.

105 E. C. Meljumyan, G. G. Kosach and T. B. Nosenko, 'Russia in the Foreign Policy Priorities of the Council of Cooperation of the Arabian Gulf States after the Events of the "Arab Spring"', 142.

106 Katz, *Russia and Arabia*, 171.

107 The UAE declared its independence on 2 December 1971 and included the shaykhdoms of Abu Dubai, Dubai, Ajman, Fujairah, Sharjah and Umm al-Quwain.

108 Yodfat, *The Soviet Union and the Arabian Peninsula*, 13.

109 Ibid.

110 Katz, *Russia and Arabia*, 178.

111 Yodfat, *The Soviet Union and the Arabian Peninsula*, 12.

112 Katz, *Russia and Arabia*, 180.

113 Yodfat, *The Soviet Union and the Arabian Peninsula*, 103.

114 Katz, *Russia and Arabia*, 181.

115 Yodfat, *The Soviet Union and the Arabian Peninsula*, 13.

116 Ibid.

117 Katz, *Russia and Arabia*, 182.

118 Yodfat, *The Soviet Union and the Arabian Peninsula*, 103.

119 Ibid., 13.

120 Ibid., 25.

121 Katz, *Russia and Arabia*, 122.

122 Katz, *Russia and Arabia*, 123.

123 E. C. Meljumyan, G. G. Kosach and T. B. Nosenko, 'Russia in the Foreign Policy Priorities of the Council of Cooperation of the Arabian Gulf States after the Events of the "Arab Spring"', 141.

124 Khaled Mohamed Ali al-Tamimi, 'Cooperation Between Russia and Bahrain in the Field of Regional Security' [Sotrudnichsetvo mechdu Rossiye i Bahreinom v oblasti obespecheniya regionalnoy bezopasnosti], *Vestnik MGIMO -Universiteta* 4, no. 55 (2017): 194.

125 Khaled Mohamed Ali al-Tamimi, 'Cooperation between Russia and Bahrain in the Field of Regional Security', 194.

126 Ibid.

127 M. Almaqbali, 'Russia's Relations with Gulf States and Their Effect on Regional Balance in the Middle East', *RUDN Journal of Political Science* 20, no. 4 (2018): 536.

128 For details on historical relations between Russia and the Middle East, see Aaron S. Klieman, *Soviet Russia and the Middle East* (Baltimore, London: The Johns Hopkins Press, 1970), 27–37.

129 Vladimir Lenin, *A Caricature of Marxism and Imperialist Economism: Collected Works* (Moscow: Progress Publishers, 1968), 34. For more on Lenin's views in support of national liberation movements and on relations with the countries of the East, see O. Gorbatov and L. Cherkasskiy, Cooperation of the USSR with the Countries of the Arab East and Africa (Moscow: Nauka, 1973), 3–14.

130 Alexey Vasiliev, *Russia's Middle East Policy: From Lenin to Putin* (Abingdon: Routledge, 2018), 14.

Also see V. Gusarov and N. Semin, 'Socialist Countries are Faithful Friends of the Arab People' [Strany Socializma – vernye druzya Arabskyh narodov'] (Moscow: Publishing House of Political Literature, 1971).

131 Wilbur Green, *Soviet Strategy in the Middle East* (Carlisle Barracks: Army War College, 1973), 4.

132 The significance of Turkey for the USSR is linked to its geographical location, geostrategic interests and other geopolitical factors. For details on Turkey–Soviet relations, see Galia Golan, *The Soviet Union and Turkey* (Cambridge: Cambridge University Press, 1990), 244–57; on relations since the Second World War, see George S. Harris, 'The Soviet Union and Turkey', in *The Soviet Union and the Middle East: The Post-World War II Era*, ed. Ivo J. Lederer and Wayne S. Vucinich (Stanford: Hoover Institution Press, Stanford University, 1974), 25–54.

133 Soviet interests in Iran were linked to the days of the Russian Empire, prior to the discovery of oil, and thus, to some extent, predating the vulnerability of the West, at least in this regard. Due to its strategic location, Iran remained important for the Soviets. For more on relations between the Soviets and Iran, see Galia Golan, *Soviet Policies in the Middle East from World War II to Gorbachev* (Cambridge: Cambridge University Press, 1990), 176–96; Firuz Kazemzadeh, 'Soviet-Iranian Relations: A Quarter-Century of Freeze and Thaw', in *The Soviet Union and the Middle East: The Post-World War II Era*, ed. Ivo J. Lederer and Wayne S. Vucinich, 55–77.

134 Details of Soviet policies towards Turkey, Iran and Afghanistan – which are called 'the Northern Tier' by Malcolm Yapp – can be found in Malcolm Yapp, 'Soviet Relations with Countries of the Northern Tier', *The Soviet Union in the Middle East*, ed. Adeed Dawisha and Karen Dawisha, 24–44.

135 Vasiliev, *Russia's Middle East Policy: From Lenin to Putin*, 19.

136 Aaron Klieman, *Soviet Russia and the Middle East* (Baltimore: The Johns Hopkins Press, 1970), 34.

137 Mark Katz, 'Russia and Iran', *Middle East Policy* 19, no. 4 (Winter, 2012): 54.

138 Vladimir Belyakov, *Sovetsko-Egipetskie otnosheniya 1943–1955: документы и материалы* [*Soviet-Egyptian relations, 1943–1955: Documents and Materials*] (Saint Petersburg: Aletelia, 2019).

139 Vasiliev, *Russia's Middle East Policy: From Lenin to Putin*, 34.

140 Ibid., 26.

141 Talal Nizameddin, *Russia and the Middle East Towards a New Foreign Policy* (London: Hurst & Company, 1999), 16.

142 Ibid.

143 Robert O. Freedman, *Moscow and the Middle East: Soviet Policy Since the Invasion of Afghanistan* (New York, 1991).

144 Nizameddin, *Russia and the Middle East*, 16.

145 Ibid.

146 George W. Breslauer, 'Soviet Policy in the Middle East, 1967–72: Unalterable Antagonism or Collaborative Competition?' in *Soviet Strategy in the Middle East*, ed. George W. Breslauer (London: Boston Unwin Hyman, 1990).

147 For example, see Robert Freedman, 'Détente and US-Soviet Relations in the Middle East during the Nixon Years (1969–1974)' in *Dimensions of Détente*, ed. Della W. Sheldon (New York: Praeger, 1978); Abraham S. Becker, Bent Hansen and Malcolm H. Kerr, *The Economics and Politics of the Middle East* (New York: American Elsevier Publishing Co., 1975); Alvin Z. Rubinstein, *Red Star on the Nile* (Princeton, NJ: Princeton University Press, 1977).

148 George W. Breslauer, 'Soviet Policy in the Middle East, 1967–72', 24.

149 Carol R. Saivetz, 'Gorbachev's Middle East Policy: The Arab Dimension', in *The Decline of the Soviet Union and the Transformation of the Middle East*, ed. David H. Goldberg and Paul Marantz (Oxford: Westview Press, 1994).

150 Nizameddin, *Russia and the Middle East*, 64–5.

151 Ibid., 64–7.

152 Alexander Rahr, 'New Thinking Takes Hold in Foreign Policy Establishment', *RFE/RL Report on the USSR* 1, no. 1 (January 1989): 4.

153 J. C. Hurewitz, 'Origins of Rivalry', in *Soviet-American Rivalry in the Middle East*, ed. J. C. Hurewitz (New York: Frederick A. Praeger Publishers, 1969), 1.

154 Ibid.

155 On the political and military dimensions of superpower competitions, see Chubin, 'Soviet-American Rivalry in the Middle East', 124–33; and Jonathan Alford, 'Soviet-American Rivalry in the Middle East: The Military Dimension', in *The Soviet Union in the Middle East*, ed. Adeed Dawisha and Karen Dawisha, 134–46.

156 Rosemary Hollis, 'Introduction: Sliding into a New Era', in *The Soviets, Their Successors and the Middle East Turning Point*, ed. Rosemary Hollis (US: St. Martin's Press, 1993), 3.
     However, Galia Golan analysing 'new thinking' in Soviet foreign policy under Gorbachev considers the shift and stresses that this idea of new thinking links with global interdependence, which led to a 'de-ideologization' of foreign policy and a quest for a balance of interests between Moscow and the West (Washington) rather than the aspiration of zero-sum-game competition. See Galia Golan, *Moscow and the Middle East: New Thinking on Regional Conflict* (London: Chatham House, 1992), 4. On Arab–Israeli conflict during the Gorbachev period, see ibid., 10–46.

157 Hurewitz, 'Origins of Rivalry', 1.

158 Rosemary Hollis, 'Introduction: Sliding into a New Era', in *The Soviets, Their Successors and the Middle East Turning Point*, ed. Rosemary Hollis, 3.

159 See the note from the head of the Middle East countries of the USSR minister of Foreign Affairs, Kiselev, to the deputy minister of Foreign Affairs of the USSR, Malikov, on 13 December 1961, where relations between the USSR and Israel were stated.

See Vitaly Naumkin, *Blizhniy Vostok: Iz dokumentov vneshney politiki* [*Middle East: From Foreign Policy Archive Documents*]. Available at: http://history-library.com/index.php?id1=3&category=voennaya-istoriya&author=naumkin-vv&book=2003&page=220.

160 Hurewitz, 'Origins of Rivalry', 2.

161 Fred Halliday, 'Gorbachev and the "Arab syndrome": Soviet Policy in the Middle East', *World Policy Journal* 4, no. 3 (1987): 415. For detailed Soviet views of pre-1952 Egypt and until 1966, see Aryeh Yodfat, *Arab Politics in the Soviet Mirror* (Jerusalem: Israel Universities Press), 32–102.

162 For more on Soviet economic aid, see Franklyn D. Holzman, 'Soviet Trade and Aid Policies', in *Soviet-American Rivalry in the Middle East*, ed. J. C. Hurewitz; Gur Ofer, 'Economic Aspects of Soviet Involvement in the Middle East' in *The Limits to Power*, 67–97; Moreover, Alan H. Smith explains the importance of trade in relations between the USSR and the region, see Alan H. Smith, 'The Influence of Trade on Soviet Relations with the Middle East', in *The Soviet Union in the Middle East*, ed. Adeed Dawisha and Karen Dawisha, 103.

163 For further details on Soviet–Egyptian relations, see Galia Golan, *Soviet Policies in the Middle East: From World War II to Gorbachev* (Cambridge: Cambridge University Press, 1990), 44–57; for, specifically, the USSR–Egypt relations during the Nasser era, see P. J. Vatikiotis, 'The Soviet Union and Egypt: The Nasser Years', in *The Soviet Union and the Middle East: The Post-World War III Era*, ed. Ivo J. Lederer and Wayne S. Vucinich, 121–33.

164 Vitaly Naumkin, *Blizhniy Vostok: Iz dokumentov vneshney politiki* [*Middle East: From Foreign Policy Archive Documents*]. Available at: http://history-library.com/index.php?id1=3&category=voennaya-istoriya&author=naumkin-vv&book=2003&page=1.

165 Ibid.

166 Elizabeth Monroe Collection, Articles on the Arab Bureau and Monroe, accounts of Monroe's travels in Italy, Algeria and Morocco, GB165-0207, B. 447 (R), April (1957): 8.

167 On strategies of offering military aid by the Soviets and the United States during 1945–67, and how it affected the rivalry of the two Superpowers in the Middle East, see Geoffrey Kemp, 'Strategy and Arms Levels, 1945–1967', in *Soviet-American Rivalry in the Middle East*, ed. J. C. Hurewitz; Lincoln P. Bloomfield and Amelia C. Leiss, 'Arms Transfers and Arms Control', in *Soviet-American Rivalry in the Middle East*, ed. J. C. Hurewitz; Amnon Sella examines the USSR military policy in the Middle East after 1973, se Amnon Sella, 'Changes in Soviet Political Military Policy in the Middle East after 1973', in *The Limits to Power: Soviet Policy in the Middle East*, ed. Yaacov Ro'I, 32–64.

168 Vasiliev, *Russia's Middle East Policy: From Lenin to Putin*, 61.

169 Hurewitz, 'Origins of Rivalry', 4.

170 Ibid., 4.

171 Ibid.

172 Ibid.

173 See Husain M. Albaharna, *The Legal Status of the Arabian Gulf States: A Study of Their Treaty Relations and Their International Problems* (Manchester: Manchester University Press, 1968).

174 Shohei Sato, *Britain and the Formation of the Gulf States: Embers of Empire* (Manchester: Manchester University Press, 2016), 1.

175 Ibid., 5–28.

176 H. R. P. Dickson, Box 3 File 1, Collection of articles, correspondence, press cuttings and so on – Kuwait and the Middle East in general, 1930s-1950s, Box 3/1/12.

177 Shohei Sato, *Britain and the Formation of the Gulf States*, 5–28.

178 See Anthony H. Cordesman, *The Gulf and the Search for Strategic Stability: Saudi Arabia, the Military Balance in the Gulf, and Trends in the Arab-Israeli Military Balance* (Boulder: Westview Press; London: Mansell Publishing Limited, 1984).

179 Shohei Sato, *Britain and the Formation of the Gulf States*, 5–28.

180 Simon C. Smith, *Britain's Revival and Fall in the Gulf: Kuwait, Bahrain, Qatar, and the Trucial States, 1950–1971* (London, New York: Routledge, 2013).

181 Shohei Sato, *Britain and the Formation of the Gulf States*, 5–28.

182 Ibid.

183 Jeffrey R. Macris, 'The Anglo-American Gulf: Britain's departure and America's arrival in the Persian Gulf', *PhD Dissertation, Johns Hopkins University*, April, 2007, 55.

184 Administration report of the Kuwait Political Agency for the year 1932, H. R. P. Dickson Box 3, File 3, Administrative reports of the Kuwait Political Agency. 1928–32.
DN 3/3/168, p. 34.

185 Macris, 'The Anglo-American Gulf'.

186 See Helene von Bismarck, *British Policy in the Persian Gulf, 1961–1968* (London: Palgrave Macmillan, 2013).

187 David Reynolds, 'A "Special Relationship?" America, Britain and the International Order since the Second World War', *International Affairs* 62, no. 1 (1986): 2.

188 See Simon C. Smith, *Britain's Revival and Fall in the Gulf: Kuwait, Bahrain, Qatar, and the Trucial States* (London and New York: Routledge, 2013), 119–28.

189 Macris, 'The Anglo-American Gulf', 97.

190 Ibid.

191 Chubin, 'Soviet-American Rivalry in the Middle East', 56.

192 Macris, 'The Anglo-American Gulf', 131.

193 Ibid.

194 Macris, 221. Also see Simon C. Smith, *Britain's Revival and Fall in the Gulf Kuwait, Bahrain, Qatar, and the Trucial States,* 129–50.

195 Macris, 'The Anglo-American Gulf', 253.

196 Shohei Sato, *Britain and the Formation of the Gulf States: Embers of Empire,* 29. Also on British withdrawal from the Gulf, see Simon C. Smith, 'Britain's Decision to Withdraw from the Persian Gulf: A Pattern Not a Puzzle', *The Journal of Imperial and Commonwealth History* 44, no. 2 (2016): 328–51.

197 Macris, 'The Anglo-American Gulf', 306.

198 Ibid., 306.

199 Chubin, 'Soviet-American Rivalry in the Middle East', 60.

200 Macris, 'The Anglo-American Gulf', 326.

201 Ibid., 328.

202 See Anthony H. Cordesman, *The Gulf and the Search for Strategic Stability: Saudi Arabia, the Military Balance in the Gulf, and Trends in the Arab-Israeli Military Balance* (Boulder: Westview Press; London: Mansell Publishing Limited, 1988); Markus Kaim, ed., *Great Powers and Regional Orders: The United States and the Persian Gulf* (Burlington: Ashgate Publishing Company, 2008).

Chapter 4

1 John W. Slocum, 'A Sovereign State Within Russia? The External Relations of the Republic of Tatarstan', *Global Society* 13, no. 1 (1999): 58.

2 'Trans-border regional paradiplomacy involves contacts between geographically contiguous subunits of adjacent countries, and typically involves issues of border crossings, immigration, smuggling, environmental problems, or economic integration.' Ivo D. Duchacek, 'Perforated Sovereignties: Towards a Typology of New Actors in International Relations', in *Federalism and International Relations: The Role of Subnational Units,* ed. Hans J. Michelmann and Panayotis Soldatos (Ingles: Praeger, 1990), 20.
'Trans-regional paradiplomacy involves contacts between non-contiguous regions of neighbouring countries. These sorts of interactions are generally limited to economic and cultural co-operation, and typically raise more difficult issues of diplomatic protocol on the part of the central governments of the regions involved. The third category, global paradiplomacy, involves contacts between subnational governments of one state and governments of regions in distant countries, or direct contacts with the federal governments of distant states.' See Slocum, 'A Sovereign State Within Russia?' 70.

3 Gul'nara Shaikhutdinova, 'Dogovorno-pravovaia praktika Respubliki Tatarstan na sovremennom etape', *Panorama* 2 (October 1995): 16–18; Slocum, 'A Sovereign State within Russia?' 64.

4 'Mezhpravitel'stvennye soglasheniia Respubliki Tatarstan s Turetskoi Respublikoi', *Panorama-Forum* 4, no. 1 (1996): 152–3. Cited in Oktay Firat Tanrisever, 'The Politics of Tatar Nationalism and Russian Federation: 1992–1999', PhD Thesis, School of Slavonic and East European Studies University College London, 2002, 169.

5 'Turkey Opened Its General Consulate, which is the First Foreign Diplomatic Mission in Tatarstan', *Respublika Tatarstan*, 12 October 1996.

6 Dr Rafael Khakimov can be identified as among the political elites under the first president of the Republic of Tatarstan, Mintimer Shaimiev, and was his chief adviser. He was also the director of the Institute of History at the Academy of Sciences of the Republic of Tatarstan.

7 The statistics cited in this paragraph are from the Republic of Tatarstan's official website. Available at: http://www.tatar.ru/english; more detailed data from 1996 may be found in Ministerstvo Vneshnikh Ekonomicheskikh sviazei Respubliki Tatarstan, *Vneshneekonomicheskaia diaatelnost' respubliki Tatarstan v 1996 godu* (Kazan, 1997), 25–6.

8 Slocum, 'A Sovereign State within Russia?' 60.

9 Ibid.

10 Republic of Tatarstan, 'Attraction of Foreign Investment'. Available at: http://www .tatar.ru/English/00000061.html.

11 Tatar-inform, 6–15 June 1998. Available at: http://www.tatar.ru/english/ti000028 .html.

12 Gulnaz Sharafutdinova, 'Paradiplomacy in the Russian Regions: Tatarstan's Search for Statehood', *Europe-Asia Studies* 55, no. 4 (2003): 618–19.

13 Marat Gatin has extensive knowledge and experience of the developments of Tatarstan's relations in the Eastern direction. Educated at al-Azhar University, he worked as the chief adviser of the sector of the countries of Asia and Africa of the Department of Foreign Relations of the President of the Republic of Tatarstan (2006–9); this was followed by his appointment as the head of the Sector for Asian and African Countries of the Department of Foreign Relations of the president of the Republic of Tatarstan (2009–10), and the head of the Office of the President of the president of the Republic of Tatarstan for Interaction with Religious Associations (2010–12).

14 Similarly to the Tatars, most GCC states have majority Sunni populations (except Bahrain). Tatars follow Hanafi madhhab (school of Islam jurisprudence). While Maliki madhhab is followed by the UAE, Kuwait and Sunnis in Bahrain, Qatar and the north-eastern parts of Saudi Arabia, the madhhab of Ibadi is followed in Oman. Saudi Arabia and Qatar follow Hanbali madhhab, along with the demographic majority in four emirates of the UAE; large minorities of Hanbali followers are also found in Bahrain and Oman.

15 Matthew Allen Derrick, 'Placing Faith in Tatarstan, Russia: Islam and the Negotiation of Homeland', PhD Thesis, University of Oregon, March 2012, 3.

16 Ibid.

17 Ibid.

18 Galina Yemelianova, 'Shaimiev's "Khanate" on the Volga and its Russian Subjects', *Asian Ethnicity* 1, no. 1 (2000): 48.

19 Marat Gatin, 2020, interviewed by author.

20 Babay (single) – babai (plural) – in Tatar literally means 'grandfather'; however, the interviewee uses it in the meaning of the older generation of religious people/ religious authorities.

21 Valiulla Yakupov was a prominent Muslim cleric in Tatarstan and the deputy to the Muslim province's chief Mufti. He was known as a strong critic of radical Islamist organizations which advocate Salafism. Yakupov was shot dead in 2012; Russia's Council of Muftis has branded this murder as a terror attack.

22 According to the Council of Religious Affairs of Tatarstan, in the 1990s about 200 Muslims from Tatarstan received a religious education abroad. In 2001, sixty Muslims from Tatarstan were studying theology abroad in the following countries: Egypt (37 students), Saudi Arabia (16), Syria (4), Turkey (2), Tunisia (2), Yemen (2), Malaysia (1), Sudan (1) and Libya (1). Derrick, 'Placing Faith in Tatarstan, Russia', 152.

23 Derrick, 'Placing Faith in Tatarstan, Russia', 152.

24 Marat Gatin, 2020, interviewed by author.

25 Russian Islamic University is Russia's first official Islamic university, which was established in 1998 in Kazan. Among other important initiatives for returning to the traditional theological school was the establishment of Bolgar Islamic Academy in 2016.

26 Kamil Samigullin has acted as the chairman of the Spiritual Board of Muslims of the Republic of Tatarstan since 2013. Being very knowledgeable in religious studies and knowing Oriental languages (Arabic and Turkish), he has earned the respect of Muslims throughout the country. He is the author of the following popular books: *Anyone Can Become a Qur'an-Hafiz*; *Eternal Love*; *Islam in Questions and Answers*; *What Do We Know About the Jinn and Their Word*; *The Muslim World*, as well as other vital publications.

27 Kamil Samigullin, 2020, interviewed by author.

28 Marat Gatin, 2020, interviewed by author.

29 Russia-Islamic Group of Strategic Vision, 'The Group of Strategic Vision "Russia-Islamic World" Presents the Updated Development Strategy', 11 June 2019. Available at: https://russia-islworld.ru/en/novosti//the-group-of-strategic-vision -russia-islamic-world-presents-the-updated-development-strategy/.

30 Realnoe vremya, 'Pozvat' v gosti Korolya: kak razvivalis' vzaimootnosheniya Tatarstana I Saudovskoy Aravii', ['To Invite the King to Visit: How Relations between Tatarstan and Saudi Arabia Developed'], 5 October 2017. Available at: https://realnoevremya.ru/articles/78308-kak-razvivalis-otnosheniya-tatarstana-i -saudovskoy-aravii

31 Russia-Islamic Group of Strategic Vision, 'The Group of Strategic Vision "Russia-Islamic World" Presents the Updated Development Strategy'.

32 Taliya Minullina can be classed among the political and economic elites under current president Rustam Minnikhanov. Prior to leading the Tatarstan Investment Development Agency, she worked at the Ministry of Economy of Tatarstan Republic (specialist in Investment Department, leading adviser, leading consultant, Head of Department) (2007–10), and in the Office of the President of Republic of Tatarstan (head of division, head of department of civil service department) (2010–14).

33 Taliya Minullina, 2020, interviewed by author.

34 Abdulrahman bin Mohammad bin Rashid al-Khalifa, 2022, interviewed by author.

35 Press Service of the Group of Strategic Vision 'Russia-Islamic World', *About the VI Annual Meeting of the Group of Strategic Vision 'Russia-Islamic World'*, 30 January 2020. Available at: https://russia-islworld.ru/en/main//about-the-vi-annual -meeting-of-the-group-of-strategic-vision-russia-islamic-world/.

36 RIA Novosti, *The Meeting of the Group of Strategic Vision 'Russia-Islamic World' Will Take Place in Saudi Arabia, [Zasedanie gruppy 'Rossiya -Islamskiy mir' proidet v Saudovskooy Aravii]*, 9 June 2021. Available at: https://ria.ru/20210609/islam -1736333229.html

37 Embassy of the Russian Federation in the Kingdom of Saudi Arabia, About the visit of the president of Tatarstan Republic, The chairman of the Group of strategic Vision 'Russia-Islamic World', R. N. Minnikhanov to Saudi Arabia [*O visite Presdienta Respubliki Tatarstan, Predsedatelya Gruppy strategicheskogo videniya 'Rossiya – islamsky mir' R.N. Minnikhanova v Saudovskuy Araviu*], 25 November 2021. Available at: https://riyadh.mid.ru/ru/press-centre/news/o_vizite_prezidenta _respubliki_tatarstan_predsedatelya_gruppy_strategicheskogo_videniya_rossiya _isla/

38 Middle East Online, 'President Putin: Russia's Positions on Many Difficult Issues are Close to Islamic Countries' [الرئيس بوتين: مواقف روسيا بشأن العديد من القضايا الصعبة متقاربة مع الدول الإسلامية], November 24 (2021). Available at: https://aawsat.com/home/article ‏/3322306‏الرئيس-بوتين-مواقف-روسيا-بشأن-العديد-من-القضايا-الصعبة-متقاربة-مع-الدول‏utm? _source=dlvr.it&utm_medium=twitter

39 See Alekhbariyatv, Speech at the meeting of the Strategic Vision delivered by the president of the Republic of Tatarstan [فيديو | كلمة #بوتين في اجتماع مجموعة الرؤية الاستراتيجية #روسيا_والعالم_الإسلامي يلقيها رئيس جمهورية تتارستان], November 24 (2021). Available at: https://twitter.com/alekhbariyatv/status/1463424545197641729?s=21

40 Kamil' Samigullin, 2021, interviewed by author.

41 Embassy of the Russian Federation in the Kingdom of Saudi Arabia, About the visit of the president of Tatarstan Republic, The chairman of the Group of strategic Vision 'Russia-Islamic world', R. N. Minnikhanov to Saudi Arabia [*O visite Presdienta Respubliki Tatarstan, Predsedatelya Gruppy strategicheskogo videniya*

'Rossiya – islamsky mir' R.N. Minnikhanova v Saudovskuy Araviu], 25 November 2021. Available at: https://riyadh.mid.ru/ru/press-centre/news/o_vizite_prezidenta_respubliki_tatarstan_predsedatelya_gruppy_strategicheskogo_videniya_rossiya_isla/

42 Almowaten.net, 'President of Tatarstan Performs Umrah', [رئيس تتارستان يؤدي مناسك العمرة], 23 November 2021. Available at: https://www.almowaten.net/2021/11/
رئيس-تتارستان-يؤدي-مناسك-العمرة/

43 Minullina, 2020, interviewed by author.

44 Ibid.

45 Marat Gatin, 2020, interviewed by author.

46 Samigullin, 2021, interviewed by author.

47 Official of Tatarstan, Rustam Minnikhanov met with the ambassador extraordinary and plenipotentiary of the Kingdom of Saudi Arabia to the Russian Federation [*Rustam Minnikhanov vstretilsya s Chesvychinym I Polnomochnym Poslom Korolevstva Saudovskaya Aravia v Rossiyskoy Federacii*], 20 June 2011. Available at: https://tatarstan.ru/index.htm/news/93482.htm

48 Realnoe vremya, 'Pozvat' v gosti Korolya: kak razvivalis' vzaimootnosheniya Tatarstana I Saudovskoy Aravii'.

49 Ibid.

50 Ibid.

51 Asharq al-Awsat, 'Custodian of the Two Holy Mosques Holds a Session of Talks with the President of Tatarstan on Prospects for Cooperation; President Rustam Minnikhanov Received at al-Yamamah palace', [https://aawsat.com/home/article
خادم-الحرمين-يعقد-جلسة-مباحثات-مع-رئيس-تتارستان-تناولت-آفاق-التعاون/849321/], 8 February 2017. Available at: https://aawsat.com/home/article/849321/
خادم-الحرمين-يعقد-جلسة-مباحثات-مع-رئيس-تتارستان-تناولت-آفاق-التعاون

52 Marat Gatin, 2020, interviewed by author.

53 Tatarstan President's Press Office, 'Business Forum "Tatarstan-Saudi Arabia" Held at the End of the Official Visit of Rustam Minnikhanov to Saudi Arabia', *Government of the Republic of Tatarstan*, 8 February 2017. Available at: https://prav.tatarstan.ru/eng/index.htm/news/840254.htm.

54 Realnoe vremya, 'Pozvat' v gosti Korolya: kak razvivalis' vzaimootnosheniya Tatarstana I Saudovskoy Aravii'.

55 Minullina, 2020, interviewed by author.

56 Ibid., 2020.

57 The Government of Tatarstan Republic, '*Rustam Minnikhanov pribyl s rabochim visitom v Korolevstvo Saudovskaya Araviya*', [*Rustam Minnikhanov Arrived on a Working Visit to the Kingdom of Saudi Arabia*], 6 February 2017. Available at: https://prav.tatarstan.ru/index.htm/news/838682.htm.

58 RIA Novosti, '*Tatarstan mozhet stat' exporterom c/hh produkcii v Saudovskyu Araviu*', [*Tatarstan May Become an Exporter of Agricultural Products to Saudi Arabia*], 18 March 2013. Available at: https://ria.ru/20130318/927734028.html.

59 The Government of Tatarstan Republic, 'Rustam Minnikhanov pribyl s rabochim visitom v Korolevstvo Saudovskaya Araviya', [*Rustam Minnikhanov Arrived on a Working Visit to the Kingdom of Saudi Arabia*].

60 Jon, Hoffman, 'The Evolving Relationship Between Religion and Politics in Saudi Arabia', 20 April 2022. Available at: https://arabcenterdc.org/resource/the-evolving-relationship-between-religion-and-politics-in-saudi-arabia/.

61 Kristian, Coates Ulrichsen and Annelle, R. Sheline, 'Mohammed bin Salman and Religious Authority and Reform in Saudi Arabia', 19 September 2019. Available at: https://www.bakerinstitute.org/media/files/files/516a1378/bi-report-092319-cme-mbs-saudi.pdf.

62 Jon, Hoffman, 'The Evolving Relationship between Religion and Politics in Saudi Arabia'.

63 Ibid.

64 Realnoe vermya, 'Kvotu na Hajd v Mekku I Medinu dlya Rossiayn mogut uvelichit' do 25 tysych mest' [The quota for the Hajj to Mecca and Medina for Russians can be increased to 25 thousand places], 8 October 2017. Available at: https://realnoevremya.ru/news/78547-kvotu-na-hadzh-v-mekku-i-medinu-dlya-rossiyan-mogut-uvelichit-do-25-tysyach-mest.

65 Sneg, 'Kamil Samigullin: Korolya Saudovskoy Aravii v Rossii vstretili po-carski', ['Kamil Samigullin: The King of Saudi Arabia in Russia was greeted like a King'], 9 October 2017. Available at: https://sntat.ru/news/kamil-samigullin-korolya-saudovskoy-aravii-v-rossii-vstretili-po-tsarski-5634577.

66 Kamil Samigullin, 2021, interviewed by author.

67 Al-Bayan, 'The President of the Republic of Tatarstan in an exclusive interview with al-Bayan: Zayed created an economic miracle on the banks of the Gulf, our oil production is 26 million tons annually and the price of $20 a barrel is fair', [رئيس جمهورية تتارستان في حديث خاص لـ البيان : زايد صنع معجزة اقتصادية, على ضفاف الخليج ، إنتاجنا النفطي 26 مليون طن سنويا وسعر 20 دولارا للبرميل عادل], 5 April 2000. Available at: https://www.albayan.ae/economy/2000-04-05-1.1049884?ot=ot.AMPPageLayout.

68 Marat Gatin, 2020, interviewed by author.

69 Minullina, 2020, interviewed by author.

70 Marat Gatin, 2020, interviewed by author.

71 Albawaba, Dubai Islamic Economy Development Centre Signs MOU With Tatarstan Investment Development Agency at Kazan Summit 2018, 13 May 2018. Available at: https://www.albawaba.com/business/pr/dubai-islamic-economy-development-centre-signs-mou-tatarstan-investment-development-agen.

72 TIDA is responsible for the economic bloc of the Group, as noted earlier, specifically with organizing the Kazan Summit annually.

73 Albawaba, Dubai Islamic Economy Development Centre Signs MOU With Tatarstan Investment Development Agency at Kazan Summit 2018.

74 Al-Khaleej, 'UAE and Tatarstan Discuss Developing Economic Relations' [الإمارات وتتارستان تبحثان تطوير العلاقات الاقتصادية], 22 February (2021). Available at: https://www.alkhaleej.ae/2021-02-22/ الإمارات-وتتارستان-تبحثان-تطوير-العلاقات-الاقتصادية/أسواق-الإمارات/اقتصاد

75 Al-bayan, 'The UAE Calls for a Global Partnership to Benefit from the Halal Industry', [الإمارات تدعو لشراكة عالمية للاستفادة من صناعة الحلال], 2 August (2021). Available at: https://www.albayan.ae/economy/uae/2021-08 -02-1.4219160?ot=ot.AMPPageLayout. As noted in the section 4.2.1., the UAE usually has among the biggest delegations at the Kazan Summit. For details of strategic investment partnerships between UAE and Tatarstan discussed at the Kazan Summit 2014, see al-Bayan, 'UAE and Tatarstan Move Towards Strategic Investment Partnerships', [الإمارات وتتارستان نحو شراكات استراتيجية استثمارية], 7 June 2014. Available at: https://www.albayan.ae/economy/local-market/2014-06 -07-1.2139507?ot=ot.AMPPageLayout.

76 TIDA, Annual Investment Meeting, 3 April 2017. Available at: https://invest .tatarstan.ru/news/annual-investment-meeting/.

77 RIA Novosti, *Minnikhanov prinimaet uchastie vo Vsemirnom samite tolerantnosti v OAE* [*Minnikhanov Takes Part in the World Summit of Tolerance in the UAE*], 14 October 2019. Available at: https://ria.ru/20191114/1560935647.html.

78 Tatar-inform, '*Tatarstan stanet pervym rossiyskim regionom predstavlennym na vystavke Expo Dubai 2020*' ['*Tatarstan will be the First Russian Region Presented at Expo Dubai 2020*'], 27 September 2021. Available at: https://www.tatar-inform.ru/ news/tatarstan-stanet-pervym-rossiiskim-regionom-predstavlennym-na-vystavke -expo-dubai-2020-5837722.

79 Business Online, *Minnikhanov, Kadyrov I nasledniy princ Saudovskoy Aravii posetili Gran-pri 'Formuly-1' v OAE*, [*Minnikhanov, Kadyrov and the Crown Prince of Saudi Arabia Attended the Formula 1 Grand Prix in the UAE*], 25 November 2018. Available at: https://m.business-gazeta.ru/news/403769.

80 TIDA, 2020.

81 Gulf News, *UAE, Russia Forge Strategic Partnership*, 1 June 2018. Available at: https://gulfnews.com/uae/government/uae-russia-forge-strategic-partnership-1 .2230246.

82 Marat Gatin, 2020, interviewed by author.

83 RBK, Tatarstan pomozeht Kataru podgotov' Chempionat mira po futbolu v 2022 godu, [Tatarstan will Help Qatar Prepare for the World Cup in 2022], 25 May 2018. Available at: https://www.google.co.uk/amp/s/amp.rbc.ru/regional/tatarstan/ freenews/5b07ad3c9a79476f3ff618be.

84 Qatar Chamber, 'The Chamber is Looking to Enhance Trade Cooperation with Tatarstan' [الغرفة تبحث تعزيز التعاون التجاري مع تتارستان], 23 July (2017). Available at: https://www.qatarchamber.com/-الغرفة-تبحث-تعزيز- التعاون-التجاري-مع-ت/?lang=ar.

85 Marat Gatin, 2020, interviewed by author.

86 For example, see the meeting of the president of Tatarstan, Rustam Minnikhanov and the vice-president of the Supreme Council for Islamic Affairs in Bahrain, Shaykh Abdul Rahman bin Mohammad bin Rashid al-Khalifa; on the sidelines of the Group of the Strategic Vision 'Russia-Islamic world' in 2016, see Al-wasat, 'The President of Tatarstan discusses with the Vice President of the Supreme Council for Islamic Affairs in Bahrain the strengthening of bilateral relations' [رئيس تتارستان يبحث مع نائب رئيس «الأعلى للشئون الإسلامية» تعزيز العلاقات الثنائية], 27 May (2016). Available at: http://www.alwasatnews.com/news/1119440.html.

87 For example, at the 2021 Kazan Summit, leaders of the Small and Medium Enterprises Association in Bahrain and the Bahrain Chamber of Commerce and Industry participated as the Bahraini delegation. See Al-ayam Newspaper, *Investment Opportunities with Tatarstan and the Russian Regions* [فرص استثمارية مع تتارستان والأقاليم الروسية], August 2021. Available at: https://www .alayam.com/alayam/economic/920324/amp.html?amp=1; Al-bilad newspaper, *Bahrain Chamber of Commerce and Industry Signs Two Memoranda of Understanding with Tatarstan*, 28 July 2021. Available at: https:// www.albiladpress.com/news/2021/4671/finance/717327.html.

88 Abdulrahman bin Mohammad bin Rashid al-Khalifa, 2022, interviewed by author.

89 See Vneshnaya Torgovlya Rossii [Russian Foreign Trade]. Available at: https:// russian-trade.com/ The information was provided to the author by the official response of the Tatarstan Investment Development Agency (TIDA).

90 Robert Mogeilnicki, 'Oil Price War Tests Saudi-Russian Investment Cooperation', *AGSIW*, 3 April 2020. Available at: https://agsiw.org/oil-price-war-tests-saudi -russian-investment-cooperation/.

91 The information was provided to the author by the official response of the Tatarstan Investment Development Agency (TIDA).

92 Al-bilad newspaper, *Bahrain Chamber of Commerce and Industry Signs Two Memoranda of Understanding with Tatarstan*, 28 July 2021. Available at: https:// www.albiladpress.com/news/2021/4671/finance/717327.html.

93 Official Tatarstan, Rustam Minnikhanov i predstaviteli Kuveita obmenyalis' mneniyami po voprosam dalneyshego sotrudnichestva [Rustam Minnikhanov and Representatives of Kuwait Exchanged Views on Further Cooperation], 5 October 2009. Available at: https://tatarstan.ru/index.htm/news/41158.htm.

94 RBK, *Bahrein i Oman gotovy eksportirovat' produkciu halal iz Tatarstana*, [Bahrain and Oman are Ready to Export Halal Products from Tatarstan], 27 February 2017. Available at: https://rt.rbc.ru/tatarstan/27/02/2017/58b433279a7947f 9fcb11fbf.

95 Izverstya, *V Kazani otkroetsya general'noe konsulstvo Saudovskoy Aravii [Consul General of Saudi Arabia to Open in Kazan]*, 13 February 2020. Available at: https://

iz.ru/975699/2020-02-13/v-kazani-otkroetsia-generalnoe-konsulstvo-saudovskoi
-aravii.

96 Kamil Samigullin, 2021, interviewed by author.

97 See Russian Direct Investment Fund, *Overview*. Available at: https://rdif.ru/Eng
_About/

98 Minullina, 2020, interviewed by author.

99 This refers to sanctions imposed by the European Union, the United States
and other countries in 2014 over Russia's annexation of Crimea. Sanctions had
continued even before the Ukraine conflict (discussed in Chapter 7); for example,
under the Trump administration alone, sanctions against Russia were announced
forty-six times. As well as following the invasion of Ukraine, these sanctions have
been in response to allegations of malicious cyber activities, human rights abuses
and corruption, the use of a chemical weapon, and Syria-related sanctions.
See Thomas Heidemann, 'EU Extends Sectoral Sanctions Against Russia', *CMS*.
Available at: https://cms.law/en/rus/publication/eu-extends-sectoral-sanctions
-against-russia; Richard Nephew, 'Evaluating the Trump Administration's
Approach to Sanctions: Russia', *Columbia Centre on Global Energy Policy*,
13 February 2020. Available at: https://www.energypolicy.columbia.edu/research/
commentary/evaluating-trump-administration-s-approach-sanctions-russia.

100 L. S. Mokina, 'Assessment of Development of Islamic Banking as Alternative
Instrument of Financing and Possibility of Its Application in Russia', *Russian
Journal of Entrepreneurship*, 18, no. 16, August 2017.

101 Business Online, *V Tatarstane sozdana investicionnaya kompaniya, rabotaushaya
po normam shariata*, [*An Investment Company Operating in Accordance with
Shari'a Norms was Established in Tatarstan*], 7 December 2009. Available at: https://
www.business-gazeta.ru/news/17870.

102 Realnoe vremya, '"*Proekt okazalsya neudachnym*": *kak umirala Tatarstanskaya
mezhdunarodnaya investicionaya kompaniya*' ['"*The Project Turned Out to be
Unsuccessful*": *How the Tatarstan International Investment Company Died*'],
26 March 2020. Available at: https://realnoevremya.ru/articles/169835-eksperty-o
-smerti-tmik-i-prichinah-provala-proekta.

103 Realnoe vremya, '"*Proekt okazalsya neudachnym*": *kak umirala Tatarstanskaya
mezhdunarodnaya investicionaya kompaniya*' ['"*The Project Turned Out to be
Unsuccessful*": *How the Tatarstan International Investment Company Died*'].

104 Aydar Shagimardanov has been acting president of the Association of Muslim
Entrepreneurs of Russia since 2016; between 2014 and 2016 he was vice-president
and executive director of the Association. He has extensive experience in business,
working in top positions for joint Russian and international companies. For
example, since 2010 he has been general director of the international company
ELIF Construction and investment, along with government positions in Tatarstan.
Between 2009 and 2014 he was assistant to the chairman of the Committee on

Ecology, Nature Management and Agrarian Issues of the State Council of the
Republic of Tatarstan.

105 The financial house Amal was established in 2010. Available at: https://fdamal.ru/
about/.

106 The association had 4672 members and partners by 2020 from forty-six different
regions of Russia. Members are representatives of medium and small businesses
in Russia, operating in the main sectors of the Russian economy: tourism,
construction, oil and gas production and processing, woodworking, IT, retail,
manufacturing and agriculture. Available at: https://apmrf.ru/o-nas/.

107 Kamil Samigullin, 2021, interviewed by author.

108 Il'kham Nurullin, 2020, interviewed by author.

109 Aydar Shagimardanov, 2020, interviewed by the author.

Chapter 5

1 Stephen Page, *The USSR and Arabia: The Development of Soviet Policies and
Attitudes Towards the Countries of the Arabian Peninsula, 1955–1970* (Michigan:
University of Michigan, 1971), 2.

2 John W. Slocum, 'A Sovereign State within Russia? The External Relations of the
Republic of Tatarstan', *Global Society* 13, no. 1 (1999): 53.

3 For more details on the dynamics of the collapse of the Soviet Union, examining
the cascade of sovereignty declarations issued by republics of the USSR and by
autonomous republics and other subunits of the Russian republic in 1990–1,
with particular focus on Tatarstan, see Jeff Kahn, 'The Parade of Sovereignties:
Establishing the Vocabulary of the New Russian Federalism', *Post-Soviet Affairs* 16,
no. 1 (2000): 58–89.

4 See Vladimir Schlapentokh, Roman Levita and Mikhail Loiberg, *From Submission
to Rebellion: The Provinces versus the Centre in Russia* (Boulder: Westview Press,
1997), 89–91.

5 Nicole Balkind, 'A Model Republic? Trust and Authoritarianism on Tatarstan's
Road to Autonomy', *MA thesis University of North Carolina* (2009): 35.

6 Dilyara Suleymanova, 'International Language Rights Norms in the Dispute over
Latinization Reform in the Republic of Tatarstan', *Caucasus Review of International
Affairs* 4, no. 1 (Winter 2010): 46.

7 Slocum, 'A Sovereign State within Russia?' 54.

8 Ibid., 55.

9 See Sergei Kondrashov, 'Nationalism and the Drive for Sovereignty in Tatarstan,
1988–1992: Origins and Development', PhD Thesis, University of Manchester,
1995.

10 Slocum, 'A Sovereign State within Russia?', 55.

11 Ibid.

12 Galina Yemelianova, 'Islam and Nation Building in Tatarstan and Dagestan of the Russian Federation', *Nationalist Papers* 27, no. 4 (1999): 613.

13 Balkind, 'A Model Republic?', 35.

14 Kondrashov, 'Nationalism and the Drive for Sovereignty in Tatarstan, 1988–1992: Origins and Development'.

15 The current version of Article 6 of the Constitution of the Republic of Tatarstan is 'The Republic of Tatarstan shall be entitled within its powers to enter into international and foreign economic relations with subjects and administrative-territorial units of foreign states, conclude international agreements, exchange diplomatic representatives, participate in the activity of international organisation'. Available at: https://tatarstan.ru/file/old/html/Constitution%20of%20the%20Republic%20of%20Tatarstan.pdf.

16 See Jennifer-Anne Davidson, 'Power Dynamics in Russian-Tatarstan Relations: A Case Study', MA Thesis, University of Victoria, 2008.

17 Slocum, 'A Sovereign State within Russia?', 56.

18 'Twelve Agreements Between Russia and Tatarstan', *Journal of South Asian and Middle Eastern Studies* 18, no. 1 (1994): 73–4.

19 Alexander Sabovyi, 'Primiril li dogovor dve knostitutsii', *Literaturnaia gazeta*, 30 March 1994, 12.

20 Sergey Sergeev, 'The Republic of Tatarstan: Reduced to a Common Denomination?' *Russian Social Science Review* 62, nos. 1–3 (2021): 214.

21 Christopher Williams, 'Tatar Nation Building since 1991: Ethnic Mobilisation in Historical Perspective', *Journal of Ethnopolitics and Minority Issues in Europe* 10, no. 1 (2011): 113.

22 Ibid., 114.

23 R. Ortung, 'Putin's Political Legacy', *Russian Analytical Digest* 36, no. 4 (2008): 2–5.

24 K. E. Graney, *Of Khans and Kremlins: Tatarstan and the Future of Ethno-Federalism in Russia* (Plymouth: Lexington Books, 2009), 138.

25 Williams, 'Tatar Nation Building since 1991', 115.

26 Graney, *Of Khans and Kremlins*, 139.

27 Sergeev, 'The Republic of Tatarstan: Reduced to a Common Denominator?' 219–20.

28 Petr Kozlov, 'Kreml tthhe prodlit dogovor s Tatarstanom. Izmenit li eto cho-to?', ['The Kremlin Will Not Renew the Agreement with Tatarstan. Will this Change Anything?' *BBC News*, 11 August 2017. Available at: https://www.bbc.com/russian/features-40904692.

29 Sergeev, 'The Republic of Tatarstan', 212.

30 Ibid., 217.

31 N. Zubarevich, *Otnosheniia tsentr-regiony: chto izmenilos' za chetyre goda krizisa,* [*Relations between Centre and Regions: What has Changed During Four Years of Crisis?*]. Available at: http://www.counter-point.org//11_zubarevich/

32 Sergeev, 'The Republic of Tatarstan', 217.

33 Business Online, *Rustam Minnikhanov: 'Raskulachivanie bylo uzhe, my posledstviia videli . . .* [*Rustam Minnkihhanov: Raskulachivanie Already Occurred, We Saw the Consequences . . .*]', 26 December 2016. Available at: www.busines-gazeta.ru/video /333026.

34 Realnoe vremya, 'The Economic Growth Pace Can be Kept if Only a Miracle Happens', 22 April 2020. Available at: https://realnoevremya.com/articles/4426 -how-tatarstan-and-russia-should-support-economy-in-crisis.

35 See Plenipotentiary Representation of the Republic of Tatarstan in the Republic of Turkey, *Sotrudnichestvo Tatarstana i Turcii* [*Cooperation between Tatarstan and Turkey*], 7 April 2020. Available at: https://tatturk.tatarstan.ru/sotrudnichestvo _tatartsan_turkey.

36 Tuba Shahin, 'Tatarstan-Turkey Trade Relations are Growing "Confidently"', **AA**, 9 August 2021. Available at: https://www.aa.com.tr/tr/ekonomi/tataristan-turkiye -ticari-iliskileri-guvenle-buyuyor/23290222.

37 Government of the Republic of Tatarstan, 'Rustam Minnikhanov otvetil na voprosy churnalistov o sotrudnichestve s tureckimi partnerami, o situacii s obmanutymi dolshikami I o sisteme "Platon"' [*Rustam Minnkihanov Answered Journalists' Questions About Cooperation with Turkish Partners, about the Situation with Defrauded Equity Holders and about the Platon System*], 21 December 2015. Available at: https://prav.tatarstan.ru/index.htm/news/525008.htm.

38 Alexei Malashenko, 'Islam in Russia', *Carnegie Moscow Center*, 23 September 2014. Available at: https://carnegie.ru/2014/09/23/islam-in-russia-pub-57048. In Tatarstan, the main opposition to Shaimiev's government was from nationalists. The Tatar Independence Party, known as *Ittifaq*, was a radical wing that broke off from the All-Tatar Public Centre (ATPC) in 1990. They demanded 'Tatarstan for Tatars'. *Ittifaq* promoted ideas of complete independence for Tatarstan, hoping one day to regain the glory of the 'Tatar-Mongol Yoke'. They also published the newspaper, *Altyn Urda* ('The Golden Horde'), and maintained branches in more than thirty regions of Tatarstan. The group also had a subsidiary youth organization, Azatliq ('Freedom'). The leader of *Ittifaq* is Fauzia Bayramova, who was the former co-chairman of the ATPC and acted in the Tatarstan parliament from 1990 to 1995. Overall, nationalists were a secular movement; however, Islam was stressed as part of cultural identity and used to combine ethnic minorities in order to get public support. The head of the ATPC stated this about the links between Islam and Tatar culture in 1991: The history of Tatar culture and enlightenment, the entire way of life, is closely connected to Islam. Therefore, Islam cannot be separate from national policy or from the national movement, and is closely connected to and cooperates

with them. For more on the subject, see Hunter, Thomas and Melikishvili, *Islam in Russia: The Politics of Identity and Security* (New York: Centre for Strategic and International Studies, 2004); Andrey Schberbak, 'Nationalism in the USSR: A Historical and Comparative Perspective', *Nationalities Papers* 43, no. 6 (2015): 866–85; Anatoly M. Khazanov, 'Ethnic Nationalism in the Russian Federation', *Daedalus* 126, no. 3 (Summer 1997); Yemelianova, 'Islam and Nation Building in Tatarstan and Dagestan of the Russian Federation', 605–30.

39 Malashenko, 'Islam in Russia'.

40 See Andrej Kreutz, *Russia in the Middle East: Friend or Foe?* (Praeger: Westport, 2009); Alexei Malashenko and Akhmed Yarlykapov, 'Radicalisation of Russia's Muslim Community', *Ethno-Religious Conflict in Europe*, working paper 9 (May, 2009): 159–92.

41 M. Fredholm, 'Central Asian Sunni Islamic Extremism and Its Links to the Gulf', in *Russian & CIS Relations with the Gulf Region: Current Trends in Political and Economic Dynamics*, ed. M. Terterov (Dubai: Gulf Research Center, 2009), 345.

42 Sherrie Steiner, 'Religious Soft Power as Accountability Mechanism for Power in World Politics: The InterFaith Leaders' Summit(s)', *SAGE Open*, 2011. Available at: https://journals.sagepub.com/doi/10.1177/2158244011428085.

43 Sophie Lambroschini, 'Russia: Putin Tells OIC That Muslims are "Inseparable" Part of A Multiethnic Nation', *RadioFreeEurope*, 16 October 2003. Available at: https://www.rferl.org/a/1104687.html.

44 Kreutz, *Russia in the Middle East: Friend or Foe?*, 44–5.

45 See A. Rahr, *Between Reform and Restoration: Putin on the Eve of his Second Term* (Berlin: Korber Department, 2004); M. Sapronova, 'Russian-Arab Cooperation Before and After the "Arab Spring"', *Vestnik MGIMO-Universiteta* 36, no. 3 (2014): 27–36.

46 Kreutz, *Russia in the Middle East: Friend or Foe?* 46.

47 Ibid.

48 Vladimir Putin, 'Speech and the Following Discussion at the Munich Conference on Security Policy', *President of Russia*, 10 February 2007. Available at: http://en.kremlin.ru/events/president/transcripts/24034.

49 R. Dannreuther, 'Russia and the Middle East: A Cold War Paradigm?' *Europe-Asia Studies* 64, no. 3 (2012): 543–60.

50 Malashenko Alexei, 'Islam in Russia', *Carnegie Moscow Center*, 23 September 2014. Available at: https://carnegie.ru/2014/09/23/islam-in-russia-pub-57048.

51 Ibid.

52 Russia-Islamic World, 'The Group of the Strategic Vision "Russia-Islamic World" Presents the Updated Development Strategy', 11 June 2019. Available at: https://russia-islworld.ru/en/novosti//the-group-of-strategic-vision-russia-islamic-world-presents-the-updated-development-strategy/.

53 See Russia-Islamic World, 'Russia-Islamic World: New Facts of Cooperation', 10 July 2019. Available at: https://russia-islworld.ru/en/main//russia-islamic-world -new-facets-of-cooperation/.

54 Kreutz, *Russia in the Middle East: Friend or Foe?* 39.

55 See Matthew Gray, 'A Theory of "Late Rentierism" in the Arab States of the Gulf', *CIRS Georgetown University*, 2011. Available at: https://repository.library .georgetown.edu/bitstream/handle/10822/558291/CIRSOccasionalPaper7Matthew Gray2011.pdf.

56 See Mehran Kamrava, *Qatar: Small State, Big Politics* (New York: Cornell University Press, 2013); Khalid AlMezaini and Jean-Marc Rickli, ed., *The Small Gulf States: Foreign and Security Policies before and after the Arab Spring* (New York: Routledge, 2017).

57 L. Watanabe, 'Gulf States' Engagement in North Africa: The Role of Foreign Aid', in *The Small Gulf States: Foreign and Security Policies Before and After the Arab Spring*, ed. Khalid Almezaini and Jean-Marc Rickli (New York: Routledge, 2017), 168–81.

58 Mehran Kamrava, ed. *Fragile Politics: Weak States in the Greater Middle East* (New York: Oxford University Press, 2016).

59 Eugene Rumer states that 'Russia has returned to the Middle East as a major power player. Yet its toolkit is modest'. See Eugene Rumer, 'Russia in the Middle East: Jack of All Trades, Master of None', *Carnegie Endowment for International Peace*, 31 October 2019. Available at: https://carnegieendowment.org/2019/10/31/russia -in-middle-east-jack-of-all-trades-master-of-none-pub-80233.

60 See Mark N. Katz, 'Better than Before: Comparing Moscow's Cold War and Putin Era Policies Toward Arabia and the Gulf', *Durham Middle East Paper*, 96/ Sir William Luce Fellowship Paper, 19, Institute for Middle Eastern and Islamic Studies, Durham University, August 2018. Available at: https://dro.dur.ac.uk /25863/1/25863.pdf; Elaine Pasquini, 'Russia's Balancing Act in the Middle East', *The Washington Report on Middle East Affairs* 39, no. 6 (2020): 58; Diana Galeeva, 'How have Russia's Policies in the Middle East Changed Since the Arab Uprisings?' *Middle East Institute*, 21 April 2021. Available at: https://www.mei .edu/publications/how-have-russias-policies-middle-east-changed-arab-uprisings -0.

61 Raphael Lefevre, 'The Pitfalls of Russia's Growing Influence in Libya', *The Journal of North African Studies* 22, no. 3 (27 May 2017): 331.

62 See Diana Galeeva, 'Russia in the Middle East in 2021: Learning from 2020', *LSE Blog*, 21 January 2021. Available at: https://blogs.lse.ac.uk/mec/2021/01/21/russia -in-the-middle-east-in-2021-learning-from-2020/

63 Alexei Malashenko, 'Islam, Politics, and the Security of Central Asia, Russian Politics & Law', *Russian Politics & Law* 42, no. 4 (2004): 312.

64 See Karim Mezran and Arturo Varvelli, eds., 'The MENA Region: A Great Power Competition', *ISPI/ Atlantic Council*, 2019. Available at: https://www.atlanticcouncil .org/wp-content/uploads/2019/10/MENA-Region-Great-Power-Competition -Report-Web-2.pdf.

65 Li-Chem Sim, 'Russia's Return to the Gulf', in *External Powers and the Gulf Monarchies*, ed. Jonathan Fulton and Li-Chen Sim (Routledge: Abingdon, 2018), 21.

66 Alexander Shumilin and Inna Shumilina, 'Russia as a Gravity Pole of the GCC's New Foreign Policy Pragmatism', *The International Spectator* 52, no. 2 (3 April 2017): 122.

67 Sinem Cengiz, 'Saudi Arabia and Russia in the Syrian Crisis: Divergent Policies, Similar Concerns', in *The Syrian Crisis Effects on the Regional and International Relations*, ed. Dania K. Khatib (Singapore: Springer Nature, 2021), 105–21.

68 Also see on the subject, Anton Mardason and Andrey Korotayev, 'Russia-GCC Relations and the Future of Syria: Political Process and Prospects for the Economic Reconstruction', in *Russia's Relations with the GCC and Iran*, ed. Nikolay Kozhanov (Singapore: Palgrave Macmillan, 2020), 205–28.

69 Ibid., 120–1.

70 Samuel Ramani, 'Russia and the UAE: An Ideational Partnership', *Middle East Policy* XXVII, no. 1 (Spring 2020): 125–40.

71 Sami Moubayed, 'Syria and Qatar Silently Mend Broken Fences', *Gulf News*, 25 April 2019. Available at: https://gulfnews.com/world/gulf/qatar/syria-and-qatar -silently-mend-broken-fences-1.63545446.

72 Al Jazeera, 'Bahrain Appoints First Ambassador to Syria in Over a Decade', 30 December 2021. Available at: https://www.aljazeera.com/news/2021/12/30/ bahrain-appoints-first-ambassador-to-syria-in-over-a-decade.

73 Ufuk Tasci, 'How the UAE, Russia and France Have Teamed Up in Libya', *TRT World*, 22 December 2020. Available at: https://www.trtworld.com/magazine/how -the-uae-russia-and-france-have-teamed-up-in-libya-42583.

74 Leonid Issaev and Nikolay Kozhanov, 'Diversifying Relationships: Russian Policy Towards GCC', *International Politics*, 2021. Available at: https://link.springer.com/ article/10.1057/s41311-021-00286-4.

75 Leonid Issaev and Andrey Koroyayev, 'Russia's Policy Towards the Middle East: The Case of Yemen', *The International Spectator* 55, no. 3 (2020): 143.

76 Katz, 'Better Than Before'.

77 See Giorgio Cafiero and Theodore Karasik, 'Qatar and Russia: What Do They See in Each Other?' *Middle East Policy Council*, 11 October 2017. Available at: https:// mepc.org/commentary/qatar-and-russia-what-do-they-see-in-each-other.

78 See Patrick Wintour, 'Saudi Kings' Visit to Russia Heralds Shift in Global Power Structures', *The Guardian*, 5 October 2017. Available at: https://www.theguardian .com/world/2017/oct/05/saudi-russia-visit-putin-oil-middle-east.

79 See Al Jazeera, *Qatari emir in Russia to Discuss Syrian Crisis,* 25 March 2018. Available at: https://www.aljazeera.com/news/2018/3/25/qatari-emir-in-russia-to -discuss-syrian-crisis.

80 See The National, *Sheikh Mohammed bin Zayed in Russia on Two-Day Official Visit,* 31 May 2018. Available at: https://www.thenationalnews.com/uae/ government/sheikh-mohammed-bin-zayed-in-russia-on-two-day-official-visit-1 .735764.

81 See Arab News, UAE and Russia sign deals worth $1.3 bn during Putin's Abu Dhabi visit, 15 October 2019. Available at: https://www.arabnews.com/node /1569171/middle-east.

82 Ministry of Foreign Affairs of Russia, *O vstreche checpredstavitelya Prezidenta Rossiskoya Federacii po Blichnemu Vostoku I stran Afriki, zamestittlya Ministra innostrannyh del Rossii M.L.Bogdanova s Gensekretarem MID Katara A.H. al-Hamadi* [*On the Meeting of the Special Representative of the President of the Russian Federatiion for the Middle East and African Countries, Deputy Minister of Foreign Affairs of Russia Mikhail Bogdanov with the Secretary General of the Ministry of Foreign Affairs of Qatar A. H. al-Hamadi*], 19 October 2019. Available at: https://www.mid.ru/ru/maps/qa/-/asset_publisher/629HIryvPTwo/content/id /3858289.

83 See Courtney Freer, *Rentier Islamism: The Influence of the Muslim Brotherhood in Gulf Monarchies* (Oxford: Oxford University Press, 2018); David Roberts, 'Qatar and the Muslim Brotherhood: Pragmatism or Preference?' *Middle East Policy* 21, no. 3 (2014): 84–94.

84 Rahr, *Between Reform and Restoration.*

85 Christopher Davidson, *Shadow Wars: The Secret Struggle for the Middle East* (London: Oneworld Publications Ltd, 2016), 78.

86 T. Figenschou, *Al Jazeera and the Global Media Landscape: The South Is Talking Back* (London: Routledge, 2013).

87 Dannreuther, 'Russia and the Middle East', 543–60.

88 J. Dargin, 'Qatar's Natural Gas: The Foreign-Policy Driver', *Middle East Policy* 14, no. 3 (2007): 136–42.

89 Malashenko, 'Islam in Russia', 313.

90 Dannreuther, 'Russia and the Middle East', 553.

91 Malashenko, 'Islam in Russia', 313.

92 K. Oskarsson, and S. Yetiv, 'Russia and the Persian Gulf: Trade, Energy, and Interdependence', *Middle East Journal* 67, no. 3 (2013): 381–403.

93 Alexey Khlebnikov, 'Why Biden's Gulf Policy Will Not Disturb Russia-GCC Relations', *Gulf International Forum*, 17 March 2021. Available at: https://gulfif.org/ why-bidens-gulf-policy-will-not-disturb-russia-gcc-relations/.

94 See Ann M. Simmons, 'Russia has been Assad's greatest ally – as it was to his father before him', 6 April 2017. Available at: https://www.latimes.com/world/middleeast/

la-fg-syria-russia-20170406-story.html; Roy Allison, 'Russia and Syria: Explaining Alignment with a Regime in Crisis', *International Affairs* 89, no. 4 (2013): 795–823. Available at: https://www.latimes.com/world/middleeast/la-fg-syria-russia -20170406-story.html

95 Khlebnikov, 'Why Biden's Gulf Policy Will Not Disturb Russia-GCC Relations'.

96 D. Smith, S. Siddiqui and P. Beaumont, *Gulf Crisis: Trump Escalates Row by Accusing Qatar of Sponsoring Terror*, 9 June 2017. Available at: https://www.theguardian.com/ us-news/2017/jun/09/trump-qatar-sponsor-terrorism-middle-east.

97 Tracey Shelton, 'US and Qatar Ink Deals for "Tremendous Amounts" of Military Weapons and Boeing Planes', *News*, 10 July 2019. Available at: https://www.abc .net.au/news/2019-07-10/qatar-donald-trump-military-and-commercial-deals /11294500.

98 Gideon Rose, ed., 'Trump's Middle East', *Foreign Affairs* 98, no. 6 (Nov/Dec 2019): 9.

99 Steven A. Cook, 'Trump's Middle East Legacy is Failure', *Foreign Policy*, 28 October 2020. Available at: https://foreignpolicy.com/2020/10/28/trumps-middle-east -legacy-is-failure/.

100 The Telegraph, 'Joe Biden says "America is Back" – But Stresses It Won't be an "Obama Third Term"', 25 November 2020. Available at: https://www.telegraph.co .uk/news/2020/11/25/joe-biden-says-america-back-stresses-wont-obama-third -term/.

101 Bruce Riedel, 'It's Time to Stop US Arms Sales to Saudi Arabia', *Brookings*, 4 February 2021. Available at: https://www.brookings.edu/blog/order-from-chaos /2021/02/04/its-time-to-stop-us-arms-sales-to-saudi-arabia/.

102 BBC News, 'Biden Raises Human Rights in Call with Saudi King Salman', 26 February 2021. Available at: https://www.bbc.co.uk/news/world-us-canada -56204449.

103 Izvestiya, *Peskov otvetil na voporos o rukopochatii Putina s Princem Saudovskoy Arabii* [*Peskov Answered the Question about Putin's Handshake with the Prince of Saudi Arabia*], 3 December 2018. Available at: https://iz.ru/819363/2018-12-03/ peskov-otvetil-na-vopros-o-rukopozhatii-putina-s-printcem-saudovskoi-aravii.

104 Kommersant, 'Sergeu Lavrovy prishla blizhnevostochnaya povestka' ['*Sergei Lavrov Received the Middle East Agenda*'], 11 March 2021. Available at: https://www .kommersant.ru/doc/4722278.

105 Javier Blas and Ilya Arkhipov, 'Russia and Saudi Arabia Step Up Oil Diplomacy', *Bloomberg*, 17 October 2020. Available at: https://www.bloomberg.com/news/articles /2020-10-17/russia-saudi-arabia-ready-to-keep-energy-market-stable-kremlin.

106 Vitaly Naumkin, 'Russia and the Arab Uprisings', *MEC Friday Seminars*, Oxford University, February 2021.

107 John Duke Anthony and Fahad Naser, 'GCC-US Relations Under a Trump Administration', *National Council on US-Arab Relations*, 13 December 2016.

Available at: https://ncusar.org/aa/2016/12/gcc-us-relations-under-trump
-administration/.

108 Trevor Richardson, 'The Decline of the Pax Americana', *The Organisation for World Peace*, 28 January 2021. Available at: https://theowp.org/the-decline-of-the-pax -americana/.

109 Christopher Layne, 'The End of Pax Americana: How Western Decline Became Inevitable', 26 April 2012. Available at: https://www.theatlantic.com/international /archive/2012/04/the-end-of-pax-americana-how-western-decline-became -inevitable/256388/.

110 Mohammad Yaghi, 'What Drives President Biden's Middle East Policies? And What Are Their Impacts on the Gulf States?' *Konrad Adenauer Stiftung*, Policy Report no. 22, May 2021. Available at: https://www.kas.de/documents/286298 /8668222/Policy+Report+No+22+What+Drives+President+Biden's+Middle+ East+Policies.pdf/98bac5dc-abc0-a108-18ef-32ff9f156873?version=1.1&t=162186 4193248.

111 Carla Norrlöf, 'Is COVID-19 the End of US Leadership? Public Bads, Leadership Failures and Monetary Hegemony', *International Affairs* 96, no. 5 (2020): 1281.

112 Natalia Starichkova, 'Russia and Saudi Arabia: New Friendship', *Rosbalt.ru*, 9 October 2003.

113 Andrej Kreutz, 'Russia and the Arabian Peninsula', *Journal of Military and Strategic Studies* 7, no. 2 (2004): 47.

114 Ibid., 58.

115 Ibid., 59.

116 M. Barabanov, 'Russian Arms Trade with the Gulf Monarchies', in *Russian & CIS Relations with Gulf Region: Current Trends in Political and Economic Dynamics*, ed. M. Terterov (Dubai, UAE: Gulf Research Center, 2009), 371–90.

117 Malashenko, 'Islam in Russia', 318.

118 Barabanov, 'Russian Arms Trade with the Gulf Monarchies', 374.

119 Kreutz, 'Russia and the Arabian Peninsula', 61.

120 Barabanov, 'Russian Arms Trade with the Gulf Monarchies', 387.

121 See The World Bank, 'Russia's Economy Loses Momentum Amid COVID-19 Resurgence, Says New World Bank Report', 16 December 2020. Available at: https://www.worldbank.org/en/news/press-release/2020/12/16/russias-economy -loses-momentum-amid-covid-19-resurgence-says-new-world-bank-report.

122 Jake Cordell, '6 things You Need to know About OPEC+. What does Russia want from this week's meeting in Vienna?', 4 December 2019. Available at: https://www .themoscowtimes.com/2019/12/04/6-things-opec-russia-a68409.

123 MFA Russia, 'Foreign Policy Concept of the Russian Federation', 1 December 2016. Available at: https://www.mid.ru/en/foreign_policy/official_documents/-/asset _publisher/CptICkB6BZ29/content/id/2542248.

124 Abdulrahman bin Mohammad bin Rashid al-Khalifa, 2022, interviewed by author.

125 See Vneshnaya Torgovlya Rossii [*Russian Foreign Trade*]. Available at: https://russian-trade.com/.

126 Ibid.

127 Theodore Karasik, 'Why is Qatar Investing so Much in Russia?', 8 March 2017. Available at: https://www.mei.edu/publications/why-qatar-investing-so-much-russia.

128 Robert Mogeilnicki, 'Oil Price War Tests Saudi-Russian Investment Cooperation', *AGSIW*, 3 April 2020. Available at: https://agsiw.org/oil-price-war-tests-saudi-russian-investment-cooperation/.

129 Arab News, *Russian President Vladimir Putin off to UAE after successful Saudi Arabia visit*, 15 October 2019. Available at: https://www.arabnews.com/node/1569186/saudi-arabia.

130 See Saeed Azhar and Kanishka Singh, 'Saudi Wealth Fund Boosts US Holdings With Stakes in Citi, Boeing, Facebook', *Reuters,* 16 May 2020. Available at: https://www.reuters.com/article/us-saudi-pif-idUSKBN22S0BQ.

131 Interfax-ABN, *Rossiya planiruet podpisat' soglashenie o voennom sotrudnichsetve s Saudovskoyy Araviei* [*Russia Plans to Sign a Military Cooperation Agreement with Saudi Arabia*], 22 February 2021. Available at: https://www.militarynews.ru/story.asp?rid=1&nid=545977&lang=RU.

132 Interfax-ABN, *Zamministra oborony rf obsudil s poslom OAE sotrudnichsetvo po voennoy linii* [*Deputy Minister of Defense of the Russian Federation Discussed Military Cooperation with the Ambassador of the UAE*], 14 September 2020. Available at: https://www.militarynews.ru/story.asp?rid=1&nid=537821&lang=RU.

133 Interfax, *Posol Katara v RF rasskazal o perspektivah voennogo sotrudnichstva s Rossiei* [*The Ambassador of Qatar to the Russian Federation Spoke About the Prospects for Military Cooperation with Russia*], 28 April 2021. Available at: https://www.interfax.ru/world/763610.

134 Samuel Ramani, 'Russia and the Middle East: Diplomacy and Security Russia and the GCC: A Rising Partnership?' *RIAC*, 29 March 2017. Available at: https://russiancouncil.ru/en/blogs/samuel-ramani-en/russia-and-the-gcc-a-rising-partnership/.

135 Giorgio Cafiero and Colby Connelly, 'Russia and the Arab Gulf States: Current Energy Variables', *Gulf International Forum*, 19 March 2019. Available at: https://gulfif.org/russia-and-arab-gulf-states-current-energy-variables/.

136 Ibid.

137 Rosemary Griffin, 'Russia, UAE Sign New Energy Cooperation Agreements', 15 October 2019. Available at: https://www.spglobal.com/platts/en/market-insights/latest-news/oil/101519-russia-uae-sign-new-energy-cooperation-agreements.

138 Ibid.

139 NS Energy, 'Lukoil, Gazprom and Tatneft to Jointly Develop Hard-to-Recover Reserves in Russia', 30 June 2020. Available at: https://www.nsenergybusiness.com/news/lukoil-gazprom-tatneft-hard-recover-reserves/.

140 S&P Global, Qatar, *Russia Adjust Tactics for European LNG Exports in March*,
3 April 2020. Available at: https://www.spglobal.com/platts/en/market-insights
/latest-news/natural-gas/040320-qatar-russia-adjust-tactics-for-european-lng
-exports-in-march.

141 Xinhuanet, 'Russia to Coordinate Energy Policy with Qatar: FM', 3 May 2019.
Available at: http://www.xinhuanet.com/english/2019-03/05/c_137868857.htm.

Chapter 6

1 In 2014, the United Nations recognized Crimea as part of Ukraine, though it has
now been annexed and is governed by Russia. The Ukraine conflict of 2022 only
adds further complications to this status.

2 Galina Yemelianova, 'Islam in Russia: An Historical Perspective', in *Islam in
Post-Soviet Russia: Public and Private Faces*, ed. Hilary Pilkington and Galina
Yemelianova (London; New York: Routledge Curzon, 2003), 28.

3 Ibid.

4 Ibid.

5 Ibid.

6 Mikhail Roshchin, 'Sufism and Fundamentalism in Dagestan and Chechnya',
CEMOTI 38 (2004): 61–72.

7 Galina Yemelianova, 'Islam and Nation Building in Tatarstan and Dagestan of the
Russian Federation', *Nationalities Papers* 27, no. 4 (December 1999): 609.

8 Moshe Gammer, 'Between Mecca and Moscow: Islam, Politics, and Political Islam
in Chechnya and Dagestan', *Middle Eastern Studies* 41, no. 6 (November 2005): 833.

9 Ibid., 834.

10 Ibid., 835.

11 Yemelianova, 'Islam and Nation Building in Tatarstan and Dagestan of the Russian
Federation'.

12 Gammer, 'Between Mecca and Moscow', 836.

13 Ibid., 833.

14 Melih Demirtas, 'Understanding Impacts of "Russian Orientalism" on Post-Soviet
Elite-Management in the Republic of Bashkortostan', *Cappadocia Journal of Area
Studies (CJAS)* 2, no. 1 (2020): 44.

15 Yalcin Deniz, 'Federal Bargaining in Post-Soviet Russia: A Comparative Study on
Moscow's Negotiations with Tatarstan and Bashkortostan', Unpublished Master's
thesis, Graduate School of Social Sciences, Eurasian Studies of Middle East
Technical University, 2005.

16 See Alexei Malashenko, 'Islam in Russia', *Social Research* 76, no. 1 (Spring 2009):
321–58; Andrej Kreutz, *Russia in the Middle East: Friend or Foe?* (Westport: Praeger,

2009); Alexei Malashenko and Akhmed Yarlykapov, 'Radicalisation of Russia's Muslim Community', *Ethno-Religious Conflict in Europe*, working paper 9 (May, 2009): 159–92.

17 Igor Dobaev, 'Islamic Radicalism in the Northern Caucasus', *Central Asia and the Caucasus*, 2000. Available at: https://www.ca-c.org/online/2000/journal_eng/eng06 _2000/09.dobae.shtml.

18 M. Fredholm, 'Central Asian Sunni Islamic Extremism and Its Links to the Gulf', in *Russian & CIS Relations with the Gulf Region: Current Trends in Political and Economic Dynamics*, ed. M. Terterov (Dubai: Gulf Research Center, 2009), 327–47.

19 Alexei Malashenko, 'Islam, Politics, and the Security of Central Asia, Russian Politics & Law', *Russian Politics & Law* 42, no. 4 (2004): 6–20.

20 Fredholm, 'Central Asian Sunni Islamic Extremism and Its Links to the Gulf', 345.

21 Kreutz, *Russia in the Middle East: Friend or Foe?* 46.

22 Ibid., 49.

23 Pavel Luzin, 'Ramzan Kadyrov: Russia's Top Diplomat', *Riddle*, 19 April 2018. Available at: https://www.ridl.io/en/ramzan-kadyrov-russias-top-diplomat/.

24 Ria Novosti, *Kadyrov: visit Putina v Er-Riyad ukrepiy sotrudnichsetvo dvuh stran* [*Kadyrov: Putin's Visit to Riyadh Will Strengthen Cooperation Between the Two Countries*], 14 October 2019. Available at: https://ria.ru/20191014/1559766501 .html.

25 Jon Gambrell, 'Russia's Putin Visits Saudi Arabia on Mideast Trip', *AP*, 14 October 2019. Available at: https://apnews.com/article/09fe0e9931904b5da91fd38 dddae915e.

26 Patrick Wintour, 'Saudi King's Visit to Russia Heralds Shift in Global Power Structures', *The Guardian*, 5 October 2017. Available at: https://www.theguardian .com/world/2017/oct/05/saudi-russia-visit-putin-oil-middle-east.

27 Ria Novosti, *Kadyrov v Abu-Dhabi obsudit ukreplenie otnosheniy mechdy OAE i Chechney* [*Kadyrov in Abu Dhabi to Discuss Strengthening Relations Between the UAE and Chechnya*], 17 February 2019. Available at: https://ria.ru/20190217 /1550989847.html.

28 Business Online, *Minnikhanov, Kadyrov i naslednyi prince Saudovskoy Aravii posetili gran-pri 'Formuly -1' v OAE* [*Minnikhanov, Kadyrov and the Crown Prince of Saudi Arabia Attend the Formula 1 Grand Prix in the UAE*], 25 November 2018. Available at: https://m.business-gazeta.ru/news/403769.

29 Tatar-inform, *Minnikhanov pruibyl na mechdunarodnyu visttavku voorucheniy v Abu-Dhabi* [*Minnikhanov Arrives at the International Arms Exhibition in Abu Dhabi*], 21 February 2021. Available at: https://www.tatar-inform.ru/news/official /21-02-2021/minnihanov-pribyl-na-mezhdunarodnuyu-vystavku-vooruzheniy-v -abu-dabi-5808222

30 TASS, *Nasledniy prince Bahraina ppribyl v Chechnu s drucheskim vizitom* [*Crown Prince of Bahrain Arrives in Chechnya on a Friendly Visit*], 8 November 2019. Available at: https://tass.ru/v-strane/7094904

31 The Irish Times, *Kadyrov had Enemies in Chechnya and Russia*, 9 May 2004. Available at:https://www.irishtimes.com/news/kadyrov-had-enemies-in-chechnya -and-russia-1.978780.

32 Elena Rodina and Dmitryi Dligach, 'Dictator's Instagram: Personal and Political Narratives in a Chechen Leader's Social Network', *Caucasus Survey* 7, no. 2 (2019): 95.

33 Marat Gatin, 2020, interviewed by author.

34 Muslim World League, *The Muslim World League Launches its International Conference in Moscow with the Participation of 43 Countries*, 30 March 2019. Available at: https://themwl.org/en/node/36002.

35 Maikbek Vatchagaev, 'Chechen and Ingush Leaders Feud over Burial of Slain Insurgents', *The Jamestown Foundation*, 15 November 2012. Available at: https://jamestown.org/ program/chechen-and-ingush-leaders-feud-over-burial-of-slain-insurgents-2/.

36 See 'The Grozny Fatwa', *The Minbar of Islam* 3–4 (2016): 49–62. Available at: http:// www.idmedina.ru/pdf/web/viewer.html?file=/pdf/content/minaret/minaret-3-4 -2016.pdf#49.

37 Martin Chulov, 'I Will Return Saudi Arabia to Moderate Islam, Says Crown Prince', *The Guardian*, 24 October 2017. Available at: https://www.theguardian.com/world /2017/oct/24/i-will-return-saudi-arabia-moderate-islam-crown-prince.

38 Rym Ghazal, 'Emirates Praised for Promoting True Principles of Islam', *The National*, 8 September 2008. Available at: https://www.thenational.ae/uae/emirates -praised-for-promoting-true-principles-of-islam-1.498720.

39 Islam News, 'Ramzan Kadyrov vystupil s rechyu v Saudovskoi Aravii', 27 May 2019. Available at: https://islamnews.ru/news-ramzan-kadyrov-vystupil-s-rech-yu-v -saudovskoj-aravii/.

40 RIA Novosti, *'Kadyrov rasskazal ob investiciyah Saudovskoq Aravii v ekonomu Chechni'*.

41 See Smart Building, 'Project Summary'. Available at: https://smbuil.ru/en/what-we -do/grozny-international-university7922/o-proekte-giu/.

42 WAM, 'Zayed Fund for Innovation and Entrepreneurship launched in Chechnya', 29 May 2017. Available at: https://aviamost.ae/en/zayed-fund-innovation-and -entrepreneurship-launched-chechnya.

43 Liz Fuller, *Chechen Leader Kadyrov Challenges Moscow Over Budget Subsidies*, 17 November 2016. Available at: https://www.rferl.org/a/chechnya-kadyrov -challenges-moscow-budget-subsidies/28123822.html.

44 Binsal Abdulkader, *Russian Official Appreciates UAE's Support for Chechen Economy*, 17 October 2019. Available at: https://wam.ae/en/details/1395302795517.

45 Reliefweb, *UAE: Humanitarian Aid and Efforts to Combat COVID-19*, 12 May 2020. Available at: https://reliefweb.int/report/world/uae-humanitarian-aid-and-efforts -combat-covid-19-12-may-2020-enar.

46 Maxim Suchkov, 'What's Chechnya Doing in Syria?' *Al-Monitor*, 26 March 2017. Available at: https://www.al-monitor.com/pulse/originals/2017/03/russia-syria -chechnya-ramzan-kadyrov-fighters.html.

47 Aurelie Campana, 'Chechens Fighting in Ukraine: Putin's Psychological Weapon Could Backfire', *The Conversation*, 18 March 2022. Available at: https:// theconversation.com/chechens-fighting-in-ukraine-putins-psychological-weapon -could-backfire-179447

48 Magomet Evloev, '*Evkurov vstretilsya s generalnym secretarem vsemirnogo souza musulmanskih unchenyh Ali al-Qaradagh*' [*Evkurov Met with General Secretary of the World Muslim Union ali al-Qaradagh*], *Gazeta Ingugushetii*, 6 February 2019. Available at: https://gazetaingush.ru/news/evkurov-vstretilsya-s-generalnym -sekretarem-vsemirnogo-soyuza-musulmanskih-uchenyh-ali.

49 Alexander Iskandaryan, *The Implications of Redrawing the Chechnya-Ingushetia Border*, 11 December 2019. Available at: https://www.ponarseurasia.org/memo/ implications-redrawing-chechnya-ingushetia-border.

50 Artur Priymak, 'Shaykh of Qatar Increased Ratings of Ingushetia' [*Sheikh iz Katara podnimaet reiting Ingushetii*], 21 February 2018. Available at: https://www.ng.ru/ng _religii/2018-02-21/13_437_qatar.html.

51 TASS, 'Ingushetia and Qatar Agreed to Establish Working Group on Development of Investment Projects', [*Ingushetia and Katar dogovorilis' o sozdanii rabochey gruppy po prodvizheniu investproektov*], 6 February 2018. Available at: https://tass.ru /ekonomika/4934413.

52 Priymak, 'Shaykh of Qatar Increased Ratings of Ingushetia'.

53 Islam Today, 'Qatar to Build the Largest Islamic Complex in Ingushetia' [*Katar postriot krupneyshiy v Ingushetii Islamskyi complex*], 27 February 2018. Available at: https://islam-today.ru/novosti/2018/02/27/katar-postroit-krupnejsij-v-ingusetii -islamskij-kompleks/.

54 Government of the Republic of Ingushetia, 'An Islamic Complex with a Cathedral Mosque to be Built in the Capital of Ingushetia' [*V stolice Ingushetii budet postroen Islamskiy complex s Sobornoy mechetuy*], 29 December 2009. Available at: http:// pravitelstvori.ru/news/detail.php?ID=690.

55 Natalya Remmer, 'UAE to Help Build the First Cathedral Mosque in Ingushetia' [*OAE pomogut postroit' pervuy sobornyu mechet' v Ingushetii*], 4 December 2020. Available at: https://businessemirates.ae/news/uae-property-news/oae-pomogut -postroit-pervuyu-sobornuyu-mechet-v-ingushetii/.

56 Ibid.

57 Ibid.

58 TASS, *Ingushetia and Saudi Arabia Establish Cooperation in Agriculture* [*Ingushetia and Saudovskaya Araviya nalazhivaut sotrudnichsetvo v selskom hozyastve*], 31 October 2016. Available at: https://tass.ru/ekonomika/3749157.

59 Republic of Ingushetia, *Head of Ingushetia Yunus-bek Yevkurov Met with King of Saudi Arabia Salman bin Abdel Aziz al-Sa'ud* [*Glava Ingushetii Unus-Bek Evkurov vstretilsya s Korolem Saudovskoy Aravii Salmanom bin Abdel Azizom al-Saudom*], 2 November 2011. Available at: https://ingushetia.ru/news/glava_ingushetii_yunus _bek_evkurov_vstretilsya_s_korolem_saudovskoy_aravii_salmanom_ben_abdel _azizom/.

60 Portal Severnogo Kavkaza, *500 Residents of Ingushetia Will Participate in the Hajj to Saudi Arabia* [*Uchastniki hadja v Saudovskuy Araviu stanut 500 zhiteley Ingushetii*], 8 May 2019. Available at: https://sevkavportal.ru/news/pub/kultura/item/40922 -uchastnikami-khadzha-v-saudovskuyu-araviyu-stanut-500-zhitelej-ingushetii .html.

61 This view was expressed during the interview with Gadzhiamin Ramaldanov, who was by that time especially responsible for economic and trade collaborations with foreign actors. He has extensive experience in the Dagestan government, such as from 2013 to 2014 being an adviser to the Government of the Republic. From 2014 to 2018 he was deputy secretariat of the Government of the Republic of Dagestan and deputy of the Government of the Republic of Dagestan. From 2018 to 2019 he served as head of the Secretariat of the Government of the Republic of Dagestan and its deputies. From 2019 to 2021 he was deputy minister of Economy and Territorial Development of the Republic of Dagestan. Currently, he is deputy head of Derbent city.

62 For example, recent discussions have touched on cooperation in importing meat, juices and tea, and in the field of tourism. For example, see RIA Dagestan, *UAE Will Study Possibility to Import Products from Dagestan* [*Obedinennye Arabskye Emiraty izuchat vozmozhnost' importirovaniya pordukcii Dagestana*], 20 March 2021. Available at: https://riadagestan.ru/news/economy/obedinennye_arabskie_emiraty _izuchat_vozmozhnost_importirovaniya_produktsii_dagestana/.

63 For example, discussions on hajj remain central in relations between Dagestan and Saudi Arabia. See RIA Dagestan, *Kingdom of Saudi Arabia and Dagestan Began to Cooperate in the Field of Tourism*, 15 September 2021. Available at: https:// riadagestan.ru/news/society/korolevstvo_saudovskaya_araviya_i_dagestan_stali _sotrudnichat_v_sfere_turizma/.

64 Importantly, the history of Islam in modern Russia traces its origins from Dagestan and its most ancient cities, including Derbent. The particular interest of tourists from Arabia is linked with the fact that forty companions of the Prophet Muhammad brought their new faith to the Caucasus almost 1500 years ago; they were buried in what is now the sacred Muslim cemetery of Kirkhlyar.

65 Gadzhiamin Ramaldanov, 2020, interviewed by author.

66 See Iwona Kaliszewska, 'Halal Landscapes of Dagestani Entrepreneurs in Makhachkala', *Ethnicities, Special Issue: Normative Orders and the Remaking of Muslim Spaces and Selves in Contemporary Russia*, 20, no. 4 (2020): 708–30.

67 Akhmet Yarlykapov, 'The North Caucasus (Chechnya, Dagestan, Ingushetia) and the Islamic World', *Online Conference on Russia and the Muslim World: Through the Lens of Shared Islamic Identities,* 18–19 March 2021.

68 Al Jazeera, 'Qatar Blockade: Five Things to Know About the Gulf Crisis', *Al Jazeera,* 5 June 2020. Available at: https://www.aljazeera.com/news/2020/6/5/qatar-blockade -five-things-to-know-about-the-gulf-crisis.

69 Yarlykapov, 'The North Caucasus (Chechnya, Dagestan, Ingushetia) and the Islamic World'.

70 Ibid.

71 Ruslan Mirsaiapov, 2020, interviewed by author.

72 Ibid.

73 Timur Rakhmatullin, 'Shaimiev Said that Millions of Muslims in Russia Need Contacts with the Islamic World', *Realnoe Vremya*, 2 December 2019. Available at: https://realnoevremya.com/articles/4018-ufa-hosts-russia-islamic-world-strategic -vision-groups-meeting.

74 Ibid.

75 Ainur Akkulov, 2020, interviewed by author.

76 Yury Barmin, 'Russian Energy Policy in the Middle East', *Insight Turkey* 19, no. 4 (2017): 125–36.

77 Ibid., 125–6.

78 Ainur Akkulov, 2020, interviewed by author.

79 Timur Rakhmatullin, 'In Saudi Arabia the Presentation by the Republic of Bashkortostan will be Conducted' ['V Saudovskoy Aravii Proydet Prezentaziya Bashkortostana'], *Bashinform.RF*, 23 March 2011. Available at: https://www .bashinform.ru/m/news/349585-v-saudovskoy-aravii-proydet-prezentatsiya -bashkortostana/.

80 Bashinform.rf, 'Rustem Khamitov Invited the Ambassador of Saudi Arabia to Bashkortostan' ['Rustem Khakimov priglasil Posla Saudvskoy Aravii posetit' Bashkortastan'], 8 October 2017. Available at: https://www.bashinform.ru/m /news/1058439-rustem-khamitov-priglasil-posla-saudskoy-aravii-posetit -bashkortostan/.

81 Gtrk.tv, 'Rustem Khamitov Conducted Working Meeting with the King of Saudi Arabia' ['Rustem Khamitov porvel rabochyu vstrechu s Korolem Saudovskoy Aravii'], 8 October 2017. Available at: https://gtrk.tv/novosti/59974-rustem -hamitov-provel-rabochuyu-vstrechu-korolyom-saudovskoy-aravii.

82 Ainur Akkulov, 2020, interviewed by author.

83 Ruslan Mirsaiapov, 2020, interviewed by author.

84 Expo Events Consulting, '"Packer" Takes Part in the International Exhibition of the Oil and Gas Industry ADIPEC, Which Takes Place in Abu Dhabi (UAE) Between 11 to 14 November' [NPF 'Packer' prinimaet uchastie v mechdunarodnoy vystavke neftynoi I gazovoy promyshlennosti ADIPEC, kotoraya prohodit s 11 po 14 noyabry v Abu Dabi (OAE)], 13 November 2019. Available at: http://www.eec-emirates.com/ru/npf-packer-at-the-international-exhibition-adipec-2019-in-abu-dhabi/.

85 Ministry of Industry and Innovation Policy Regarding the Republic of Bashkortostan, 25 February 2020. Response to the author's request.

86 Ibid.

87 Ibid.

88 Ministry of Foreign Economic Relations and Congress Activities of the Republic of Bashkortostan, *In Kuwait the Economic Potential of Bashkortostan is Presented* [*V Kuveite predstavlen ekonomicheskiy potencial Bashkortostana*], 27 September 2018. Available at: https://foreign.bashkortostan.ru/presscenter/news/58048/.

89 Bashinform.rf, 'Bashkir Kumis is Planned to be Delivered to the Countries of the Persian Gulf' [*V strany Persidskogo Zaliva planiruetsya postavlit' BAshkiskyi kumys*], 5 November 2019. Available at: https://www.bashinform.ru/news/economy/2019-11-05/v-strany-persidskogo-zaliva-planiruetsya-postavlyat-bashkirskiy-kumys-2109576.

90 Ministry of Industry and Innovation Policy Regarding the Republic of Bashkortostan, 2020.

91 Ruslan Mirsaiapov, 2020, interviewed by author.

92 Ainur Akkulov, 2020, interviewed by author.

93 Kaliszewska, 'Halal Landscapes of Dagestani Entrepreneurs in Makhachkala', 708–30.

94 Ruslan Mirsaiapov, 2020, interviewed by author.

Chapter 7

1 This manuscript generally applies the term 'Russian-Ukraine conflict'; Russia calls it 'a special military operation', while the Western position calls it the '2022 Russian Invasion of Ukraine'.

2 Galeeva Diana, '"Zero-Sum" or "Win-Win?": Russia's Next Steps in the Middle East', *InterRegional for Strategic Analysis*, 19 April 2022. Available at: https://www.interregional.com/en/zero-sum-or-win-win/

3 Yossi Alpher, 'The Ukraine/Crimea Crisis: Ramifications for the Middle East', *OpenDemocracy*, 8 May 2014. Available at: https://www.opendemocracy.net/en/north-africa-west-asia/ukrainecrimea-crisis-ramifications-for-middle-east/.

4 Ukrinform, 'Ukraine Invites Bahrain to Join Crimean Platform Summit', 13 July 2021. Available at: https://www.ukrinform.net/rubric-polytics/3279640-ukraine-invites-bahrain-to-join-crimean-platform-summit.html.

5 Hamad Amani, 'Bahrain's King, Russia's Putin Discuss Conflict in Ukraine', *Al Arabiya News*, 15 March 2022. Available at: https://english.alarabiya.net/News/gulf/2022/03/15/Bahrain-s-King-Russia-s-Putin-discuss-diplomatic-solutions-for-Ukraine-conflict.

6 Foreign Ministry of Oman, 25 January 2022. Available at: https://fm.gov.om/sultanate-of-oman-expresses-concern-over-ukraine-crisis/.

7 Asharq al-Awsat, 'Lavrov Visits Oman, Says Russia Does Not Want War in Europe', 12 May 2022. Available at: https://english.aawsat.com/home/article/3641006/lavrov-visits-oman-says-russia-does-not-want-war-europe.

8 Austin Bodetti, 'Oman Strives for Neutrality in the Middle East', *Yale Global Online*, 7 January 2020. Available at: https://archive-yaleglobal.yale.edu/content/oman-strives-neutrality-middle-east.

9 Times of Oman, 'Oman Oil Poised to Touch $100 Amid Ukraine Crisis', 22 February 2022. Available at: https://timesofoman.com/article/113617-oman-oil-poised-to-touch-100-amid-ukraine-crisis.

10 Kuwait News Agency, 'Kuwait Calls for Respecting Ukraine's Independence, Sovereignty', 24 February 2022. Available at: https://www.kuna.net.kw/ArticleDetails.aspx?id=3027315.

11 Cockburn Patrick, 'Putin's Advance into Ukraine Compares with Saddam Hussein's Invasion of Kuwait – A Disaster for Russia', *World*, 22 February 2022. Available at: https://inews.co.uk/news/world/putin-advance-russia-ukraine-compare-saddam-hussein-kuwait-invasion-disaster-1476212.

12 Volodymyr Zelensky, 24 February 2022. Available at: https://twitter.com/ZelenskyyUa/status/1496736576780521472.

13 Doha Forum, Agenda 2022. Available at: https://dohaforum.org/doha-forum-2022/program.

14 Faucon Benoit, Said Summer and Kalin Stephen, 'Europe Woos Qatar for an Alternative to Russian Gas', *WSJ*, 30 March 2022. Available at: https://www.wsj.com/articles/europe-woos-qatar-as-alternative-to-russian-gas-11648649463.

15 Patrick Wintour, 'Germany Agrees Gas Deal with Qatar to Help End Dependency on Russia', *The Guardian*, 20 March 2022. Available at: https://www.theguardian.com/world/2022/mar/20/germany-gas-deal-qatar-end-energy-dependency-on-russia.

16 Michael Young, 'Power to Which People?', 30 March 2022. Available at: https://carnegie-mec.org/diwan/86757.

17 D'emilio Frances and Moulson Geir, 'Kremlin Demands Rubles for Gas, EU Leaders Push Back', *AP News*, 31 March 2022. Available at: https://apnews.com/article/russia-ukraine-putin-business-germany-europe-039156dc49ded4754877a3a9c99eaa52.

18 Spivak Vita, 'Can the Yuan Ever Replace the Dollar for Russia?', *Carnegie*, 2 August 2021. Available at: https://carnegiemoscow.org/commentary/85069.

19 Arab News, 'Frankly Speaking, Prince Turki Al-Faisal, Former Chief of the General Intelligence Directorate'. 16 May 2022. Available at: https://www.arabnews.com/node/2074106/frankly-speaking-s4-e1-prince-turki-al-faisal-former-chief-general-intelligence.

20 Markets Insider. Available at: https://markets.businessinsider.com/commodities/oil-price?type=wti.

21 Daou Marc, 'Attacks on the UAE: "A New Chapter has Begun in the Yemen Conflict"', *France*, 24, 25 January 2022. Available at: https://www.france24.com/en/middle-east/20220125-attacks-on-the-uae-a-new-chapter-has-begun-in-the-yemen-conflict.

22 DW, 'Houthi Attacks Expose Saudi Arabia's Defense Weakness'. Available at: https://www.dw.com/en/houthi-attacks-expose-saudi-arabias-defense-weakness/a-61294825.

23 Mason Robert, 'Security, Energy and Identity Dominate Gulf Positions on Ukraine', *AGSIW*, 25 February 2022. Available at: https://agsiw.org/security-energy-and-identity-dominate-gulf-positions-on-ukraine/.

24 Javier Blas, 'Ukraine Crisis Creates a Winner in Saudi Arabia', *Bloomberg*, 15 February 2022. Available at: https://www.bloomberg.com/opinion/articles/2022-02-15/saudi-arabia-isn-t-wasting-the-ukraine-crisis-wielding-influence-in-washington.

25 Chatham House, 'How is the War in Ukraine Affecting Middle East Oil Production?', 1 May 2022. Available at: https://twitter.com/CH_MENAP/status/1520761346765332480.

26 Pazzanese Christina, 'Biden May Regret Releasing Report on Khashoggi Murder', *The Harvard Gazette*, 27 February 2021. Available at: https://news.harvard.edu/gazette/story/2021/02/biden-may-regret-releasing-report-on-khashoggi-murder-says-expert/.

27 Chmaytelli Maher, 'Saudi Crown Prince Says He Does Not Care If Biden Misunderstands Him – The Atlantic', *Reuters*, 3 March 2022. Available at: https://www.reuters.com/world/saudi-crown-prince-says-do-not-care-if-biden-misunderstands-him-atlantic-2022-03-03/.

28 Nissenbaum Dion, Kalin Stephen and S. Cloud David, 'Saudi, Emirati Leaders Decline Calls With Biden During Ukraine Crisis', *WSJ*, 8 March 2022. Available at: https://www.wsj.com/articles/saudi-emirati-leaders-decline-calls-with-biden-during-ukraine-crisis-11646779430.

29 Khalid Al-Jabri and Sheline Annelle, 'Biden Should Punish Saudi Arabia for Backing Russia', *Foreign Policy*, 22 March 2022. Available at: https://foreignpolicy.com/2022/03/22/biden-mbs-oil-saudi-arabia-russia-ukraine/.

30 Al-Faisal Prince Turki, 'America Should Laugh with the Kingdom, Not Scowl', *Arab News*, 15 April 2022. Available at: https://www.arabnews.com/node/2064041.

31 Coates Ulrichsen Kristian, 'The GCC and the Russia-Ukraine Crisis', Arab Center, Washington DC. Available at: https://arabcenterdc.org/resource/the-gcc-and-the-russia-ukraine-crisis/.

32 MOFAIC, 'H. H. Sheikh Abdullah bin Zayed, Russian Foreign Minister Discuss Friendship Relations, Strategic Partnership', 23 February 2022. Available at: https://www.mofaic.gov.ae/en/mediahub/news/2022/2/23/23-02-2022-uae-russia.

33 Narayanan Ayush, 'UAE Foreign Minister, US Secretary of State Discuss Russian Invasion: State Dept', *Al Arabiya*, 25 February 2022. Available at: https://english.alarabiya.net/News/gulf/2022/02/25/UAE-foreign-minister-US-secretary-of-state-discuss-Russian-invasion-State-dept.

34 *The Economic Times*, 'India Along with China and UAE Abstain from US-Backed UNSC Resolution Condemning Russia', 26 February 2022. Available at: https://economictimes.indiatimes.com/news/international/world-news/india-along-with-china-and-uae-abstain-from-us-backed-unsc-resolution-ondemning-russia/articleshow/89839770.cms.

35 Ayush Narayanan, 'UAE Calls for Immediate De-escalation and Cessation of Hostilities in Ukraine', *Al Arabiya English*, 26 February 2022. Available at: https://english.alarabiya.net/News/gulf/2022/02/26/UAE-calls-for-immediate-de-escalation-and-cessation-of-hostilities-in-Ukraine.

36 Ebtesam Al-Ketbi, 'Prospects of UAE-US Relations in a New Strategic Environment', *Emirates Policy Center*, 22 April 2022. Available at: https://epc.ae/en/details/scenario/prospects-of-uae-us-relations-in-a-new-strategic-environment.

37 Ibid.

38 Al-Ketbi, 'Prospects of UAE-US Relations in a New Strategic Environment'.

39 Baharoon Mohammed, 'UAE-U.S. Relations: What Went Wrong?' *AGSIW*, 22 April 2022. Available at: https://agsiw.org/uae-u-s-relations-what-went-wrong/.

40 Ibid.

41 Rahman Fareed, 'UAE and Russia Trade Set to Rise 21% to Hit $4bn in 2021', *The National*, 12 December 2021. Available at: https://www.thenationalnews.com/business/economy/2021/12/12/uae-and-russia-trade-set-to-rise-21-to-hit-4bn-in-2021/.

42 Mohammed, 'UAE-U.S. Relations: What Went Wrong?'

43 Financial Times, 'Gulf States' Neutrality on Ukraine Reflects Deeper Russian Ties'. Available at: https://www.ft.com/content/5e3b0998-705f-46c4-8010-9972b3c8a847.

44 Mohammed, 'UAE-U.S. Relations: What Went Wrong?'

45 Al-Ketbi, 'Prospects of UAE-US Relations in a New Strategic Environment'.

46 European Council of the European Union, 'EU Restrictive Measures Against Russia over Ukraine (since 2014)'. Available at: https://www.consilium.europa.eu/en/policies/sanctions/restrictive-measures-against-russia-over-ukraine/.

47 BBC News, 'What Sanctions Are Being Imposed on Russia over Ukraine Invasion?', 4 May 2022. Available at: https://www.bbc.co.uk/news/world-europe-60125659.

48 Shaji Mathew and Nicolas Parasie, 'Abu Dhabi Wealth Fund Mubadala Pauses Investments in Russia', *Bloomberg*, 28 March 2022. Available at: https://www .bloomberg.com/news/articles/2022-03-28/abu-dhabi-wealth-fund-pauses -investments-in-russia-reuters-says.

49 Ibid.

50 Arab News, 'Abu Dhabi's Mubadala and Qatar Investment Authority Holding on to Russian Assets for Now: Bloomberg', 1 March 2022. Available at: https://www .arabnews.com/node/2033906/business-economy.

51 Ibid.

52 Hyatt John, 'Russian Oligarchs Fleeing Sanctions Are House Hunting in Dubai', *Forbes*, 8 April 2022. Available at: https://www.forbes.com/sites/johnhyatt/2022 /04/08/russian-oligarchs-fleeing-sanctions-are-house-hunting-in-dubai/?sh =6e1b89f058ce.

53 Ibid.

54 Business Online, *Pochemy 'Business Online' prodolzhit nazyvat' Minnikhanova prezidentom'*, [*Why Business Online will continue to call Minnikhanov president*], 9 November 2021. Available at: https://m.business-gazeta.ru/article/528476. Also see, for example, Business Online, *Federacia nepreemlima dlya Rossii!' : kak v Gosdume iz glav regionov delali 'rabov lampy'*, [*The Federation is Unacceptable for Russia: How in the State Duma They Made 'Slaves of the Lamp' from the Heads of Regions*], 13 November 2021. Available at: https://www.business-gazeta.ru/article /529104.

55 See Joel Gunter, 'China Committed Genocide Against Uyghurs, Independent Tribunal Rules', *BBC News*, 9 December 2021. Available at: https://www.bbc.com/ news/world-asia-china-59595952?piano-modal.

56 Braginskaia Ekaterina, '"Domestication" or Representation?: Russia and the Institutionalism of Islam in Comparative Perspective', *Europe-Asia Studies* 64, no. 3 (2012): 597–620.

57 Ibid.

Bibliography

Abdala al-Tajir, Mahdi. *Bahrain, 1920–1945: Britain, the Shaikh and the Administration*, London, New York, Sydney: Croom Helm, 1987.

Abdulkader, Binsal, *Russian Official Appreciates UAE's Support for Chechen Economy*, 17 October 2019. Available at: https://wam.ae/en/details/1395302795517

Abdulrahman, bin MOHAMMAD bin Rashid al-Khalifa, 2022, interviewed by author.

Administration report of the Kuwait Political Agency for the year 1932, H. R. P. Dickson Box 3, File 3, Administrative reports of the Kuwait Political Agency. 1928–32. DN 3/3/168, p. 34.

Ainur, Akkulov, 2020, interviewed by author.

Akchura, Usuf. *Three Policies [Üç Tarzı Siyaset]*, edited by H. B. Parsoy, Abington: Routledge, 1995.

al-aher, Isam, *Kuwait – The Reality*, Pittsburgh: Dorrance Publishing Co, Inc, 1995.

al-Awsat, Asharq, 'Custodian of the Two Holy Mosques Holds a Session of Talks with the President of Tatarstan on Prospects for Cooperation. President Rustam Minnikhanov Received at al-Yamamah Palace', [https://aawsat.com/home/article خادم-الحرمين-يعقد-جلسة-مباحثات-مع-رئيس-تتارستان-تناولت-آفاق-التعاون/849321/], February 8 2017. Available at: https://aawsat.com/home/article/849321/-خادم-الحرمين-يعقد-جلسة-مباحثات-مع-رئيس-تتارستان-تناولت-آفاق-التعاون

al-Awsat, Asharq, 'Lavrov Visits Oman, Says Russia Does Not Want War in Europe', 12 May 2022. Available at: https://english.aawsat.com/home/article/3641006/lavrov -visits-oman-says-russia-does-not-want-war-europe

Al-Ayam Newspaper, *Investment Opportunities with Tatarstan and the Russian Regions* [فرص استثمارية مع تتارستان والأقاليم الروسية], August 2021. Available at: https://www .alayam.com/alayam/economic/920324/amp.html?amp=1

Albaharna, Husain M., *The Legal Status of the Arabian Gulf States: A Study of Their Treaty Relations and Their International Problems*, Manchester: Manchester University Press, 1968.

Albawaba, Dubai Islamic Economy Development Centre Signs MoU With Tatarstan Investment Development Agency at Kazan Summit 2018, 13 May 2018. Available at: https://www.albawaba.com/business/pr/dubai-islamic-economy-development -centre-signs-mou-tatarstan-investment-development-agen

Al-Bayan, 'The President of the Republic of Tatarstan in an Exclusive Interview with al-Bayan: Zayed Created an Economic Miracle on the Banks of the Gulf, Our Oil Production is 26 Million Tons Annually and the Price of $20 a Barrel is Fair', [رئيس جمهورية تتارستان في حديث خاص لـ البيان : زايد صنع معجزة اقتصادية على ضفاف الخليج ، إنتاجنا]

النفطي 26 مليون طن سنويا وسعر 20 دولارا للبرميل عادل], April 5 2000. Available at: https://
www.albayan.ae/economy/2000-04-05-1.1049884?ot=ot.AMPPageLayout

Al-Bayan, 'UAE and Tatarstan Towards Strategic Investment Partnerships',
الإمارات وتتارستان نحو شراكات استراتيجية استثمارية], June 7 (2014). Available at:
https://www.albayan.ae/economy/local-market/2014-06-07-1.2139507?ot=ot
.AMPPageLayout

Al-Bayan, 'The UAE Calls for a Global Partnership to Benefit from the Halal Industry',
الإمارات تدعو لشراكة عالمية للاستفادة من صناعة الحلال], August 2 2021. Available at: https://
www.albayan.ae/economy/uae/2021-08-02-1.4219160?ot=ot.AMPPageLayout

Al-Bilad Newspaper, *Bahrain Chamber of Commerce and Industry Signs Two
Memoranda of Understanding with Tatarstan*, 28 July 2021. Available at: https://www
.albiladpress.com/news/2021/4671/finance/717327.html.

Alekhbariyatv, Speech at the Meeting of the Strategic Vision Delivered by the President
of the Republic of Tatarstan [روسيا_# فيديو | كلمة #بوتين في اجتماع مجموعة الرؤية الاستراتيجية
والعالم_الإسلامي يلقيها رئيس جمهورية تتارستان], November 24 2021. Available at: https://
twitter.com/alekhbariyatv/status/1463424545197641729?s=21

al-Enazy, Askar H. *The Creation of Saudi Arabia: Ibn Saud and British Imperial Policy,
1914–1927*, London; New York: Routledge, 2010.

Al-Faisal, Prince Turki, 'America Should Laugh with the Kingdom, Not Scowl', *Arab
News*, 15 April 2022. Available at: https://www.arabnews.com/node/2064041.

Alford, Jonathan, 'Soviet-American Rivalry in the Middle East: The Military Dimension',
in *The Soviet Union in the Middle East: Policies and Perspectives*, edited by Adeed
Dawisha and Karen Dawisha, 134–46, New York: Holmes & Meier Publishers, 1982.

Ali al-Tamimi, Khaled Mohamed, 'Cooperation between Russia and Bahrain in the
Field of Regional Security' [Sotrudnichsetvo mechdu Rossiye i Bahreinom v oblasti
obespecheniya regionalnoy bezopasnosti], *Vestnik MGIMO -Universiteta* 4, no. 55
(2017): 194.

Al-Jabri, Khalid and Sheline Annelle, 'Biden Should Punish Saudi Arabia for backing
Russia', *Foreign Policy*, 22 March 2022. Available at: https://foreignpolicy.com/2022
/03/22/biden-mbs-oil-saudi-arabia-russia-ukraine/.

Al-Jazeera, *Qatari Emir in Russia to Discuss Syrian Crisis*, 25 March 2018. Available at:
https://www.aljazeera.com/news/2018/3/25/qatari-emir-in-russia-to-discuss-syrian
-crisis

Al-Jazeera, *Putin Visits Saudi Arabia in Sign of Growing Ties*, 14 October 2019. Available
at: https://www.aljazeera.com/news/2019/10/14/putin-visits-saudi-arabia-in-sign-of
-growing-ties

Al-Jazeera, *Russia's Putin Signs Deals Worth $1.3.bn During UAE Visit*, 15 October 2019.
Available at: https://www.aljazeera.com/economy/2019/10/15/russias-putin-signs
-deals-worth-1-3bn-during-uae-visit

Al-Jazeera, 'Qatar Blockade: Five Things to Know About the Gulf Crisis', *Al Jazeera*,
5 June 2020. Available at: https://www.aljazeera.com/news/2020/6/5/qatar-blockade
-five-things-to-know-about-the-gulf-crisis

Al-Jazeera, *Bahrain Appoints First Ambassador to Syria in Over a Decade*, 30 December 2021. Available at: https://www.aljazeera.com/news/2021/12/30/bahrain-appoints -first-ambassador-to-syria-in-over-a-decade

Al-Ketbi, Ebtesam, 'Prospects of UAE-US Relations in a New Strategic Environment', *Emirates Policy Center*, 22 April 2022. Available at: https://epc.ae/en/details/scenario /prospects-of-uae-us-relations-in-a-new-strategic-environment.

Al-Khaleej, UAE and Tatarstan Discuss Developing Economic Relations [الإمارات وتتارستان تبحثان تطوير العلاقات الاقتصادية], February 22 (2021). Available at: https://www.alkhaleej.ae/2021-02-22/الإمارات-وتتارستان-تبحثان-تطوير-العلاقات-الاقتصادية/أسواق-الإمارات/اقتصاد

Allen, Calvin H. and W. Lynn Rigsbee, II, *Oman under Qaboos: From Coup to Constitution, 1970–1996*, London, Portland: Frank Cass, 2000.

Allison, Roy, 'Russia and Syria: Explaining Alignment with a Regime in Crisis', *International Affairs* 89, no. 4 (2013): 795–823. Available at: https://www.latimes .com/world/middleeast/la-fg-syria-russia-20170406-story.html

Almaqbali, M, 'Russia's Relations with Gulf States and Their Effect on Regional Balance in the Middle East', *RUDN Journal of Political Science* 20, no. 4 (2018): 536–47.

al-Mezaini, Khalid and Rickli Jean-Marc, *The Small Gulf States: Foreign and Security Policies before and after the Arab Spring*, New York: Routledge, 2017.

Almowaten.net, 'President of Tatarstan Performs Umrah', [رئيس تتارستان يؤدي مناسك العمرة], November 23 2021. Available at: https://www.almowaten.net/2021/11/رئيس-تتارستان-يؤدي-مناسك-العمرة/

Almushev, Khamidulla, *Hajj-Name [Hadj–Name]*. Available at: http://www.idmedina.ru /books/history_culture/hadjj/1/almushev.htm.

Alov, A. A., N. G. Vladimirov and F. G. Ovsienko, *Mirovie Religii*, Moscow: Nauka, 1998.

Alpher, Yossi, 'The Ukraine/Crimea Crisis: Ramifications for the Middle East', *OpenDemocracy*, 8 May 2014. Available at: https://www.opendemocracy.net/ en/north-africa-west-asia/ukrainecrimea-crisis-ramifications-for-middle-east/

al-Rasheed, Madawi, *A History of Saudi Arabia*, Cambridge: Cambridge University Press, 2012.

Al-Wasat, 'The President of Tatarstan Discusses with the Vice President of the Supreme Council for Islamic Affairs in Bahrain the Strengthening of Bilateral Relations', [رئيس تتارستان يبحث مع نائب رئيس «الأعلى للشئون الإسلامية» تعزيز العلاقات الثنائية], May 27 2016. Available at: http://www.alwasatnews.com/news/1119440.html

Anthony, John Duke and Naser Fahad, 'GCC-US Relations Under a Trump Administration', *National Council on US-Arab Relations*, 13 December 2016. Available at: https://ncusar.org/aa/2016/12/gcc-us-relations-under-trump-administration/

Arab News, *UAE and Russia Sign Deals Worth $1.3 bn During Putin's Abu Dhabi Visit*, 15 October 2019. Available at: https://www.arabnews.com/node/1569171/ middle-east

Arab News, *Russian President Vladimir Putin off to UAE After Successful Saudi Arabia Visit*, 15 October 2019. Available at: https://www.arabnews.com/node/1569186/saudi-arabia

Arab News, *Frankly Speaking, Prince Turki Al-Faisal, Former Chief of the General Intelligence Directorate*, 16 May 2022. Available at: https://www.arabnews.com/node/2074106/frankly-speaking-s4-e1-prince-turki-al-faisal-former-chief-general-intelligence

Arab News, 'Abu Dhabi's Mubadala and Qatar Investment Authority Holding on to Russian Assets for Now: Bloomberg', 1 March 2022. Available at: https://www.arabnews.com/node/2033906/business-economy

Arapov, U., *Islam in the Russian Empire (Legislative Acts, Descriptions, Statistics)* [*Islam v Rossiyskoy imperii (zakonodatelnye akty, opisaniya, statistika)*], Akademkniga: Moscow, 2001.

Arhiv vnseshnei politiki Rossii [Archive of Foreign Policy of Russia], F. 110, Op. 2, D. 6, p. 233; cited in Ruslan Khayretdinov, 'Karim Khakimov – Revolutionary, Diplomat' [Karim Khakimov – Revolutioner, Diplomat], PhD, Bashkir State University, 2006, 19.

Arhiv vnseshnei politiki Rossii [Archive of Foreign Policy of Russia], F.25859, Op. 1., D. 51, p. 66; cited in Ruslan Khayretdinov, 'Karim Khakimov – Revolutionary, Diplomat' [Karim Khakimov – Revolutioner, Diplomat], PhD, Bashkir State University, 2006, 19.

Arhiv vnseshnei politiki Rossii [Archive of Foreign Policy of Russia], 'From the Personal Case of Karim Khakimov': 9, cited in Ruslan Khayretdinov, 'Karim Khakimov – Revolutionary, Diplomat' [Karim Khakimov – Revolutioner, Diplomat], PhD, Bashkir State University, 2006, 20.

Arhiv vnseshnei politiki Rossii [Archive of Foreign Policy of Russia], F.180, Op.517/2, D. 5322, II., 203–203ob.

Arhiv vnseshnei politiki Rossiskoi imperii [*Archive of Foreign Policy of Russian Empire*], f. 149 (Turetski stol) [*Turkish Table*], op. 502a, d. 425, II, 3-4, 9-10; f. 180 (Posol'stvo v Kostabtinopole) [*Embassy in Constantinople*], op. 517/2, d.5322, 1. 97.

Arhiv vnseshnei politiki SSSR [Archive of Foreign Policy of the USSR], X, Doc. 77, Moscow, 1965, 134.

Artamonov, Mikhail, *History of Khazars [Istoria Khazar]*, Leningrad: Izd-vo Gos. Ermitazha, 1962.

Article 6 of the Constitution of the Republic of Tatarstan. Available at: https://tatarstan.ru/file/old/html/Constitution%20of%20the%20Republic%20of%20Tatarstan.pdf

Arzamaskin, Uryi, 'Government-Muslim Relations of the USSR in 1944–1949' [Gosudarstvenno-Musulmanskie Otnosheniya v SSSR v 1944-1949 godu], *Islam in the Modern World* 13, no. 4 (December 2017): 25–35.

Azhar, Saeed and Kanishka, Singh, 'Saudi Wealth Fund Boosts US Holdings with Stakes in Citi, Boeing, Facebook', *Reuters*, 16 May 2020. Available at: https://www.reuters.com/article/us-saudi-pif-idUSKBN22S0BQ

Baharoon, Mohammed, 'UAE-U.S. Relations: What Went Wrong?' *AGSIW*, 22 April 2022. Available at: https://agsiw.org/uae-u-s-relations-what-went-wrong/.

Balkind, Nicole, 'A Model Republic? Trust and Authoritarianism on Tatarstan's Road to Autonomy', MA thesis, University of North Carolina, 2009.

Barabanov, M, 'Russian Arms Trade with the Gulf Monarchies', in *Russian & CIS Relations with Gulf Region: Current Trends in Political and Economic Dynamics,* edited by M. Terterov, 371. Dubai: Gulf Research Center, 2009.

Barmin, Yury, 'Russian Energy Policy in the Middle East', *Insight Turkey* 19, no. 4 (2017): 125–36.

Bashinform.rf, 'Rustem Khamitov Invited the Ambassador of Saudi Arabia to Bashkortostan' ['Rustem Khakimov priglasil Posla Saudvskoy Aravii posetit' Bashkortostan'], 8 October 2017. Available at: https://www.bashinform.ru/m /news/1058439-rustem-khamitov-priglasil-posla-saudovskoy-aravii-posetit -bashkortostan/

Bashinform.rf, 'Bashkir Kumis is Planned to be Delivered to the Countries of the Persian Gulf' [V strany Persidskogo Zaliva planiruetsya postavlit' Bashkiskyi kumys], 5 November 2019. Available at: https://www.bashinform.ru/news/economy /2019-11-05/v-strany-persidskogo-zaliva-planiruetsya-postavlyat-bashkirskiy -kumys-2109576

BBC News, 'Biden Raises Human Rights in Call with Saudi King Salman', 26 February 2021. Available at: https://www.bbc.co.uk/news/world-us-canada-56204449.

BBC News, 'What Sanctions are Being Imposed on Russia over Ukraine Invasion?', 4 May 2022. Available at: https://www.bbc.co.uk/news/world-europe-60125659.

Becker, Abraham, Bent Hansen and Malcolm H. Kerr. *The Economics and Politics of the Middle East*, New York: American Elsevier Publishing Co., 1975.

Bekkin, Renat, 'The Central Spiritual Administration of the Muslims of Russia (TSDUM) and Its Strategy of Subordinate Partnership in Dialogue with the Russian Orthodox Church', *Journal of Interdisciplinary Studies* 4, no. 2 (2017): 7–28.

Belyakov, Vladimir. *Sovetsko-Egipetskie otnosheniya 1943–1955: dokumenty i materialy* [*Soviet-Egyptian Relations 1943–1955: Documents and Materials*], Saint Petersburg: Aletelia, 2019.

Benningsen, Alexander and Broxup Marie. *The Islamic Threat to the Soviet State*, London: Croom Helm, 1983.

Bennigsen, Alexander, B. Henze Paul, K. Tanham George and S. Enders Wimbush. *Soviet Strategy and Islam*, London: The Macmillan Press Ltd, 1989.

Bigiev, Musa, 'Hajj Performance of Musa Bigiev' [Musa Bigievnen 1927–nche elgy hachnamese], *Hajj of Russian Muslims [Hajj Rosiyskyh Musulman]* 8 (2017): 15–53.

von Bismarck, Helene, *British Policy in the Persian Gulf, 1961–1968*, London: Palgrave Macmillan, 2013.

Blas, Javier, 'Ukraine Crisis Creates a Winner in Saudi Arabia', *Bloomberg*, 15 February 2022. Available at: https://www.bloomberg.com/opinion/articles/2022-02-15/saudi -arabia-isn-t-wasting-the-ukraine-crisis-wielding-influence-in-washington

Blas, Javier and Arkhipov Ilya, 'Russia and Saudi Arabia Step Up Oil Diplomacy', *Bloomberg*, 17 October 2020. Available at: https://www.bloomberg.com/news /articles/2020-10-17/russia-saudi-arabia-ready-to-keep-energy-market-stable -kremlin

Bloomfield, Lincoln P. and Amelia C. Leiss, 'Arms Transfers and Arms Control', in *Soviet-American Rivalry in the Middle East*, edited by J. C. Hurewitz, 3–754, New York: Frederick A. Praeger, Publishers, 1969.

Bodetti, Austin, 'Oman Strives for Neutrality in the Middle East', *Yale Global Online*, 7 January 2020. Available at: https://archive-yaleglobal.yale.edu/content/oman -strives-neutrality-middle-east

Braginskaia, Ekaterina, '"Domestication" or Representation? Russia and the Institutionalism of Islam in Comparative Perspective', *Europe-Asia Studies* 64, no. 3 (2012): 97–620.

Breslauer, George W, 'Soviet Policy in the Middle East, 1967–72: Unalterable Antagonism or Collaborative Competition?', in *Soviet Strategy in the Middle East*, edited by George W. Breslauer, London: Boston Unwin Hyman, 1990.

Bukharaev, Ravil, *The Model of Tatarstan under President Mintimer Shaimiev*, New York: St. Martin's Press, 1999.

Bukharaev, Ravil, *Islam in Russia: The Four Seasons*. Richmond: Curzon Press, 2000.

Bukharaev, Ravil, *Tatarstan: A 'Can-Do' Culture – President Mintimer Shaimiev and the Power of Common Sense*. Kent: Global Oriental, 2007.

Burbiel, Gustav, *The Tatars and the Tatar ASSR: Handbook of the Major Soviet Nationalities*. London: The Free Press, 1975.

Business Online, *Pochemy "Business Online" prodolzhit nazyvat' Minnikhanova prezidentom*', [*Why Business Online Will Continue to Call Minnikhanov President*], 9 November 2021. Available at: https://m.business-gazeta.ru/article/528476.

Business Online, *Federacia nepreemlima dlya Rossii!' : kak v Gosdume iz glav regionov delali "rabov lampy"*, [*The Federation is Unacceptable for Russia: How in the State Duma They Made 'Slaves of the Lamp' from the Heads of Regions*], 13 November 2021. Available at: https://www.business-gazeta.ru/article/529104

Business Online, *Minnikhanov, Kadyrov I nasledniy princ Saudovskoy Aravii posetili Gran-pri 'Formuly-1' v OAE*, [*Minnikhanov, Kadyrov and the Crown Prince of Saudi Arabia attended the Formula 1 Grand Prix in the UAE*], 25 November 2018. Available at: https://m.business-gazeta.ru/news/403769

Business Online, *V Tatarstane sozdana investicionnaya kompaniya, rabotaushaya po normam shariata*, [*An Investment Company Operating in Accordance with Shari'a Norms was Established in Tatarstan*], 7 December 2009. Available at: https://www .business-gazeta.ru/news/17870

Business Online, *Rustam Minnikhanov: 'Raskulachivanie bylo uzhe, my posledstviia videli . . . [Rustam Minnkihhanov: Raskulachivanie Already Occurred, We Saw the Consequences . . .]*', 26 December 2016. Available at: www.busines-gazeta.ru/video /333026.

Business Online, *Minnikhanov, Kadyrov i naslednyi prince Saudovskoy Aravii posetili gran-pri 'Formuly –1' v OAE [Minnikhanov, Kadyrov and the Crown Prince of Saudi Arabia Attend the* Formula 1 *Grand Prix in the UAE]*, 25 November 2018. Available at: https://m.business-gazeta.ru/news/403769

Bustanov, Alfrid, 'The Language of Moderate Salafism in Eastern Tatarstan', *Islam and Christian Muslim Relations* 28, no. 2 (2017): 183–201.

Bustanov, Alfrid, 'Shihabaddin Marjani and the Muslim Archive in Russia', *Islamology* 9, no. 1–2 (2019): 138.

Cafiero, Giorgio and Connelly Colby, 'Russia and the Arab Gulf States: Current Energy Variables', *Gulf International Forum*, 19 March 2019. Available at: https://gulfif.org/russia-and-arab-gulf-states-current-energy-variables/

Cafiero, Giorgio, and Karasik Theodore, 'Qatar and Russia: What Do They See in Each Other?', *Middle East Policy Council*, 11 October 2017. Available at: https://mepc.org/commentary/qatar-and-russia-what-do-they-see-each-other.

Campana, Aurelie, 'Chechens Fighting in Ukraine: Putin's Psychological Weapon Could Backfire', *The Conversation*, 18 March 2022. Available at: https://theconversation.com/chechens-fighting-in-ukraine-putins-psychological-weapon-could-backfire-179447

Cengiz, Sinem, 'Saudi Arabia and Russia in the Syrian Crisis: Divergent Policies, Similar Concerns', in *The Syrian Crisis Effects on the Regional and International Relations*, edited by Dania K. Khatib, 105–21. Singapore: Springer Nature, 2021.

Charap, Samuel, 'Is Russia an Outside Power in the Gulf?', *Survival* 57, no. 1 (2015): 153–70.

Chatham House, 'How is the War in Ukraine Affecting Middle East Oil Production?', 1 May 2022. Available at: https://twitter.com/CH_MENAP/status/1520761346765332480

Chicherin – Stalinu [Chicherin to Stalin], 18 December 1923, Arhiv vnseshnei politiki Rossii [Archive of Foreign Policy of Russia], F. 0127, Op. 1, p. 1, d. 2., pp. 6–7., cited in Naumkin, 2018, 81–82.

Chmaytelli, Maher, 'Saudi Crown Prince Says He Does Not Care If Biden Misunderstands Him – The Atlantic', *Reuters*, 3 March 2022. Available at: https://www.reuters.com/world/saudi-crown-prince-says-do-not-care-if-biden-misunderstands-him-atlantic-2022-03-03/

Christie, J., 'History and Development of the Gulf Cooperation Council: A Brief Overview', in *The Gulf Cooperation Council: Moderation and Stability in an Interdependent World*, edited by J. A. Sandwick, 1–14. Colorado: Westview Press, 1987.

Chubin, Shahram, 'Soviet-American Rivalry in the Middle East: The Political Dimension', in *The Soviet Union in the Middle East: Policies and Perspectives*, edited by Adeed Dawisha and Karen Dawisha, 124–33, New York: Holmes &. Meier Publishers.

Chulov, Martin, 'I will return Saudi Arabia to Moderate Islam, Says Crown Prince', *The Guardian*, 24 October 2017. Available at: https://www.theguardian.com/world/2017/oct/24/i-will-return-saudi-arabia-moderate-islam-crown-prince

Cockburn, Patrick, 'Putin's Advance into Ukraine Compares with Saddam Hussein's Invasion of Kuwait – A Disaster for Russia', *World*, 22 February 2022. Available at: https://inews.co.uk/news/world/putin-advance-russia-ukraine-compare-saddam -hussein-kuwait-invasion-disaster-1476212

Confino, Michael and Shimon Shamir, *The USSR and the Middle East*, New York: J. Wiley, 1973.

Cook, Steven A, 'Trump's Middle East Legacy Is Failure', *Foreign Policy*, 28 October 2020. Available at: https://foreignpolicy.com/2020/10/28/trumps-middle-east-legacy -is-failure/

Cordell, Jake, *6 things You Need to Know About OPEC+. What Does Russia Want from this Week's Meeting in Vienna?*, 4 December 2019. Available at: https://www .themoscowtimes.com/2019/12/04/6-things-opec-russia-a68409

Cordesman, Anthony H., *The Gulf and the Search for Strategic Stability: Saudi Arabia, the Military Balance in the Gulf, and Trends in the Arab-Israeli Military Balance*, Boulder: Westview Press; London: Mansell Publishing Limited, 1984.

Crystal, Jill. *Kuwait: The Transformation of an Oil State*, Boulder: Westview Press Inc, 1992.

Czaplicka, M. A., *The Turks of Central Asia in History and at the Present Day*, Oxford: Clarendon Press, 1918.

Daishev, *History of TASSR [Tatarstan ASSR tarihy]*, Kazan, 1960.

Dannreuther, R., 'Russia and the Middle East: A Cold War Paradigm?', *Europe-Asia Studies* 64, no. 3 (2012): 543–60.

Daou, Marc, 'Attacks on the UAE: "A New Chapter has Begun in the Yemen Conflict"', *France 24*, 25 January 2022. Available at: https://www.france24.com/en/middle -east/20220125-attacks-on-the-uae-a-new-chapter-has-begun-in-the-yemen -conflict

Dargin, J., 'Qatar's Natural Gas: The Foreign-Policy Driver', *Middle East Policy* 14, no. 3 (2007): 136–42.

Davidson, Christopher M., *Abu Dhabi: Oil and Beyond*, London, Oxford: Hurst & Co. / Oxford University Press, 2011.

Davidson, Christopher M., *Shadow Wars: The Secret Struggle for the Middle East*, London: Oneworld Publications Ltd, 2016.

Davidson, Jennifer-Anne, 'Power Dynamics in Russian-Tatarstan Relations: A Case Study', MA Thesis, University of Victoria, 2008.

D'emilio, Frances and Moulson Geir, 'Kremlin Demands Rubles for Gas, EU Leaders Push Back', *AP News*, 31 March 2022. Available at: https://apnews.com/article/russia -ukraine-putin-business-germany-europe-039156dc49ded4754877a3a9c99eaa52

Demirtas, Melih, 'Understanding Impacts of "Russian Orientalism" on Post-Soviet Elite-management in the Republic of Bashkortostan', *Cappadocia Journal of Area Studies (CJAS)* 2, no. 1 (2020): 44.

Derrick, Matthew Allen, 'Placing Faith in Tatarstan, Russia: Islam and the Negotiation of Homeland', PhD Thesis, University of Oregon, 2012.

Devin, DeWeese, *Islamization and Native Religion in the Golden Horde: Baba Tükles and Conversion to Islam in Historical and Epic Tradition*, University Park: Pennsylvania State University Press, 1994.

Dobaev, Igor, 'Islamic Radicalism in the Northern Caucasus', *Central Asia and the Caucasus*, 2000. Available at: https://www.ca-c.org/online/2000/journal_eng/eng06 _2000/09.dobae.shtml

Documents from the KGD of Tatarstan in 'East is a Delicate Matter' [Vostok-delo tonkoe], Echo of centuries [Eko vekov], 1 no. 2 (1998). Available at: http://www .archive.gov.tatarstan.ru/magazine/go/anonymous/main/?path=mg:/number s/1998_1_2/07/1/&searched=1

Documenty vneshnei politiki SSSR [Documents of Foreign Policy of the USSR], 1, Moscow: Gospolitizdat, 1957, 34–35, cited in Alexey Vasiliev, *Russia's Middle East Policy: From Lenin to Putin*, Abingdon: Routledge, 2018, 11.

Documenty vneshnei politiki SSSR [Documents of Foreign Policy of the USSR], 3, Moscow: Gospolitizdat, 1959, 598–601, cited in Alexey Vasiliev, *Russia's Middle East Policy: From Lenin to Putin*, Abingdon: Routledge, 2018, 18.

Doha Forum, Agenda 2022. Available at: https://dohaforum.org/doha-forum-2022/ program

Duchacek, Ivo D., 'Perforated Sovereignties: Towards a Typology of New Actors in International Relations', in *Federalism and International Relations: The Role of Subnational Units*, edited by Hans J. Michelmann and Panayotis Soldatos, 20, Singapore: Palgrave Macmillan, 1990.

DW, 'Houthi Attacks Expose Saudi Arabia's Defense Weakness'. Available at: https:// www.dw.com/en/houthi-attacks-expose-saudi-arabias-defense-weakness/a -61294825

El-Solh, Raghid. *The Sultanate of Oman, 1939–1945*, Reading: Ithaca Press, 2000.

The Economist, 'Can Joe Biden Get America Out of the Middle East?', 4 March 2021. Available at: https://www.economist.com/united-states/2021/03/03/can-joe-biden -get-america-out-of-the-middle-east

The Economic Times, 'India Along with China and UAE Abstain from US-backed UNSC Resolution Condemning Russia', 26 February 2022. Available at: https:// economictimes.indiatimes.com/news/international/world-news/india-along-with -china-and-uae-abstain-from-us-backed-unsc-resolution-ondemning-russia/ articleshow/89839770.cms.

Embassy of the Russian Federation in the Kingdom of Saudi Arabia, *About the Visit of the President of Tatarstan Republic, The Chairman of the Group of strategic Vision 'Russia-Islamic World', R. N. Minnikhanov to Saudi Arabia* [*O visite Presdienta Respubliki Tatarstan, Predsedatelya Gruppy strategicheskogo videniya 'Rossiya – islamsky mir' R. N. Minnikhanova v Saudovskuy Araviu*], 25 November 2021. Available at: https://riyadh.mid.ru/ru/press-centre/news/o_vizite_ prezidenta_respubliki_tatarstan_predsedatelya_gruppy_strategicheskogo_ videniya_rossiya_isla/

Embassy of the Russian Federation in the Kingdom of Saudi Arabia, *About the Visit of the President of Tatarstan Republic, The Chairman of the Group of Strategic Vision 'Russia-Islamic World', R. N. Minnikhanov to Saudi Arabia* [*O visite Presdienta Respubliki Tatarstan, Predsedatelya Gruppy strategicheskogo videniya 'Rossiya – islamsky mir' R. N. Minnikhanova v Saudovskuy Araviu*], 25 November 2021. Available at: https://riyadh.mid.ru/ru/press-centre/news/o_vizite_prezidenta_ respubliki_tatarstan_predsedatelya_gruppy_strategicheskogo_videniya_rossiya_isla/

European Council of the European Union, 'EU Restrictive Measures Against Russia over Ukraine (since 2014)'. Available at: https://www.consilium.europa.eu/en/ policies/sanctions/restrictive-measures-against-russia-over-ukraine/.

Evloev, Magomet, *Evkurov vstretilsya s generalnym secretarem vsemirnogo souza musulmanskih unchenyh Ali al-Qaradagh'* [*Evkurov met with General Secretary of the World Muslim Union Ali al-Qaradagh*], *Gazeta Ingushetii*, 6 February 2019. Available at: https://gazetaingush.ru/news/evkurov-vstretilsya-s-generalnym -sekretarem-vsemirnogo-soyuza-musulmanskih-uchenyh-ali

Expo Events Consulting, *'Packer' Takes Part in the International Exhibition of the Oil and Gas Industry ADIPEC, Which Takes Place in Abu Dhabi (UAE) Between 11 to 14 November* [*NPF 'Packer' prinimaet uchastie v mechdunarodnoy vystavke neftynoi I gazovoy promyshlennosti ADIPEC, kotoraya prohodit s 11 po 14 noyabry v Abu Dabi (OAE)*], 13 November 2019. Available at: http://www.eec-emirates.com/ru/npf -packer-at-the-international-exhibition-adipec-2019-in-abu-dhabi/

Fahretdinovich, Fahretdinov Rizeddin. Available at: https://kitap.tatar.ru/ru/site /42317029a/pages/Fahretdin/

Faizullin, Almaz, 'Conditions and Activities of the Tatar-Muslims after the February Revolution in the Government of Kazan (February–October 1917) [Polozhenie I deyatelnost' Tatar-Musuulman posle Fevralskoy Revolucii v kazanskoy Gubernii (Fevral' -Octyabr' 1017 goda)]', *Islam in the Modern World* 15, no. 3 (2019): 138–49.

Faucon, Benoit, Said Summer and Kalin Stephen, 'Europe Woos Qatar for an Alternative to Russian Gas', *WSJ*, 30 March 2022. Available at: https://www.wsj.com/ articles/europe-woos-qatar-as-alternative-to-russian-gas-11648649463.

Figenschou, T., *Al Jazeera and the Global Media Landscape: The South is Talking Back*, London: Routledge, 2013.

File 3666/1925, 'Arabia: Printed Correspondence, 1924–28', IOR/L/PS/10/1155: 27 December 1924–28, October 1929. Available at: https://searcharchives.bl .uk/primo_library/libweb/action/display.do?tabs=detailsTab&ct=display&doc =IAMS040-000546630&displayMode=full&vid=IAMS_VU2&_ga=2.110433856 .413039908.1626276110-1358129400.1626276110

File 61/11 II (D 42), 'Relations between Nejd and Hijaz', IOR/R/15/1/565: 7 November 1924–10 July 1925. Available at: https://searcharchives.bl.uk/primo_library/libweb/ action/display.do?tabs=detailsTab&ct=display&fn=search&doc=IAMS040-000228024 &indx=2&recIds=IAMS040-000228024&recIdxs=1&elementId=1&renderMode =poppedOut&displayMode=full&frbrVersion=&dscnt=0&scp.scps=scope%3A

%28BL%29&frbg=&tab=local&dstmp=1626276466337&srt=rank&mode=Basic&
&dum=true&vl(freeText0)=Soviet%20Muslims%20%20and%20Arabia&vid=IAMS_
VU2

Financial Times, 'Gulf States' Neutrality on Ukraine Reflects Deeper Russian Ties'.
Available at: https://www.ft.com/content/5e3b0998-705f-46c4-8010-9972b3
c8a847

Foreign Ministry of Oman. 25 January 2022. Available at: https://fm.gov.om/sultanate
-of-oman-expresses-concern-over-ukraine-crisis/

Frank, Allen, *Islamic Historiography and 'Bulghar' Identity among the Tatars and
Bashkirs of Russia*, Leiden: Brill, 1998.

Fredholm, M., 'Central Asian Sunni Islamic Extremism and Its Links to the Gulf',
in *Russian & CIS Relations with the Gulf Region: Current Trends in Political and
Economic Dynamics*, edited by M. Terterov, 327–47, Dubai: Gulf Research Center,
2009.

Freedman, Robert O., 'Détente and US-Soviet Relations in the Middle East during the
Nixon Years (1969–1974)', in *Dimensions of Détente*, edited by Della W. Sheldon,
New York: Praeger, 1978, pp. 110–130.

Freedman, Robert O., *Moscow and the Middle East: Soviet Policy Since the Invasion of
Afghanistan*, New York: Praeger Special Studies, 1991.

Freedman, Robert, 'Russia and the Middle East under Yeltsin, Part II', *Milwaukee* 6,
1997, pp. 58–90.

Freer, Courtney, *Rentier Islamism: The Influence of the Muslim Brotherhood in Gulf
Monarchies*, Oxford: Oxford University Press, 2018.

Friedberg, Aaron L., 'The Future of US-China Relations: Is Conflict Inevitable?',
International Security 30, no. 2 (2005): 34.

Fromherz, Allen, *Qatar: A Modern History*, London: I.B. Tauris, 2010.

Fuller, Liz, *Chechen Leader Kadyrov Challenges Moscow Over Budget Subsidies*, 17
November 2016. Available at: https://www.rferl.org/a/chechnya-kadyrov-challenges
-moscow-budget-subsidies/28123822.html

Gadilov, L. and F. Gumerov , *Karim Khakimov* [*Kerim Khakimov*], Ufa: Bashknigoizdat,
1966.

Gadilov, L. Z. and G. G. Amiri. *Memories of Karim Khakimov* [*Vospominaniya o Karime
Khakimove*], Ufa: Bashkir book publisher, 1982.

Gadilov, L. Z. and F. H. Gumerov, *Karim Khakimov – Revolutionary, diplomat* [*Karim
Khakimov – Revlucioner, Diplomat*], Ufa: Bashkir book publisher, 1966.

Galeeva, Diana, 'How National Identity Will Shape the Future of Liberalism: The
Consequences of Brexit in the EU, and of the 2017 Crisis in the GCC', *Al Mesbar*, 5
February 2018. Available at: https://mesbar.org/national-identity-will-shape-future
-liberalism-consequences-brexit-eu-2017-crisis-gcc/

Galeeva, Diana, 'Russia in the Middle East in 2021: Learning from 2020', *LSE Blog*,
21 January 2021. Available at: https://blogs.lse.ac.uk/mec/2021/01/21/russia-in-the
-middle-east-in-2021-learning-from-2020/

Galeeva, Diana, 'How have Russia's Policies in the Middle East Changed since the Arab Uprisings?', *Middle East Institute*, 21 April 2021. Available at: https://www.mei.edu/publications/how-have-russias-policies-middle-east-changed-arab-uprisings-0.

Galeeva, Diana. *Qatar: The Practice of Rented Power*, Abingdon: Routledge, 2022.

Galeeva, Diana, '"Zero-Sum" or "Win-Win?": Russia's Next Steps in the Middle East', *InterRegional for Strategic Analysis*, 19 April 2022. Available at: https://www.interregional.com/en/zero-sum-or-win-win/

Gambrell, Jon, 'Russia's Putin Visits Saudi Arabia on Mideast Trip', *AP*, 14 October 2019. Available at: https://apnews.com/article/09fe0e9931904b5da91fd38dddae915e

Gammer, Moshe, 'Between Mecca and Moscow: Islam, Politics, and Political Islam in Chechnya and Dagestan, *Middle Eastern Studies* 41, no. 6 (November 2005): 833.

Gatin, Marat, 2020, interviewed by author.

Ghazal, Rym, 'Emirates Praised for Promoting True Principles of Islam', *The National*, 8 September 2008. Available at: https://www.thenational.ae/uae/emirates-praised-for-promoting-true-principles-of-islam-1.498720.

Gideon, Rose, 'Trump's Middle East', *Foreign Affairs* 98, no. 6 (November/December 2019): n/a.

Glesler, Rodney. *The Story of Kuwait*, 1959.

Golan, Galia, *Soviet Policies in the Middle East: From World War Two to Gorbachev*, Cambridge: Cambridge University Press, 1990.

Golan, Galia, *Moscow and the Middle East: New Thinking on Regional Conflict*, London: Chatham House, 1992.

Golden, P., *Khazar Studies: A Historical-Philological Inquiry into the Origins of the Khazars*, Budapest: Bibliotheca Orientalist Hunarica, 1980.

Gorbatov, O. and L. Cherkasskiy, *Cooperation of the USSR with the Countries of the Arab East and Africa*, Moscow: Nauka, 1973.

Gordlevskii, V. A., *Pamiati Akademika Ol'denburga*, Moscow: Nauka, 1934.

Government of the Republic of Tatarstan. Available at: https://prav.tatarstan.ru/eng/

Government of the Republic of Tatarstan, *Rustam Minnikhanov otvetil na voprosy churnalistov o sotrudnichestve s tureckimi partnerami, o situacii s obmanutymi dolshikami I o sisteme 'Platon'* [Rustam Minnikhanov Answered Journalists' Queations about Cooperation with Turkish Partners, about the Situation with Defrauded Equity Holders and About the Platon System], 21 December 2015. Available at: https://prav.tatarstan.ru/index.htm/news/525008.htm

The Government of Tatarstan Republic, *Rustam Minnikhanov pribyl s rabochim visitom v Korolevstvo Saudovskaya Araviya* [Rustam Minnikhanov Arrived on a Working Visit to the Kingdom of Saudi Arabia], 6 February 2017. Available at: https://prav.tatarstan.ru/index.htm/news/838682.htm

Graney, K. E., *Of Khans and Kremlins: Tatarstan and the Future of Ethno-Federalism in Russia*. Plymouth: Lexington Books, 2009.

Gray, Matthew, 'A Theory of "Late Rentierism" in the Arab States of the Gulf', *CIRS Georgetown University*, 2011. Available at: https://repository.library.georgetown .edu/bitstream/handle/10822/558291/CIRSOccasionalPaper7MatthewGray2011 .pdf

Green, Wilbur, *Soviet Strategy in the Middle East*, Carlisle Barracks: Army War College, 1973.

Griffin, Resemary, 'Russia, UAE Sign New Energy Cooperation Agreements', 15 October 2019. Available at: https://www.spglobal.com/platts/en/market-insights/latest-news/ oil/101519-russia-uae-sign-new-energy-cooperation-agreements

Group of the Strategic Vision, 'Russia-Islamic World', Karim Hakimov – 'Red Pasha' and the Arabian Vizier of the Kremlin, 25 May 2020. Available at: https://russia-islworld .ru/kultura//karim-hakimov-red-pasha-and-the-arabian-vizier-of-the-kremlin/

'The Grozny Fatwa', *The Minbar of Islam*, 3–4, 2016, 49–62. Available at: http://www .idmedina.ru/pdf/web/viewer.html?file=/pdf/content/minaret/minaret-3-4-2016.pdf #49

Gtrk.tv, 'Rustem Khamitov Conducted Working Meeting with the King of Saudi Arabia' ['Rustem Khamitov porvel rabochyu vstrechu s Korolem Saudovskoy Aravii'], 8 October 2017. Available at: https://gtrk.tv/novosti/59974-rustem-hamitov-provel -rabochuyu-vstrechu-korolyom-saudovskoy-aravii

Gulf News, *UAE, Russia Forge Strategic Partnership*, 1 June 2018. Available at: https:// gulfnews.com/uae/government/uae-russia-forge-strategic-partnership-1.2230246

Gunter, Joel, 'China Committed Genocide Against Uyghurs, Independent Tribunal Rules', *BBC News*, 9 December 2021. Available at: https://www.bbc.com/news/world -asia-china-59595952?piano-modal

Gusarov, V. and N. Semin, *Socialist Countries are Faithful Friends of the Arab People* [*Strany Socializma – vernye druzya Arabskyh narodov*], Moscow: Publishing House of Political Literature, 1971.

Guseva, U., 'The Gloomy Echo of the "TsDUM Affair" : "The Chain of the Qur'an" and the Repressions against the Muslims Elite in the USSR, 1940,' ['Mrachnoe echo "Dela TsDUM": Cep' Korana" I Repressii protiv msuslmanskoy elity v SSSR (1940)'], *Novyi Istoriceskij Vestnik* 52, no. 2 (2017): 85.

Halliday, Fred, 'Gorbachev and the "Arab Syndrome": Soviet Policy in the Middle East', *World Policy Journal* 4, no. 3 (1987): 415.

Hamad, Amani, 'Bahrain's King, Russia's Putin Discuss Conflict in Ukraine', *Al Arabiya News*, 15 March 2022. Available at: https://english.alarabiya.net/News/gulf/2022/03/15 /Bahrain-s-King-Russia-s-Putin-discuss-diplomatic-solutions-for-Ukraine-conflict

Harris, George S., 'The Soviet Union and Turkey', in *The Soviet Union and the Middle East: The Post-World War II Era*, edited by Ivo J. Lederer and Wayne S. Vucinich, 1–32, Stanford: Hoover Institution Press, Stanford University, 1974.

Heidemann, Thomas, 'EU Extends Sectoral Sanctions Against Russia', *CMS*. Available at: https://cms.law/en/rus/publication/eu-extends-sectoral-sanctions-against -russia

Hoffman, Jon, *The Evolving Relationship Between Religion and Politics in Saudi Arabia*, 20 April 2022. Available at: https://arabcenterdc.org/resource/the-evolving -relationship-between-religion-and-politics-in-saudi-arabia/

Hollis, Rosemary, 'Introduction: Sliding into a New Era', in *The Soviets, Their Successors and the Middle East Turning Point*, edited by Rosemary Hollis, 1–15, New York: St. Martin's Press, 1993.

Holzman, Franklyn D., 'Soviet Trade and Aid Policies', in *Soviet-American Rivalry in the Middle East*, edited by J. C.Hurewitz, 104–20, New York: Frederick A.Praeger Publishers, 1969.

Hostler, Charles Warren, *Turkism and the Soviets : The Turks of the World and Their Political Objectives*, London: George Allen & Unwin, 1957.

H. R. P. Dickson, Box 3, File 3, Administrative reports of the Kuwait Political Agency, 1928–32, DN3/3/135: VI.

H. R. P. Dickson, Box 3, File 1, Collection of articles, correspondence, press cuttings etc. – Kuwait and the Middle East in general, 1930s–1950s, Box 3/1/12.

Hunter, Thomas and Alexander, Melikishvili. *Islam in Russia: The Politics of Identity and Security*, New York: Centre for Strategic and International Studies, 2004.

Hurewitz, J. C., 'Origins of Rivalry', in *Soviet-American Rivalry in the Middle East*, edited by J. C. Hurewitz, New York: Frederick A. Praeger Publishers, 1969.

Hyatt, John, 'Russian Oligarchs Fleeing Sanctions Are House Hunting in Dubai', *Forbes*, 8 April 2022. Available at: https://www.forbes.com/sites/johnhyatt/2022/04/08/ russian-oligarchs-fleeing-sanctions-are-house-hunting-in-dubai/?sh=6e1b89f058ce

Interfax, *Posol Katara v RF rasskazal o perspektivah voennogo sotrudnichstva s Rossiei* [*The Ambassador of Qatar to the Russian Federation Spoke about the Prospects for Military Cooperation with Russia*], 28 April 2021. Available at: https://www.interfax .ru/world/763610

Interfax-ABN, *Zamministra oborony rf obsudil s poslom OAE sotrudnichsetvo po voennoy linii* [*Deputy Minister of Defense of the Russian Federation Discusesd Military Cooperation with the Ambassador of the UAE*], 14 September 2020. Available at: https://www.militarynews.ru/story.asp?rid=1&nid=537821&lang=RU

Interfax-ABN, *Rossiya planiruet podpisat' soglashenie o voennom sotrudnichsetve s Saudovskoyy Araviei* [*Russia Plans to Sign a Military Cooperation Agreement with Saudi Arabia*], 22 February 2021. Available at: https://www.militarynews.ru/story .asp?rid=1&nid=545977&lang=RU

Iskhakyi, Gayaz. *Idel-Ural*, Kazan: Tatarskoe knizhnoe izd-vo, 1991.

Islam News, *Ramzan Kadyrov vystupil s rechyu v Saudovskoi Aravii*, 27 May 2019, https://islamnews.ru/news-ramzan-kadyrov-vystupil-s-rech-yu-v-saudovskoj -aravii/

Islam Today, *Qatar to Build the Largest Islamic Complex in Ingushetia* [*Katar postroit krupneyshiy v Ingushetii Islamskyi complex*], 27 February 2018. Available at: https:// islam-today.ru/novosti/2018/02/27/katar-postroit-krupnejsij-v-ingusetii-islamskij -kompleks/

Ikenberry, G. John, *Liberal Leviathan: The Origins, Crisis, and Transformation of the American World Order*, Princeton: Princeton University Press``, 2012.

The Irish Times, *Kadyrov Had Enemies in Chechnya and Russia*, 9 May 2004. Available at:https://www.irishtimes.com/news/kadyrov-had-enemies-in-chechnya-and-russia-1.978780

Ishtvan, Z., 'Volzhskie Bulgary I Islam' ['Volga Bolgars and Islam'], *Minbar Islamic Studies* 4, no. 2 (2011): 52–6. Available at: https://www.minbar.su/jour/article/view/92

Iskandaryan, Alexander. *The Implications of Redrawing the Chechnya-Ingushetia Border*, 11 December 2019. Available at: https://www.ponarseurasia.org/memo/implications-redrawing-chechnya-ingushetia-border

Islamgulova, Ilmira, 'Political view of Mirsaid Sultan-Galiev' [Politichsekie vzlyady Mirsaida Sultan-Galieva], PhD Thesis, Bashkir State University, 2005.

Ismail-zade, Hajj to Mecca [Palomnichestvo v Mekku], New East [Novyi Vostok] 8, no. 9 (1925): 230–43.

Issaev, Leonid and Koroyayev Andrey, 'Russia's Policy towards the Middle East: The Case of Yemen', *The International Spectator* 55, no. 3 (2020): 143.

Issaev, Leonid and Kozhanov Nikolay, 'Diversifying Relationships: Russian Policy toward GCC', *International Politics* 58, no. 6 (2021): 884–902.

Izverstya, *V Kazani otkroetsya general'noe konsulstvo Saudovskoy Aravii [Consul General of Sauid Arabia to open in Kazan]*, February 13 2020. Available at: https://iz.ru/975699/2020-02-13/v-kazani-otkroetsia-generalnoe-konsulstvo-saudovskoi-aravii.

Izvestiya, *Peskov otvetil na voporos o rukopochatii Putina s Princem Saudovskoy Arabii [Peskov Answered the Question About Putin's Handshake with the Prince of Saudi Arabia]*, 3 December 2018. Available at: https://iz.ru/819363/2018-12-03/peskov-otvetil-na-vopros-o-rukopozhatii-putina-s-printcem-saudovskoi-aravii

Jones, Jeremy and Ridout Nicholas, *A History of Modern Oman*, Cambridge: Cambridge University Press, 2015.

Joyce, Miriam. *The Sultanate of Oman: A Twentieth-Century History*, Westport: Praeger Publishers, 1995.

Kahn, Jeff, 'The Parade of Sovereignties: Establishing the Vocabulary of the New Russian Federalism', *Post-Soviet Affairs* 16, no. 1 (2000): 58–89.

Kaim, Markus, *Great Powers and Regional Orders: The United States and the Persian Gulf*, Burlington: Ashgate Publishing Company, 2008.

Kaliszewska, Iwona, 'Halal Landscapes of Dagestani Entrepreneurs in Makhachkala', *Ethnicities, Special Issue: Normative Orders and the Remaking of Muslim Spaces and Selves in Contemporary Russia* 20, no. 4, (2020): 708–30.

Kamrava, Mehran, *Qatar: Small State, Big Politics*, New York: Cornell University Press, 2013.

Kamrava, Mehran, *Fragile Politics: Weak States in the Greater Middle East*, New York: Oxford University Press, 2016.

Karasik, Theodore, 'Why is Qatar Investing so Much in Russia?', 8 March 2017. Available at: https://www.mei.edu/publications/why-qatar-investing-so-much-russia

Karimi, F., *Compliments from Istanbul* [*Istambul maktuplary*], Orenburg: n/a, 1913.

Kasymov, G., *Essays about Religious and Antireligious Movements Among Tatars Before and After Revolution* [*Ocherki po relizioznomu I antireligioznomu dvicheniy sredi Tatar do I posle revolucii*], Kazan: Tatizdat, 1931.

Katz, Mark, *Russia and Arabia: Soviet Foreign Policy Toward the Arabian Peninsula*, Baltimore: Johns Hopkins University Press, 1986.

Katz, Mark, 'Saudi-Russian Relations since the Abdullah-Putin Summit', *Middle East Policy* 16, no. 1 (2009): 113–20.

Katz, Mark, 'Russia and Iran', *Middle East Policy* 19, no. 4 (Winter, 2012): 54.

Katz, Mark N., 'Better than Before: Comparing Moscow's Cold War and Putin Era Policies toward Arabia and the Gulf', *Durham Middle East Paper*, 96/ Sir William Luce Fellowship Paper, 19, Institute for Middle Eastern and Islamic Studies, Durham University, August, 2018. Available at: https://dro.dur.ac.uk/25863/1/25863.pdf.

Kazemzadeh, Firuz, *The Struggle for Transcaucasia, 1917–1921*, New York: Philosophical Library; Oxford: George Ronald, 1951.

Kazemzadeh, Firuz, 'Soviet-Iranian Relations: A Quarter-Century of Freeze and Thaw', in *The Soviet Union and the Middle East: The Post-World War II Era*, edited by Ivo J. Lederer and Wayne S. Vucinich, 55–77, Stanford: Hoover Institution Press, Stanford University, 1974.

Kemp, Geoffrey, 'Strategy and Arms Levels, 1945–1967', in *Soviet-American Rivalry in the Middle East*, edited by J. C. Hurewitz, 21–36, New York: Frederick A. Praeger Publishers, 1969.

Kemper, Michael, *Sufis und Gelehrte in Tatarien und Baschkirien, 1789–1889: Der Islamische Diskurs unter russischer Herrschaft*, Berlin: Klaus Swartz Verlag, 1998.

Kemper, Michael, 'From 1917 to 1937: The Mufti, the Turkologist, and Stalin's Terror', *Die Welt Des Islam* 57 (2017): 162–91.

Kemper, Michael and S. Shikhaliev, 'Qadidism and Jadidism in Twentieth-century Dagestan', *Asiatische Studien* 69, no. 3 (2015): 593–624.

Keohane, Robert O., *After Hegemony*, Princeton: Princeton University Press, 2005.

Khabutdinov, Aydar, 'All-Russian Muslim Congresses of 1917, the National Assembly and Their Importance: Declaration of National Autonomy in 1917–1918', in *The History of The Tatars Since Ancient Times: Tatars and Tatarstan in the 20ᵗʰ-Beginning of the 21ˢᵗ Centuries*, 7, Kazan: Academy of Sciences of the Republic of Tatarstan Sh. Marjani Institute of History, 2017.

Khabutdinov, Aydar, 'Organs of Tatar Autonomy in 1917–1919', in *The History of The Tatars Since Ancient Times: Tatars and Tatarstan in the 20ᵗʰ-Beginning of the 21ˢᵗ Centuries*, 7, Kazan: Academy of Sciences of the Republic of Tatarstan Sh. Marjani Institute of History, 2017.

Khabutdinov, Aydar, 'Kazan from the February Revolution until the Creation of the Tatar Autonomous Republic (1920) [Kazan ot Fevralskoy Revolucii 1917 goda do sozdaniya Avtonomnoy Tatarskoy Respubliki v 1920 godu], *Islam in the Modern World* 13, no. 3 (September 2017): 115–36.

Khabutdinov, Aydar, *Spiritual Boards During World Wars and Totalitarianism (1917–1950)* [*Spiritual Boards in the Years of World Wars and Totalitarianism (1917–1950)*]. Available at: http://www.idmedina.ru/books/history_culture/minaret/5/habutdin .htm?

Khabutdinov, A. U. and Fakhretdinov Rizeddin (1859–1936) 'About the Model of State in Modern Time' ['Rizeddin Fakhretdinov (1859–1936) O Modeli Gosudarstva Novogo Vremeny'], *Islam in the Modern World* 17, no. 3 (2021): 107–19.

Khairutdinov, Aydar, 'Unique Notes of Musa Bigiev's Performance of Hajj in 1927 [Unikalniy zapisi Musy Bigieva o ego hadje 1927 goda]', *Hajj of Russian Muslims [Hajj Rosiyskyh Musulman]* 8 (2017): 7–14.

Khakimov, Rafael, 2020, interviewed by author.

Khalikov, Alfred, *Tatars and their Accessors* [*Tatarskii narod I ego predki*], Kazan: Tatarskoe knizhnoe izd-vo, 1989.

Khayretdinov, D., and B. Ahmadullin, *Manifestations of the Repressive-Ideological Dictatorship of the Authorities on the Muslims of Moscow During the Years of Soviet Rule* [*Proyavleniya repressivno-ideologicheskogo diktata vlastei na musulman Moskvy v gody sovetskoy vlasti*]. Available at: http://www.idmedina.ru/books/materials/ faizhanov/5/hist_haretdinov.htm?

Khayretdnov, Ruslan, Karim Khakimov – Revolutionary, Diplomat [Karim Khakimov – Revolucioner, Diplomat], PhD Thesis, Bashkir State University, 2006. Available at: https://www.dissercat.com/content/karim-khakimov-revolyutsioner-diplomat/read

Khayretdinov, R. F., 'Unknown Heroes of the Past. Karim Khakimov [Neizvestniye geroi proshlogo. Karim Khakimov]', *Vestnik of Bashkir State University* 15, no. 4 (2010): n/a.

Khayri, Anvar. *Writings of Ahmad Ibn Fadlan of his Travels to the Bolgar Government in 921–922* [*Ahmed ibne Fadlannyn 92n–922 ellarda Bolgar deuletene kulgende yazgan seyahetlere*]. Kazan: Suz, 2013.

Khazanov, Anatoly M., 'Ethnic Nationalism in the Russian Federation', *Daedalus*, 126, no. 3, Summer 1997.

Khlebnikov, Alexey, 'Why Biden's Gulf Policy Will Not Disturb Russia-GCC Relations', *Gulf International Forum*, 17 March 2021. Available at: https://gulfif.org/why-bidens -gulf-policy-will-not-disturb-russia-gcc-relations/

Khodorovsky, I., *What is the Tatar Soviet Republic?* [*Chto takoe Tatarskaya Sovetskaya Respublika?*], Kazan: Gosudarstvennoe Izdatelstvo: 1920, 5. Available at: https:// kitaphane.tatarstan.ru/file/kitaphane/File/1.%20Inv_18459_93.pdf; p. 5.

Khudyakov, M., *Essays on the History of the Kazan Khanate* [*Ocherki po istorii Kazanskogo khanstva*]. Kazan: State Publisher, 1923.

Khusainov, Salavat, 'Riza Fakhretdinnov about Main World Religions [Riza Fakhretdinov on the Main Religions of the World]', *Educational Traditions of Islam in the Ural-Volga Region: First Fakhretdinov Readings*, 15 April 2009. Available at: http://www.idmedina.ru/books/materials/?1237

Klieman, Aaron S., *Soviet Russia and the Middle East*, Baltimore, London: The Johns Hopkins Press, 1970.

Klimov, I., *Establishment and Development of Tatar ASSR [Obrazovanie I razvitie tatarskoy ASSR]*, Kazan: Kazan University Press, 1960.

Kramer, Martin, *Islam Assembled: The Advent of the Muslim Congresses*, New York: Dayan Center for Middle Eastern and African Studies, 1986.

Kreutz, Andrej, 'Russia and the Arabian Peninsula', *Journal of Military and Strategic Studies* 7, no. 2 (2004): 47.

Kreutz, Andrej, *Russia in the Middle East: Friend or Foe?* Praeger: Praeger Security International, 2007.

Kommersant, *Sergeu Lavrovy prishla blizhnevostochnaya povestka [Sergei Lavrov Received the Middle East Agenda]*, 11 March 2021. Available at: https://www .kommersant.ru/doc/4722278

Kondrashov, Sergei, 'Nationalism and the Drive for Sovereignty in Tatarstan, 1988–1992: Origins and Development', PhD Thesis, University of Manchester, 1995.

Kosach, G., 'Karim Khakimov: Years of Life in Orenburg (a person and his time)' ['Karim Khakimov: Gody zhizni v Orenburge (chelovek I ego vremya)'], in *Unknown Pages of Russian Oriental Studies [Neizvestnye stranicy otechest-vennogo vostokovedeniya]*, edited by V. Naumkin and I. Smilyanskaya, 2, 125–48, n/a, 2004.

Kosach, G., 'Saudi Arabia: Power and Religion [Saudovskaya Aravia: Vlast' I Religiya]', *Politichsekaya nauka*, 2, (2013): 110–25.

Kostiner, Joseph, *The Making of Saudi Arabia, 1916–1936: From Chieftaincy to Monarchical State*, Oxford, New York: Oxford University Press, 1993.

Kozhanov, Nikolay, *Russia's Relations with the GCC and Iran*, Singapore: Palgrave Macmillan, 2021.

Kozlov, Petr, 'Kremlin ne Prodlit Dogovor s Tatarstanom. Izmenit li eto cho-to? [The Kremlin will Not Renew the Agreement with Tatarstan. Will this Change Anything?], *BBC News*, 11 August 2017. Available at: https://www.bbc.com/russian/ features-40904692

Kudrina, Olga, 'Rustam Minnikhanov Boosts Links with the Muslim World [Rustam Minnikhanov ukreplyaet svizi s Islamskim mirom]', *Kommersant*, 8 February 2017. Available at: https://www.kommersant.ru/doc/3213546

Kuwait News Agency, 'Kuwait Calls for Respecting Ukraine's Independence, Sovereignty', 24 February 2022. Available at: https://www.kuna.net.kw/ArticleDetails .aspx?id=3027315

Lambroschini, Sophie, 'Russia: Putin Tells OIC That Muslims Are 'Inseparable' Part of a Multiethnic Nation', *RadioFreeEurope*, 16 October 2003. Available at: https://www .rferl.org/a/1104687.html

Landis, Lincoln, *Politics and Oil: Moscow in the Middle East*, New York; London: Dunelen Publishing Company, 1973.

Laruelle, Marlene, 'Russia's Islamic Diplomacy', *CAP Paper* 220 (2019), 'Islam in Russia, Russia in the Islamic World' Initiative, Central Asia Program, Institute for European, Russian, and Eurasian Studies of the George Washington University. Available at: https://centralasiaprogram.org/wp-content/uploads/2019/07/CAP-paper-220-Russia -Islamic-Diplomacy.pdf

Layne, Christopher, 'The End of Pax Americana: How Western Decline Became Inevitable', 26 April 2012. Available at: https://www.theatlantic.com/international/ archive/2012/04/the-end-of-pax-americana-how-western-decline-became-inevitable /256388/

Lazzerini, Edward J., 'Ethnicity and the Uses of History: The Case of the Volga Tatars and *Jadidism*', *Central Asian Survey* 1 (1982): 61–9.

Lederer, Ivo J., 'The Soviet Union and the Middle East: The post-World War II era', in *Historical Introduction*, edited by Ivo J. Lederer and Wayne S. Vucinich, 8, Stanford: Hoover Institution Press, 1974.

Lefevre, Raphael, 'The Pitfalls of Russia's Growing Influence in Libya', *The Journal of North African Studies* 22, no. 3 (27 May 2017): 331.

Lenczowski, George. *Soviet Advances in the Middle East*, Washington: American Enterprise Institute for Public Policy Research, 1972.

Lenin, Vladimir, *A Caricature of Marxism and Imperialist Economism: Collected Works*, Moscow: Progress Publishers, 1968.

Lobell, Steven, Ripsman Norrin and Taliaferro Jeffrey. *Neoclassical Realism, the State, and Foreign Policy*, Cambridge: Cambridge University Press – M.U.A., 2009.

Long, David E., *The Kingdom of Saudi Arabia*. Gainesville: University Press of Florida, 1997.

Luzin, Pavel, *Ramzan Kadyrov: Russia's Top Diplomat, Riddle*, 19 April 2018. Available at: https://www.ridl.io/en/ramzan-kadyrov-russias-top-diplomat/

Macris, Jeffrey R, 'The Anglo-American Gulf: Britain's Departure and America's Arrival in the Persian Gulf', PhD Dissertation, Johns Hopkins University, 2007.

Malashenko, Alexei, 'Islam, Politics, and the Security of Central Asia, Russian Politics & Law', *Russian Politics & Law* 42, no. 4 (2004): 6–20.

Malashenko, Alexei, 'Islam in Russia', *Social Research* 76, no. 1 (Spring 2009): 321–58.

Malashenko, Alexei, 'Islam in Russia', *Carnegie Moscow Center*, 23 September 2014. Available at: https://carnegie.ru/2014/09/23/islam-in-russia-pub-57048.

Malashenko, Alexei and Yarlykapov Akhmed, 'Radicalisation of Russia's Muslim Community', *Ethno-religious Conflict in Europe*, working paper 9 (2009): 159–92.

Mardanova, D., 'Controversy as a Mechanism for Search and Approval of Truth (The Case of Debate on 'Aqibah Between Shihabetdin Marjani and His Opponents in the Volga Region in the Last Third of the 19th Century)', *RUDN Journal of Russian History* 17, no. 3 (2018): 513–37.

Mardason, Anton, and Korotayev Andrey, 'Russia-GCC Relations and the Future of Syria: Political Process and Prospects for the Economic Reconstruction', in *Russia's*

Relations with the GCC and Iran, edited by Nikolay Kozhanov, 205–28. Singapore: Macmillan, 2020.

Markets Insider. Available at: https://markets.businessinsider.com/commodities/oil -price?type=wti

Masanov, E. A., 'Sh. M. Ibragimov – drug Ch.Ch. Valikhanova', *Vestnik Akademii nauk Kazakhskoi SSR [Kazakh SSR]* 9 (1964): 53–60.

Mason, Robert, 'Security, Energy and Identity Dominate Gulf Positions on Ukraine', *AGSIW*, 25 February 2022. Available at: https://agsiw.org/security-energy-and -identity-dominate-gulf-positions-on-ukraine/.

Mearsheimer, John, *The Tragedy of Great Power Politics*, New York: W. W. Norton & Company, 2001.

Medina, *The Hajj of Russian Muslims and the Sanitary Conditions of the Pilgrimage [O hajje russkih musulman i o sanitarnyh usloviyah palomnichestva]*. Available at: http://www.idmedina.ru/books/history_culture/hadjj/2/glava-5.htm?

Melkumyan, E., G. Kosach and T. Nosenko, *Russia in the Foreign Policy Priorities of the Council of Cooperation of the Arabian Gulf States After Events of the Arab Spring [Roosiya vo vneshnepolitichsekih prioritetah Soveta Sotrudnichestva Arabskih Gosudarst zaliva posle sobytiy 'arabskoy vesny]*, *Vestnik MGIMO-Universiteta*, 4, no. 55 (2017): 139–53.

'Mezhpravitel'stvennye soglasheniia Respubliki Tatarstan s Turetskoi Respublikoi', *Panorama-Forum* 4, no. 1 (1996): 152–3.

Mezran, Karim and Varvelli Arturo, eds., 'The MENA Region: A Great Power Competition', *ISPI/ Atlantic Council*, 2019. Available at: https://www.atlanticcouncil .org/wp-content/uploads/2019/10/MENA-Region-Great-Power-Competition -Report-Web-2.pdf

MFA Russia, *Foreign Policy Concept of the Russian Federation*, 1 December 2016. Available at: https://www.mid.ru/en/foreign_policy/official_documents/-/asset _publisher/CptICkB6BZ29/content/id/2542248

MicROFILM, 'Relations between Nejd and Hijaz From 7-11-24 to 7-25', R/15/1/565, 10R, NEG 9871, F. 61/11-II, D. 244: 7-8.

MicROFILM, 'Relations between Nejd and Hijaz From 7-11-24 to 7-25', R/15/1/565, 10R, NEG 9871, F. 61/11-II, D. 253: 5.

MicROFILM, 'Relations between Nejd and Hijaz From 7-11-24 to 7-25', R/15/1/565, 10R, NEG 9871, F. 61/11-II, D. 1.

MicROFILM, 'Relations between Nejd and Hijaz From 7-11-24 to 7-25', R/15/1/565, 10R, NEG 9871, F. 61/11-II, D. 28.

Middle East Centre Archive St Antony's College, *Guide to Collections Regarding the Gulf*, 1 February 2020, 3. Available at: https://www.sant.ox.ac.uk/sites/default/files/ mec-archive-gulf-guide.pdf

Middle East Centre Archive St Antony's College, *Guide to Collections Regarding the Gulf*, 1 February 2020, 2. Available at: https://www.sant.ox.ac.uk/sites/default/files/ mec-archive-gulf-guide.pdf

Middle East Centre Archive St Antony's College, *Guide to Collections Regarding the Gulf*, 1 February 2020, 2. Available at: https://www.sant.ox.ac.uk/sites/default/files/mec-archive-gulf-guide.pdf

Middle East Centre Archive St Antony's College, *Guide to Collections Regarding the Gulf*, 1 February 2020, 1. Available at: https://www.sant.ox.ac.uk/sites/default/files/mec-archive-gulf-guide.pdf

Middle East Online, 'President Putin: Russia's Positions on Many Difficult Issues are Close to Islamic Countries [الرئيس بوتين: مواقف روسيا بشأن العديد من القضايا الصعبة متقاربة مع الدول الإسلامية], November 24 (2021). Available at: https://aawsat.com/home/article/3322306/الرئيس-بوتين-مواقف-روسيا-بشأن-العديد-من-القضايا-الصعبة-متقاربة-مع-الدول?utm_source=dlvr.it&utm_medium=twitter

Ministerstvo Vneshnikh Ekonomicheskikh sviazei Respubliki Tatarstan, *Vneshnee-konomicheskaia diaatelnost' respubliki Tatarstan v 1996 godu (Kazan)*, 1997, 25–6.

Ministry of Foreign Affairs of Russia, *O vstreche checpredstavitelya Prezidenta Rossiskoya Federacii po Blichnemu Vostoku I stran Afriki, zamestittlya Ministra innostrannyh del Rossii M. L. Bogdanova s Gensekretarem MID Katara A.H. al-Hamadi* [*On the meeting of the Special Representative of the President of the Russian Federation for the Middle East and African Countries, Deputy Minister of Foreign Affairs of Russia Mikhail Bogdanov with the Secretary General of the Ministry of Foreign Affairs of Qatar A. H. al-Hamadi*], 19 October 2019. Available at: https://www.mid.ru/ru/maps/qa/-/asset_publisher/629HIryvPTwo/content/id/3858289

Ministry of Foreign Affairs of the Russian Federation, *Documents of the USSR's Foreign Policy* [*Dokumenty vneshney politiki SSSR*], 2 January–31 August 1943. Available at: https://idd.mid.ru/dokumental-nye-publikacii/-/asset_publisher/5H3VC9AbCsvL/content/publikacii-podgotovlennye-istoriko-dokumental-nym-departamentom-v-2004-2015-gg-?inheritRedirect=false&redirect=https%3A%2F%2Fidd.mid.ru%3A443%2Fdokumental-nye-publikacii%3Fp_p_id%3D101_INSTANCE_5H3VC9AbCsvL%26p_p_lifecycle%3D0%26p_p_state%3Dnormal%26p_p_mode%3Dview%26p_p_col_id%3Dcolumn-2%26p_p_col_count%3D1

Ministry of Foreign Economic Relations and Congress Activities of the Republic of Bashkortostan, *In Kuwait the economic potential of Bashkortostan is presented* [*V Kuveite predstavlen ekonomicheskiy potencial Bashkortostana*], 27 September 2018. Available at: https://foreign.bashkortostan.ru/presscenter/news/58048/

Minullina, Taliya, 2020, interviewed by author.

Mirsaiapov, Ruslan, 2020, interviewed by author.

MOFAIC, 'H. H. Sheikh Abdullah bin Zayed, Russian Foreign Minister Discuss Friendship Relations, Strategic Partnership', 23 February 2022. Available at: https://www.mofaic.gov.ae/en/mediahub/news/2022/2/23/23-02-2022-uae-russia

Mogeilnicki, Robert, 'Oil Price War Tests Saudi-Russian Investment Cooperation', *AGSIW*, 3 April 2020. Available at: https://agsiw.org/oil-price-war-tests-saudi-russian-investment-cooperation/

Mokina, L. S., 'Assessment of Development of Islamic Banking as Alternative Instrument of Financing and Possibility of Its Application in Russia', *Russian Journal of Entrepreneurship* 18, no. 16 (August 2017): 2399–412.

Monroe, Elizabeth, Collection, Articles on the Arab Bureau, and Monroe, accounts of Monroe's travels in Italy, Algeria and Morocco, GB165-0207, B. 447 (R), April (1957): 8.

Morgenthau, Hans J., *Politics Among Nations: The Struggle for Power and Peace.* 3rd edn., Chicago: University of Chicago Press, 1954.

Morsy Abdullah, Muhammad. *The United Arab Emirates: A Modern History*, London; New York: Croom Helm, 1978.

Moubayed, Sami, 'Syria and Qatar Silently Mend Broken Fences', *Gulf News*, 25 April 2019. Available at: https://gulfnews.com/world/gulf/qatar/syria-and-qatar-silently -mend-broken-fences-1.63545446

Mukhamadeeva, L. A. and A. R. Faizullin, 'The Anti-Religious Policy of the Tatarstan Government (1920s) [Antireligioznaya politika v Tatarstane (1920s)]', *Minbar: Islamic Studies* 12, no. 2 (2019): 438–50.

Mukhametshin, Rafiq, *Islam in the Social and Political Life of Tatarstan: Ethnicity and Confessional Tradition in the Volga-Ural Region, [Islam v obshchestvenno-politicheskoy zhizni Tatarstana: Etnichnost' i konfessional'naya traditsiya v Volgo-Ural'skom regione]*, Moscow: Vostochnaya Literature, 1998.

Mukhametshin, Radik, 'Riza Fakhretdinov and Some Aspects of Religious and World Outlook in the Tatar Theological Thought of the Beginning of the XX Century [Riza Fakhretdinov and nekotorye aspecyt religiozno-mirovozzrencheskih iskaniy v Tatarskoi bogoslovskoy mysli nachala XX veka]', *Innovative Resources of Muslim Education and Culture: Second Fakhretdinov Readings*, 31 May 2011. Available at: http://www.idmedina.ru/books/materials/?2355.

Mukhametzynova, Dina, 'Kadimist Education System in the Writings of Rizeddin Fakhretdinov [Kadimistkaya sistema obrazovaniya v trudah Rizeddina Fakhretdinova], *Educational traditions of Islam in the Ural-Volga Region: First Fakhretdinov Readings*, 15 April 2009. Available at: http://www.idmedina.ru/books/ materials/?1241

Mukhetdinov, Damir, 'Rizeddin Fakhretdinov: Ideas of Reforms in the Muslim World of Russia [Rizeddin Fakhretdinov: idei reform musulmanskogo mira Rossii], *Educational Traditions of Islam in the Ural-Volga Region: First Fakhretdinov Readings*, 15 April 2009. Available at: http://www.idmedina.ru/books/materials/?1209.

Muslim World League, *The Muslim World League Launches Its International Conference in Moscow with the Participation of 43 Countries*, 30 March 2019. Available at: https://themwl.org/en/node/36002

Mustafin, Rafael. *Tatars Who Were Repressed [Repressiyalengen Tatar ediplery]*, Kazan: Tatarstan Kitab Neshriyaty, 2009.

Naganawa, Norihiro, 'The Red Sea Becoming Red? The Bolsheviks', commercial enterprise in the Hijaz and Yemen, 1924–38 (n/a).

Nakhleh, Emile A., *Bahrain*, Toronto, London: Lexington Books, 1938.

Narayanan, Ayush, 'UAE Foreign Minister, US Secretary of State Discuss Russian Invasion: State Dept', *Al Arabiya*, 25 February 2022. Available at: https://english .alarabiya.net/News/gulf/2022/02/25/UAE-foreign-minister-US-secretary-of-state -discuss-Russian-invasion-State-dept

Narayanan, Ayush, 'UAE Calls for Immediate De-Escalation and Cessation of Hostilities in Ukraine', *Al Arabiya English*, 26 February 2022. Available at: https:// english.alarabiya.net/News/gulf/2022/02/26/UAE-calls-for-immediate-de-escalation -and-cessation-of-hostilities-in-Ukraine

The National, *Sheikh Mohammed bin Zayed in Russia on two-day official visit*, 31 May 2018. Available at: https://www.thenationalnews.com/uae/government/sheikh -mohammed-bin-zayed-in-russia-on-two-day-official-visit-1.735764

National Archive of the Republic of Tatarstan, File R-873, List 1, Act 4, Sheet 33.

National Archive of the Republic of Tatarstan, Fund R-873, List 1, Act 93, Sheet 58.

National Library of the Republic of Tatarstan. *Electronic Collections of Books for 100-year Anniversary of TASSR*. Available at: https://kitaphane.tatarstan.ru/TASSR100/ elibrary.htm

National Library of the Republic of Tatarstan, *Statistics of Collections [Collection Statistics]*. Available at: https://kitap.tatar.ru/ru/ssearch/ecollection/

Naumkin, Vitaly, *Failed Partnership: Soviet Diplomacy towards Saudi Arabia between the World Wars [Nesostoyavsheesya partnerstvo Sovetskaya diplomatiya v Saudovskoy Aravii mezhdu mirovymi voynami]*, Moscow: Aspect Press, 2018.

Naumkin, Vitaly, 'Russia and the Arab Uprisings', *MEC Friday Seminars*, Oxford University, February 2021.

Naumkin, Vitaly, (ed.) *Middle East: From Foreign Policy Archive Documents [Blizhnevostochniy conflict: Iz dokumentov arhiva vneshney politiki]*, Moscow: MFD, 2003. Available at: http://history-library.com/index.php?id1=3&category=voennaya -istoriya&author=naumkin-vv&book=2003&page=220

Naumkin, Vitaly, *Blizhniy Vostok: Iz dokumentov vneshney politiki [Middle East: From Foreign Policy Archive Documents]*. Available at: http://history-library.com/index.php ?id1=3&category=voennaya-istoriya&author=naumkin-vv&book=2003&page=220

Nephew, Richard, 'Evaluating the Trump Administration's Approach to Sanctions: Russia', *Columbia Centre on Global Energy Policy*, 13 February 2020. Available at: https://www.energypolicy.columbia.edu/research/commentary/evaluating-trump -administration-s-approach-sanctions-russia

Neumann, Iver B., *Uses of the Other: 'The East' in European Identity Formation*, Manchester: Manchester University Press, 1998.

Nikonov, O. B., 'The USSR's Role in Forming the State Sovereignty of the Kingdom of Saudi Arabia [Rol' SSSR v stanovlenii gosudarstvennogo suvereniteta korolevsta Sauvskaya Aravia]', *Prepodavatel 21 vek* 94, no. 53 (2017): 302–16.

Nissenbaum, Dion, Kalin Stephen and S. Cloud David, 'Saudi, Emirati Leaders Decline Calls With Biden During Ukraine Crisis', *WSJ*, 8 March 2022. Available at: https://

www.wsj.com/articles/saudi-emirati-leaders-decline-calls-with-biden-during
-ukraine-crisis-11646779430.

Nizameddin, Talal, *Russia and the Middle East Towards a New Foreign Policy*, London:
Hurst & Company, 1999.

Norrlöf, Carla, 'Is COVID-19 the End of US Leadership? Public Bads, Leadership
Failures and Monetary Hegemony', *International Affairs* 96, no. 5 (2020): 1281.

NS Energy, 'Lukoil, Gazprom and Tatneft to Jointly Develop Hard-to-Recover Reserves
in Russia', 30 June 2020. Available at: https://www.nsenergybusiness.com/news/
lukoil-gazprom-tatneft-hard-recover-reserves/

Nurimanov, Ildar, 'Hajj of Russian Muslims: From Past to Present [Hajj
Musulman Rossii. Iz proshlogo k nastoyzshemu]', *Medina al-Islam* 1, no. 25 (2007).
Available at: http://www.idmedina.ru/books/history_culture/hadjj/1/nurimanov
.htm

Nurimanov, Ildar, 'Hajj in Soviet Period [Hadzh v Sovetskiy Period]', *Hajj of Russian
Muslims no. 4, Annual Collection of Hajj Travel Notes [Jadzh rossiskih musulman
№4 Ezhegodniy sbornik putevyh zametok o hadzhe]*, 7 September 2012. Available at:
http://www.idmedina.ru/books/history_culture/?4751

Nurimanov, Ildar, 'Meccan Congress and Hajj in 1926: Based on the Travel Notes of
Abdrakhman Umerov [Mekkanskiy Kongress i hajj 1926 goda: Po motivam putevyh
zapisok Abdrahmana Umerova]', *Islam in the Modern World* 17, no. 1 (2021): 148–9.
Available at: http://www.idmedina.ru/pdf/web/viewer.html?file=/pdf/content/ism/
ism-1-2021.pdf#139

Nurullin, Ilham, 2020, interviewed by author.

Nye, Joseph S., *The Paradox of American Power: Why the World's Only Superpower Can't
Go It Alone*, USA: Oxford University Press, 2003.

Ocherki, *Islam and Muslim Culture in the Middle Volga Region: Past and Present [Islam
and Musulmanskaya kultura v Srednem Povolzhie: istoriya i sovremennnost']*, Kazan:
Master Lain, 2002.

Ofer, Gur, 'Economic Aspects of Soviet Involvement in the Middle East', in *The Limits
to Power: Soviet Policy in the Middle East*, edited by Yaacov Ro'I, 67–97. London:
Croom Helm, 1979.

*Official Tatarstan, Rustam Minnikhanov i predstaviteli Kuveita obmenyalis' mneniyami
po voprosam dalneyshego sotrudnichestva [Rustam Minnikhanov and Representatives
of Kuwait Exchanged Views on Further Cooperation]*, 5 October, 2009. Available at:
https://tatarstan.ru/index.htm/news/41158.htm

*Official Tatarstan, Rustam Minnikhanov met with the Ambassador Extraordinary and
Plenipotentiary of the Kingdom of Saudi Arabia to the Russian Federation [Rustam
Minnikhanov vstretilsya s Chesvychinym I Polnomochnym Poslom Korolevstva
Saudovskaya Aravia v Rossiyskoy Federacii]*, 20 June 2011. Available at: https://
tatarstan.ru/index.htm/news/93482.htm

Ogonek, no. 23 (167), 1926: 13.

Ortung, R., 'Putin's Political Legacy', *Russian Analytical Digest* 36, no. 4 (2008): 2–5.

Oskarsson, Katerina and Yetiv Steven, 'Russia and the Persian Gulf: Trade, Energy, and Interdependence', *The Middle East Journal* 67, no. 3 (2013): 381–403.

Owtram, Francis, *A Modern History of Oman: Formation of the State since 1920*, London; New York: I.B.Tauris, 2004.

Ozerov, Oleg, *Karim Khakimov: Chronicle of his Life* [*Karim Khakimov: letopis' zhini*], LitRes: Samizdat, 2020.

Page, Stephen, *The USSR and Arabia: The Development of Soviet Policies and Attitudes towards the Countries of the Arabian Peninsula, 1955–1970*, Michigan: University of Michigan, 1971.

Pasquini, Elaine, 'Russia's Balancing Act in the Middle East', *The Washington Report on Middle East Affairs* 39, no. 6 (2020): 58.

Peterson, J. E. *Saudi Arabia under Ibn Saud: Economic and Financial Foundations of the State*, London, New York: I.B. Tauris, 2018.

Pilkington, Hilary and Galina Yemelianova . *Islam in Post-Soviet Russia: Public and Private Faces*, London: Routledge, 2003.

Plenipotentiary Representation of the Republic of Tatarstan in the Republic of Turkey, *Sotrudnichestvo Tatarstana i Turcii* [*Cooperation between Tatarstan and Turkey*], 7 April 2020. Available at: https://tatturk.tatarstan.ru/sotrudnichestvo_tatartsan _turkey

Portal Severnogo, Kavkaza, *500 residents of Ingushetia will participate in the Hajj to Saudi Arabia* [*Uchastniki hadja v Saudovskuy Araviu stanut 500 zhiteley Ingushetii*], 8 May 2019. Available at: https://sevkavportal.ru/news/pub/kultura/item/40922 -uchastnikami-khadzha-v-saudovskuyu-araviyu-stanut-500-zhitelej-ingushetii.html

President of the Republic of Tatarstan. Available at: https://president.tatarstan.ru/eng/.

Press Service of the Group of Strategic Vision 'Russia-Islamic World', About the VI Annual Meeting of the Group of Strategic Vision 'Russia-Islamic World', 30 January 2020. Available at: https://russia-islworld.ru/en/main//about-the-vi-annual-meeting-of -the-group-of-strategic-vision-russia-islamic-world/.

Primakov, Evgeny, *Russia and the Arabs: Behind the Scenes in the Middle East from the Cold War to the Present*, New York: Basic Books, 2009.

Priymak, Artur, *Shaykh of Qatar Increased Ratings of Ingushetia* [*Sheikh iz Katara Podnimaet Reiting Ingushetii*], 21 February 2018. Available at: https://www.ng.ru/ng _religii/2018-02-21/13_437_qatar.html

Publishing House, 'Medina'. Available at: http://www.idmedina.ru/about/concept/

Putin, Vladimir, 'Speech and the Following Discussion at the Munich Conference on Security Policy', *President of Russia*, 10 February 2007. Available at: http://en.kremlin .ru/events/president/transcripts/24034

Qatar Chamber, 'The Chamber is Looking to Enhance Trade Cooperation with Tatarstan' [الغرفة تبحث تعزيز التعاون التجاري مع تتارستان], July 23 2017. Available at: https:// www.qatarchamber.com/الغرفة-تبحث-تعزيز-التعاون-التجاري-مع-ت/?lang=ar

Racius, Egdunas, *Islam in Post-communist Eastern Europe: Between Churchification and Securitization*, Leiden, Boston: Brill, 2020.

Rahman, Fareed, 'UAE and Russia Trade Set to Rise 21% to hit $4bn in 2021', *The National*, 12 December 2021. Available at: https://www.thenationalnews.com/business/economy/2021/12/12/uae-and-russia-trade-set-to-rise-21-to-hit-4bn-in -2021/.

Rahr, A., 'New Thinking Takes Hold in Foreign Policy Establishment', *RFE/RL, Report on the USSR*, 1, no. 1 (January 1989): 4.

Rahr, A., *Between Reform and Restoration: Putin on the Eve of his Second Term*, Berlin: Korber Department, 2004.

Rakhmatullin, Timur, 'In Saudi Arabia the Presentation by the Republic of Bashkortostan will be Conducted [V Saudovskoy Aravii Proydet Prezentaziya Bashkortostana]', *Bashinform.RF*, 23 March 2011. Available at: https://www .bashinform.ru/m/news/349585-v-saudovskoy-aravii-proydet-prezentatsiya -bashkortostana/.

Rakhmatullin, Timur, 'Shaimiev Said That Millions of Muslims in Russia Need Contacts with the Islamic World', *Realnoe Vremya*, 2 December 2019. Available at: https:// realnoevremya.com/articles/4018-ufa-hosts-russia-islamic-world-strategic-vision -groups-meeting.

Ramaldanov, Gadmiamin, 2020, interviewed by author.

Ramani, Samuel, 'Russia and the Middle East: Diplomacy and Security in Russia and the GCC: A Rising Partnership?', *RIAC*, 29 March 2017. Available at: https://russiancouncil .ru/en/blogs/samuel-ramani-en/russia-and-the-gcc-a-rising-partnership/

Ramani, Samuel, 'Russia and the UAE: An Ideational Partnership', *Middle East Policy*, XXVII:1, Spring 2020.

Rasuli, Gabdurrahman, 'Trip to Hajj in 1945' [Poezdka v hajj v 1945 godu], *Hajj of Russian Muslims no. 4, Annual Collection of Hajj Travel Notes [Jadzh rossiskih musulman №4 Ezhegodniy sbornik putevyh zametok o hadzhe]*, 7 September 2012. Available at: http://www.idmedina.ru/books/history_culture/?4752.

RBK, *Bahrein i Oman gotovy exportirovat' produkciu halal iz Tatarstana, [Bahrain and Oman are ready to export halal products from Tatarstan]*, 27 February 2017. Available at: https://rt.rbc.ru/tatarstan/27/02/2017/58b433279a7947f9fcb11fbf

RBK, *Tatarstan pomozeht Kataru podgotov' Chempionat mira po futbolu v 2022 godu, [Tatarstan will Help Qatar Prepare for the World Cup in 2022]*, 25 May 2018. Available at: https://www.google.co.uk/amp/s/amp.rbc.ru/regional/tatarstan/ freenews/5b07ad3c9a79476f3ff618be

Readings, Ramazanov, *Ramazanovskiy Chteniya*, 25 May 2020. Available at: http://www .idmedina.ru/ramazan/

Realnoe vremya, *Pozvat' v gosti Korolya: kak razvivalis' vzaimootnosheniya Tatarstana I Saudovskoy Aravii [To Invite the King to Visit: How Relations Between Tatarstan and Saudi Arabia Developed]*, 05 October 2017. Available at: https://realnoevremya.ru/ articles/78308-kak-razvivalis-otnosheniya-tatarstana-i-saudovskoy-aravii

Realnoe vermya, *Kvotu na Hajd v Mekku I Medinu dlya Rossiayn mogut uvelichit' do 25 tysych mest [The Quota for the Hajj to Mecca and Medina for Russians*

can be Increased to 25 Thousand Places], 8 October 2017. Available at: https://
realnoevremya.ru/news/78547-kvotu-na-hadzh-v-mekku-i-medinu-dlya-rossiyan
-mogut-uvelichit-do-25-tysyach-mest

Realnoe vremya, *'Proekt okazalsya neudachnym': kak umirala Tatarstanskaya
mezhdunarodnaya investicionaya kompaniya* [*'The* Project Turned Out to Be
Unsuccessful': How *the Tatarstan International Investment Company Died*], 26 March
2020. Available at: https://realnoevremya.ru/articles/169835-eksperty-o-smerti-tmik
-i-prichinah-provala-proekta

Realnoe vremya, *The Economic Growth Pace Can Be Kept if Only a Miracle Happens*,
22 April 2020. Available at: https://realnoevremya.com/articles/4426-how-tatarstan
-and-russia-should-support-economy-in-crisis

Reliefweb, *UAE: Humanitarian Aid and Efforts to Combat COVID-19*, 12 May 2020.
Available at: https://reliefweb.int/report/world/uae-humanitarian-aid-and-efforts
-combat-covid-19-12-may-2020-enar

Remmer, Natalya, *UAE to Help Build the First Cathedral Mosque in Ingushetia* [*OAE
pomogut postroit' pervuy sobornyu mechet' v Ingushetii*], 4 December 2020. Available
at: https://businessemirates.ae/news/uae-property-news/oae-pomogut-postroit
-pervuyu-sobornuyu-mechet-v-ingushetii/

Republic of Bashkortostan, *The Friend of the King, Soviet Diplomat* [*Drug korolya, soviet
diplomat*], 30 October 2020. Available at: https://resbash.ru/articles/cotsium/2020-10
-30/drug-korolya-sovetskiy-diplomat-758145

Republic of Ingushetia, *Head of Ingushetia Yunus-bek Yevkurov met with King of
Saudi Arabia Salman bin Abdel Aziz al-Sa'ud* [*Glava Ingushetii Unus-Bek Evkurov
vstretilsya s Korolem Saudovskoy Aravii Salmanom bin Abdel Azizom al-Saudom*],
2 November 2011. Available at: https://ingushetia.ru/news/glava_ingushetii_yunus
_bek_evkurov_vstretilsya_s_korolem_saudovskoy_aravii_salmanom_ben_abdel
_azizom/

Republic of Tatarstan, *Attraction of Foreign Investment*. Available at: http://www.tatar.ru
/English/00000061.html.

Reynolds, David, 'A 'Special Relationship?' America, Britain and the International
Order since the Second World War', *International Affairs* 62, no. 1 (1986): 2.

RIA Dagestan, *UAE Will Study Possibility to Import Products from Dagestan* [*Obedinennye
Arabskye Emiraty izuchat vozmozhnost' importirovaniya pordukcii Dagestana*],
20 March 2021. Available at:https://riadagestan.ru/news/economy/obedinennye
_arabskie_emiraty_izuchat_vozmozhnost_importirovaniya_produktsii_dagestana/

RIA Dagestan, *Kingdom of Saudi Arabia and Dagestan Began to Cooperate in the Field
of Tourism*, 15 September 2021. Available at: https://riadagestan.ru/news/society/
korolevstvo_saudovskaya_araviya_i_dagestan_stali_sotrudnichat_v_sfere_turizma/

RIA Novosti, *The Meeting of the Group of Strategic Vision 'Russia-Islamic World' will
Take Place in Saudi Arabia*, [*Zasedanie gruppy 'Rossiya -Islamskiy mir' proidet
v Saudovskooy Aravii*], 9 June 2021. Available at: https://ria.ru/20210609/islam
-1736333229.html

RIA Novosti, *Tatarstan mozhet stat' exporterom c/hh produkcii v Saudovskyu Araviu,* [*Tatarstan May Become an Exporter of Agricultural Products to Saudi Arabia*], 18 March 2013. Available at: https://ria.ru/20130318/927734028.html

RIA Novosti, *Minnikhanov prinimaet uchastie vo Vsemirnom samite tolerantnosti v OAE* [*Minnikhanov Takes Part in the World Summit of Tolerance in the UAE*], 14 October 2019. Available at: https://ria.ru/20191114/1560935647.html

RIA Novosti, *Kadyrov: visit Putina v Er-Riyad ukrepiy sotrudnichsetvo dvuh stran* [*Kadyrov : Putin's Visit to Riyadh Will Strengthen Cooperation Between the Two Countries*], 14 October 2019. Available at: https://ria.ru/20191014/1559766501.html

RIA Novosti, *Kadyrov v Abu-Dhabi obsudit ukreplenie otnosheniy mechdy OAE i Chechney* [*Kadyrov in Abu Dhabi to Discuss Strengthening Relations Between the UAE and Chechnya*], 17 February 2019. Available at: https://ria.ru/20190217/1550989847.html

RIA Novosti, *The Meeting of the Group of Strategic Vision 'Russia-Islamic World' will Take Place in Saudi Arabia* [*Zasedanie gruppy 'Rossiya -Islamskiy mir' proidetv Saudovskooy Aravii*], 9 June 2021. Available at: https://ria.ru/20210609/islam-1736333229.html

Richardson, Trevor, 'The Decline of the Pax Americana', *The Organisation for World Peace*, 28 January 2021. Available at: https://theowp.org/the-decline-of-the-pax-americana/

Riedel, Bruce, 'It's Time to Stop US Arms Sales to Saudi Arabia', *Brookings*, 4 February 2021. Available at: https://www.brookings.edu/blog/order-from-chaos/2021/02/04/its-time-to-stop-us-arms-sales-to-saudi-arabia/

Roberts, David, 'Qatar and the Muslim Brotherhood: Pragmatism or Preference?', *Middle East Policy* 21, no. 3 (2014): 84–94.

Roberts, David, *Qatar: Securing the Global Ambitions of a City-State*, London: C. Hurst & Co, 2017.

Rodina, Elena and Dligach Dmitryi, 'Dictator's Instagram: Personal and Political Narratives in a Chechen leader's Social Network', *Caucasus Survey* 7, no. 2 (2019): 95.

Rodriguez, A, *Establishment of the Trade Relations between the Soviet Union and the States of the Arabian Peninsula (1920–1930)* [*Y istokov vneshnetorgovyh svyzei SSSR so stranami Araviyskogo poluostrova' (1920-1930)*] Vostk-Zapad: Kontakty i Protivorechiya.

Rorlich, Azade-Ayse. *The Volga Tatars: A Profile in National Resilience*, Stanford: Hoover Institution Press, 1986.

Rose, Gideon, 'Neoclassical Realism and Theories of Foreign Policy', *World Politics* 51, October (1998): 144–72.

Roshchin, Mikhail, 'Sufism and Fundamentalism in Dagestan and Chechnya', *CEMOTI* 38 (2004): 61–72.

Rubinstein, Alvin Z., *Red Star on the Nile*, Princeton: Princeton University Press, 1977.

Rumer, Eugene, 'Russia in the Middle East: Jack of All Trades, Master of None', *Carnegie Endowment for International Peace*, 31 October 2019. Available at: https://

carnegieendowment.org/2019/10/31/russia-in-middle-east-jack-of-all-trades-master
-of-none-pub-80233

Russia-Islamic Group of Strategic Vision, *The Group of Strategic Vision 'Russia-Islamic World' Presents the Updated Development Strategy*, 11 June 2019. Available at: https:// russia-islworld.ru/en/novosti//the-group-of-strategic-vision-russia-islamic-world -presents-the-updated-development-strategy/

Russia-Islamic World, *The Group of the Strategic Vision 'Russia-Islamic World' Presents the Updated Development Strategy*, 11 June 2019. Available at: https://russia-islworld .ru/en/novosti//the-group-of-strategic-vision-russia-islamic-world-presents-the -updated-development-strategy/

Russia-Islamic World, *Russia-Islamic World: New Facets of Cooperation*, 10 July 2019. Available at: https://russia-islworld.ru/en/main//russia-islamic-world-new-facets-of -cooperation/

Russian Direct Investment Fund, *Overview*. Available at: https://rdif.ru/Eng_About/

SA HPD TR, Fund 15, Inventory 5, File 1844b, Sheet 1.

Sabovyi, Alexander, 'Primiril li dogovor dve knostitutsii', *Literaturnaia gazeta*, 30 March 1994, 12.

Said, Edward W., *Orientalism*, New York: Pantheon Books, 1978.

Saivetz, Carol R., *The Soviet Union and the Gulf in the 1980s*, Boulder, San Francisco, London: Westview Press, 1989.

Saivetz, Carol R., 'Gorbachev's Middle East Policy: The Arab Dimension', in *The Decline of the Soviet Union and the Transformation of the Middle East*, edited by David H. Goldberg and Paul Marantz, 1–30, Oxford: Westview Press, 1994.

Samigullin, Kamil, 2021, interviewed by author.

Samoylovich, A., *About the History of the Tatar Crimean Language* [*K istorii Krysko-Tatarskogo literaturnogo yazyka*]. *Vestnok nauchnogo obshestva Tatarovedeniya 7*, Kazan: Academy of the Centre of the People's Commissariat of Education of the TSSR, 1927.

Sapronova, M. 'Russian-Arab Cooperation Before and After the "Arab Spring"', *Vestnik MGIMO-Universiteta* 36, no. 3 (2014): 27–36.

Sato, Shohei, *Britain and The Formation of The Gulf States: Embers of Empire*, Manchester: Manchester University Press, 2016.

Schberbak, Andrey, 'Nationalism in the USSR: A Historical and Comparative Perspective', *Nationalities Papers* 43, no. 6 (2015): 866–85.

Schlapentokh, Vladimir, Levita Roman and Loiberg Mikhail. *From Submission to Rebellion: The Provinces versus the Centre in Russia*, Boulder: Westview Press, 1997.

Sella, Amnon, 'Changes in Soviet Political Military Policy in the Middle East after 1973', in *The Limits to Power: Soviet Policy in the Middle East'*, edited by Yaacov Ro'i', 32–64. London: Croom Helm, 1979.

Sella, Amnon, 'The Soviet Union, Israel and the PLO: Policy Shift in the 1980s', in *The Soviets, Their Successors and the Middle East Turning Point*, edited by Rosemary Hollis, 19–54. US: St. Martin's Press, 1993.

Sergeev, Sergey, 'The Republic of Tatarstan: Reduced to a Common Denomination?', *Russian Social Science Review* 62, nos. 1–3 (2021): 214.

Shagimardanov, Aydar, 2020, interviewed by the author.

Shahin, Tuba, *Tatarstan-Turkey Trade Relations are Growing 'Confidently'* [*Tataristan-Türkiye ticari ilişkileri "güvenle" büyüyor*], AA, 9 August 2021. Available at: https://www.aa.com.tr/tr/ekonomi/tataristan-turkiye-ticari-iliskileri-guvenle-buyuyor/2329022

Shaikhutdinova, Gul'nara, 'Dogovorno-pravovaia praktika Respubliki Tatarstan na sovremennom etape', *Panorama* 2 (October 1995): 16–18.

Sharaf, Asma, *Memories of My Father. Rizeddin Fakhretdinov: Scientific-Bibliographic Collection* [*Vsopominaniya ob otce. Rizeddin Fakhretdinov: nauchno-bibliographicheskiy sbornik*], Kazan: Kazan University Press, 1999.

Sharafutdinova, Gulnaz, 'Paradiplomacy in the Russian Regions: Tatarstan's Search for Statehood', *Europe-Asia Studies* 55, no. 4 (2003): 618–19.

Shelton, Tracey, 'US and Qatar Ink Deals for "Tremendous Amounts" of Military Weapons and Boeing Planes', *News*, 10 July 2019. Available at: https://www.abc.net.au/news/2019-07-10/qatar-donald-trump-military-and-commercial-deals/11294500

Shireen, Hunter, Thomas Jeffrey and Alexander Melikishvili, *Islam in Russia: The Politics of Identity and Security*, New York; London: Armonk, 2004.

Shirin, Akiner, *Islamic Peoples of the Soviet Union*, London: Kegan Paul International, 1983.

Shumilin, Alexander and Shumilina Inna, 'Russia as a Gravity Pole of the GCC's New Foreign Policy Pragmatism', *The International Spectator* 52, no. 2 (2017): 115–29.

Sim, Li-Chem, 'Russia's Return to the Gulf', in *External Powers and the Gulf Monarchies*, edited by Jonathan Fulton and Li-Chen Sim, 1–21, Abingdon: Routledge, 2018.

Simmons, Ann M., *Russia Has been Assad's Greatest Ally – as It Was to His Father Before Him*, 6 April 2017. Available at: https://www.latimes.com/world/middleeast/la-fg-syria-russia-20170406-story.html

Slocum, John W., 'A Sovereign State Within Russia? The External Relations of the Republic of Tatarstan', *Global Society* 13, no. 1 (1999): 58.

Smart Building, 'Project Summary'. Available at: https://smbuil.ru/en/what-we-do/grozny-international-university7922/o-proekte-giu/

Smith, Alan H., 'The Influence of Trade on Soviet Relations with the Middle East', in *The Soviet Union in the Middle East: Policies and Perspectives*, edited by Adeed Dawisha and Karen Dawisha, 103–23, New York: Holmes&Meier Pub, 1982.

Smith, D., S. Siddiqui and P. Beaumont. *Gulf Crisis: Trump Escalates Row by Accusing Qatar of Sponsoring Terror*, 9 June 2017. Available at: https://www.theguardian.com/us-news/2017/jun/09/trump-qatar-sponsor-terrorism-middle-east

Smith, Simon C. *Britain's Revival and Fall in the Gulf: Kuwait, Bahrain, Qatar, and the Trucial States, 1950–1971*, London; New York: Routledge, 2013.

Smith, Simon C., 'Britain's Decision to Withdraw from the Persian Gulf: A Pattern Not a Puzzle', *The Journal of Imperial and Commonwealth History* 44, no. 2 (2016): 328–51.

Smolin, V., *To the Opening of the List of Works of Ibn Fadlan* [*K otkrytiu spiska sochineniyya Ibn – Fadlana*]. Vestnik narodnogo obshestva Tatarovedeniya 1–2, January–April, Kazan: Academy of the Centre of the People's Commissariat of Education of the TSSR, 1925.

Sneg, *Kamil Samigullin: Korolya Saudovskoy Aravii v Rossii vstretili po-carski* [*Kamil Samigullin: The King of Saudi Arabia in Russia was Greeted Like a King*], 9 October 2017. Available at: https://sntat.ru/news/kamil-samigullin-korolya-saudovskoy -aravii-v-rossii-vstretili-po-tsarski-5634577

S&P Global, Qatar, *Russia Adjust Tactics for European LNG Exports in March*, 3 April 2020. Available at: https://www.spglobal.com/platts/en/market-insights/latest -news/natural-gas/040320-qatar-russia-adjust-tactics-for-european-lng-exports-in -march

Speranskyi, Aristah, *Kazan Tatars* [*Kazanskie Tatary*]. Kazan: Central Publisher, 1914. Available at: https://kitap.tatar.ru/ru/dl/nbrt_tatarica_Inv_F_1633843

Spivak, Vita, 'Can the Yuan Ever Replace the Dollar for Russia?', *Carnegie*, 2 August 2021. Available at: https://carnegiemoscow.org/commentary/85069

Stacpoole, Anthony, 'Energy as a Factor in Soviet Relations with the Middle East', in *The Soviet Union in the Middle East: Policies and Perspectives*, edited by Adeed Dawisha and Karen Dawisha, 85–102, New York: Holmes&Meier Pub, 1982.

Starichkova, Natalia, 'Russia and Saudi Arabia: New Friendship', *Rosbalt.ru*, 9 October 2003.

Steiner, Sherrie, 'Religious soft Power as Accountability Mechanism for Power in World Politics: The InterFaith leaders' Summit(s)', *SAGE Open*, 2011. Available at: https:// journals.sagepub.com/doi/10.1177/2158244011428085

Strohmeier, Martin, 'The Exile of Husayn b. Ali, ex-Sharif of Mecca and ex-king of the Hijaz, in Cyprus (1925–1930)', *Middle Eastern Studies* 55, no. 5 (2019): 733–55.

Suchkov, Maxim, 'What's Chechnya doing in Syria?', *Al-Monitor*, 26 March 2017. Available at: https://www.al-monitor.com/pulse/originals/2017/03/russia-syria -chechnya-ramzan-kadyrov-fighters.html

Suleymanova, Dilyara, 'International Language Rights Norms in the Dispute over Latinization Reform in the Republic of Tatarstan', *Caucasus Review of International Affairs* 4, no. 1 (Winter 2010): 43.

Tanrisever, Oktay Firat, 'The Politics of Tatar Nationalism and Russian Federation: 1992–1999', PhD Thesis, School of Slavonic and East European Studies University College London, 2002.

Tasci, Ufuk, 'How the UAE, Russia and France Have Teamed Up in Libya', *TRT World*, 22 December 2020. Available at: https://www.trtworld.com/magazine/how-the-uae -russia-and-france-have-teamed-up-in-libya-42583

TASS, *Ingushetia and Saudi Arabia establish cooperation in agriculture* [*Ingushetia and Saudovskaya Araviaya nalazhivaut sotrudnichsetvo v selskom hozyastve*], 31 October 2016. Available at: https://tass.ru/ekonomika/3749157

TASS, 'Ingushetia and Qatar Agreed to Establish Working Group on Development of Investment Projects' [*Ingushetia and Katar dogovorilis' o sozdanii rabochey gruppy po prodvizheniu investproektov*], 6 February 2018. Available at: https://tass.ru/ekonomika/4934413

TASS, *Nasledniy prince Bahraina ppribyl v Chechnu s drucheskim vizitom* [*Crown prince of Bahrain arrives in Chechnya on a friendly visit*], 8 November 2019. Available at: https://tass.ru/v-strane/7094904

Tatar-inform, *Minnikhanov pruibyl na mechdunarodnyu visttavku vooruchenyi v Abu-Dhabi* [*Minnikhanov arrives at the international arms exhibition in Abu Dhabi*], 21 February 2021. Available at: https://www.tatar-inform.ru/news/official/21-02-2021/minnihanov-pribyl-na-mezhdunarodnuyu-vystavku-vooruzheniy-v-abu-dabi-5808222

Tatar-inform, 6–15 June 1998. Available at: http://www.tatar.ru/english/ti000028.html.

Tatar-inform, '*Tatarstan stanet pervym rossiyskim regionom predstavlennym na vystavke Expo Dubai 2020*' ['*Tatarstan Will Be the First Russian Region Presented at Expo Dubai 2020*'], 27 September 2021. Available at: https://www.tatar-inform.ru/news/tatarstan-stanet-pervym-rossiiskim-regionom-predstavlennym-na-vystavke-expo-dubai-2020-5837722

Tatarstan President's Press Office, 'Business Forum "Tatarstan- Saudi Arabia" Held at the End of the Official Visit of Rustam Minnikhanov to Saudi Arabia', *Government of the Republic of Tatarstan*, 8 February 2017. Available at: https://prav.tatarstan.ru/eng/index.htm/news/840254.htm

The Telegraph, 'Joe Biden Says "America is Back" – but Stresses It Won't Be an 'Obama Third Term', 25 November 2020. Available at: https://www.telegraph.co.uk/news/2020/11/25/joe-biden-says-america-back-stresses-wont-obama-third-term/

Tewari, J. G., *Muslims under The Czars and the Soviet*, Lucknow, India: Academy of Islamic Research and Publications, 1984.

Times of Oman, 'Oman Oil Poised to Touch $100 Amid Ukraine Crisis', 22 February 2022. Available at: https://timesofoman.com/article/113617-oman-oil-poised-to-touch-100-amid-ukraine-crisis

Togan, Zeki Velidi, 'Unification Cases of Turks' ['Türkistanlıların Birleşme Davaları'], *Serdengeçti*, 15–16, 1952.

Trepalov, V. V., 'Vostochnie Elementy Rossisskoi Gosudartvennosti', *Rossiia i Vostok, Problemy Vzaimodeistviia*, 1: 38–59.

Troeller, Gary, *The Birth of Saudi Arabia: Britain and the Rise of the House of Sa'ud*. The Garden City Press Limited: Letchworth, 1976.

Tuimetov, J. G., 1893. Available at:: https://ru.openlist.wiki/Туйметов_Юсуф_ Галяутдинович_(1893)

Tuna, Mustafa, '"Pillars of the Nation": The Making of a Russian Muslim Intelligentsia and the Origins of Jadidism', *Kritika: Explorations in Russian and Eurasian History* 18, no. 2 (Spring 2017): 257–81.

'Twelve Agreements Between Russia and Tatarstan', *Journal of South Asian and Middle Eastern Studies* 18, no. 1 (1994): 73–4.

Ukrinform, *Ukraine Invites Bahrain to Join Crimean Platform Summit*, 13 July 2021. Available at: https://www.ukrinform.net/rubric-polytics/3279640-ukraine-invites -bahrain-to-join-crimean-platform-summit.html

Ulrichsen, Kristian Coates, *The United Arab Emirates: Power, Politics and Policy-Making*, Abingdon: Routledge, 2016.

Ulrichsen, Kristian Coates and R. Sheline Annelle, *Mohammed bin Salman and Religious Authority and Reform in Saudi Arabia*, 19 September 2019. Available at: https://www.bakerinstitute.org/media/files/files/516a1378/bi-report-092319-cme -mbs-saudi.pdf

Ulrichsen, Kristian Coates, 'The GCC and the Russia-Ukraine Crisis', Arab Center, Washington, DC. Available at: https://arabcenterdc.org/resource/the-gcc-and-the -russia-ukraine-crisis/

Umerov, A., 'Based on the Travel Notes of Abdrakhman Umerov [Po motivam putevyh zapisok Abdrahmana Umerova]', *Hajj of Russian Muslims* 10 (2021): 8–67. Available at: http://www.idmedina.ru/pdf/web/viewer.html?file=/pdf/content/hajj/hajj-10-r .pdf#27

Unusova, Aysilu, 'Riza Fakhretdinov's Activities to Preserve the Teaching of Religious Doctrine in Bolshevik Russia [Deyatelnost' Rizy Fakhretddinova po sohraneniu prepodavaniya religioznogo verouchheniya v bolshevistskoy Rossii]', *Educational Traditions of Islam in the Ural-Volga Region: First Fakhretdinov Readings*, 15 April 2009. Available at: http://www.idmedina.ru/books/materials/?1213

Usmanova, Dilyara, 'The Kazan Muslim Congresses and the Proclamation of "Cultural National Autonomy"', in *The History of The Tatars Since Ancient Times: Tatars and Tatarstan in the 20th–Beginning of the 21st Centuries*, 7, edited by Kazan: Academy of Sciences of the Republic of Tatarstan Sh. Marjani Institute of History, 2017.

Usmanova, Dilyara, 'The National Assembly and National Autonomy Projects', in *The History of The Tatars Since Ancient Times: Tatars and Tatarstan in the 20th–Beginning of the 21st Centuries*, 7, edited by Kazan: Academy of Sciences of the Republic of Tatarstan Sh.   Marjani Institute of History, 2017.

Uzeev, Aydar, 'Islamism, Turkism and Tatarism in Components of the Social-Political Establishment of Tatar at the Beginning of the XXth Century ['Islamism, Turkism and Tatarism kaka komponenty obshestvenno-politicheskogo coznaniya tatar nachala 20 veka']', *Islam in the Modern World* 14, no. 1 (March, 2018), 175.

Valeev, Ramzi, 'Projects of National State-Building and the Establishment of the Tatar Autonomous Soviet Socialist Republic', in *The History of The Tatars Since Ancient Times: Tatars and Tatarstan in the 20ᵗʰ–Beginning of the 21ˢᵗ Centuries*, 7, edited by Kazan: Academy of Sciences of the Republic of Tatarstan Sh. Marjani Institute of History, 2017.

Vasiliev, Alexei, *The History of Saudi Arabia (1745–1973)* [*Istoria Saudovskoy Aravii (1745–1973)*], Moscow: Nauka, 1982.

Vasiliev, Alexei, *Russia's Middle East Policy: From Lenin to Putin*, Abingdon: Routledge, 2018.

Vatchagaev, Maikbek, 'Chechen and Ingush Leaders Feud over Burial of Slain Insurgents', *The Jamestown Foundation*, 15 November 2012. Available at: https://jamestown.org/program/chechen-and-ingush-leaders-feud-over-burial-of-slain-insurgents-2/

Vatikiotis, P. J., 'The Soviet Union and Egypt: The Nasser Years', in *The Soviet Union and the Middle East: The Post-World War II Era*, edited by Ivo J. Lederer and Wayne S. Vucinich, 121–33, New York: Hoover Inst Pr, 1975.

Vneshnaya Torgovlya Rossii [*Russian Foreign Trade*]. Available at: https://russian-trade.com/

Walt, Stephen. *The Origins of Alliances*, Ithaca and London: Cornell University Press, 1987.

Waltz, Kenneth N. *Theory of International Politics*, Reading, MA: Addison-Wesley, 1979.

WAM, *Zayed Fund for Innovation and Entrepreneurship Launched in Chechnya*, 29 May 2017. Available at: https://aviamost.ae/en/zayed-fund-innovation-and-entrepreneurship-launched-chechnya

Watanabe, L., 'Gulf States' Engagement in North Africa: The Role of Foreign Aid', in *The Small Gulf States: Foreign and Security Policies Before and After the Arab Spring*, edited by Khalid Almezaini and Jean-Marc Rickli, 168–81, New York: Routledge, 2017.

Wendt, Alexander, 'Collective Identity Formation and the International State', *American Political Science Review* 88, no. 2 (1994): 384–96.

Wendt, Alexander, 'Constructing International Politics', *International Security* 20, no. 1 (1995): 71–81.

Wendt, Alexander, *Social Theory of International Politics*, Cambridge: Cambridge University Press, 1999.

Wigglesworth-Baker, Teresa, 'Language Policy and Post-Soviet Identities in Tatarstan', *New York, USA: Cambridge University Press, Nationalities Papers* 44, no. 1 (2016): 20–37.

Williams, Christopher, 'Tatar Nation Building Since 1991: Ethnic Mobilisation in Historical Perspective', *Journal of Ethnopolitics and Minority Issues in Europe* 10, no. 1 (2011): 113.

Wintour, Patrick, 'Saudi King's Visit to Russia Heralds Shift in Global Power Structures', *The Guardian*, 5 October 2017. Available at: https://www.theguardian.com/world/2017/oct/05/saudi-russia-visit-putin-oil-middle-east

Wintour, Patrick, 'Germany Agrees Gas Deal with Qatar to Help End Dependency on Russia', *The Guardian*, 20 March 2022. Available at: https://www.theguardian.com/world/2022/mar/20/germany-gas-deal-qatar-end-energy-dependency-on-russia

The World Bank, 'Russia's Economy Loses Momentum Amid COVID-19 Resurgence, Says New World Bank Report', 16 December 2020. Available at: https://www.worldbank.org/en/news/press-release/2020/12/16/russias-economy-loses-momentum-amid-covid-19-resurgence-says-new-world-bank-report

Xinhuanet, 'Russia to Coordinate Energy Policy with Qatar: FM', 3 May 2019. Available at: http://www.xinhuanet.com/english/2019-03/05/c_137868857.htm

Yaghi, Mohammad, 'What Drives President Biden's Middle East Policies? And What are Their Impact on the Gulf States?', *Konrad Adenauer Stiftung, Policy Reportno*, 22 May 2021. Available at: https://www.kas.de/documents/286298/8668222/Policy+Report+No+22+What+Drives+President+Biden's+Middle+East+Policies.pdf/98bac5dc-abc0-a108-18ef-32ff9f156873?version=1.1&t=1621864193248

Yalcin, Deniz, 'Federal Bargaining in Post-Soviet Russia: A Comparative Study on Moscow's Negotiations with Tatarstan and Bashkortostan', Unpublished Master's thesis, Graduate School of Social Sciences, Eurasian Studies of Middle East Technical University, 2005.

Yapp, Malcolm, 'Soviet Relations with Countries of the Northern Tier', in *The Soviet Union in the Middle East: Policies and Perspectives*, edited by Adeed Dawisha and Karen Dawisha, 24–44. London: Royal Institute of International Affairs, 1982.

Yarlykapov, Akhmet, 'The North Caucasus (Chechnya, Dagestan, Ingushetia) and the Islamic World', *Online Conference: Russia and the Muslim World: Through the Lens of Shared Islamic Identities*, 18–19 March 2021.

Yemelianova, Galina, 'The National Identity of the Volga Tatars at the Turn of the 19th Century: Tatarism, Turkism and Islam', *Central Asian Survey* 16, no. 4 (1997): 543–72.

Yemelianova, Galina, 'Islam and Nation Building in Tatarstan and Dagestan of the Russian Federation', *Nationalist Papers* 27, no. 4 (1999): 605–30.

Yemelianova, Galina, 'Shaimiev's "Khanate" on the Volga and its Russian Subjects', *Asian Ethnicity* 1, no. 1 (2000): 48.

Yemelianova, Galina, *Russia and Islam: A Historical Survey*, New York: Palgrave, 2002.

Yemelianova, Galina, Islam in Russia: An Historical Perspective', in *Islam in Post-Soviet Russia: Public and Private Faces*, edited by Hilary Pilkington and Galina Yemelianova, 15–60, London, New York: Routledge Curzon, 2003.

Yemelianova, Galina, 'Islam, Nationalism and State in the Muslim Caucasus', *Caucasus Survey* 1, no. 2 (2014): 5.

Yodfat, Aryeh Y., *The Soviet Union and the Arabian Peninsula: Soviet Policy Towards the Persian Gulf and Arabia*, London: Palgrave Macmillan, 1983.

Yodfat, Aryeh, *Arab Politics in the Soviet Mirror*, Jerusalem: Israel Universities Press, 32–102.

Young, Michael, 'Power to Which People?', 30 March 2022. Available at: https://carnegie-mec.org/diwan/86757

Zelensky, Volodymyr, 24 February 2022. Available at: https://twitter.com/ZelenskyyUa/status/1496736576780521472

Zenkovsky, Serge A., *Pan-Turkism and Islam in Russia*, Cambridge: Harvard University Press, 1960.

Znamenskoy, P., *Kazan Tatars* [*Kazanskie Tatary*]. Kazan: Publisher of Imperator's University, 1910. Available at: https://kitap.tatar.ru/ru/dl/nbrt_tatarica_Inv_373_63

Zubarevich, N., *Otnosheniia tsentr-regiony: chto izmenilos' za chetyre goda krizisa*, [*Relations Between Centre and Regions: What has Changed During Four Years of Crisis?*]. Available at: http://www.counter-point.org//11_zubarevich/

Index